'A Slashing Man of Action'

'A Slashing Man of Action'

The Life of Lieutenant-General Sir Aylmer Hunter-Weston MP

ELAINE MCFARLAND

PETER LANG
Oxford · Bern · Berlin · Bruxelles · Frankfurt am Main · New York · Wien

Bibliographic information published by Die Deutsche Nationalbibliothek
Die Deutsche Nationalbibliothek lists this publication in the Deutsche National-
bibliografie; detailed bibliographic data is available on the Internet at http://
dnb.d-nb.de.

A catalogue record for this book is available from the British Library.

Library of Congress Cataloging-in-Publication Data:

McFarland, E. W. (Elaine W.)
 "A slashing man of action" : the life of Lieutenant-General Sir Aylmer Hunter-Weston MP / Elaine McFarland.
   pages cm
 Includes bibliographical references and index.
 ISBN 978-3-0343-0290-6 (alk. paper)
 1. Hunter-Weston, Aylmer, 1864-1940. 2. Generals--Great Britain--Biography. 3. World War, 1914-1918--Campaigns. 4. Great Britain. Army--Officers--Biography. 5. Legislators--Great Britain--Biography. I. Title. II. Title: Life of Lieutenant-General Sir Aylmer Hunter-Weston MP.
 DA69.3.H77M34 2014
 940.4'1241092--dc23
 [B]
                    2014024854

Cover picture: Lieut.-General Sir Aylmer Gould Hunter-Weston by Francis Dodd, 1917. By courtesy of the Imperial War Museum (Art.IWM ART 1811).

ISBN 978-3-0343-0290-6 (print)
ISBN 978-3-0353-0788-7 (eBook)

© Peter Lang AG, International Academic Publishers, Bern 2014
Hochfeldstrasse 32, CH-3012 Bern, Switzerland
info@peterlang.com, www.peterlang.com, www.peterlang.net

All rights reserved.
All parts of this publication are protected by copyright.
Any utilisation outside the strict limits of the copyright law, without
the permission of the publisher, is forbidden and liable to prosecution.
This applies in particular to reproductions, translations, microfilming,
and storage and processing in electronic retrieval systems.

This publication has been peer reviewed.

Printed in Germany

Contents

List of Plates   vii

Acknowledgements   ix

Introduction   1

CHAPTER ONE
Hunters and Westons   7

CHAPTER TWO
A Gentleman and a Soldier   13

CHAPTER THREE
Small Wars   21

CHAPTER FOUR
Hunting the Boer   39

CHAPTER FIVE
Brain of the Army   65

CHAPTER SIX
'A Brigadier and a Band of Brothers'   79

CHAPTER SEVEN
Winter in the Trenches   107

CHAPTER EIGHT
'A Second Crimea' – The Road to Gallipoli   121

CHAPTER NINE
Achieving the Impossible – The Beaches and Beyond   145

CHAPTER TEN
A Dealer in Hope – The Last Battles   177

CHAPTER ELEVEN
A Day of Disaster   211

CHAPTER TWELVE
Holding On   249

CHAPTER THIRTEEN
Breaking Through   273

CHAPTER FOURTEEN
The Man That Gets Things Done   297

Bibliography   315

Index   329

Plates

Illustrations

1. The infant Aylmer on his pet donkey
2. Grace Strang Steel, Lady Hunter-Weston
3. Hunter-Weston at St Yves, the scene of his failed counter-attack in November 1914
4. 11th Brigade troops fraternise at Ploegsteert during the Christmas ceasefire, 1914
5. Hunter-Weston pictured outside his Gallipoli dugout
6. 52nd Division Bathing Parade, Gallipoli
7. Major-General Henry de Beauvoir De Lisle, KCB, DSO
8. Planning the Somme: Hunter-Weston and VIII Corps Staff
9. Hunter-Weston and Reginald Pinney, April 1918
10. Local MP – the Hunter-Weston Masonic Bowling Trophy, 1927

Maps

1. 11th Brigade at Le Cateau, 26 August 1914
2. Operations on the Aisne, 12 September–7 October 1914
3. Hunter-Weston's Campaign in Gallipoli, 25 April to 13 July 1915
4. VIII Corps Sector at the Somme, 1 July 1916

Acknowledgements

My thanks are firstly due to the Hunter family for their kind permission to consult the Hunter papers at Hunterston House. I would also like to thank the staff and trustees of the following institutions for their invaluable assistance during my research for this book: the National Library of Scotland, the Liddell Hart Centre for Military Archives, the Imperial War Museum, the British Library, the National Archives, the National Army Museum, the Churchill Archives Centre, Churchill College Cambridge, the West Kilbride Museum. I have attempted to locate current holders of copyright in text, but I apologise for any omissions that may have occurred in this respect and will ensure amendments are made in any future edition.

I am grateful to Colin Cumming for proof reading and his many excellent suggestions; also thanks to Michael Hopcroft for his hard work with the maps.

My apologies to colleagues in the GCU battlezone who have been subjected to many inspiring parallels from the career of Hunter-Weston over the last few years: Annie Tindley, Stewart Davidson, Fraser Duncan, Ross Campbell, Ben Shepherd, Vicky Long, and Karly Kehoe.

Finally, thanks to Jim Whiston for his continuing tolerance and unflagging support (and help with photographs).

Introduction

> The one thing that a General thinks about all the time is sparing his men's lives – never does a General attack unless he thinks by so doing he will in the end save [lives]; that is what our job is, we are very careful on the question of loss of life and the human suffering which must occur. Actually speaking if an attack is well thought out, even if you lose life you will probably save life in the end, because you keep the other people apprehensive and they will not be able to concentrate on you and attack you with overwhelming force.[1]

The comments made by Sir Aylmer Gould Hunter-Weston at the Dardanelles Commission in February 1917 came from a soldier who has since earned a reputation as one of the most brutal, callous and incompetent commanders of the Great War. His case is one that powerfully illustrates the manner in which that destructive conflict has become embedded in the popular memory. There is no doubt that for some contemporaries, he was a 'butcher', a jovial 'mountebank', who was perhaps even 'not quite sane'.[2] However, this colourful testimony has often been uncritically absorbed into the historical record, so that even the latest revisionist treatments that seek to provide a more nuanced account of the tactical transformation of

---

[1] Hunter-Weston, 'Evidence to Dardanelles Commission', 12 February 1917, Hamilton Papers, 8/2/50, Liddell Hart Centre for Military Archives, King's College London, (LHCMA).

[2] Notable accounts in published memoirs include: Charles Carrington, *Soldier from the Wars Returning* (London: Hutchinson, 1965), 104; Captain J. C. Dunn, *The War the Infantry Knew, 1914–19* (London: Abacus, 1994), 50–5, 408, 412, 432–3; Eric Harrison, *Gunners, Game and Gardens: An Autobiography* (London: Leo Cooper, 1978), 50–1; Llewelyn Wyn Griffith, *Up to Mametz ... and Beyond* (Oxford: Casement, 2010).

the British Army present him as a bullying eccentric; a convenient counterpoint to the 'learning curve' displayed by more successful commanders.[3]

The intention of this biography is to provide a more rounded portrait of the soldier and the man. Four main themes are explored in order to capture the complexities of a commander who began the Great War as one of the British Army's rising stars: command in context, personality and performance, the political soldier, reputation and memory. Taking each in turn, the obvious starting point is to trace the 'making' of Hunter-Weston as a commander, examining his upbringing, training, early military service and his years as a peacetime staff officer. Once the cultural and environmental influences that shaped his development are taken into account, he emerges less as a pantomime villain and more as a transitional figure, overwhelmed by a war that confounded his expectations. The creation of a mass army boosted many careers, but Hunter-Weston experienced the fastest promotion of any 1914 infantry brigade commander, advancing from substantive Colonel to temporary Lieutenant-General by May 1915. In practice, this meant exchanging a 1,000-yard trench sector in Flanders for the command of a large and complex combined-arms formation on the Helles front at Gallipoli. Described by Sir Ian Hamilton as 'a slashing man of action; an acute theorist', he set out to be a modern solider, believing that war could only be won by the application of military science.[4] Yet, while he was fascinated by the potential of technology in warfare, he also believed that all new inventions would find their place in the military machine, modifying but not undermining 'well-established principles'.[5] He was far

---

[3] See, for example, Simon Robbins, *British Generalship on the Western Front 1914–18: Defeat into Victory* (London: Frank Cass, 2005), 14, 32; Andy Simpson, *Directing Operations: British Corps Command on the Western Front, 1914–18* (Stroud: Spellmount, 2006), 198–9. For an unusually sympathetic and perceptive short treatment, see Elizabeth Balmer, 'General Hunter-Weston's Appreciation of the Dardanelles Situation', *Stand To!* 79, (April 2007), 5–8.

[4] Sir Ian S. M. Hamilton, *Gallipoli Diary*, vol. 1 (London: E. Arnold, 1920), 3.

[5] Aylmer Hunter-Weston (HW) to Grace Hunter-Weston (GHW), 7 October 1914, Hunter-Weston, Private War Diary, Vol. IX, 4 Aug. 1914–15 Feb. 1915, Add. MS 48363, British Library [HW Private War Diary, 48363, BL].

Introduction

from alone in this traditional reasoning, but while other senior commanders struggled to grasp the tactical implications of the firepower revolution, few were as persistent as Hunter-Weston in continuing to expound the 'all costs' logic of offensive warfare with such brutal clarity. In fact, it his own bombastic talkativeness contributed significantly to earning him the 'butcher' epithet, while obscuring the extent to which he was capable of adaptation and innovation.

Although this study examines the various command situations that Hunter-Weston faced, it is not exclusively concerned with his generalship. Some biographers have found their military subjects 'personally ... of no great interest', but it is impossible to understand Hunter-Weston's encounters with the modern battlefield without reference to character traits that were mirror images of the 'terse' and 'aloof' Douglas Haig.[6] In an age when most generals were little more than 'brass hats' to their soldiers, he was unmistakably a personality. Cheeriness was an article of faith in the British army and he became one of its chief exponents, privately criticising King George V for his 'doleful face'.[7] His commitment to the ideals of heroic personal leadership meant that he found glory where others saw only grind and suffering. He also benefited from a powerful physical presence. Reckoned to be the best-dressed officer on the Western Front, he was below average height with a remarkable hawk–like nose and glittering eyes, and possessed one of the finest moustaches in the senior ranks of the British army, a creation that became larger and more impressive with age.[8] The considerable element of theatricality in his nature also meant that he was something of a showman, actively seeking out close contact with his troops. Not surprisingly, a whole cycle of stories were told about him, enough to form 'a volume like the Norse sagas, in which Hunter-Weston takes the place of the mythical heroes of old.'[9] As his active military role

---

6   Robin Prior and Trevor Wilson, *Command on the Western Front: The Military Career of Sir Henry Rawlinson 1914–18* (Oxford: Blackwell, 1992), 5.
7   HW to GHW, 8 August 1918: Hunter-Weston Private War Diary, Vol. XIII, 1 Jan.–11 Nov. 1918, Add. MS 48367, British Library [HW Private War Diary, 48367, BL].
8   *The Sketch*, 29 September 1929.
9   *Ardrossan and Saltcoats Herald*, 17 May 1918.

diminished after the disastrous performance of his corps on the first day of the Somme, his idiosyncrasies assumed a life of their own, and the 'Hunter-Bunter' anecdotes subsequently multiplied.[10]

One of the main tasks in writing this biography has been to cut through the colourful mythology which has built up over the years in order to confront Hunter-Weston on his own terms. There is no shortage of primary material, as he was acutely concerned with the management of his public image. Despite his claims to be a 'plain, blunt soldier', he grasped the politicisation of the war effort with impressive dexterity. An astute networker, he was elected as an MP while still a Corps Commander, later reinventing himself as a populist politician once he had left the army. He was devoted to both careers and meticulously – almost obsessively – documented their progress in impeccably ordered volumes of newspaper clippings. He also preserved eight volumes of his official war diaries; typically, one of his priorities on returning from Gallipoli was to have his papers bound by a celebrated London firm. A further six volumes of his personal war diary were compiled retrospectively by his admiring and unflagging wife, Lady Grace Hunter-Weston. These include selections from the letters that he sent her almost daily during the war – a remarkable correspondence that sometimes included highly sensitive military information. In retirement, he began to revisit this material, as well as his other personal papers from his service in South Africa and his time as a staff officer, often vigorously annotating them.

While he also had a clear idea of how he wished to be remembered, his efforts to shape posterity were less effective than he intended. Hunter-Weston often emerges from his writings as vainglorious, self-congratulatory

---

10 He had originally been known as 'The Count' while at the School for Military Engineering at Chatham, a reference to his distinguished appearance, but he had become 'Hunter-Bunter' by the time he joined Staff College in 1897; the affectionate nickname was unconnected with the Billy Bunter character who first made his appearance in *The Magnet* in 1908. The resulting confusion led to Hunter-Weston being assigned a weight problem in one 'comical' history: Nigel Cawthorne, *The Beastly Battles of Old England: The Misguided Manoeuvres of the British at War* (London: Piatkus, 2013).

Introduction 5

and insensitive, but at the same time he can also appear as intelligent, professional, brave and loyal. Well-schooled in the paternalism of the old army, he ardently sought the approval of his men, as well as his superiors, and was capable of spontaneous acts of kindness when faced with the troubles of individual soldiers.[11] Tragically, however, the wars of empire had poorly prepared his generation of commanders for the realities of high-pressure decision-making in which a single ill-judged order could have catastrophic consequences. Together they have gained popular notoriety as 'bunglers', but among this dubious company, Hunter-Weston stands out as the perfect caricature of a 'Donkey' general. Separating substance from recycled rumour and pejorative comment is not an easy task, but in tackling a figure who is so at odds with modern sensibilities, it seems wise to remember Bidwell and Graham's injunction that we should treat all human subjects with 'equal respect for their frailties, their handicaps and their achievements'.[12]

---

[11] For example, when a Gunner named Casey got a lady in Newcastle pregnant, he left his post to marry her. When tried for desertion, he was convicted and given the lenient sentence of one year's hard labour. Hunter-Weston later commuted the sentence and sent the new Mrs Casey a £2 cheque for her wedding present: HW to Mrs Casey, 17 December 1917. Hunter-Weston, Private War Diary, Vol. XII, 8th Army Corps, Ypres, Flêtre and Passchendaele. 1 Jan–31 Dec. 1917, Add MS 48366, British Library, [HW Private War Diary, 48366, BL].

[12] Shelford Bidwell and Domenick Graham, *Fire-Power: The British Army Weapons and Theories of War, 1904–45* (Barnsley: Pen & Sword, 2004), 64.

CHAPTER ONE

Hunters and Westons

In the half century before the Great War, the British officer corps was a remarkably self-contained body. Although there had been a gradual broadening of its membership, there was still a high degree of self-recruitment involving the sons of professional officers, as well as a strong representation of the gentry and aristocracy, for whom military service was traditionally a well-regarded career.[1] Often less financially secure than their southern counterparts, Scottish landed families made a sizable contribution to this confident and cohesive elite – by 1914 some 17 per cent of generals were from Scotland, a proportion well beyond its share of the UK population.[2] For all his individual flamboyance and striking traits of character, Aylmer Gould Hunter-Weston personified this shared patrician profile. It was a background that shaped his values, his lifestyle, and his friendships, as well as his professional destiny.

An immediate familial military connection existed through Hunter-Weston's father, Gould Read Weston. Born in 1823, Gould was the second son of a Dorsetshire gentleman, James Willis Weston, but could claim direct descent from an ancient Staffordshire family who had been resident in the county since the reign of Henry II.[3] After attending the East India

---

1   Robbins, *British Generalship on the Western Front*, 3–8; Simon Robbins, *British Generalship during the Great War: The Military Career of Sir Henry Horne (1861–1929)* (Farnham: Ashgate, 2010), 1–8; Edward Spiers, *The Late Victorian Army, 1868–1902* (Manchester: Manchester University Press, 1992), 94.
2   Stuart Allan and Allan Carswell, *The Thin Red Line: War, Empire and Visions of Scotland* (Edinburgh: National Museum of Scotland, 2004), 105.
3   Volume of obituary notices of Gould Weston, 1904, Hunter of Hunterston Papers, Hunterston House, NRAS852/4/17. See also William Low, *Lieutenant-Colonel Gould Hunter-Weston of Hunterston, Knight of Justice and honorary commander of*

Company's Military Seminary, he followed a familiar path for younger sons. Gazetted as an ensign in the 65th Native Infantry, he sailed for India in April 1840, where he spent the next eighteen years. During an eventful career in the army of the Bengal Presidency he took on a variety of demanding diplomatic and military appointments.[4] The high point of his career came in July 1857, when he served under Sir Henry Lawrence at the siege of Lucknow. As it did for many officers, the Indian Munity provided Gould's 'essential knightly moment'.[5] He displayed great personal courage in the defence of the Lucknow Residency, and subsequently headed General Sir James Outram's Intelligence Department during its recapture. He was mentioned in dispatches for these services, but the collapse of his health hastened his retirement from the army in October 1861 with the honorary rank of Lieutenant-Colonel.[6]

Gould's first wife was a young Lancashire lady, Frances Crooke Freeman, who died with their new-born son after less than a year of marriage.[7] Two years later, the widower found a new bride, Jane Caldwell Hunter, fourteen years his junior, the eldest daughter and heiress of Robert Caldwell Hunter, 25th Laird of Hunterston.[8] Intermarriage between English and Scottish landed families had become common, but the Hunters – with their family motto *Cursum Perficio* (I will complete the course) – remained acutely conscious of their ancient lineage.[9] Compared with the settled gentility of the Westons, they certainly boasted a colourful pedigree. According to family

---

the Order of St John of Jerusalem in England, one of the defenders of Lucknow during the Indian Mutiny 1857–8: a biographical sketch (Selkirk: Scottish Chronicle Office, 1914).

4 These included setting up a military police force in the province of Oude; *Illustrated London News*, 14 May 1853 shows him presiding over the trial of a 'thug'.

5 John Mackenzie, *Imperialism and Popular Culture* (Manchester: Manchester University Press, 1986) 116–18.

6 L. E. Ruutz Rees, *A Personal Narrative of the Siege of Lucknow* (Oxford: Oxford University Press, 1858) 109, 145; *London Gazette*, 22 May 1858.

7 *Blackburn Standard*, 17 July 1861.

8 *Ardrossan and Saltcoats Herald*, 11 July 1863.

9 In 1856 Jane's father superintended the painstaking compilation of his family's genealogy, work that was later continued by Gould Weston and his son, Aylmer: *Some*

tradition, the first Hunter laird, Willielmo Venator (William the Hunter) was summoned by King David I from his native Normandy at the end of the eleventh century to become Royal Huntsman to the Scottish Court. The power base of the Hunter family was located on the northern coast of Ayrshire. Built in the thirteenth century, their castle at Hunterston was a bluff, pugnacious tower, commanding a strategic position overlooking the Firth of Clyde. From this stronghold, the Hunters contributed to Scottish efforts to repel repeated Viking incursions. This martial tradition continued during the middle ages and beyond. One authenticated forbear, 'Aylmere Le Huntar', for whom Aylmer Hunter-Weston was named, was a signatory of the notorious submission to King Edward of England in 1296. Later generations proved more dogged in their loyalty to the Scottish Crown: John Huntar (the 14th Laird) died with King James IV at Flodden in 1513 and Mungo Huntar (the 16th Laird) followed the standard of Mary, Queen of Scots and died at the Battle of Pinkie Cleugh in 1547. The family's tradition of military service continued after the Act of Union and during the early growth of Britain's colonial empire. General Robert Hunter (1666–1734), grandson of the 20th Laird, served under Marlborough at Blenheim and Ramillies. Like many of the Scottish gentry, the family's landholdings contracted during the excesses of the eighteenth century, but their relative financial decline was quickly reversed by more prudent Hunter lairds who accumulated wealth through imperial trade and improved their estates. By 1799, the 24th Laird, Eleanora Hunter, had begun the construction of Hunterston House (where Gould and Jane were married), a handsome new family dwelling. Entering a boom period for Scottish agriculture in the mid-nineteenth century, these achievements were consolidated by Jane's formidable father who had abandoned his career as an advocate to manage the family estate of nearly nine hundred acres of prime arable land.[10]

---

family papers of the Hunters of Hunterston (edited for Lt.-General Sir Aylmer Hunter-Weston of Hunterston by M. S. Shaw W.S.) (Edinburgh: J. Skinner, 1925).

10 F. H. Groome, *Ordnance Gazetteer of Scotland. A Study of Scottish Topography. Statistical, Biographical and Topographical*, vol. 1 (London: William Mackenzie, 1892), 278.

Gould and Jane's first child, a boy who was originally christened Aylmer Gould Weston, was born on 23 September 1864 at Annanhill House, near Kilmarnock, Ayrshire, which had earlier been the scene of the couple's honeymoon.[11] A second child, Reginald Hugh, followed five years later. Indeed, it would be 'Reggie's' fate to follow his older brother along various paths in life for many years to come. For the Hunters, the birth of their first son was an auspicious event, as the family had recently had a patchy record in producing male heirs. One of the earliest photographs of Aylmer, aged eighteen months, shows a cherished child on his pet donkey, surrounded by the family servants. Much of his later boyhood would be spent in the beautiful wooded setting of his grandfather's estate. The only exception to the pleasantness of his existence were the dreary Sabbaths, where lengthy family prayers were followed by 'interminable and senseless' services in the local kirk.[12]

His parents travelled extensively on the continent during the early years of their marriage. In 1869 their full-length portraits were painted by Francesco Didoni, and exhibited in the Brera in Milan.[13] Their Ayrshire links were reinforced in March 1880, when Jane became the 26th Laird of Hunterston following the death of Robert Hunter. Gould also assumed the Hunter name as a prefix by royal license, thus fulfilling the conditions of a family contract which stipulated that the spouses of female Hunter heirs had to bear the family name before they could inherit.[14] A capable and strong-minded woman, Jane took over the running of the estate. She proved a shrewd manager in continuing her father's improvements but she

11 *Ardrossan and Saltcoats Herald*, 1 October 1864.
12 *Ardrossan and Saltcoats Herald*, 7 July 1925.
13 Hunter of Hunterston Papers, NRAS852/511. The paintings remain on display in the house – a small, petticoat-clad Aylmer features in his mother's portrait.
14 *London Gazette*, 21 May 1880. This was not enough for Jane's aunt, Miss Margaret Hunter, who launched an unsuccessful legal challenge, claiming that their adoption of the 'Hunter-Weston' surname was insufficient to meet the conditions of entail placed by her grandfather on the estate: see *Glasgow Herald*, 28 June, 1881.

was also an energetic patron of philanthropic and charitable initiatives and gained a local reputation for 'good works'.[15]

Their marriage seems to have grown into a strong partnership. There could be no doubt of Gould's former profession. He was a strikingly handsome figure, with an impressive dark moustache and an unmistakable military bearing. A 'Lucknow hero', he could now happily turn to the duties and amusements of a country gentleman. Away from his public responsibilities as the Deputy Lieutenant of Ayrshire, he balanced his exertions on the hunting field with the more gentle occupations of sketching and collecting works of art.[16] Both he and Jane also shared an interest in the Venerable Order of St John of Jerusalem. This was an exclusive chivalric body whose cachet among the British Royal Family and aristocracy grew from the late 1880s. While the order undertook important charitable work, it also offered the Hunter-Westons a point of entry into court circles. Their eldest son, who was personally appointed a 'Knight of Justice' by the sovereign on his coming of age, would make this most of this linkage during his military career.[17]

Clearly, the young Aylmer Hunter-Weston knew the security that came from inherited wealth, but his parents also made him aware of the various expectations that accompanied an elevated social position in Victorian society. One of the first of these was that he should leave the sequestered comfort of his family home and enter the world of the English public school.

15   *Ardrossan and Saltcoats Herald*, 21 October 1911.
16   List of the art collection of Lieutenant-Colonel Gould Weston, Kerriston Papers, 0924/6/1, City of Westminster Archives Centre. The collection includes William Blake's *Elijah in the Chariot of Fire*.
17   Gould claimed descent from Sir William Weston, Grand Prior of the Knights of St John in England during the sixteenth century; Jane was created an honorary Lady of Justice by Queen Victoria in 1895: *London Gazette*, 23 March 1895.

CHAPTER TWO

A Gentleman and a Soldier

Hunter-Weston's birth and family background may have conferred social standing, but it was his education which confirmed him in the rank of a gentleman. It was through his formal schooling that he was expected to acquire the self-belief and sense of purpose that would equip him to lead in any situation. As the 'embodiment of instant tradition', public schools in England were at the peak of their influence and mystique during the last half of the nineteenth century and their numbers had multiplied accordingly.[1]

It is unclear when Hunter-Weston decided that he wanted to become a solider, or the extent to which this was an independent decision.[2] However, for a boy who had serious ambitions towards an army career, the choice of school was fairly obvious – on the eve of the Great War, more than one third of the officers in the British Army's High Command had been educated at either Eton, Wellington, Harrow, Marlborough or Charterhouse.[3] Hunter-Weston's parents chose the newest of these schools, Wellington College. Originally founded in 1859 for the benefit of army families of limited means, it was moving into the first rank by the 1870s, with fees second only to Eton.[4]

---

[1] W. J. Reader, *'At Duty's Call': A Study in Obsolete Patriotism* (Manchester: Manchester University Press, 1988), 86.
[2] Besides the obvious precedent of his father, his grandfather, Robert Hunter, had also wanted to join the army as a young man and had only entered the legal profession as a result of his mother's pleas. For his obituary, see *Ardrossan and Saltcoats Herald*, 20 March 1880.
[3] Robbins, *British Generalship*, 11.
[4] G. F. H. Berkeley, *My Recollections of Wellington College* (Newport: R. H. Johns Ltd, 1945), 23; David Newsome, *A History of Wellington College, 1859–1959* (London: John Murray, 1959), 201.

Short, robust and cheerful, Hunter-Weston entered Wellington in the Michaelmas Term of 1877. He was determined to make an impression with his turnout. According to family legend, he was discovered in the butler's inner sanctum on the morning before he left home, polishing his boots so that they would shine to his own exacting standards.[5] Looking up at the school's lofty, red-brick buildings, new boys were left little doubt of its martial origins – the motto carved above the doorway stated that 'The Path of Duty is the Way to Glory'.[6] He was one of forty-four new entrants that autumn – eighteen were from service families and twenty-two would go on to military careers.[7] Among them was R. W. Breeks, who would serve as his artillery commander at Gallipoli, while another prominent 'Old Wellingtonian' on the peninsula was Sir Ian Hamilton, who had enrolled in 1867.[8]

The young Hunter-Weston entered a busy but strangely secluded world. Bullying was interwoven into the fabric of life at the school, whose dormitories functioned as austere little parishes divided by strong rivalries and intense group loyalties.[9] The school day was long and unvaried; work began at seven and on midwinter mornings pupils shivered in poorly lit classrooms. Yet, there was another side to Wellington. As one of the new generation of public schools, it had continued to invest in the 'Modern Side' of the curriculum in order to prepare pupils not only for army entrance exams, but also for a range of careers across the Empire. The disciplinary regime became rather more humane during the late 1870s, with an emphasis on instilling civility into boys who had previously been regarded by

---

5   *Ardrossan and Saltcoats Herald*, 7 August 1925.
6   He was assigned to Orange dormitory, which had a particularly strong games culture: *The Wellington College Register 1859–1923* (Wellington College: The Old Wellingtonian Society, 1926), 97.
7   *Wellington College Register*, 97–8.
8   He and Hunter-Weston celebrated the hundredth anniversary of Waterloo over a dish of crayfish, with Turkish guns booming in the distance: Hamilton, *Gallipoli Diary*, *(1)*, 318; Compton Mackenzie, *Gallipoli Memories* (London: Cassell, 1929), 149.
9   F. S. Horan, *From the Crack of the Pistol: A Personal Saga* (Dorchester: Longmans, 1955), 26 J. L. Bevir, *The Making of Wellington College* (London: Edward Arnold, 1920), v–x.

A Gentleman and a Soldier 15

observers as 'somewhat boorish'.[10] The formation of character was viewed as the school's most important function. The basic rules of conduct were strictly enforced, but within these limits pupils were expected to work out their own solutions, drawing on the school's pervasive Christian, military and imperial values. Special prestige was reserved for physical prowess and sporting achievement.[11]

Hunter-Weston retained a great affection for Wellington, later becoming one of its governors through Ian Hamilton's intervention.[12] It was a boisterous school environment in which all of his resilient temperament was needed for him to prosper. By the time his school career ended in June 1881, he had repaid the investment of his parents. His sporting achievements included colours in rugby, association football and athletics, but he also won a Senior Scholarship in successive years, as well as the School's Chemistry and Electricity Prize.[13] In short, he had come to embody the much-vaunted 'Wellingtonian type' – a sturdy all-rounder who regarded military service as 'a happy, sporting, out-of doors existence, with always a chance of glory'.[14]

While the path to a gentleman's estate was narrow and prescribed by convention, there were various routes to becoming a regular officer in the British Army. Although Hunter-Weston's brother Reginald, who had followed him to Wellington, was later forced to adopt the 'back-door' approach by first obtaining a Militia commission, the route chosen by Aylmer was more direct and demanding.[15] Rather than a glamorous kilted battalion, or the relaxed amateurism of a fashionable cavalry regiment, he decided to seek a commission in the Royal Engineers (RE). Traditionally a non-purchase corps, it had become an integral part of the army since

10 R. S. Talboys, *A Victorian School: The Story of Wellington College* (Oxford: Basil Blackwell, 1944), 36.
11 Talboys, *Victorian School*, 30.
12 Ian Hamilton to HW, 22 June 1925, Hamilton Papers, 13/III, LHCMA.
13 *The Times*, 3 July 1880; 20 June 1881; *Wellington College Register*, 97–8.
14 Berkeley, *My Recollections*, 36.
15 He was initially gazetted Second Lieutenant in the Worcestershire Regiment, before joining the Seaforth Highlanders: *London Gazette*, 12 June 1892.

coming under the control of the Commander-in-Chief in 1855. By the early 1880s, senior officers such as Sir Charles Warren were regularly appointed to independent active service commands, while the fighting reputation of the corps had recently been boosted by the exploits of John Chard VC, defender of Rorke's Drift. Still somewhat lacking in social status, it had nevertheless become a magnet for an intelligent type of officer candidate who was seriously bent on a professional army career.[16]

Entrance to the Royal Military Academy at Woolwich, which trained both engineers and artillerymen, was by open competition, and required success in a difficult examination in which mathematics was compulsory. Only forty places were available for each six-monthly intake. Having spent the summer in preparation, Hunter-Weston passed the exam in November 1881, gaining a solid eighteenth place in the order of merit.[17] He joined as a gentleman cadet at the beginning of the next year. The spirit of competition was immediately carried into his new studies, since only the top cadets in each cohort would gain a Royal Engineers commission, the remainder being assigned to the Royal Artillery. Known as 'the Shop', his new institution displayed some of the more unpleasant aspects of the public school system in a particularly intense form. Despite an overall atmosphere of restrained elegance in its premises, the living conditions were cramped and spartan, while an undercurrent of casual menace was felt among the cadets, who maintained a strict code of honour. Although some improvement in discipline could be detected during the 1880s, J. E. Edmonds, a brilliant near contemporary, remembered Woolwich with his customary rancour as 'a rough place'.[18]

---

16 Reader, *Duty's Call*, 89; David French, *Military Identities: the Regimental System, the British Army, and the British People c. 1870–2000* (Oxford: Oxford University Press, 2005), 165.

17 *Morning Post*, 24 December 1881: he scored a total of 6113 marks, compared to the top candidate's 7975. Herbert Kitchener, who passed the exam in 1868, came twenty-eighth out of fifty-six successful candidates.

18 J. E. Edmonds, 'The "Shop" sixty years ago', *The Royal Engineers Journal*, December 1940, 527. He was a cadet from 1879 to 1881.

Hunter-Weston's sociability and self-confidence meant that he confronted these challenging conditions head-on. He was appointed one of the three 'Under Officers' in his year, a position that gave him some authority over his boisterous colleagues. He also maintained the judicious balance between sporting and academic achievement that had distinguished his Wellington career. For many cadets, drill, gymnastics, riding and artillery exercises absorbed the energy formerly directed at team games, but Hunter-Weston also represented the College at rugby, soccer and the half mile.[19] More importantly for his future career, he improved on his entrance examination placing, ultimately graduating seventh in a class of thirty-eight and winning the prize for chemistry and physics (for which he was awarded a travelling bag). As a result, he 'got sappers', joining the top eighteen cadets – including five old Wellingtonians – who were presented to the dyspeptic old Duke of Cambridge in February 1884 to receive their commissions as Lieutenants in the Royal Engineers.[20]

These were exhilarating times for any new RE officer. Only a few weeks before, Major-General Charles Gordon had left for the Sudan on his fatal mission. In reality, however, a high placing on the graduation list was little guarantee of future success.[21] In fact, Woolwich was only the first stage in the training of a scientific officer. Hunter-Weston's next posting was to the School of Military Engineering at Chatham in February 1884, where he would remain for over two years. Considered to be the most advanced school of its type in Europe, it provided highly specialised study in traditional areas such as field fortifications, but its syllabus also grasped the

---

19 *Morning Post*, 10, 15 and 17 December 1883; See Hunter-Weston's CV (undated): Hunter-Weston Papers, 65/03/39/12, National Army Museum (NAM).
20 *The Standard*, 19 June 1884.
21 The officer who graduated top of the class of 1884 was still a Captain fifteen years later, despite holding a War Office appointment: W. Baker Brown, *History of the Corps of Engineers*, vol. 4 (Chatham: Institution of Royal Engineers, 1952) 168–9; 206.

military potential of new technology, with courses also offered in telegraphy, electricity, photography, and photolithography.[22]

The corps itself was about to enter a period of expansion and reorganisation during the late 1880s, bringing it into line with the duties expected of engineers in the modern army.[23] For new officers, this meant a growing range of opportunities to broaden their professional expertise. During his first posting, Hunter-Weston was able to pursue his interest in electricity and electronic communications by joining the 1st Division of the Telegraph Battalion, at Aldershot in March 1886. He was soon leading a telegraphist detachment, providing useful assistance during operations to strengthen the defenses of Milford Haven in September 1886.[24] Promotion, however, was quite another matter. Although he had already passed his Captain's exam by October 1885 at the age of twenty-one, he was well aware that he had not yet accrued sufficient seniority in the corps to actually attain this rank. While higher rates of pay provided some compensation, the rules for retirement meant that advancement could be glacially slow, even after attempts at reform in the early 1880s. As the careers of his Woolwich contemporaries demonstrated, the long professional apprenticeship of almost five years in the corps could place its officers at a disadvantage compared with their counterparts in line regiments, who were more frequently exposed to early career-enhancing opportunities across the Empire.

Hunter-Weston's own service in the south of England was busy but uneventful. He continued to hone his professional skills, returning to Chatham for a construction course in the spring of 1889. Here, his painstaking project and drawing work revealed a noticeable thoroughness and attention to detail which his instructors found praiseworthy, if rather excessive for the purpose intended.[25] But, as always, there were plenty of

---

22 Col. B. R. Ward, *The School of Military Engineering, 1812–1909* (Chatham: Royal Institute of Engineers, 1909); French, *Military Identities*, 154.
23 Baker Brown, *History of the Corps of Engineers*, 1–12.
24 *Morning Post*, 6 September 1886. See Records of Service for War Office and Roorkee, Hunter of Hunterston Papers, NRAS852/336. *The Times*, 6 September 1886.
25 Construction Course at Chatham – Engineering Projects, Hunter-Weston Papers, 65/03/39/1, NAM. Projects included the construction of a barracks and a sergeants' mess.

other diversions. He was reckoned to be one of the best RE cricketers, also representing both the corps and the county of Kent at football, while finding time to make his debut in amateur theatricals at Colchester Theatre.[26] Meanwhile, he made the most of his family's social connections, with a formal presentation to the Prince of Wales at St James Palace in July 1884.[27] This may all have been agreeable, but it was hardly the life for an ambitious young officer. The answer was India – the crucible of British military power. After volunteering for service in an Indian Engineer Corps on the North West Frontier, he left England in December 1899.[28]

26   *The Essex Standard, West Suffolk Gazette, and Eastern Counties' Advertiser*, 11 April 1885; *Morning Post*, 25 March 1887; *Essex Standard, West Suffolk Gazette, and Eastern Counties' Advertiser*, 28 September 1889.
27   *The Times*, 9 July 1884.
28   *Ardrossan and Saltcoats Herald*, 8 December 1905.

CHAPTER THREE

Small Wars

Soldiering on the North West Frontier was a high-risk rite of passage, but as Hunter-Weston knew from his father's experience, the display of a cool resolve under fire was indispensable to building a reputation in the service. At the same time, campaigning in mountainous border territory also revealed the mechanisms of war, enabling him to build a knowledge of topography, supply and logistics. Having already acquired a modern technological education at Woolwich and Chatham, the frontier now taught him another time-honoured lesson – how to make the correct decision in a dangerous situation.

The North West Frontier

Hunter-Weston's restored career mobility was the product of the British Empire's 'scientific frontier' policy. Replacing the former system of tribal management, this involved the region's highly independent tribes being brought firmly to heel to allow the construction of advanced military posts, necessitating a growing number of punitive expeditions.[1] These 'small wars' have been dismissed by historians as anachronistic and unequal contests, but effective resistance from the Pathaan tribesmen underlined the need

---

1   Cuthbert Collin Davies, *The Problem of the North West Frontier, 1890–1908* (Cambridge: Cambridge University Press, 1932), 71; Leslie Harris, 'A Scientific Frontier for India: Background to the "Forward Policy of the Nineties"', *Canadian Journal of History* 1/1 (1966), 46–71.

for carefully controlled fire and manoeuvre, while placing a growing premium on the tactical dispersion, skill and self-reliance of imperial troops.[2]

In common with most branches of the Indian Army, the corps that Hunter-Weston joined in December 1889 had recently undergone a process of modernisation. Formed in 1803, the Bengal Miners and Sappers had once been regarded within the Royal Engineers as a refuge for inefficient colleagues.[3] However, from 1885 onwards each of the three Indian Engineer corps had been comprehensively reorganised and retrained in order to re-establish them as highly effective specialist units. After the reorganisation, sapper companies were led exclusively by Royal Engineers officers. Encouraged by the prospect of adventurous frontier service, as well as a rich social and sporting life, there was eager competition for the twenty officer posts available in each corps.

The expanded role of military engineers in colonial warfare was well illustrated by Hunter-Weston's first active service campaigns. During the early 1890s, an increase in border raids by Orakzai tribesmen led to the dispatch of two punitive expeditions to the Miranzai Valley.[4] The first was carried out by a force of 5,000 men led by Sir William Lockhart, an expert in Indian mountain warfare. One of the most widely recognisable military personalities of his day, the veteran Scottish soldier was also an early model for Hunter-Weston's own dramatic leadership style: 'a dashing captain, full of life and humour, and a strong love of adventure'.[5]

Concentrating at Kohat, Lockhart began operations in January 1891, traversing the Miranzai country in various directions and establishing fortified posts on the Samana. Later attacks on these posts lead to a further expedition in April which recaptured the ridge and quelled the further

---

[2] Tim Moreman, 'The British and Indian Armies and North West Frontier Warfare, 1849–1914', *Journal of Imperial and Commonwealth History* 20/1 (1992), 35–64.

[3] Lieut.-Col. E. W. C. Sandes, *The Indian Sappers and Miners* (Chatham: Institution of Royal Engineers, 1948), 282.

[4] Capt. H. L. Neville, *Campaigns on the North-West Frontier* (London: John Murray, 1912), 124–9.

[5] G. W. Forrest, *Sepoy Generals, Wellington to Roberts* (Edinburgh: Blackwoods, 1901), 344.

pockets of resistance. For one RE colleague, the campaign was 'another not inglorious little war'.[6] The country was wild and mountainous, fragrant with wild herbs and studded with mulberry and poplar trees and woods of thorn and tamarisk. Notwithstanding this bucolic setting, the enemy was formidable and Lockhart's force faced night attacks and guerilla warfare tactics from an estimated 25,000 Orakzais. Not only were there many natural obstacles to be overcome before the tribesmen could be tackled, but the enemy's increased armament also meant that better protection would be required for the advanced camps and posts from which the new advanced frontier line could easily be occupied. The age of the 'engineer war' had arrived. During the expedition, the work of Hunter-Weston's sappers involved blasting roads out of solid rock, systematically demolishing at least seventy of the enemy's defensive towers.

With the region subdued, Hunter-Weston reluctantly returned to corps training and other routine duties.[7] His men were mostly employed in civil engineering and communications projects, including road building on the Assam border and the construction of a new water supply system in the Punjab.[8] His Indian service was already bringing rewards: promoted to Captain at the age of twenty-seven, just before the second Miranzai expedition, he now took over command of 3rd Company, a post which carried the status of Field Engineer.[9] The plentiful supply of tigers and elephants on the Manipur Road project also meant excellent opportunities for shooting. Indeed, while a ban on 'poodle-faking' – over-attentiveness to ladies – was strictly in force for the Sappers and Miners, young officers were expected to chase game as much as possible. Hunter-Weston lived

---

6   Capt. A. H. Mason, 'The Miranzai Expedition of 1891', *Journal of the Royal United Services Institution* XXXVI/168 (1892), 109–23.

7   He had attempted to remain with Lockhart, but there had been no vacancy for him and his corps wished him to return: W. Lockhart to HW, 10 September 1892, Hunter of Hunterston Papers, NRAS852/292.

8   *History and Digest of Service of the 1st King George's Own Sappers & Miners* (Roorkee: 1st King's Own Press, c. 1911), 56–7.

9   *London Gazette*, 24 May 1891; E. W. C. Sandes, *The Military Engineer in India*, vol. 1 (Chatham: Institute of Royal Engineers, 1933), 394.

up to his name and a large oorial (wild goat) claimed its place among the sporting trophies hanging in the RE Mess at Roorkee.[10]

By this point in his career, his personality and personal characteristics were already well formed. Something of a dandy, he was sociable and extrovert, blessed by an apparently unshakeable self-belief. Relaxing in Simla, the summer capital of British India, he was 'as good a looking a young soldier as anyone would wish to see'.[11] He was deemed quite a capable actor, and his chestnut hair and moustache ensured that he was much in demand as romantic lead in amateur theatricals. Although his addition of a St John of Jerusalem decoration to his uniform drew comment from some fellow officers, he was popular enough to gain election to the Order of the Black Heart, a club of 'hospitable bachelors' who laid on tasteful social entertainments during the summer season. Yet beneath the bonhomie, at least one Simla grand dame discerned a true career soldier, commenting that 'that young man has only one consuming fire, and that is ambition'.[12] Another incident from this period suggests a junior officer who had the confidence and presence of mind to stand up for the welfare of his troops. Rejecting the transport assigned to his sappers to convey them down the Brahmaputra River during the spring of 1893, Hunter-Weston simply refused to embark and instead commandeered the mail boat. He remained unrepentant, and despite howls of protest from the Director of the Indian Marine, he was cleared of all blame for this extraordinary burst of initiative.[13]

Hunter-Weston's military apprenticeship resumed during operations in Waziristan during 1894–5. This campaign involved specialist boundary

---

10 He also found time for botanical activities, spending his first leave in 1890 gathering rare Himalayan wildflowers in the province of Baltistan, which he then deposited with the Royal Botanical Gardens at Kew. The 113 specimens included the genus *Astragalus var. pilosus* (a type of vetch): S. I. Ali, 'Notes on the Genus Astragalus Linn. from West Pakistan', *Kew Bulletin* vol. 13/2 (1958), 104.
11 *Town Topics*, 25 September 1914; E. I. Buck, *Simla Past and Present* (Calcutta: Thackray, Spinks and Co., 1904) 171.
12 *Town Topics*, 25 September 1914.
13 River Transport of Sappers down the Brahmaputra River, 5 May 1893, Hunter-Weston Papers, 65/03/39/3, NAM.

Small Wars

commission work and also underlined the growing use of engineers as fighting troops. Now in command of 2nd Company, he joined the military escort of the British Delimitation Commission, charged with establishing the frontier between Afghanistan and India in the south of Waziristan. It began as another hot and weary assignment, spent in the company of 'a hundred swearing, snarling, restive camels' – the querulous beast that had become emblematic of Indian field service.[14] Hunter-Weston soon saw action, as the local Mahsud Waziris were deeply suspicious of what they interpreted as an overture to annexation. At dawn on 3 November, the tribesmen launched a series of desperate attacks on the Commission's camp at Wana, which had been poorly situated on open ground and was surrounded by ravines. Yelling and beating drums, a thousand men crashed into the left flank of the camp before the defenders had left their tents. The situation was only stabilised when the Gurkhas formed a rallying square. Hunter-Weston's energy and appetite for work in the aftermath impressed the Delimitation Escort commander, Brigadier-General A. H. Turner, who gave him his first mention in despatches.[15] A more practical reward was the role he was assigned in the inevitable punitive expedition that followed. Again led by Lockhart, the three mixed brigades of the Waziristan Field Force began a coordinated invasion of Mahsudi territory in early December 1894. In addition to his own company, Hunter-Weston was now in overall command of all the Miners and Sappers who accompanied the force.

Waziristan presented a typically harsh frontier environment, a mountainous landscape overlooking a blistering, featureless plain with boulder-strewn river beds which could quickly become raging torrents.[16] For Hunter-Weston, the expedition involved blowing up more towers and building the small, square mud-plastered forts that served as fortified posts. The road making was exceptionally difficult on this campaign, as the sappers were required to blast their way through narrow gorges with vertical

---

14 *Scotsman*, 22 December 1894.
15 *London Gazette*, 14 June 1894.
16 Hugh Beattie, *Imperial Frontier: Tribe and State in Waziristan* (Richmond: Curzon, 2002), 82–93.

cliffs rising hundreds of feet on either side.[17] These activities could hardly go uncontested by the Mahsuds, who were armed with weapons that could kill at 1,500 yards. During one expedition to destroy the enemy defences at Karam and Guralkot, Hunter-Weston was lucky to narrowly escape with only a slight wound, from a bullet which left a permanent scar over his left ear.[18]

The achievement of his corps in removing many of the physical difficulties facing the Field Force won Lockhart's praise and a second mention in despatches. Service in Waziristan also brought the first clasp for Hunter-Weston's Indian service medal. Such rewards were important compensation, given the constraints on promotion in the Victorian army, but in Hunter-Weston's case the decoration was combined with advancement to the brevet rank of Major in August 1895.[19] He now benefited from the notoriously clumsy 'fast-track' system, which gave him unpaid seniority on the Army List, but not within the Royal Engineers. Entitled to the badges and accoutrements of the higher rank, the seniority he accumulated would also transfer with him if he were to be promoted to Major in his own corps. Despite its inconsistencies, this advance in rank was an important acknowledgement of his recent service.

India had broken the health of his brother Reginald, who was forced to resign his commission and return home in 1895.[20] While garrison duty in the softer climate of Southern India may have encouraged a seductive languor in military life, for an officer of Aylmer Hunter-Weston's energy six years of frontier service had been an ideal posting. He was able to show himself to be a highly professional officer, ready to suggest improvements to every aspect of colonial warfare, from the sappers' personal equipment

---

17 Report on the Engineering Operations, Waziristan Field Force, 1884–5, Hunter-Weston Papers, 65/03/39/5, NAM.
18 Waziristan Field Force. 'Return of Casualties during the Expedition from 17th December, 1894, to 30th March, 1895' *London Gazette*, 2 July 1895.
19 *London Gazette*, 2, 18 June 1895.
20 *The Standard*, 12 October 1895.

to the positioning of mules.[21] The combination of danger, hard work and sport he encountered also gave him membership of a tightly knit circle of service acquaintances. Overt careerism was still frowned upon among the officer corps, but his display of professional competence had caught the attention of his superiors, marking him out as an officer of promise.

Dongola

In India, Hunter-Weston had been involved thus far in limited operations which were quickly terminated and highly effective. His next active service was in the northern Sudan where the risks and rewards were similar, but the logistical challenges were even greater. On 10 April 1896, he was one of six 'Indian' officers who were ordered to proceed immediately to Egypt to join the force under Sir Herbert Kitchener RE, who had commenced his long-awaited reconquest of this unforgiving territory.[22]

After the fall of Khartoum in 1884, pressure among the press and public to seize the initiative in the Sudan had scarcely abated. However, the sudden launch of a plan to invade the province of Dongola in March 1896 reflected more immediate political events. The defeat of the Italians at the Battle of Adowa had raised fears for British interests in the eastern Sudan, prompting support for a diversionary expedition up the Nile. This expedition – or 'advance', as it was referred to by politicians at home – was always intended as more than a demonstration in the interests of a friendly power. For Kitchener, it was nothing less than the first stage of a personal crusade to avenge the death of Gordon.[23]

---

21   Report on the Engineering Operations, Waziristan Field Force, 1884–5, Hunter-Weston Papers, 65/03/39/5, NAM.
22   *The Times*, 30 April 1896.
23   F. I. Maxse, *Seymour Vandeleur: the story of a British officer: being a memoir of Brevet-Lieutenant-Colonel Vandeleur, D.S.O., Scots Guards and Irish Guards, with a general*

The other less emotive theme of the Dongola campaign was parsimony. Financed by the Egyptian treasury, its main object was to bring hostilities to a successful conclusion as quickly and as cheaply as possible.[24] The principle of economy extended equally to camels, men, telegraph wire and railway sleepers – and certainly to 'Special Service Officers' like Hunter-Weston. Since the latter were funded by the War Office, Kitchener was anxious to maximise their numbers, while the War Secretary, Lord Landsdowne, was equally committed to supplying additional resources only on the basis of necessity.[25] As the prospects of a short, successful campaign encouraged the usual flood of applications, Hunter-Weston was lucky to emerge from this gentlemanly tug-of-war on the list of the thirty-one approved officers, a number slightly short of Kitchener's original request. The highly personalised nature of command and leadership in the late Victorian army encouraged the formation of well-documented 'rings' around rival commanders, a system that even percolated down to the employment of junior officers. In Hunter-Weston's case, it was lucky that he was still on leave in England when the crisis broke and was therefore able to lobby personally for inclusion.[26]

In joining Kitchener's contingent, he found himself among a group of young men already considered to be among the most promising in the army. The conspicuous presence of military engineers in their number also hinted at the extraordinary nature of the Dongola campaign. Like the North West Frontier, this would be a war against nature, involving

---

description of his campaigns (London: National Review, 1905), 147–8; Trevor Royle, *The Kitchener Enigma* (London: M. Joseph, 1985), 96.

24 Michael Asher, *Khartoum: The Ultimate Imperial Adventure* (Harmonsworth: Penguin, 2006), 298–319; Henry Keown-Boyd, *A Good Dusting: A Centenary Review of the Sudan Campaigns, 1883–99* (London: Leo Cooper, 1986), 156–75.

25 Ian Beckett, 'Kitchener and the Politics of Command' in Edward Spiers, ed., *The Sudan: The Reconquest Reappraised* (London: Frank Cass, 1998), 41.

26 He may have exploited his connection with Colonel Archibald Hunter, a 'Wolselyite' and close associate of Kitchener, who was a West Kilbride neighbour: *Ardrossan and Saltcoats Herald*, 8 December 1905; Archie Hunter, *Kitchener's Sword Arm: The Life and Campaigns of General Sir Archibald Hunter* (Staplehurst: Spellmount, 1996), 3–4.

huge distances and with even greater difficulties of climate and terrain. The power of the Mahdists had waned since the days of Gordon, but they were still fearless opponents who could quickly mass and launch frontal attacks, then melt back into the desert with equal speed. Victory in the Sudan would be won by endurance and planning rather than tactical brilliance. Kitchener's main idea was straightforward: he planned to use his mobile force to bring the enemy into open battle. His chief problem was the deployment and movement of supplies, a problem which at times almost eclipsed the actual military operations.[27] This would be solved by a laborious step-by-step advance into the enemy's heartland, maximising the advantages of river navigation and camel convoys while also creating a lifeline through the rebuilding and extension of the railway.

As the new Egyptian Army did not contain engineering troops, he was forced to rely on a handful of RE officers, including the subalterns who became known as his 'Band of Boys'.[28] Being more senior in rank, he assigned Hunter-Weston to general duties, keeping him under his hand for any operational tasks that might arise.[29] Arriving in Egypt in early May, he was initially attached to the staff of the Commandant at Wadi Halfa. Perched on the banks of the Nile amid scorching heat and roaring dust storms, the filthy barrack town was known as 'Bloody Hell-Fire' by its garrison; ominously, the British cemetery had plenty of room for new occupants and was full to capacity by the end of the campaign.[30] At first sight, this seemed a disappointing posting, but he was under orders to survey and dynamite the Nile cataracts, a mission which would be vital to the progress of the whole expedition, as Kitchener needed to gain full command of the

---

27 *The Sudan Campaign 1896–99 [by An Officer]*, (London: Chapman & Hall, 1899), 11–12.
28 E. W. C. Sandes, *The Royal Engineers in Egypt and the Sudan* (Chatham: Institution of Royal Engineers, 1937) 153–4; H. S. L. Alford and W. D. Sword, *The Egyptian Soudan: its Loss and Recovery* (London and New York: Macmillan, 1898), 200.
29 Scrapbook of the Sudan Expedition and the Boer War, Hunter of Hunterston Papers, NRAS852/501.
30 Alford and Sword, *Egyptian Soudan*, 63; Sandes, *Royal Engineers*, 157.

river before he could move to destroy the enemy.[31] The cataracts, teeth-like ridges of black and red granite between Halfa and Firket, were formidable obstacles to navigation which prevented boats from passing at low tide. Hunter-Weston began his reconnaissance beyond the Second Cataract in early May, preparing a survey that would inform the efforts of Royal Naval transport team. As crocodiles looked on, he employed methods unheard of at Chatham:

> I started my work alone, assisted by such of the natives as were likely to have a special knowledge of the subject. As I was a fairly good swimmer and had had experience of using *mashaks* (inflated skins) in India, I was able to carry out reconnaissance to Kitchener's satisfaction. My costume was simple, artistic and well suited to the purpose, for it consisted only of a large helmet, a sun umbrella and my birthday suit![32]

Initiative and improvisation were hallmarks of British colonial service, but this eye-catching ingenuity also provided ideal copy for the weekly papers, appearing as an illustration in *The Graphic* – Hunter-Weston's first taste of publicity.[33]

His survey report revealed a labyrinth of channels, three-miles long, of which only the eastern channel provided any realistically navigable option.[34] Having completed the task, he moved on to join Kitchener's staff at Akasha, a deserted mud-walled village which had been converted into a fortress. Here, the British officers' tents were pitched in a dry ravine where a few scrubby acacia trees offered some respite from temperatures reaching over 120 degrees in the shade.[35]

His new chief made an immediate impact. Bronzed from years of colonial service and impeccably uniformed, Kitchener at the age of forty-six

---

31   *Daily News*, 23 May 1896.
32   Sandes, *Royal Engineers*, 159.
33   *The Graphic*, 5 September 1896.
34   Draft of a Report on the Second Cataract with a view to selection by which to take steamers, 31st May 1896, Hunter-Weston Papers, 65/03/39/6, NAM.
35   A. H. Atteridge, *Towards Khartoum: The Story of the Soudan War of 1896* (London: A. D. Innes & Co, 1897), 142–5.

had become one of the empire's most instantly recognisable personalities.[36] With his forces concentrated by early June, the time had come for him to pounce on the Mahdist stronghold of Firket. The job of marshaling the two columns which would attack the fortified village in a pincer movement now devolved on Hunter-Weston.[37] This was a huge organisational challenge, as the plan demanded speed, surprise and perfect timing. The columns moved off quietly from Akasha on 6 June; the infantry followed a narrow, plunging track along the right bank of the Nile, while the mounted desert column made a wide detour inland to prepare for a flank and rear offensive.[38]

Hunter-Weston's first battle became a rout. Firket lay at the southern end of the 'Belly of Stones', some of the roughest country in the northern Sudan. Displaying impeccable march discipline, both columns arrived at the village at dawn the next day, just as the garrison had finished their morning prayers. They then executed a simple plan of attack with precision and ferocity. Artillery shells, Maxim rounds and rifle volleys all poured into the enemy camp and within two hours it had been surrounded and overrun at bayonet point. The basic application of modern technology did its work, and as the correspondent of the *Daily Chronicle* wandered among the enemy dead, he was relieved to see very little blood, thanks to the precision of the Martini bullet.[39]

Firket was the decisive battle of the campaign, as it forced the Mahdists from large areas of the Nile Valley. It would be three months before Kitchener's force saw action again, during which time human enemies were superseded by disease and extreme weather conditions. The Sudanese summer that year was the hottest on record, fuelled by a furnace-like wind from the south, and dysentery and cholera swept the British base during July and August.[40] Working as a cog in the 'Sudan machine' could certainly be

---

36 G. W. Steevens, *With Kitchener to Khartum* (Edinburgh: Dodd, Mead & Co., 1898), 45.
37 Alford and Sword, *Egyptian Soudan*, 87; Sandes, 163.
38 Hunter, *Kitchener's Sword-Arm*, 45–8; Royle, *Kitchener Enigma*, 108.
39 *Sudan Campaign*, 32–3; Atteridge, Towards Khartoum, 220.
40 Alford and Sword, *Egyptian Soudan*, 95–101; Hunter, *Kitchener's Sword-Arm*, 50.

frustrating. Kitchener's habit of maintaining a less than sufficient staff meant that capable officers like Hunter-Weston were required to take responsibility for crucial logistical components of the expedition without a clear sense of his overall plans being shared with them. Yet despite his reputation as a hard driver of men, he was also famous for the interest he took in their careers.[41] Already impressed by Hunter-Weston's military efficiency, he encouraged him to apply for Staff College and provided him with the necessary testimonials. A total of sixty-three officers sat the qualifying examination that August, facing a range of reportedly 'catchy' papers in mathematics, tactics, military law, topography and a language.[42] Hunter-Weston wrote his answers 'while sitting in a small tent, covered with sweat, at a table, covered with dust, on which the sweat dropped and formed mud'; despite these conditions, he was one of forty successful candidates, even though his mark of 2853 was well adrift from the top mark recorded.[43]

For the moment, campaigning took precedence. At the end of the month, the army at last began a series of gruelling desert marches. The enemy's defensive positions at Hafir were pounded on 19 September, clearing the way to Dongola. In a disappointing anti-climax, Kitchener's entire force marched into the fortified town three days later, only to find it deserted. The expedition had been exactly the sort of preemptive 'small war' prescribed in C. E. Callwell's manual of colonial campaigning, published in the same year as the expedition.[44] It had cost the Egyptian Treasury £E. 715,000 – a sum which could be considered a small price to pay for the first stage of the reconquest of Sudan.[45] For its part, the War Office had reached the limits

---

41 Royle, *Kitchener Engima*, 93–4; John Pollock, *Kitchener: The Road To Omdurman* (London: Constable, 1998), 108.
42 *Morning Post*, 28 September 1896.
43 Sandes, *Royal Engineers* 160; *Pall Mall Gazette*, 6 October 1896; *Report of the Examination for Admission at Staff College Held in August, 1896* (London: HMSO, 1896).
44 C. E. Calwell, *Small Wars: Their Principles and Practice* (London: HMSO, 1896).
45 Earl of Cromer, *Modern Egypt* (London: Macmillan, 1908), vol. II, 91.

of its generosity. By the middle of October, the Special Service Officers had been recalled to their units.[46]

The previous six months had been another important step in shaping Hunter-Weston's future. His Sudan service earned him another special mention in dispatches and a medal clasp struck for the battle of Firket, which had been classed as a 'general action': he was also one of fourteen offices who were selected to receive the Imperial Order of the Medjidie of the Fourth Class, awarded by the Khedive of Egypt.[47] This was not a bad haul in the wake of a blazing, disease-ridden campaign that had provided relatively few opportunities for combat. Victory had been won by superior planning, technology and firepower rather than a direct clash of armies on the battlefield but despite this, it was the role of charismatic personal leadership that caught the popular imagination. Although its emphasis had been on economy and practicality, the war in the Sudan helped power the romantic cult of the general towards its zenith – Kitchener rose to the status of imperial icon, while even 'Archie' Hunter, his truculent second in command, was hailed as a 'twentieth century Crusader ... a paladin drifted into the wrong century'.[48]

Staff College

Rather than joining the march on Omdurman, Hunter-Weston soon began his studies at the Staff College. He had been in no hurry to return to India, but despite passing his entrance exam in the Sudan, there had been no immediate place for him, as the Engineers and Artillery were assigned a strict quota of entrants to ensure that their talented officers did not swamp

---

46   *The Times*, 21 October 1896.
47   *The Standard*, 10 April 1897.
48   Steevens, *With Kitchener to Khartum*, 55.

every intake.[49] Instead, he was one of ten students to gain a nomination from the Commander in Chief, Sir Garnet Wolseley, joining the new cohort in January 1897; far from being a disadvantage, this was in fact held to be the most privileged route of admission, promising the pick of future staff jobs.[50]

Although its buildings were allegedly mistaken for Broadmoor Criminal Lunatic Asylum, the Staff College at Camberley was rather more congenial than Wellington or Woolwich. Established in 1858, the new foundation was initially regarded with suspicion by regimental officers, who viewed it as 'a forcing house for unpleasant people'.[51] However, by the 1890s its standing had been boosted by internal modernisation and a more progressive spirit among the officer corps as a whole. Attendance required considerable personal investment, as an officer's pay was stopped on entrance; nor was there any guarantee of a staff job upon completion of the course, despite the number of graduates being insufficient to fill the available staff vacancies. Even so, the letters '*p.s.c.*' after an officer's name – 'Passed Staff College' – had begun to decorate the narrow gateway to accelerated promotion. The College also began to attract more able and ambitious students, a significant number of whom would go on to reach the peak of their profession during the Great War.

Hunter-Weston missed the vintage 'Diamond Jubilee' cohort which included Douglas Haig, Edmund Allenby and J. E. Edmonds, but his own year of entry was still highly competitive thanks to the Sudan campaign.[52] His new colleagues were a band of committed professionals who would go on to achieve notable success in their careers. The intake of thirty-one

---

49   Baker Brown, *Corps of Engineers*, 307. For the fraught issue of his return to Indian service, see Loan of Brevet Major A. G. Hunter-Weston, R. E. for service under Egyptian government: India Office Records and Private Papers, IOR/L/MIL/7/672, Collection 5/22, British Library.
50   *The Times*, 4 October 1897; 19 January 1898; J. E. Edmonds, 'Four generations of Staff College students – 1896 to 1952. I, 1896', *Army Quarterly* LXV/1 (1952), 42.
51   Brian Bond, *The Victorian Army and the Staff College, 1854–1915* (London: Eyre Methuen, 1972), 82; A. R. Godwin-Austen, *The Staff and the Staff College* (London: Constable, 1927), xi.
52   Godwin-Austen, *Staff and the Staff College*, 278. He calculates that only a third of infantry applicants gained entry: *Morning Post*, 19 January 1898.

produced one Field Marshal (G. F. Milne, Commander of the Army in Salonika from 1916, and Chief of the Imperial General Staff, 1926–33); one General (W. P. Braithwaite, Chief of Staff, Mediterranean Expeditionary Force, 1915); two Lieutenant-Generals (Hunter-Weston and Sir John Fowler, Director of Signals for the British Expeditionary Force, 1914–18) and six Major-Generals (including Sir Arthur Lynden-Bell, who succeeded Braithwaite at Gallipoli and later became Director of Staff Duties at the War Office, 1918–21). A further five officers reached the rank of Brigadier-General, among them the military historians J. V. H. Crowe and C. R. Ballard.

There was general agreement that one of the College's most valuable functions lay in bringing together the future leaders of the army to share their expertise. As a Brevet Major, Hunter-Weston was the most senior of officer his year, most of whom were Captains. Their corps and regimental backgrounds were more limited than normal, but his colleagues brought with them an impressive range of recent service on the North West Frontier, and in Burma, China and the Sudan.[53] Attendance at Camberley also broadened informal networks; indeed, for G. F. Milne, the 'freemasonry of good fellowship, hard work and a sense of duty' acquired at Staff College was second only to pride in one's regiment or corps.[54]

For any officer who had passed through Woolwich and Chatham, the wide-ranging curriculum at Camberley was quite familiar. The students studied fortification and artillery, topography and reconnaissance, minor tactics, staff duties and military administration, as well as military history and a compulsory language; Hunter-Weston was one of eight officers to gain a first-class interpreter's qualification in German at the end of his first year.[55] Under the dynamic regime of Henry Hildyard, the Commandant from 1893 to 1898, the practice of cramming for formal examinations had been swept away and students were instead encouraged to solve practical

---

53 His year produced six artillerymen, two engineers, nineteen infantrymen and four Indian Staff Corps officers, without any representatives in either the Guards or the Cavalry.
54 Godwin-Austen, *Staff and the Staff College*, vii.
55 *The Times*, 7 December 1898.

problems of strategy, tactics and organisation in the field as well as the classroom, using techniques which enthusiasts of modern pedagogy would recognise as 'group learning' and 'role playing'.[56]

Hunter-Weston was also exposed to the teaching of G. F. R. Henderson, whose passionate lectures on military history were intended to develop the students' judgment by presenting them with real command situations. Only two of the exercises that Hunter-Weston wrote for 'Henders' survive, but while his tutor's painstaking annotations in red ink are noteworthy, even more remarkable are the pencilled ripostes added at a later date by his pupil. Whether he was driven by confidence in his own abilities or a high sensitivity to criticism, Hunter-Weston was unabashed in challenging the assessments of one of Britain's leading military theorists. His first paper was a situation appraisal written from the perspective of a Union staff officer at the outset of the Peninsular Campaign in March 1862. Although the piece was generally well executed, Henderson did not find its reasoning very conclusive, but Hunter-Weston defensively countered that poor guidance from his tutor was really at fault, as: 'I did not know what was wanted and the "instructions" rather misled me'. His second effort was much more poised. Adopting the role of one of Napoleon's staff officers on the eve of Waterloo, he was required to draw up his proposed plan of action along with appropriate orders. His account tried to grasp how the psychology of commanders such as Marshal Ney might have shaped their command decisions. Henderson found it a 'good, clear and well thought out memoir', but took exception to Hunter-Weston's typically exhaustive attempts to establish 'possible outcomes', reminding him that 'it is useless to try to lay down implicit instructions for all eventualities. It is always the unexpected that happens'. This was good advice, but Hunter-Weston's admiration of his own work was unqualified: 'An excellent appreciation, framed upon the right lines, with the issues well put'.[57]

The traditional emphasis on character and leadership was further enshrined in the students' leisure pursuits. Riding was a military necessity,

---

56 Bond, *Victorian Army*, 154.
57 Hunter-Weston Papers, 65/03/39/2, NAM.

because as Sir Evelyn Wood observed, even the most gifted staff officer was useless unless he was at home in the saddle; but the hunting field also offered opportunities to meet officers from every branch of the service, even from the Royal Navy.[58] Enthusiasm for the cult of the Staff College Drag Hounds went beyond such practicalities. Founded in 1871, 'the Drag' quickly generated its own mystique. It would be difficult to find a better example of the spirit of the old professional army, united by the rigours of imperial service and a shared approach to tactics, but equally bound by the gentlemanly ideals of honour, courage and sportsmanship. Participation in this 'school of manliness' was viewed as the most important pastime for officers, not only for building esprit de corps, but also as it fostered individual qualities of stamina and decisiveness.[59] Hard riding was reckoned to be essential to get a staff job, and even in the 1930s, students firmly believed that becoming a master or whip was a 'sure stepping stone' to rapid advancement. Hunter-Weston's election as Master of the Drag by his fellow students for the 1898–9 season was therefore a credit both to his horsemanship and to the impact that his powerful personality had had on his colleagues. The first engineer to hold the position, his success followed an earlier victory in the Staff College Point to Point, placing him in the exalted company of Allenby, Horace Smith-Dorrien, Henry Rawlinson, Arthur Godley and Hubert Gough. It would remain one of his proudest achievements.[60]

The Staff College system did have its weaknesses. After Hildyard stepped down to be replaced by the placid H. S. G. Miles the new syllabus remained, but much of the reforming momentum was lost. Although the College was intended as preparation for high command, this objective was never systematically pursued despite the high quality of entrants in the late 1890s.[61] The 'schemes' which Hunter-Weston and his colleagues developed

---

58   Godwin-Austen, *Staff and the Staff College*, 240.
59   Ian Beckett and Steven Corvi, eds, *Haig's Generals* (Barnsley: Pen & Sword, 2006), 20. For an illustrated diary of a memorable season, see: *The Staff College Drag Hunt, 1895–6* (1896).
60   Both the election and the point-to-point win are recorded in Hunter-Weston's CV: Hunter-Weston Papers, 65/03/39/12, NAM.
61   Bond, *Victorian Army*, 162.

while riding their pneumatic cycles through the Surrey countryside may have strengthened their powers of reasoning, but they were mostly related to minor tactical operations involving a small mixed force rather than a brigade or division. The experience of studying at Camberley also remained highly segmented; no Royal Navy officers participated, and as a result any 'combined operations' exercises were extremely artificial.

More seriously, Tim Travers has argued that in the case of Haig's generation, Staff College training tended to confirm rather than challenge the key tenets of 'normal' warfare.[62] Although some attempt had been made to adapt the curriculum to military realities, he suggests that the concentration on the lessons of past campaigns may have diverted attention from how new forms of military technology might shape the battlefields of the future. Modern weapons and increased firepower were acknowledged as requiring flexible tactics, but it was thought to be possible to control and overcome these challenges by bravery, stamina and towering morale. The message was also that while disciplined leadership was crucial, it was the function of the senior commander to develop his guiding idea and set out his strategic decisions, leaving their implementation to his subordinates. At the same time, the dead hand of Camberley was not the whole story. Sheffield, for example, has argued that the pragmatism and improvisation that were also central to the culture of the British army tended to undermine any instilled nostrums.[63] In fact, the concept of war as mobile and ultimately controllable was as much the product of recent experience in colonial campaigns like Waziristan or Dongola as of classroom teaching. Whatever their origins, there is little doubt that doctrines such as delegated command – deference to 'the man on the spot' – had important consequences for Hunter-Weston and some of his classmates like Walter Braithwaite, not least at the Gallipoli landings.

---

62 Tim Travers, *The Killing Ground: The British Army, the Western Front and the Emergence of Modern War, 1900–1918* (Barnsley: Pen & Sword, 1987), 85–97.
63 Gary Sheffield, *The Chief: Douglas Haig and the British Army* (London: Aurum, 2011) 27–8.

CHAPTER FOUR

Hunting the Boer

In normal circumstances, Hunter-Weston would have left Camberley at the end of 1899 and taken up a comfortable staff appointment. Instead, he was plunged into a colonial conflict which tested the standards of command and staff work in the British army as never before. By the close of hostilities in May 1902, British casualties in the Second South African War amounted to 21,842; among the fallen were four of Hunter-Weston's Staff College classmates. The war may have proved deadly for many men, but it was also Hunter-Weston's hour of opportunity. Displaying a powerful blend of professionalism and self-promotion, he began to build a reputation with a British public hungry for heroes.

Field Troop

As a thirty-five year old Brevet Major, Hunter-Weston was hardly party to the *arcana imperii* that were driving events between Capetown and London. Nevertheless, he became acutely aware of its impact on the ordered life of the peacetime army. The South African crisis had built up slowly during the summer. Continued diplomatic machinations by the British High Commissioner, Sir Alfred Milner, to re-establish supremacy in the region encountered determined resistance from the governments of the Transvaal and Orange Free State. Following the breakdown of negotiations over 'Uitlander' voting rights in June, Milner pressed for military reinforcements to overawe the Boer republics. Within weeks a 'special service draft' had been despatched from Staff College to augment local staffs and train mounted infantry in Cape Colony and Natal.[1] The fears of some that they would be left behind in the classroom were soon dispelled as Britain began to assemble its largest expeditionary force for over a century. The momentum of events was unstoppable. The arrival of the first of Sir Redvers Buller's 47,000 men at Cape Town on 9 October was pre-empted by the delivery of President Kruger's ultimatum demanding the withdrawal of all British troops from the Transvaal's borders. Seizing the initiative, the Boers launched their offensive almost immediately, injecting Britain's war aims with moral certitude, but actually constraining the army's strategic options in the months to come.[2]

Staff College gradually emptied as instructors and students were mobilised. In a typical gesture, the gentlemen paid to feed the drag hounds in the hope of returning for the new hunting season, but by springtime the College was closed and the dogs had to be destroyed.[3] Hunter-Weston's initial assignment in October was to staff duties on the lines of communication at the Cape.[4] Had he taken up this posting, the chronic shortage of trained staff officers in South Africa would have meant steady progress, but his fate took a more exiting turn after new orders arrived a few weeks later that he was instead to lead the Royal Engineers' mounted Field Troop. His new command was a highly mobile, lightly equipped version of the standard RE Field Company, combining telegraphers, bridging specialists and even photographers. Unknown in continental armies at this point, it was still something of an experimental formation in Britain, with its roots in colonial campaigning and the large-scale manoeuvres of the Indian Army in the early 1890s.[5] The appointment was a recognition of Hunter-Weston's

---

[1] Bond, *Victorian Army*, 237; A. Farrar-Hockley, *Goughie* (London: Granada, 1975), 37.
[2] Halik Kochanski, 'Planning for the Final Years of the *Pax Britannica*, 1889–1903', in David French and Brian Holden Reid, *The British General Staff: Reform and Innovation, 1890–1939* (London: Frank Cass, 2002), 18–20.
[3] Godwin-Austen, *Staff and the Staff College*, 240.
[4] *Yorkshire Herald*, 9 October 1899.
[5] Hunter-Weston later claimed that it was his own use of 'Mounted Sappers' in India in November 1891 that had set the precedent for this: Records of Service for War Office and Roorkee, Hunter of Hunterston Papers, NRAS852/336.

early promise, while the relative novelty of the unit allowed him to put his own stamp on its development.

It was not only the proficiency of the Field Troop that secured his rapid rise during the campaign. Equally important was his attachment to General Sir John French's Cavalry Division. Seldom content with a mere supporting role, this posting gave Hunter-Weston the chance to claim the limelight by fusing the technical expertise of the military engineer with the glamour of the 'cavalry spirit'. His speciality would become the demolition raid deep into enemy territory, epitomising the boldness, enterprise and dash which was prized in all British cavalry regiments. Like many aspects of the campaign in South Africa, these independent actions combined elements of modernity and tradition, looking forward to the quick, destructive Commando Raid of World War Two, but also invoking the longer pedigree of the Cavalry Raid, where troops rode in strength through enemy territory, aiming to inflict maximum material damage.

As a 'fighting engineer', Hunter-Weston's identification with the cavalry in South Africa became total as he rose to become French's senior staff officer and the commander of various mounted columns during the guerrilla phase of the campaign. In keeping with his confident and ebullient personality and his excellent horsemanship, this process of assimilation was also well judged from a professional point of view. Cavalry, as Badsey has suggested, enjoyed a revival during the 1890s and although the South African War challenged tactical doctrine and organisation, its mobility remained precious during the campaign.[6] The later shift to column warfare also gave cavalrymen a definite career advantage, preparing the ground for officers like Haig and Allenby to rise in their profession.

On 30 October, Hunter-Weston's specialist unit left Aldershot in a train packed with a vast amount of technical equipment.[7] The day of their departure coincided with 'Mournful Monday', when Sir George White's attempt to strike out of Ladysmith met with a humiliating reverse. On a

---

6   Stephen Badsey, *Doctrine and Reform in the British Cavalry, 1880–1918* (Aldershot: Ashgate, 2008), 81.
7   *Morning Post*, 1 November 1899.

smaller scale, their own experiences soon provided further portents of the misfortunes and recriminations that would come to colour the British war effort. Cheered by immense crowds, they steamed down the Mersey aboard the transport *Rapidan* on the first leg of their voyage to Cape Town.[8] Two days later, they were back. A massive storm had overwhelmed the ship, sweeping many of the horses overboard and prompting an angry debate over War Office incompetence. To make matters worse, a thirsty steward had also taken advantage of the crisis to consume Hunter-Weston's private stock of alcohol.[9] After a hectic period of refitting during which the people of Birkenhead 'adopted' the stranded troops, the ship set off again on 13 November, again cheered by thousands on the quayside. A further embarrassing return was narrowly averted after it was forced to shelter from the weather for a second time, but it managed to resume steaming slowly en route for Cape Town. After a journey of over 6,000 miles, the Field Troop at last arrived in Table Bay on 9 of December – at which point the *Rapidan* disgraced herself once again by running aground after discharging her human and equine cargo.[10]

Hunter-Weston had spent almost a month at sea, cut off from events at the front. In the meantime the British campaign had failed to prosper. Buller was forced to disperse his troops further to deal with the various Boer sieges, rather than pushing on to deliver a decisive blow in the Orange Free State. The tenacity and ingenuity of the enemy's well-armed citizen army could no longer be doubted. As the various relief columns stumbled on, various tactical errors compounded an already weak strategic position. The disasters of 'Black Week' commenced on the day after the Field Troop landed, with successive reversals at Stormberg, Magersfontein and Colenso. Against this grim backdrop, there was only one senior officer left in a position to pursue

8   *The Times*, 2 November 1899.
9   *Liverpool Mercury*, 6 November 1899; *Bristol Mercury*, 22 November 1899. For Hunter-Weston's account of the voyage, see Scrapbook of the Sudan Expedition and the Boer War, Hunter of Hunterston Papers, NRAS852/501; *Liverpool Mercury*, 8 November 1899.
10 *Morning Post*, 13 December 1899. *The Rapidan* was certainly an unlucky ship, which eventually caught fire and sunk off the Cape of Good Hope in 1906.

active operations against the Boers. On 25 January, Hunter-Weston's unit at last arrived to join Sir John French's Cavalry Division at Arundel, where the swaggering, red-faced 'General of 'orse' was vigorously countering Boer incursions in the Cape Midlands.[11]

His new commanding officer was a cavalryman to the backbone. Exuberant, feckless with money and perfectly prepared to take advantage of his unaccountable attractiveness to women, it was difficult to imagine a greater contrast from Hunter-Weston's old chief in the Sudan. The forty-seven year old 'Johnnie' French was also, however, an instinctive tactician of great personal courage who took risks and led from the front. Showing little concern for the organisational detail that powered the modern army, he gathered an able band of staff officers around him whom Hunter-Weston would shortly join.

The Field Troop had reached French's sector just as British operations were reaching a crucial stage. An aggressive Boer presence in the area threatened to disrupt vital communication lines at the heart of Cape Colony, thereby isolating the relief column which was heading for Kimberly. Outnumbered, French's reaction was to maintain a psychological edge by aggressive patrolling and making thrusting attacks on key positions. After various harassing engagements, the Boers increasingly fell back to the strong natural defences of Colesberg. There followed a four-week duel among the dusty hills and wagon roads that surrounded the town, as French probed and manoeuvred to maintain pressure. Hunter-Weston's responsibilities grew rapidly during this time since the climate and terrain presented daunting communications and supply challenges. In addition to the Field Troop, he also acted as commander of the whole Engineer Field Force attached to the Cavalry Division, maintaining a 'perfect' telegraphic and telephonic service across twenty-eight miles of the Colesberg front.[12] Often working close up to enemy positions, he provided vital support in a fast-moving campaign of night marches and coordinated swoops on enemy convoys.

---

11   Diaries of Engineer Work with Lieutenant-General French's Cavalry Division, Christmas 1899 to early March 1901, Hunter-Weston Papers, 65/03/39/7, NAM.
12   *The Times*, 5 May 1900.

Typically restless, he remained anxious for a more direct combat role. The opportunity arose at Slingsfontein on 11 January, when French attempted to drive off a strengthened Boer force which had advanced southwards into the hills. Reconnaissance revealed that they presented a formidable obstacle and Hunter-Weston was sent to work his way round the enemy's left flank with a detachment of mounted engineers in order to cut the railway and telegraph and prevent new reinforcements from arriving.[13] He was within sight of success when he found his route to the railway blocked by a concentration of the Johannesburg commando. Although he was foiled on this occasion, he was destined to make the railway his personal battlefield. Indeed, the Slingsfontein episode would become the prototype of five more ambitious and more successful forays behind enemy lines as the British campaign recovered its confidence in the coming months.

French never captured Colesberg but his operations there have since been hailed as a 'minor military classic'.[14] By early February, the new Commander-in-Chief Lord Roberts and Kitchener, his Chief of Staff, had another mission for the Cavalry Division. French was ordered to undertake a demanding five-day march to relieve the fragile garrison at Kimberly, outflanking the enemy's defensive positions on the Modder River and heading east in an 80-mile arc to ford the river further north. Hunter-Weston was now part of a 5,000-strong flying column that included the cream of the British cavalry. They set off on 11 February, during the hottest month of the South African summer. The area of the Orange Free State they were about to invade was 4,000 feet above sea level, an exceptionally dusty land with very little surface water and with little protection for the sun's rays. Supply difficulties soon slowed their progress and finding water for the Division's thirsty horses became a constant challenge for the Field Troop.

---

13   Frederick Maurice, *History of the War in South Africa, 1899–1902* (London: Hurst and Blackett, 1906–9), vol. 1, 400 [*Official History*]; L. S. Amery, ed., *The Times History of the War in South Africa, 1899–1902* (London: Sampson, Lowe, Marsden and Company, Ltd, 1900–9), vol. 3, 139 [*Times History*]; Charles Goldman, *With General French and the Cavalry in South Africa* (London: Macmillan, 1902), 57.

14   John Terraine, *Douglas Haig. The Educated Soldier* (London: Leo Cooper, 1990), 25.

The first leg of the journey was uneventful, but the second leg required French's Cavalry Division to cross twenty-five burning miles to the drifts of the Modder River. They moved off from Ramdam on 12 February in bright moonlight, riding east in three columns, with Hunter-Weston's mounted engineers following the centre column, commanded by Brigadier T. C. Porter. They had covered only four miles when they encountered enemy gunfire. Again, Hunter-Weston made sure he was in the thick of the action as French attempted to force a crossing at Dekiel Drift. From his vantage point on the higher ground he saw the enemy rushing to seize a kopje overlooking the drift on the right. Dashing down the slope, his horse lost a shoe on the stones, but he still finished at a gallop. As French and his staff looked on, Hunter-Weston rallied a skirmishing party just in time to intercept the Boers. After half an hour's concentrated rifle fire, the enemy was driven off and the British were able to secure the position.[15]

Amid blinding dust storms, the division now moved across the veldt on a five-mile front. Crossing the Modder River early on 15 February, they came under artillery and rifle fire from low rising hills which blocked their advance. After ordering covering fire from his guns, French ordered the whole division to gallop through in an open-order charge. With their weakened horses travelling at fourteen miles per hour, they powered through the enemy's central line at Klip Drift, brushing aside crossfire. In a matter of minutes they had reached their objective. Hunter-Weston's field telegraph cart was immediately on hand for French to report his success to his chief staff officer, Douglas Haig, who relayed it to Lord Roberts.[16] This was a brilliant exploit, frequently invoked in the bitter tactical debates that followed the war. Now the road to Kimberly was clear. That same evening, Hunter-Weston was one of six staff officers invited by Cecil Rhodes to celebrate at the Sanatorium Hotel, where they drank copious amounts of champagne and ate peaches and nectarines from Rhodes' own vines; their

---

15   *Daily News*, 24, 29 March 1900; Goldman, *With French*, 78–9; Christiaan de Wet, *Three Years War* (New York: Charles Scribner, 1902), 28.
16   *Official History*, vol. 2, 31; *Times History*, vol. 3, 392–5.

enjoyment was only tempered slightly by a course of horse, which Haig found 'rather tough'.[17]

The days that followed were a disappointment. The Boers had succeeded in cutting the telegraph cable, and although his engineers quickly substituted heliograph communications, orders to pursue Cronje's large force moving eastwards towards the Modder River were delayed. The Cavalry Division was now a spent force; four of the Field Troop's horses had died of exhaustion after the massive final effort of Klip Drift.[18] French was at least able to send a brigade forwards on another punishing seventeen-mile march to block Cronje at Paardeberg Drift on 17 February, although the horses were too crippled to allow the cavalry any significant role in the subsequent battle. Attempts to capitalise on the success of Kitchener's frontal attack were hampered by a continuing reduction in the military effectiveness of the cavalry which was evidenced by the series of lacklustre operations.

Demolition Raider

By early March, Roberts' great juggernaut was tramping towards Bloemfontein, the pretty capital of the Orange Free State, as Hunter-Weston's pontoon troops smoothed the cavalry's path.[19] Fearful that any further delay would allow time for the potential arrival of Boer reinforcements, French was ordered to strike northeast to probe the enemy defences. Taking Porter's brigade, along with mounted infantry and two sections of the Field Troop, he trotted out of Venter's Vallei on the afternoon of

---

17 D. Haig to H. Jameson, 22 February 1900: Edinburgh, Haig Papers, Ms 28003, National Library of Scotland, Edinburgh (NLS); *Ardrossan and Saltcoats Herald*, 8 December 1905.
18 Diaries of Engineer Work, Hunter-Weston Papers, 1965/03/39/7, NAM.
19 *Official History*, vol. 2, 194–6; *Times History*, vol. 3, 383–5.

Hunting the Boer

12 March.[20] As his reconnaissance force fanned out under harassing rifle and pom-pom fire, one squadron pushed eastwards with the mounted engineers to disrupt railway communications at Ferriera, south of Bloemfontein.

Having shown what his troop could do, Hunter-Weston was personally ordered by French to cut the line north of the capital. Calling for volunteers from the mounted engineers and cavalry pioneers, he selected Lieutenant Ronald Charles RE, along with seven sappers and guides from French's scouts.[21] Well supplied with guncotton, the small band set off at 1 a.m. on 13 March. Even though they had picked the freshest mounts, their horses had already travelled over twenty-five miles the previous day. Moving deeper into enemy territory, they first made a wide detour round the east of Bloemfontein to avoid enemy patrols, then, feeling their way north and westward, they found the main line to Pretoria which lay about two miles north of the town. The night was now pitch black. Reaching the railway at 4.00 a.m., they began to search for a suitable site to detonate, while one sapper climbed the telegraph poles and cut the wires. Twenty minutes later, Charles was lucky to find a large double-spanned culvert, and he and Hunter-Weston fixed 10lbs of explosives at each end of the girders. They lit their fuses and ran. The charges exploded at 4.50 a.m., filling the air with fragments of iron which rained down around them and creating a din that was heard by French's staff, waiting anxiously back at Ferriera Farm.[22] Five minutes later, the news had already been relayed to Lord Roberts, who quickly began his advance.

Back at the siding, Hunter-Weston had no need to check the damage. His main priority was now to get back his men to safety. He calmly ordered them to move off at a steady trot, realising that trying to gallop on exhausted horses across a veldt seamed with steep and deep-banked water courses would be unwise. After quarter of an hour, just as the first light of dawn

20 *Official History*, vol. 2, 234.
21 Later General Sir J. R. E. Charles; his account of the episode is given in letters to his mother: Charles Correspondence, 16 March 1900, 7412/79/20/2, NAM. See also Cavalry Division Diary and Orders Vol. II, 12 March 1900, Haig Papers, Acc. 3155/35, NLS.
22 Haig Diary, 13 March 1900, Haig Papers, Acc. 3155/38, NLS.

was breaking, they suddenly came upon a strong Boer picket entrenched in one of the gullies. Hunter-Weston's Dutch-speaking guide ordered them out and they obediently rode up the side of the bank, while his own men dismounted and, gripping their carbines, led their horses across. They had ridden on only thirty yards when they heard more Boers talking in another gully. This time, bluff was not an option; nor was there any convenient cover. Hunter-Weston galloped straight at the enemy, followed by his men in single file, forcing his horse to jump down into the bed some twenty feet below. Although greatly superior in numbers, the Boers immediately rushed to their horses and retired to a neighbouring ridge, pouring heavy fire on the patrol as they escaped. Protected by the thin dawn light, they crossed a final gully accompanied by shellfire from the south and a fusillade from a nearby Boer picket. With these dangers behind him, Hunter-Weston led his patrol back to the cavalry lines, reaching camp as dawn was breaking. Not a man or a horse had been lost.

It was the success of the Bloemfontein raid that properly brought Hunter-Weston to the attention of the British public – his earlier exploit at Dekiel Drift had erroneously been credited to 'Hunter and Weston'.[23] Not only had this latest raid prevented the arrival of substantial reinforcements from the north, it had also ensured the capture of a large amount of much-needed rolling stock, standing ready to leave Bloemfontein Station.[24] Shortly after his return, Hunter-Weston strode into the Bloemfontein railway offices and sent for all the heads of department. Creating 'order out of chaos', the track southwards was quickly opened and his booty pressed into service.[25]

The war correspondents who had flocked to South Africa were eager for tales of stirring deeds in exotic locations. It was not only senior commanders like French and Roberts who benefitted from the first major 'media war'. The achievements of Hunter-Weston's tiny patrol fitted comfortably into

23 *Daily News*, 24 February 1900.
24 D. Haig to H. Jameson, 16 March 1900, Haig Papers, Acc.3155/6, NLS; *Times*, 16 March 1900; *Morning Post*, 16 March 1900.
25 Cavalry Division Diary and Orders Vol. II, 13 March 1900, Haig Papers, Acc.3155/35, NLS.

the tradition of heroic imagery built up from previous colonial campaigns. Indeed, as the son of a Lucknow defender, he already had a glamorous pedigree. Coolheaded, resourceful and with a dashing leadership style, he was presented in illustrated weeklies, popular histories – and even cigarette cards – as the ideal British officer-type, displaying 'not merely the instinctive gallantry which wins Victoria Crosses, but a far higher gallantry of calculation'.[26] However, not all of his colleagues were ready to celebrate his success. The junior officers who had managed to detonate the railway at Ferriera without him resented his assumption of personal command for the Bloemfontein raid, especially as he had recently been spending most of his time on French's staff. Privately, the friends and family of Lieutenant Charles grumbled that he should have received a DSO and that Hunter-Weston 'was there but had little to do with it'.[27] This was perhaps rather unfair, as his quest for personal glory had been accompanied by assiduous attempts to win recognition for his men, including Sergeant Englefield of the 10th Hussars who was awarded the VC for rescuing a sapper during the raid.[28]

Lord Roberts and his cavalry escort entered Bloemfontein on the morning of 13 March, preceded by the press corps. By the time French was toasting his commander's health through gritted teeth at the celebratory banquet the Boers had already melted into the veldt to begin their long and energetic campaign of resistance. Arguably, it was Robert's overemphasis of the strategic importance of the enemy's capitals that prevented him from deploying the necessary forces to encircle and annihilate the enemy at the point of capture. This miscalculation was repeated throughout the rest

26 Arthur Conan Doyle, *The Great Boer War* (London: Smith and Elder & Co., 1902), 417. The incident was extensively covered in other popular histories as well as the official campaign history: Goldman, *With French*, 138–9; *Official History*, vol. 2, 236–7; *Times History*, vol. 3, 598. For typical newspaper coverage, see: *The Graphic*, 24 March 1900. The raid also gained him a further mention in despatches: *London Gazette*, 8 February 1901.
27 J. R. E. Charles to his mother, 16 March 1900; E. Mozely to E. M. Charles, 24 March 1900, Charles Correspondence, 7412/79/20/4, NAM.
28 Various drafts of the recommendation for Englefield's award survive, along with generous commendations for other officers and men, including Charles. Hunter-Weston Papers, 65/03/39/12, NAM.

of the invasion, with thrusting excursions to cut communications substituted as a less costly alternative in terms of British lives. As a consequence, Hunter-Weston, with his trademark 'bold charge', would become one of the minor personalities of the war.

French and his staff lodged at the crowded Bloemfontein Club while the division was refitted sufficiently to launch largely futile strikes eastwards at Thaba 'Nchu and Karee Siding.[29] The rest of Robert's force was equally in need of resupply, and it was not until 3 May that he began the next stage of his advance, a blistering twenty-six day march along the line of the railway to Pretoria. Losing horses at every stage of the journey, French's brigades on the left flank encountered a series of strong rearguards. A week into the march they arrived at the Zand River, where the Free State and Transvaal armies under Louis Botha seemed determined to make a stand. An effective flank attack by the cavalry outmanoeuvred Botha, but again French's exhausted force could not move quickly enough and the Boers were able to take up another strong position south of Kroonstad, the temporary Free State capital. Intent on taking the town at minimum cost, Roberts sent French urgent orders that evening to get round to the rear and blow up the railway. Despite the condition of his horses he was able to seize the Valsch River Drift, nine miles north-west of Kroonstad, but at this point a force of 3,000 Boers emerged from the town to attack. They were only driven off by the insistence of his artillery. The situation became a stalemate – the cavalry could go no further, but the line had still to be cut.

The scene was now set for a 'Boys' Own' escapade that would not have been out of place in the juvenile literature of the period. On the night of 11 May, French sanctioned Hunter-Weston's offer to take fifty hand-picked men, along with a demolition party of mounted sappers, to penetrate enemy lines. The 'adventure of empire' flavour was reinforced by the colourful presence of Frederick Russell Burnham as scout to the patrol. A celebrated explorer, hunter and cowboy, Burnham was born on a Sioux reservation in Minnesota, and after an eventful career as a soldier of fortune in Africa, had taught scouting skills to Baden-Powell. Such was

---

29   D. Haig to H. Jameson, 16 March 1900, Haig Papers, Acc.3155/6, NLS.

Hunting the Boer 51

his reputation that Roberts had summoned from prospecting in Alaska and made him his Chief of Scouts.[30] Assigned this larger than life companion, Hunter-Weston's call for volunteers was answered by two hundred men. The plan was a simple one, apparently hatched in just a few minutes. They would ride west then north, probing for the thinnest spot in the Boer picket lines and then charging through. The cavalry would subsequently have to fight their way back while Hunter-Weston and his men would slip inside the railway lines.

Steering by the stars, his little column threaded past enemy pickets thanks to the extraordinary bushcraft skills of Burnham (skills that earned him the African nickname, 'he-who-sees-in-the-dark').[31] About a mile north of the Modderspruit, the scout detected a small patrol which would have been impossible to avoid. The cavalry divided and charged. The thud of galloping horses and the flash of sabres under bright moonlight made splendid copy for the special correspondents, although the 'patrol' actually turned out to be three Africans who quickly raised the white flag.[32] Now that the outer cordon had been breached it was time for the cavalry to turn back, while the raiding party continued to edge forward, to a point fifteen miles behind the Boer lines. It was now 4.00 am and they were at the most difficult part of their mission. They were within a quarter of a mile of the railway line. The moon had just set and they had only an hour to do their work. At Amerika Siding, the very spot where they had planned to strike, the Boers had posted a whole commando.[33] Next to the railway there was a farmhouse with a small wired pasture and a nearby wagon road, along which

---

30 See F. R. Burnham, *Scouting on Two Continents* (New York: Doubleday, 1926); *Morning Post*, 18 July 1900. Burnham's career, including his raids with Hunter-Weston are fictionalised in the biographical novel by Peter Van Wyk, *Burnham. King of Scouts: Baden-Powell's Secret Mentor* (Victoria, BC: Trafford, 2003).
31 Peter Lamb, *He-who-sees-in-the-dark; the Boys' story of Frederick Burnham, the American Scout* (London: Brewer, Warren and Putnam, 1932).
32 *The Standard*, 9 June 1900; *Pall Mall Gazette*, 15 May 1900; *The Graphic*, June 23 1900; J. R. E. Charles to his mother, 14 May 1900; Charles Correspondence, 7412/79/29/2, NAM.
33 Burnham, *Scouting*, 332.

ox carts and mounted men were constantly moving. By cutting the barbed wire they entered the pasture, surprising three scouts asleep in their blankets. Hunter-Weston held his pistol to the head of one man while Burnham and Lieutenant Charles subdued the rest. Now encumbered by prisoners, he abandoned this first attempt and decided to cut the line alone with the American scout. This time there could be no doubt about Hunter-Weston's personal role in this mission. He ordered a nervous Charles to await their return and also instructed him to fight his way back to the British lines if he should fail to reappear.

They crept back on foot, only yards away from more sleeping Boers. At last they reached the railway embankment. Setting the charge of guncotton, Burnham covered the fuse with his broad-brimmed hat, while Hunter-Weston lit it. As they retreated towards their horses, the ground trembled with a roar. In the tumult, they re-joined the patrol and trotted northwest for three miles until they were out of contact with the enemy. However, the adventure was far from over. At dawn they discovered another outpost of dismounted Boers, which they charged and captured. The enemy were now in hot pursuit. After a running fight lasting two hours, the small force was beginning to take casualties, with one sapper wounded and a horse killed. Hunter-Weston ordered everyone to gallop on while he wheeled round his horse and dismounted to cover their retreat with rifle fire. The leading Boer instantly did the same. In a duel lasting less than a minute, Hunter-Weston got his man at a distance of 300 yards, ending the pursuit. After fifteen hours in the saddle and a ride of more than fifty miles, mostly in enemy territory, they returned to base on the afternoon of 12 May.[34]

The Kroonstat raid was hailed by the press as 'one of the most stirring, gallant and self-sacrificing side-histories of this war'.[35] Militarily, it had actually achieved very little. The last train had already left the town and the demolition of the railway did nothing to stop the enemy convoys withdrawing during the night. Despite this, the bravery of the episode fur-

34   Report on the Raid on the Railway North of Kroonstat, Hunter-Weston Papers, 65/03/39/12, NAM; *Official History*, vol. 3, 61.
35   *The Times*, 9 June 1900.

Hunting the Boer

ther anchored the 'mounted sappers' in the professional and the popular imagination, encouraging the formation of another three specialist units by the end of the war.[36]

Lord Roberts had, once again, victoriously entered a town that was strategically worthless. Having outmarched his railhead he was compelled to linger until the Royal Engineers and the Railway Pioneers could repair the damage that Hunter-Weston and the retiring enemy had inflicted on the line. The enemy continued its frustrating withdrawal across the veldt. On 23 May, Hunter-Weston led another volunteer mission to cut their railway communications under cover of darkness and head them off at the Rhenoster River. He returned the next morning to report that the enemy had destroyed the culverts themselves and that their rear guard was already twenty miles north of the river, which had long since been abandoned.[37] As resistance ebbed away, the British entered Johannesburg on 31 May. Forsaking a direct attack, the Boer army was allowed to flow out of the city intact under a twenty-four hour armistice.

Convinced of the moral effect of fall of the Transvaal's capital, the pattern was repeated five days later at Pretoria, with the Boer troop trains rolling out before the British arrived. Rather than ordering French's force eastwards of the railway to block their retreat, Hunter-Weston and Burnham were despatched to cut the line with band of 200 picked men, while the bulk of the cavalry remained in the west in the hope of heading off any escape by President Kruger. Their objective, the 400-mile long Pretoria–Delagoa Railway, was the main artery for Boer munitions arriving from Germany and other friendly overseas powers, but the mission was made all the more pressing by the rumour that the enemy intended to use the line to ship out thousands of British prisoners of war to the pestilential Portuguese East African border.[38] This was intended to be a fast-paced demolition mission, blowing up tanks, bridges and culverts as fast and as far as possible.

---

36   Baker Brown, *Corps of Engineers*, 276.
37   Cavalry Division Diary and Orders Vol. II, 22 May 1900, NLS, Haig Papers, Acc. 3155/35, NLS; Goldman, *With French*, 239.
38   Cavalry Division Diary and Orders Vol. II, 1 June 1900, NLS, Haig Papers, Acc. 3155/35, NLS.

Setting off on 1 June, they moved rapidly through the night and covered twenty miles undetected. However, their good luck did not hold; as dawn broke, Burnham moved forward to reconnoitre at Bapsfontein Farm, but they had already been spotted. They found themselves attacked by a whole Boer commando who poured out of the nearby escarpment.[39] The situation seemed desperate, with survival now the main priority. Taking advantage of the uneven terrain, Hunter-Weston was able to make a running fight from one position to another, but his centre was hard pressed and his flanks not much less in danger. He now sent the intrepid Burnham to gallop through the Boer lines for help, while he rallied his exhausted men behind nearby kraal, which he transformed into an improvised fort.[40] The Boers crept up in skirmishing lines, but faltered and turned back rather than making a final assault, allowing Hunter-Weston to get his men away.

Although credited in the *Official History* with helping to intimidate President Kruger, when viewed in objective terms the Delagoa mission was undoubtedly a failure. It had taken Hunter-Weston's presence of mind and resolve under pressure to prevent his whole patrol from being cut up or taken prisoner.[41] It is difficult in retrospect to see how the enterprise could have succeeded, as the force assigned to it was too large to evade discovery, but too small to combat determined resistance. A small covert operation might have been more effective, but even this is doubtful; the following day Burnham embarked on a solo raid, after Hunter-Weston's attempts to draw off the Boers to the west of the line, but this attempt failed and resulted in his serious injury.[42]

---

39   Report on the attempted Raid on the Delagoa Bay Railway, 1–2 June 1900, Hunter-Weston Papers, 65/03/39/12, NAM.
40   Goldman, *With French*, 259.
41   *Official History*, vol. 3, 95.
42   *Daily News*, 6 June 1900.

Column Commander

The Delagoa operation was not quite the end of Hunter-Weston's career as a demolition raider – a further expedition on the night of the 5 June destroyed the railway north of Pretoria – but he returned increasingly to a more conventional role on French's staff.[43] The Cavalry Division was now despatched by Roberts into the Eastern Transvaal to prepare for the army's general advance against Botha in July. The results were predictable: retreating Boers, tired horses and failed pursuits. By the middle of August, French was ordered to hold a defensive line around Middelburg on the Delagoa Bay Railway. Here, he replayed his earlier harassing operations at Colesberg while Hunter-Weston tackled the division's transport and supply problems by improvising rolling stock from trucks and locomotives which had been commandeered from local collieries.[44] Following the railway eastwards, Roberts' advance rolled over the enemy in a final set-piece battle at Belfast on 27 August. French was given his own chance to shine with the long-awaited permission having finally arrived to mount an attack on Baberton, a well-defended supply depot and communications hub. His force crossed the mountains by bridle path, with Hunter-Weston again in charge of transport. French led from the front as the cavalry plunged down to capture the town from the heights above it in a surprise attack on 13 September.[45]

It seemed that autumn as though the conflict in South Africa was drawing to a close. Indeed, its history was already being written, with Hunter-Weston advertised as one of the contributors to an ambitious narrative being compiled by *The Times*.[46] His nine months of active service had produced the usual rewards. Mentioned in Lord Roberts' despatches, his

---

43 Goldman, *With French*, 270.
44 *Times History*, vol. 3, 435.
45 *Official History*, vol. 3, 412–18.
46 *The Times*, 24 October 1900. Rather than allowing independent authorship, drafts were actually sent to selected participants for checking: Beckett, *Victorians at War*, 86.

appointment as Deputy Assistant Adjutant General (DAAG) on French's staff was confirmed just before the capture of Baberton; this was followed by his long-awaited substantive promotion to Major in October.[47]

In fact, Hunter-Weston's war lasted another year, even though its face had already begun to change. Captain Maurice Grant's rather despairing preface to the fourth volume of the *Official History* captured the 'universal stir' which characterised the conflict's final phase. From December 1900 to May 1902, the whole theatre of operations was racked with incessant guerrilla warfare. It was inevitable that British military superiority would inevitably wear down local resistance, but as formal warfare disintegrated, Grant found it almost impossible to discern any cumulative development in the constant movement of columns and commandos, in which a flurry of hundreds of small victories and defeats followed one another in rapid succession.[48] This new kind of war, largely conducted away from the public gaze, brought both challenges and opportunities for military professionals as while the fragmentation of an elusive enemy defied conventional staff work, it also increased the possibilities for independent command.

Amid wrangles over the future direction of the war, Kitchener, the new Commander in Chief, sanctioned more drastic methods of scouring the country, with the aim of striking hard at scattered Boer detachments. Early in 1901, mounted troops began to the original self-contained infantry columns with their lumbering ox carts. Although the language was that of sport – 'drives', 'bags' and 'stops' – the new warfare posessed a systematic, industrial quality. Kitchener's approach was typically single-minded and executed on a grand scale. Converging flying columns were sent to clear areas by trapping guerrillas against fortified lines or smashing them in a pincer movement. Hunter-Weston's introduction to the new regime began in late January, when French's Division was ordered to concentrate in the Eastern Transvaal to sweep the enemy off the High Veldt.

For any trained staff officer, the challenges of the mission and the limitations of Kitchener's system must have been obvious. The vastness of

47   *Standard*, 12 September, 3 October 1900; *The Times*, 9 September 1901.
48   *Official History*, vol. 4, i–iii.

the distances involved and the level of exposure to the enemy at all points left any invading force extremely isolated and vulnerable. The countryside was destitute of supplies apart from a few scattered farms and impoverished townships, but somewhere in this wasteland roamed around 6,000 enemy soldiers, constantly dispersing like 'broken bubbles of mercury', but never regrouping long enough to be found and decisively destroyed.[49] For the next three months, French's force would repeatedly sweep the area diagonally, first eastwards while the northern exits were barred, then south-eastwards, where it was hoped to corner the commandos of Botha in a fatal cul-de-sac. Meanwhile, Boer families judged capable of providing sustenance to the enemy were removed in empty railway supply wagons for settlement in a growing number of internment camps.[50]

Hunter-Weston's responsibilities now increased significantly. On 31 December 1900 he became French's chief staff officer, following Haig's promotion to an independent column command.[51] He immersed himself in the organisational and personnel systems that enabled the force to work as a cohesive whole. Providing logistical support to maintain the mobility of the columns was in itself a massively complex undertaking, involving as it did the precise calculation of times, places and loads for supply convoys and their escorts. Success was also dependent on adequate intelligence and secure and rapid communication. Unfortunately, information on Boer movements was often out-of-date by the time it reached French's HQ and it therefore became difficult to accurately control and direct the columns using despatch riders, heliograph and telegraph.[52]

Despite these frustrations, his career continued to flourish. The slowness of French's staff to receive decorations had earlier been the source of some concern, but in April he was given another brevet promotion to

---

49 *Official History*, vol. 4, 112.
50 Narrative of Operations in the Eastern Transvaal and Natal, 27 January-16 April, Hunter-Weston Papers, 65/03/39/8, NAM.
51 Hunter-Weston CV (undated), Hunter-Weston Papers, 65/03/39/5, NAM.
52 *Official History*, vol. 4, 198.

Lieutenant-Colonel and awarded the DSO.[53] His next posting was to the Cape Colony, where French had been placed in command of field operations in early June. Tactically, the outlook here seemed more favourable than it had been in the Eastern Transvaal, as harassing operations in the centre of the region had apparently succeeded in transforming the enemy from raiders into fugitives. The next step, excluding them from the south of the region and forcing them northwards over the Orange River, seemed relatively straightforward for an overwhelming force of 15,000 men. In fact, the enemy commandos had retained their self-belief and were ably led by experienced commanders. Splitting into small bands, they filtered through the British cordon and vanished southwards into the mountains, from where they were able to strike out repeatedly at hapless British patrols.[54] For the next month, French's columns seemed unable to achieve more than to push the commandos from one corner of Cape Colony to another. A new winter offensive was urgently needed.

Hunter-Weston was one of the immediate beneficiaries of this crisis, as he was selected to lead one of columns which were organised to counter the increasing proliferation of marauding bands. His new command was an important one – columns were cavalry brigades in all but name, complete with staff, intelligence, signallers and transport. His force, was formed at Graaf Reinet in mid-July and numbered 468 mounted men, accompanied by cyclists, artillery and a machine-gun detachment.[55] Composed of detachments from the 5th (Royal Irish) Lancers and the Prince of Wales Light Horse, it bore witness to the war's voracious appetite for military manpower. The Royal Irish were Britain's oldest lancer regiment, while the Light Horse were one of the many irregular colonial corps who were now plugging the gaps in the British war effort. Although most columns of this type were assigned to rising stars of the cavalry, such as Edmund Allenby

---

53 *London Gazette*, 19 April 1901; Haig to Henrietta Jameson, 9 Jul. 1900, Haig Papers, Acc.3155/6, NLS; *Times*, NLS. At this point 'not a single staff officer from French down' had been recognised.

54 Staff Diary of Mobile Columns under Lieutenant-General Sir John French, Cape Colony, June-July, 1901, Hunter-Weston Papers, 65/03/39/9, NAM.

55 *Official History*, vol. 4, 244.

and Julian Byng, Hunter-Weston's promotion was by no means unusual, as the minute subdivision of the field force meant that the net was cast more widely across other branches of the service. These however remained highly personalised appointments over which Kitchener retained an obsessive control. They were also highly risky in career terms, as the Commander-in Chief continued to closely monitor his column commanders, with perceived poor performance resulting in speedy dismissal and a damaged reputation.

The ideal leader was described as 'almost a bushman' – an instinctive fighter who could quickly gain mastery of the terrain.[56] This was a consummate war of movement. The most frequent types of engagements were ambushes and long-range skirmishes, usually with limited casualties on either side, although during the course of the campaign Boer tactics became more flexible, even featuring mounted charges.[57] Hunter-Weston had little time to adjust to the new conditions of warfare. Concentrating his disparate force at Middelburg on 21 July, his men marched twenty-two miles west the next day, searching the households of those whom were reported to be disloyal. Conditions were harsh and the health of his troops suffered from very cold nights and lack of sleep.[58]

He would become an astute and resolute commander, capable of rapid response and master of the 'smart engagement'.[59] The new drive had begun, following rumours of a renewed Boer invasion attempt. It became increasingly necessary for French to draw the bulk of his troops towards the crossings of the Orange River, carrying out a general sweep between the midland and western lines of the railway. On the right flank, Hunter-Weston's column replaced that of Colonel Henry Scobell, one of French's most experienced commanders. By 26 July, four columns were ready to scour the countryside: Lieut.-Colonel Beauchamp Doran and Captain

---

56 Terrain, *Haig*, 29.
57 Badsey, *Doctrine and Reform*, 122.
58 Staff Diary for Hunter-Weston's Column in Cape Colony, 21 July-31 August, Hunter-Weston Papers, 65/03/39/10, NAM; *Times*, 15 July 1901; *Official History*, vol. 4, 232, 244.
59 Louis Creswick, *South Africa and the Transvaal War* (Edinburgh: T. C. and E. C. Jack, 1902), vol. 7, 138.

F. T. Lund were positioned in front, along the railway at Hanover Road and Reitfontein, with Hunter-Weston and Lieut.-Colonel W. P. Wyndham covering the rear at Richmond. Riding abreast northwards, they spread out between Beaufort West and Graaf Reinet. Although their efforts were assisted by rapid blockhouse building along over two hundred miles of the Orange River, the first phase of the drive was unsuccessful since all but one of the Boer commandos were able to break back from the frontier.

At the end of the month French decided to change tactics. The successful harrying of the commandos in the Cape Midlands had placed their incursions under manageable limits, but he felt that one decisive push could move them beyond the river and clear the Colony once and for all. The combined drive formula was now repeated on a more extensive scale in order to spring the trap on the Midland commandos. Three new columns joined the hunt, making ten in all. The plan was relatively sophisticated. On 29 July the columns first rode southwards in a feint, deliberately maintaining wide gaps between their flanks in order to encourage the Boers to break through to the north. On 2 August, Hunter-Weston's force suffered their first casualties when they began a duel with Theron's commando at Zuurfontein. Spotting the enemy transport trekking up the valley, he impulsively made a dash with the 5th Lancers. On emerging from a spruit 600 yards away from Zuurfontein Farm, he was assailed by heavy fire from both flanks and forced to retire, suffering one man killed and another wounded. Undaunted, he regrouped and pursued the enemy to the crown of the nearby hills, at which point they predictably melted away.[60]

The next day, French's columns turned round to begin the return drive. Most of the Boers were now trapped between the columns and the Orange River. Over the next few weeks they made desperate attempts to escape, braving the blockhouses and armoured trains which blocked their retreat. On the night of 16 August, the end seemed close; Doran was to the north of the enemy and Hunter-Weston behind them at Paarde Vallei, with Scobell and Kavanagh waiting to the south. Before dawn the columns

---

60 Staff Diary for Hunter-Weston's Column, Hunter-Weston Papers, 65/03/39/10, NAM.

began to converge and displaying incredible courage, the outnumbered Boers galloped out to meet them. Discovering a narrow gap between the two southern columns they charged through the darkness. By afternoon they were safely back in their redoubt in the Rhenoster Berg, leaving a trail of dead horses behind them. The chase then began all over again, as the columns had to split up to hunt down the fragmented bands until exhaustion drove them to re-equip.

French's force was still making dogged progress, wearing down the enemy by keeping them on the move and denying them fresh horses. Indeed, his achievements in the Cape Colony removed the need for further major operations to remove the civilian population. The next two months were dominated by attempts to contain Jan Smuts' audacious incursion into the Colony from the north, while at the same time combating commandos who had escaped from the August bag and who were now causing havoc. Hunter-Weston's force, which had grown to 700 men, was one of sixteen columns under French's command focusing on driving the enemy northwards back across the Orange River.[61]

These gruelling contests, in which the enemy's weather-beaten riflemen vanished as suddenly as they had appeared, tested the stamina of even the most robust commanders. Allenby felt physically and mentally drained by his column work around Pretoria, while an equally spent Scobell had to be relieved of his command at the end of 1901.[62] Hunter-Weston shared these pressures and fatigue. Hospitalised with fever during October, he nevertheless insisted on getting back in the saddle before the disease had run its course.[63] He rejoined his column just in time for the latest thrust of French's policy of attrition, which was aimed at preventing any combination with the western commandos. The columns were once again on the move, scouring the Midlands and the southern counties. Hunter-Weston's last task was to chase a marauding band of fifty Boers who had crossed the Orange

---

61 *Official History*, vol. 4, 270–90; *The Times*, 16 September 1901; *London Gazette*, 17 January 1902.
62 *Official History*, vol. 4, 369.
63 *Scotsman*, 2 November 1901.

River on 22 November. Posted near Colesberg, the region where he had begun his war service, his column left at dawn the next day and had covered forty miles by nightfall.[64] Due to faulty intelligence reports, the column was required to cover an estimated 301 miles over the next ten days, trekking mostly by night. The weather was extremely cold, windy and inhospitable, with torrential rain washing away all trace of the Boers' tracks. After a further failure in intelligence, their elusive quarry broke westwards to the shelter of the Kareekloof hills. Bitterly disappointed, Hunter-Weston was again 'very seedy with fever', but stayed post until his column was ordered to return to Philpstown, where he was forced to hand over command.[65] Invalided home, he arrived at Southampton on 17 January.[66]

Hunter-Weston's invaliding was a low-key ending to a 'good war'. He had shown great personal courage under fire and exercised determined leadership in the challenging conditions of mobile warfare. He had also developed his tactical and organisational skills, serving in a senior capacity on the staff of one of the war's more successful commanders. Active service in South Africa was, of course, a common bond among the generation of senior officers who later fought in the Great War. The South African War was, however, a complex and lengthy struggle in which personal combat experiences were diverse and sometimes contradictory. Hunter-Weston witnessed the bloody assaults against entrenched positions at Paardeburg, but he had not been involved in the great set piece battles of the opening months of the war which had challenged traditional infantry tactics and encouraged new operational procedures. Instead, his war was one of sudden strikes and rapid movement, where quickness in decision making, boldness in command and above all faith in the offensive spirit had to be maintained.

The war which had just ended was not the sort of tidy campaign that he had studied at Staff College. It was a transitional military conflict, whose 'lessons' were confusing and contested. For all the debate that it unleashed,

64 Narrative of Operations of Hunter-Weston's Column, Hunter-Weston Papers, 65/03/39/11, NAM.
65 *Official History*, vol. 4, 366; *Scotsman*, 27 December 1901.
66 *The Times*, 2, 13 January 1902.

critics at the time agreed that reform of the army was inevitable. One of the most significant products of the managerial revolution that followed was the creation of a British General Staff. Hunter-Weston knew that membership of this new body would be essential to the continued progress of his army career.

CHAPTER FIVE

Brain of the Army

After six months of convalescence, Hunter-Weston was given command of the 11th Field Company and posted to Shorncliffe Camp in Kent.[1] After being so close to the centre of events in South Africa, he found the return to routine duties frustrating. As his professional world shrank over the next few years, he also faced the risk of being leapfrogged by colleagues with equally impressive war records.[2] At the root of his problem was the British Army's fondness for operating in separate compartments. While the South African war had blunted this tendency – as his own attachment to the Cavalry Division proved – the old barriers between the different service arms soon re-asserted themselves.[3] Despite his connection with French, whose own turbulent star continued to rise during these years, his affiliation to a specialist corps now threatened to limit his opportunities, particularly as the Royal Engineers were experiencing a painful period of post-war contraction.[4] The threat of being marginalised was particularly irksome given that the debate over the army's future tactics and mission was just beginning to gain momentum. Recognising the influence of modern firepower and weaponry, the officer corps struggled to balance the destructive reality of the new military technology with a professional culture that prioritised the human factor in winning battles. A complex process of administrative reform was also underway, involving both staff work and

---

1 Records of Service for War Office and Roorkee, Hunter of Hunterston Papers, NRAS852/336.
2 William Birdwood, for example, was made a full Colonel by 1905 and a Major-General by 1911: Beckett and Corvi, *Haig's Generals*, 34.
3 Bidwell and Graham, *Firepower*, 3; Robbins, *British Generalship*, 12–13.
4 Watson, *History of the Corps of Royal Engineers*, vol. 3, 20.

command structures, as the British military establishment began to prepare for the growing likelihood of a war in Europe.[5]

Staff Officer

Before he could engage in the clash of blueprints and ideas, Hunter-Weston first had to secure a staff appointment. He began to plan his escape from Shorncliffe from late 1903 onwards, making discreet use of professional networks by lobbying both of the major rings that split the officer corps.[6] Although his war service had brought him into close association with Sir John French and with the Wolseley camp, one of his first approaches was to the Quartermaster-General, Sir Ian Hamilton, one of the foremost members of the Roberts clique. For good measure, he also wrote to the prominent Wolseleyite, Sir Henry Hildyard, former Staff College Commandant and now Director General of Military Education.[7] When neither could assist, he contacted the Military Secretary of the War Office directly; in the end it was the arch-fixer Henry Wilson, the new Deputy Director of Staff Duties and another Roberts protégé, who helped to secure his appointment as DAAG to IV Army Corps in September 1904.[8]

This was a poignant promotion for Hunter-Weston since his father had died at Hunterston the previous month.[9] Fortunately, his personal affairs soon assumed a happier outlook. Like many of his brother officers,

---

5   Tim Travers, 'The Offensive and the Problem of Innovation in British Military Thought, 1870–1915', *Journal of Contemporary History* 13/3 (1978), 531–53.
6   For a typical function of the Staff College Dinner Club attended by Hunter-Weston at the Ritz Hotel, see *The Times*, 23 June 1911.
7   I. Hamilton to HW, 23 November 1903; H. Hildyard to HW, 26 November 1903, Hunter of Hunterston Papers, NRAS852/292.
8   J. Spencer Ewart to HW, 7 March 1904; H. Wilson to HW, 13 January 1905, Hunter of Hunterston Papers, NRAS852/292; *London Gazette*, 9 September 1904.
9   *Ardrossan and Saltcoats Herald*, 19 November 1904.

Hunter-Weston had postponed matrimony, but in August 1905 he proposed to Miss Grace Strang Steel and was duly accepted.[10] It proved a good match. Aged twenty-one, Grace was twenty years his junior, a striking-looking young woman, with an abundance of dark hair. She may have lacked her husband's pedigree (her forbears were Glasgow tradesmen and Lanarkshire farmers) but her father had made a large enough fortune in the Burma trade to retire and purchase the fine old estate of Philiphaugh in Selkirkshire.[11] The marriage took place in December in the music room of the bride's home; their wedding presents included a silver bowl from French and his staff, and a painting from Sir Ian and Lady Hamilton.[12] For the next thirty-five years, Grace would be Hunter-Weston's strongest supporter; but, far from being a meek 'helpmate', she also established herself as a woman of firm, independent character and marked organisational ability.

Hunter-Weston fully repaid Wilson's confidence. He was an able staff officer, showing himself to be systematic, conscientious and above all, capable of breaking down complex tasks into a myriad of sequential detail. In keeping with the spirit of the times, IV Army Corps was reconstituted as Eastern Command in February 1905. With the formal inception of the General Staff the following year, Hunter-Weston was among a select group appointed to the first 'General Staff List'.[13]

Joining the rather slender complement of peacetime staff officers, his new role focussed on raising the standards of training throughout the command.[14] Many challenges lay ahead, not least in combating what French has termed the 'mental parochialism' of the regimental system.[15] The dispersal of units throughout an operational area covering East Anglia and

---

10   *Ardrossan and Saltcoats Herald*, 11 August 1905; Gary Sheffield and John Bourne, eds, *Douglas Haig. War Diaries and Letters, 1914–18* (London: Phoenix, 2006), 12.
11   *The Times*, 3 January 1911.
12   *Ardrossan and Saltcoats Herald*, 8 December 1905.
13   John Gooch, *The Plans of War: The General Staff and British Military Strategy, c.1900–16* (London: Routledge and Kegan Paul, 1974), 107; Records of Service for War Office and Roorkee, Hunter of Hunterston Papers, NRAS852/336.
14   Bond, *Victorian Army*, 231.
15   French, *Military Identities*, 162.

the Home Counties did not help to build a common sense of purpose, while basic funds for training were the subject of repeated wrangles with the finance department of the War Office, often resulting in half-strength troop deployment.[16]

As he plunged himself into the task of writing scenarios for army exercises and 'appreciations' of operational performance, Hunter-Weston began to build links with a number of future colleagues. Working beside Julian Byng and Colonel Thomas D'Oyly Snow, he was one of the directing staff for the staff tours that were held in the Severn Valley during 1905 and 1906. Their object was to give senior army officers practice in tactical schemes involving large formations, in the hope that they would cascade the accrued insight and experience to their subordinates.[17] The highlight of the training year, however, was the annual combined manoeuvres, which tested commanders as much as divisions and brigades; in 1907 these were held in Wiltshire, matching Ian Hamilton, now General Officer Commanding (GOC) Southern Command, against the hapless Major General Sir Frederick Stopford.[18] Hunter-Weston and a young team of staff officers spearheaded the drive for better press and public understanding of this aspect of the army's work in this area. Drawing on his recent South African experience he also took great personal pride in in creating imaginative intelligence training, while 'still only a GSO [General Staff Officer] 2nd Grade'.[19] Covering reconnaissance, interrogation and night work, these intensive, month-long courses for selected officers were also striking for their input from military personalities of the future, such as 'Johnnie' Gough VC and William 'Wully' Robertson.

Escaping from his local responsibilities, Hunter-Weston was one of a number of British staff officers invited to the *Kaisermanöver*, exercises held around the Coblenz area of Germany during September 1905. These

16 Bidwell and Graham, *Fire-Power*, 42–3.
17 Staff Tours 1905–6, with an appreciation by AHW, Hunter-Weston Papers, 65/03/39/14, NAM.
18 *The Times*, 14 July 1907.
19 Reports on the Eastern Command Intelligence and Reconnaissance Courses, 1907 and 1908, Hunter-Weston Papers, 65/03/39/15/16, NAM.

manoeuvres would soon shift towards a focus on more realistic war planning, but on this occasion they functioned as a massive stage set for the Kaiser's unmilitary meddling.[20] They also provided foreign observers with an excellent opportunity for assessing the strengths and weaknesses of the German military machine. While modern commentators have hailed the consistency and superiority of German training and command systems, Hunter-Weston on the contrary found both to be wanting.[21] He realised that the German war games were for the training of the General Staff rather than the troops, but even so he found them wildly unrealistic, featuring rather too much 'theatrical work'.[22] The infantry were kept closely in hand and made to push on 'victoriously' in thick lines with the bayonet; constant forward assaults were launched, with no attempt at flank attacks. Although the marching power of the men was remarkable, his engineer's eye noted the lack of entrenchment even in defence. While admitting the thoroughness of their staff work, overall he saw the antithesis of the pragmatic approach he had learned from his own military service. Indeed, he detected little of the tactical flexibility later associated with German army's doctrine of decentralised decision-making, believing instead that the work was so subdivided that 'red tape, lack of initiative and fear of responsibility are apt to ensue'.[23]

Despite these weaknesses, the *Kaisermanöver* offered many insights into the deadly trajectory of modern warfare. Hunter-Weston's interest in new technology reached beyond developments in his own service branch. The shooting power of the artillery's new quick-firing recoil gun fascinated him, as well as the infantry's use of machine-guns in separate batteries, rather

---

20 Annika Mombauer, *Helmuth von Moltke and the Origins of the First World War* (Cambridge: Cambridge University Press, 2001), 59–66.
21 Martin Samuels, *Command or Control?: Command, Training and Tactics in the British and German Armies, 1888–1918* (London: Frank Cass, 1999); Terence Zuber, *The Mons Myth. A Reassessment of the Battle* (Stroud: History Press, 2010), 13–62.
22 *Kaisermanöver*, 1905. Reported on by Bt. Lt.-Col. A. Hunter-Weston, Hunter-Weston Papers, 65/03/39/13, NAM.
23 *Kaisermanöver*, Hunter-Weston Papers, 65/03/39/13, NAM.

than the British practice of attaching them to battalions.[24] His appreciation of the inexorable development of firepower was accompanied by an equal awareness of the scale of the losses that this implied. Commenting on the lack of attention paid to casualty management in the German manoeuvres, he was told by his hosts that: 'in future wars there would be no attempt to remove the wounded during an action, but they would be left to lie quiet where they fell, and would be collected only at night'.[25]

High flying officers were expected to move rapidly from one staff post to another, but it may have been his courtship of Miss Strang Steel that prompted Hunter-Weston to canvass Henry Wilson again in the spring of 1905 with a view to filling a General Staff vacancy in Scotland.[26] This time Wilson could not help, and it took another three years before he was promoted join the Scottish Command at Edinburgh Castle as General Staff Officer, Grade 1 (GSO1) in the summer of 1908 – an appointment which brought hearty congratulations from Kitchener.[27] In the interim, Lord Haldane's army reform measures had begun to take effect. The regular army was now reordered as a first line expeditionary force and a Territorial Force for home defence. These sweeping administrative changes, combined with a growing apprehension that Germany would be the most likely antagonist in any continental war, set the agenda for his new appointment. Absorbed in the latest debates on army reform and compulsory military service, much of Hunter-Weston's time was dedicated to training the Territorial Force units which formed the largest part of Scottish Command, although the deteriorating international situation gave a special edge to the usual round of instructional tours and exercises.

Discovering that Territorial officers were keen and commendably self-educated in military subjects, Hunter-Weston believed that they required to be taught how to apply their knowledge in the field. Addressing one

24 Observing the 1913 Imperial German Manoeuvres, C. E. Callwell made similar criticisms: *Stray Recollections* (London: Edward Arnold & Co., 1923) vol. 2, 251.
25 *Kaisermanöver*, Hunter-Weston Papers, 65/03/39/13, NAM.
26 H. Wilson to HW, 5 April 1905, Hunter of Hunterston Papers, NRAS852/292.
27 *London Gazette*, 26 June, 10 July 1908. Kitchener to HW, 18 March 1908: Hunter of Hunterston Papers, NRAS852/327.

eager group in the autumn of 1908, he attempted to explain the interconnectedness of the modern army and the managerial demands that this imposed on commanders:

> No unit, no arm nowadays, must think only of its individual action. It must look upon itself as a constituent of an organised whole, or to put it colloquially, as part of a team ... the secret of success nowadays is <u>organisation</u>, organisation, and again organisation. Organisation is the secret of success both in the business of commerce and the business of war.[28]

These principles were put into practice at the Scottish General Manoeuvres of 1910, which were intended to prove that the Territorials could and should be taken seriously as a fighting force.[29] Hunter-Weston meticulously planned the exercises, liaising with the Admiralty to establish a detailed scenario for a simulated enemy invasion of the Fife coast, including careful preparations for a test of casualty evacuation arrangements for Scotland's 'citizen soldiers'.[30] He acted as Chief of Staff, with General Sir Bruce Hamilton, GOC Scottish Command, as overall Director. The weather was atrocious. Among of the drenched ranks of the Lowland Division that summer were some of the same troops that he would command in the July battles at Gallipoli in 1915. Their performance on this occasion was highly uneven and possibly influenced his later judgment of their capacities, as although they adapted well to the appalling conditions, there were repeated failures of communication and often little evidence of definite plans of attack.[31]

The tactical weaknesses of the new part-time force particularly attracted his attention. Enthusiastic battalions had used dangerously wide frontages in both attack and defence, with their officers needlessly leading them over

---

28 Lecture on 29th September on the organisation of a division, Scottish Command, Hunter-Weston Papers, 65/03/39/17, NAM.
29 Allan and Carswell, *Thin Red Line*, 33, 111–12.
30 War Games, 1909 and 1910, Scottish Command, Hunter-Weston Papers, 65/03/39/17, NAM.
31 *Scotsman*, 27 July 1910; Review of Training, 1910, Scottish Command, Hunter-Weston Papers, 65/03/39/17, NAM.

exposed ground and showing scant regard for cover. Hunter-Weston instead stressed the need for concentrated fire and the maintenance of cohesion as necessary conditions of movement. One of the chief lessons drawn from the exercises related to the use of covering and supporting fire; the object was to overwhelm the enemy via a hammer blow delivered at close quarters, but to do so required both high morale and great attention to fire discipline.[32]

War Office

Hunter-Weston's Scottish posting featured many pleasant interludes, not least the splendidly choreographed ceremonial duties that occupied the peacetime army. He had set up home with Grace at Crammond Bridge in Midlothian, where the couple maintained a substantial household, as befitted their social position.[33] He was profiled in the *United Services Gazette* in 1910, an indication that his reputation as an innovative and intelligent staff officer had continued to grow.[34] For an ambitious soldier still in his early forties, the lure of a War Office appointment was inescapable, and in March 1911 he became Assistant Director of Military Training.[35] Far from being distanced from political manoeuvring, as Gardiner suggests,

---

[32] Memorandum on Infantry Training, 1911, Scottish Command, Hunter-Weston Papers, 65/03/39/17, NAM.

[33] *Scotsman*, 6 June 1909. At Braehead House, they kept six house servants, a groom and a chauffeur.

[34] *United Services Gazette*, 22 September 1910. He also remained a specialist in military engineering and set exam papers for the Staff College which drew on examples from South Africa and the Russo-Japanese War: Junior Division Staff College Exam Papers 1909, Hunter-Weston Papers, 65/03/39/17, NAM.

[35] *London Gazette*, 7 March 1911.

his career was now firmly back on track, with his new post taking him to the heart of the latest developments in tactical thinking.[36]

The year 1911 marked another important stage in his personal life. With his mother's sudden death in October, he became the 27th Laird of Hunterston.[37] Shrewd to the last, Jane Hunter had settled her affairs and handed over the estate in good order. Despite later inheriting Lane House in Dorset from a Weston kinsman, the 'family seat', as he liked call it, remained closest to Hunter-Weston's heart, offering him a respite from military duties and, eventually, a launch-pad for his political career.

Hunter-Weston's new position was certainly not a Whitehall sinecure. The Department of Military Training (DMT) had been reconstituted as part of the new General Staff machine, assuming responsibility for all army education with the exception of the Staff College.[38] Initially under the direction of Sir Archibald Murray, the work involved long hours of planning army exercises and preparing training manuals. There remained the challenge of training the Territorial Force in the face of resistance from regional commanders who often disliked centralised initiatives. The frequent changes of station experienced by regular battalions coupled with the manpower demands imposed by imperial policing also curtailed the opportunities for stable divisional or brigade-level training. Further, budgetary restrictions were still in place and persistent internal rivalries prevented the creation of the 'Army Schools' which might have encouraged a more coordinated approach.[39]

An even more important issue at this point in time was the need for strategic and tactical principles upon which any training schemes could be based. Travers has argued that the search for a consistent doctrine that might have shaped these principles was impeded by a distrust of 'dogma',

---

36   Nikolas Gardner, *Trial by Fire: Command and the British Expeditionary Force in 1914* (London: Praeger, 2003), 17.
37   *Ardrossan and Saltcoats Herald*, 27 October 1911. His brother had left for New Zealand in 1895, after his breakdown in health, and became proprietor of the massive Cottesbrook sheep station in Otago.
38   Gooch, *Plans of War*, 112.
39   Bidwell and Graham, *Fire-Power*, 41.

something which Hunter-Weston shared with the great majority of his colleagues.[40] More than the simple product of military wrongheadedness, however, the 'cult of experience' was fuelled by an understandable commitment to the qualities of flexibility and initiative that had brought these officers success in many colonial campaigns. Indeed, this approach was also consonant with a deeper strain of empiricism in wider British culture that distrusted speculative theorising and extrapolation.

The arrival of Douglas Haig as Director of Military Training in 1906 meant that the work of instilling 'uniformity, efficiency and preparedness' was at last underway through practical training initiatives such as staff tours and embarkation exercises.[41] Haig's tactical precepts had the benefit of clarity, if not subtlety. The solution to the conundrum of modern firepower lay in the adoption of offensive tactics. It was the rapid tempo of advance at the bayonet point, assisted by direct fire and good leadership, which would decide the battles of the future. Training therefore acquired a new urgency, which did not flag after Haig's departure two years later. The orchestration of shock tactics and fire tactics began to preoccupy both the infantry and the cavalry arms of the army, as the unambiguous victory of Japanese forces in Manchuria superseded the much-disputed lessons of the South African War. It seemed that the army which successfully nurtured its offensive spirit, regardless of losses, would be the army that succeeded, no matter whether this was achieved by discipline or by individual morale.

This tactical orthodoxy, enshrined in successive Staff College conferences, is the one that greeted Hunter-Weston on taking up his DMT post.[42] He was not about to challenge it. Although he was keenly aware of recent technological developments and was possessed of a good analytical mind, he was not an original thinker – in any case, it would have taken a great leap of imagination to anticipate the extent to which internal logic

40   Travers, *Killing Ground*, 38.
41   Sheffield, *Haig, The Chief*, 59.
42   Michael Senior, *Lieutenant General Sir Richard Hacking: XI Corps Commander, 1915–18: A Study in Corps Command* (Barnsley: Pen & Sword: 2012), 21–6; Tim Travers, 'Technology, Tactics and Morale: Jean de Bloch, the Boer War and British Military Theory, 1900–14', *Journal of Modern History* 51 (1979), 264–86.

of technology would become the dominant factor in modern warfare. The implication that this logic might even eclipse those moral qualities of leadership which had had been the hallmarks of his own military service was even more inconceivable. Hunter-Weston was a committed career soldier in an army that often functioned on the basis of a kaleidoscope of friendships, feuds and dominant personalities. His London transfer had already done much to raise his profile, conferring membership of War Office committees and enhancing his links with court circles.[43] As the German military threat shifted into sharper focus during the last years of peace prior to 1914, he would continue the work of aligning training and tactics, with an emphasis on morale, efficiency and character.

After the departure in 1912 of Murray's successor, Sir David Henderson, Hunter-Weston became the department's Acting Director for a period, although he remained in a junior staff grade. One of the most tangible products of this period was the publication of the *Training and Manoeuvre Regulations, 1913*, which he largely composed and edited.[44] A detailed manual running to 168 pages, this document was intended to set out the practical guidelines for the army's whole military training activity. The sole object of this training, it explained, was 'to prepare our forces for war, success in battle being held in view as the ultimate aim'.[45] A progressive, devolved model was prescribed, but it stipulated that local initiative was to be balanced with the need to ensure that that training was on 'sound lines'.[46] This more codified approach was evident in the manual's warning against 'freelance' treatises, which could lead to confusion of thought; the

---

43 In 1912, for example, he served on the Committee on the Attachment of Staff College students, chaired by General Sir William Robertson: Official Papers written by, or concerning Col. A. Hunter-Weston, March 1911–January 1914, Hunter-Weston Papers, 65/03/39/19, NAM. He was awarded a Companion of the Bath in June 1911; for his royal links during the period, see *The Times*, 5, 18 March 1912; 16 June, 24 July 1913.
44 General Staff, *Training and Manoeuvre Regulations, 1913* (London, HMSO, 1913). His pride was evident in having his annotated copy bound in leather and stamped with the family crest: Official Papers, Hunter-Weston Papers, 65/03/39/19, NAM.
45 *Training and Manoeuver Regulations, 1913* (London: General Staff, War Office, 1913), 9.
46 *Training and Manoeuver Regulations*, 18, 39.

army's *Field Service Regulations*, first published in 1905, covering operational matters, organisation and administration, remained paramount.

Maintenance of the offensive spirit had become a key article of faith. As the *Training Regulations* insisted: 'There are instances ... which may preclude taking the initiative, but a purely passive attitude is seldom permissible.'[47] In keeping with the search for human-centred solutions, one of the most important functions of individual training remained unchanged, seeking 'to foster a spirit of self-reliance in the soldier, to increase his esprit de corps and patriotism, and to develop as highly as possible the mental, moral and physical qualities in each individual'.[48] The manual also made a great effort to detail the qualities that the ideal officer should display. Here, the emphasis was on serious professionalism, including the linguistic skills deemed necessary to master continental military treatises. Ultimately, however, a leader of men in war needed experience, fitness and backbone: 'He must have practice handling troops in the field, and he needs a healthy body capable of long continuous exertion, a capacity for overcoming difficulties and always appearing confident and cheerful, and finally a cultivated willpower and determination strong enough to impress itself on his men in the stress of battle'.[49]

Hunter-Weston was equally forthright on the value of collective training in engendering 'mutual confidence between units, between formations and their commanders'.[50] As someone whose career had almost been sidelined at an early stage by service specialisation, he continued to advocate the cooperation of all arms in practice as well as in theory. After observing collective training in operation at Okehampton Camp and Salisbury Plain, he pressed for the improved tactical training of artillery, prescribing 'tactical days' which would bring together all senior officers of the division in the artillery practice camp, rather than training the divisional artillery 'only in

---

47   *Training and Manoeuver Regulations*, 34.
48   *Training and Manoeuver Regulations*, 9.
49   *Training and Manoeuver Regulations*, 20.
50   *Training and Manoeuver Regulations*, 67.

a watertight compartment'.[51] These insights helped to inform an ambitious scheme in 1913 which aimed at integrating infantry and cavalry officers into artillery practice, where they could work with battery officers in outlining tactical situations and devising fire plans.[52] Despite serious divergences in strategic policy between the army and Royal Navy, the *Training Regulations* also marked out Hunter-Weston as one of small band of senior officers, including John French, Ian Hamilton and Walter Braithwaite, who had come to grasp the need for closer inter-service cooperation. Building on the tactical exercises he had developed for the Scottish Territorials, and prophetically for his future career, the *Training Regulations* made provision for 'Special Exercises', including combined naval and military manoeuvres, 'such as landing on an open beach or unprotected harbour.'[53]

The concept of war that emerges from the various schemes prescribed in the *Training Regulations* remained one that was ultimately felt to be controllable. Just as he had attempted to do in his academic work at Staff College, Hunter-Weston sought to manage contingencies by an accumulation of detail, attempting to list all the variables that might influence the attainment of his objectives and identifying the key factor or factors that could compel the enemy to conform to his will.[54] Nevertheless, his firsthand experience of army manoeuvres suggested that in reality, the exact opposite of this ordered military universe usually occurred. The pinnacle of his peacetime DMT career came in 1913, when he became acting Executive Director of the autumn Army Exercises. The chaotic potential of combat was fully realised as Sir John French launched a disastrous combined infantry and cavalry assault on an entrenched position. A general breakdown in communications led to a disjointed effort in which the principles of fire and manoeuvre were soon abandoned.[55] The unscripted decision of

---

51 Memorandum of Army Training During Collective Training Period, 1913, Official Papers, Hunter-Weston Papers, 65/03/39/19, NAM.
52 Bidwell and Graham, *Fire-Power*, 25–6.
53 *Training and Manoeuver Regulations*, 25, 78.
54 *Training and Manoeuver Regulations*, 32.
55 Report of Army Exercises 1913, Official Papers, Hunter-Weston Papers, 65/03/39/19, NAM; Holmes, *Little Field Marshal*, 149–50.

Hubert Gough, the leader of the opposing skeleton army, not to wait to be attacked, compounded French's embarrassment at the failure. Personal recriminations resulted, but more importantly, the staff-command failures witnessed that year on Salisbury Plain by King George V and numerous foreign dignitaries came back to haunt the army during the opening weeks of the war.

After almost a decade of diligent staff work, Hunter-Weston received his reward. In February 1914, he was raised to the rank of Brigadier and given command of the 11th Infantry Brigade, stationed at Colchester.[56] His interlude at the War Office had acquainted him with developments in military technology and while there, he had embraced the need for realistic training in continental warfare. Furthermore, his deepening grasp of the techniques of management and method required of modern command was strengthened by a sensible commitment to the principle of combined arms coordination. At the same time, these insights were accompanied by an emotional commitment to offensive tactics, coupled with an unshakeable faith in the role of personal leadership and individual morale. In other words, he fitted the template for the ideal officer in his own training manual – a modern professional who led from the front.

56   *London Gazette*, 13 February 1914. At this point, Brigadier was only a temporary rank in the army.

CHAPTER SIX

'A Brigadier and a Band of Brothers'

A few weeks after war broke out, the *Essex County Standard* reminded its readers of Hunter-Weston's warning to his new brigade in the spring of 1914 – 'We shall be at war with Germany before I give up this command'.[1] In the trusting spirit of the pre-war ranker, his men simply assumed he knew more about the international situation than they did. It was impossible for any of them to foresee that by the end of the year, the brigade would have suffered total casualties of 126 officers and 3,357 from other ranks.[2]

In mourning the deaths of friends and colleagues across the service, officers of Hunter-Weston's generation also grieved for the loss of the 'old army', a finely balanced mechanism whose professionalism and cohesion, which had been moulded by years of soldiering across the empire, was felt to constitute 'an irreplaceable moral asset'.[3] Confronted by modern warfare in a series of desperate actions, commanders coped with their sense of disorientation with varying degrees of success. In Hunter-Weston's case, his flamboyant personality initially encouraged him to stress the externalities of heroic leadership. He eagerly assumed 'the mask of command' and became determined to excel by demonstrating that he was the type of inspirational figure that the situation required.[4] Later in his career, this

---

1 *Essex County Standard*, 5 September 1914.
2 Brigade casualties, 2 August to 20 December, Hunter-Weston Official War Diary (11th Brigade), Vol. I, 18 Aug. 1914–14 Feb. 1915, Add. MS 48355, British Library, [HW Official War Diary, 48355, BL]. After less than five months of war, only 18 per cent of officers and 28 per cent of other ranks were still on active service.
3 Paddy Griffith, *Battle Tactics of the Western Front: the British Army's Art of Attack, 1916–18* (New Haven and London: Yale University Press, 1996), 51.
4 See John Keegan, *The Mask of Command: A Study of Generalship* (Harmondsworth: Penguin, 1988).

approach would be condemned as eccentric posturing, but in 1914 it helped him to win recognition as an aggressive soldier of some potential. For all his identification with the traditional ideals of leadership during the ferocious early months of the war, he also grasped that modern warfare demanded a more organised and managerial approach. His response was to develop another 'mask', one of technical competence and emotional detachment. In time, this too would damage his reputation.

The Old Brigade

Familiar faces were waiting to greet Hunter-Weston when he arrived to take up his new post. The 11th brigade formed part of 4th Division, one of six regular infantry divisions reorganised by the Haldane reforms as a continental intervention force. The GOC was his old colleague from Eastern Command, Thomas d'Oyly Snow, a towering, irascible, lantern-jawed officer with a reputation as a fierce disciplinarian. 'Snowball', who had made a hobby out of route marching, shared Hunter-Weston's passion for training and was determined to drive his division to the peak of its performance.[5] To this end he encouraged competitive emulation between his Brigadiers, H. F. M. 'Fatty' Wilson (12th Brigade) and the well-connected Aylmer Haldane (10th Brigade). With the addition of Hunter-Weston, he believed that had secured one of the strongest teams in the army, 'far and away better than the Brigadiers of other Divisions'; in return, Hunter-Weston, unlike Haldane, respected his chief and valued his opinion highly.[6]

---

5   J. E. Edmonds, Unpublished Draft Memoirs, Ch. XXII, 3/7/1, LHCMA; J. A. L. Haldane, *A brigade of the old army: Relating to operations of 10 Infantry Bde, France, Aug-Nov, 1914* (London: Edward Arnold, 1920), 5.

6   The story of the doings of the 4th Division B.E.F. Aug. & Sep. 1914. Maj. Gen. T. D'Oyly Snow, 76/79/1, Imperial War Museum (IWM); HW to GHW, 9 September 1914, HW Private War Diary, 48363, BL.

New battalion structures were beginning to take root during 1914, but Hunter-Weston's brigade remained a microcosm of the army's unwritten social hierarchy. Indisputably in the regimental top drawer was the exclusive 1/Rifle Brigade (Prince Consort's Own), which was already looking forward to a spell of service overseas in September 1914.[7] On the next layer below were the 1/Prince Albert's (Somerset Light Infantry) who shared both the lustre of the Rifle Brigade's royal patron and their reputation for light infantry 'smartness'.[8] Slightly further down the pecking order were the 1/Hampshire Regiment, a solid county battalion with a strong local recruiting base, who had spent the last nine years on home service.[9] Marching in the rear were the 1/East Lancashire Regiment, another perfectly sound battalion, but one whose affiliation with the north of England meant that it was deemed as rather unfashionable.[10]

Hunter-Weston now had the perfect vehicle to put his theories of training and morale into practice. From the outset he identified closely with 'his' brigade. Like most regular officers he was thoroughly paternalistic, gladly accepting responsibility for the wellbeing of his soldiers. His extrovert personality meant that he rejected the remote, mutually respectful relationship that was customary between officers and men in the peacetime army. Instead, he never tired of addressing his 'dear men' on parade and was prepared to engage them in individual conversation where circumstances allowed. Massive social, educational and professional barriers existed between commissioned officers and other ranks, but he had learned from John French's highly personalised command style in South Africa that effort invested in building even superficial bonds could pay

[7] R. Berkeley and W. W. Seymour, *History of the Rifle Brigade in War of 1914–18*, vol. 1 (London: Rifle Brigade Club, 1927), 1.
[8] Everard Wyrall, *The Somerset Light Infantry, 1914–19* (London: Methuen & Co., 1927).
[9] Christopher T. Atkinson, *The Royal Hampshire Regiment, 1914–18* (Glasgow: Maclehose & Co., 1952).
[10] E. C. Hopkinson, *Spectamur Agendo: 1st Battalion The East Lancashire Regiment. August and September, 1914* (Cambridge: W. Heffer & Sons Ltd, 1926).

dividends.[11] While regimental loyalties were the primary ties binding the army, he was determined that the brigade would develop its own identity as a unit of 'self-sufficiency and instinctive efficiency'.[12] For their part, his men admired an affable and jovial personality who was good at what he did and who made an effort to communicate with them. Hunter-Weston was quite comfortable with his 'Hunter-Bunter' nickname and was a commander who met his men's expectations of how a general should look and behave. Indeed, for the young Private Arthur Cook of the Somersets, he was simply 'one of the finest soldiers and gentlemen, you could wish to meet'.[13]

In Colchester, 29 July 1914 began unremarkably, like most days in a British garrison town. The morning's work had given way to the usual round of cricket and tennis. Most of the men had drifted into the town and only the orderly officer was left in the barracks of the East Lancashires, when a telephone call came through at 4 p.m. with the news that the 'Precautionary Period' – a term denoting the possibility of attack – had been declared.[14] The European crisis had built up slowly and the effect of this news was electric. All leave was cancelled and instead of moving to Shropshire for pre-manoeuvres training, the 11th Brigade rushed to man the coastal defences at Felixstowe and Purfleet, where enemy raids were imminently expected.[15] Rifles were overhauled, bayonets sharpened and preparations made to receive hundreds of reservists. Full mobilisation was complete by the evening of 8 August, which in hindsight was a remarkable logistical achievement. The real work now began, to train and equip men who had been dramatically removed from civilian life. Officers tackled

11 Holmes, *Little Field Marshal*, 211.
12 HW to Brig. W. D. S. Brownrigg, 17 March 1934, HW Private War Diary, 48363, BL.
13 Arthur Cook (George Molesworth, ed.), '*A Soldier's War*' (Taunton: Goodman and Sons, 1957), 1.
14 Hopkinson, *Spectamur Agendo*, 2.
15 Hunter-Weston was given a mobile strike force against this eventuality, comprised of the 20th Hussars and 14th Royal Field Artillery: HW Private War Diary, 5 August 1914, 48363, BL; Berkeley and Seymour, *Rifle Brigade*, 2.

missing boot studs and a host of similar military conundrums, relishing the novelty of handling companies and platoons at wartime strength.

War loomed with an air of unreality. 11 August was a beautiful day, and Hunter-Weston and his wife motored to a conference at the division's new HQ at Bury St Edmunds, stopping off for a picnic along the way.[16] The 4th Division was to become the temporary spearhead of home defence while the rest of the British Expeditionary Force (BEF) crossed the channel. Hunter-Weston spent the next few days inspecting blockhouses along the east coast, as day-trippers relaxed on the beaches. Events were, however, moving quickly. The division was instructed to concentrate on the playing fields of Harrow School in preparation for its embarkation. The long-awaited orders for France arrived on 21 August.

Hunter-Weston spent his last day before embarkation at Abbey House, his official Colchester residence, writing letters with Grace and arranging his affairs.[17] Arriving at Southampton at midnight, he boarded the crowded old troopship *Braemar Castle*. It was exciting even for a seasoned campaigner to watch the horses being hoisted by electric crane, and he was particularly pleased when his old hunter Solomon took the indignity in his stride. As GOC, Hunter-Weston had a comfortable saloon to himself, although the noise of his men tramping overhead and the whine of the crane meant that he slept little.[18] The ship finally slipped out of the harbour at 8.20 a.m. on 22 August, arriving off Le Havre in the evening.

As Hunter-Weston slept late and breakfasted on board, the first BEF contingent under Sir John French was already in extreme danger. Despite their lack of numbers, they were in a pivotal position to counter the massive outflanking manoeuvre of the German First and Second Armies, but their exposed deployment on the French left flank meant that they were liable to encirclement. Rejecting intelligence reports of a large German force rapidly closing in from the north, French had optimistically led them towards Mons, preparing for an early strike into Belgium. Equally uncertain

16 HW Private War Diary, 11 August 1914, 48363, BL.
17 HW Private War Diary, 11 August 1914, 48363, BL.
18 HW Private War Diary, 22 August 1914, 48363, BL.

of the location of the BEF, the advance guard of General Von Kluck's First Army ran into British positions on the morning of 23 August. The next twenty-four hours would not only test British training and discipline, but also the ability of senior British officers to handle large and complex battle formations. Falling back on their second defensive line, BEF units held off repeated German assaults while command and control above battalion level effectively disintegrated.[19] French had little option but to retire southwest the next day. While I Corps under Douglas Haig travelled down the eastern side of the Forêt de Mormal, Smith-Dorrien's exhausted II Corps, which had borne the brunt of the fighting, took the road to the west with the enemy hard on their heels.

Hot Work in the Quarries

The 4th Division may have missed Mons, but it was pitched straight into action to cover Smith-Dorrien's fighting withdrawal. After spending the day of 23 August in a dirty rest camp outside Le Havre, the 11th Brigade were packed into open cattle trucks.[20] Hunter-Weston guessed that their destination would be somewhere between Amiens and Lille, where he confidently expected his men to be ordered to concentrate and move to the front. Thanks to the slowness of the French troop transports, they began detraining early the next evening at Le Cateau, an unassuming lace-making town whose name for the moment meant nothing to them.[21] Although the information gleaned from Divisional HQ remained sketchy, the seriousness of the British situation soon began to sink in. Even though 4th Division

---

19 Zuber, *Mons Myth*, 167; Gardiner, *Trial by Fire*, 13–45; Jerry Murland, *Retreat and Rearguard 1914: The BEF's Actions from Mons to the Marne* (Barnsley: Pen & Sword, 2011), 29–30.
20 Record of the 11th [dictated by HW in January 1916], HW Private War Diary, 1914–15, 48363, BL.
21 HW Private War Diary, 23, 24 August 1914, 48363, BL.

was not fully assembled and lacked cavalry, heavy artillery, signals, ambulances and their artillery train, Snow ordered that they were to intervene between the enemy and Smith-Dorrien's hard-pressed divisions, who by this point had been retreating continuously for thirty-six hours.

There were no welcoming billets for the 11th Brigade, who at once set out northwest for the village of Briastre, a journey of five miles in the fierce evening heat. Hunter-Weston rode alongside the Somersets and the East Lancashires, praising their marching, but the bad news was already filtering through their ranks.[22] After reaching their destination, they were allowed a few hours sleep before moving off for their next objective, Solesmes, a key road junction eight miles to the north.[23] Here Snow's three brigades had been ordered to act as rearguard to allow the final retirement of II Corps. Arriving early on the morning of 25 August, Hunter-Weston ordered his battalions to take up positions on the high ground to the southwest of the town.[24] He remained anxious to encourage his troops – although his announcement to the officers of the Somersets, that they had a glorious task in front of them, 'a strategic retirement to a position around St Quentin', failed to have the desired effect.[25]

The rest of the day was uneventful, but the evidence before their eyes was grim. War was coming close. The town was shuttered and the streets barricaded, while the roads were crowded with frightened refugees, moving their belongings in everything from prams to farm carts. Meanwhile, Smith-Dorrien's tired troops and columns of military transport trudged southwards. As the afternoon wore on, the congestion increased and the boom of the German guns to the northwest became louder and more rapid. The oppressive heat gave way to a thunderstorm, and through the pouring rain

22 Hopkinson, *Spectamur Agendo*, 5–6.
23 J. E. Edmonds, *History of the Great War based on official documents by direction of the Historical Section of the Committee of Imperial Defence: Military Operations in France and Belgium, 1914. Volume I: Mons, the Retreat to the Seine, the Marne and the Aisne, August to October, 1914* (Macmillan: London, 1922), 126 [*OH 1914, (1)*].
24 HW Private War Diary, 25 August 1914, 48363, BL.
25 Brian Gillard, *Good Old Somersets: An 'Old Contemptible' Battalion in 1914* (Leicester: Matador, 2004), 13.

Hunter-Weston had an excellent view of the German horse artillery and the heavy masses of cavalry and *jägers*.[26] Dusk was beginning to fall as the 4th Division watched the last men pass through the town. Their next task was to protect the left flank of II Corps; 11th Brigade were ordered to occupy the high ground from Fontaine-au-Pire to the railway station at Cattenières, while the 12th Brigade was to continue the line to Wambaix, with the 10th Brigade in reserve at Haucourt.[27]

Hunter-Weston's brigade left Solesmes at 10 p.m. heading southwest, but not before the German guns had shelled and set fire to the eastern part of Briastre where they were assembled.[28] Tired, soaked and starving, his men stumbled in darkness along roads that had become rutted and clogged with mud. The brigade traffic stretched back for two and a half miles, as German cavalry patrols hovered and probed. Riding near the head of the column, Hunter-Weston passed through Beauvois and reached the adjoining Fontaine-au-Pire at 2.45 a.m. in torrential rain.[29] Reading his map by torchlight, he made a basic navigational error; as a result, his two leading battalions disappeared up a rough track that disappeared into sodden clover fields instead of taking the right fork towards Cattenières at the end of the village.[30]

The 4th Division now paid the price for its lack of reconnaissance support. After a brief conference with his Brigadiers, Snow agreed to halt for a few hours and continue the march to their assigned positions when the light improved, completely unaware that a large enemy force was already sweeping down towards Beauvois from the northwest.[31] The battalions who were still jammed in the village slept in the streets, forbidden to enter the abandoned houses. Breaking a great taboo of peacetime manoeuvres,

26 Record of the 11th, HW Private War Diary, 48363, BL; *OH 1914, (1)*, 128.
27 HW Official War Diary, 25 August 1914, 48355, BL.
28 *OH, 1914 (1)*, 138.
29 An Account of the Action of the 11th Infantry Brigade between Fontaine-au-Pire and Ligny-en-Cambresis, West of Le Cateau [Hunter-Weston, 16 September 1914], Hunter-Weston Papers, 6503/39/20, NAM.
30 *OH 1914, (1)*, 6.
31 4th Division B.E.F, 76/79/1, IWM.

'A Brigadier and a Band of Brothers' 87

the remainder bivouacked in the open fields to the west, some using the sweet-smelling corn sheaves as pillows, while others tried to avoid the recent evidence of grazing cattle.[32] Taking the normal precautions for local defence, Hunter-Weston sent out the Rifle Brigade in front as an outpost line, covering the ground between Beauvois and Cattenières, while other experienced units, like the East Lancashires, instinctively drew back from exposed positions.[33] As his men grabbed a fitful rest, the military situation was rapidly changing. Failing to connect with I Corps on his right, with his divisions exhausted and his left flank exposed, Smith-Dorrien's situation was precarious. He asked Snow to serve under him to resist the inevitable enemy attack, but by the time his request was received at 5 a.m., his participation had become a reality.

At 4.14 a.m. on 26 August, just as the 11th Brigade was preparing to renew the march to Cattenières, rifle, machine-gun and shell fire suddenly opened up on the Rifle Brigade companies west of the village of Beauvois.[34] For Hunter-Weston and his men, the Battle of Le Cateau had begun. In later years, his memory of his first modern battlefield was summed up by 'a Brigadier and a band of brothers [who] had to act entirely on their own initiative'.[35] Romanticism aside, this recollection contained two basic truths: the importance of esprit de corps, and the breakdown in the chain of command. While Hunter-Weston was candid about being cut off from higher authority because of failures in communication, he found it more difficult to admit the confusion of command in his own brigade. Instead, his formal report to Snow and the expanded record he dictated in January 1916 both depicted a battlefield where the troops rapidly assumed the

32 An anonymous account of the 1st Battalion East Lancashire Regiment, August – September 1914, Misc 154 (2388), IWM.
33 Hopkinson, *Spectamur Agendo*, 9.
34 Battle of August 26th, 1/Rifle Brigade War Diary, WO 95/1496, The National Archives, London (TNA).
35 HW to Brig. W. D. S. Brownrigg, 17 March 1934, HW Private War Diary, 48363, BL.

positions allotted to them by their Brigadier, and artillery cooperation was effective.[36] In reality, with only a small brigade staff and no signals section, he spent the day trying to control a disintegrating military situation through sheer force of personality. Revisiting the scene four years later as a Corps Commander, he gave his younger self a well-deserved pat on the back.[37]

In the immediate shock of the attack, the advance security precautions that Hunter-Weston had taken saved his battalions from disaster. While the Rifle Brigade held off the enemy in extended order on the left, he pushed up half of the Somersets east of Beauvois village to secure the safe passage for the brigade transport, including the vital ammunition carts. A hundred-yard dash began to reach defensive positions, which were hastily improvised on a ridge half a mile southwest of Fontaine. Their centrepiece was 'La Carrière', a heavily quarried knoll. There was no time for tactical sophistication, as battalions were thrown into action in a 'piecemeal' manner.[38] The plan was for the remaining units to retire in parallel columns, but this was difficult for the tired men to achieve. Nevertheless, the Somersets rushed up the bank to the right, defending the quarries and the line of the railway to the south east, while the Hampshires took up a good position on the left, holding the quarries on the western side and both sides of the light railway to Cambrai. Meanwhile, the East Lancashires mistook the spur that Hunter-Weston intended for them, so that he had to retrieve them and pull them forward to a covered position on the left flank. This in effect became the reserve line during the day. After holding their ground for almost two hours, the Rifle Brigade now aimed to retire to safety up the slope, which they managed at a contemptuous walking pace; Hunter-Weston again directed them to their position in the centre of the line on a sunken road on an east-west axis across the ridge.[39]

---

36 Account [Le Cateau], Hunter-Weston Papers, 6503/39/20, NAM; Record of the 11th, HW Private War Diary, 48363, BL.
37 HW to GHW, 11 October 1918, HW Private War Diary, 48367, BL.
38 Short Account of the Battle of Ligny, HW Official War Diary, 48355, BL; 1/Somerset Light Infantry War Diary, 26 August 1914, WO 95/1499, TNA.
39 Battle of August 26th, 1/Rifle Brigade War Diary, WO 95/1496, TNA.

'A Brigadier and a Band of Brothers'   89

The defensive line of 11th Brigade was meant to be temporary; Brigade HQ was in a small railwayman's cottage in the southern ravine, though in his eagerness to remain in contact with his battalions, Hunter-Weston spent much of his time in the forward line at the quarries.[40] The position had its advantages, for while the ridge was exposed to German artillery and machine-gun fire, the enemy would find it difficult to conceal their approach. Its uneven landscape, pitted with the quarries on the reverse slope, also gave ample natural cover, enabling the brigade to fight without dug-in positions for most of the day; behind them was the natural defensive screen of the Warnelle Ravine, offering another good reserve position if required. The most pressing danger came from the vulnerable position of the 4th Division as a whole, compounded by the continuing lack of combat support troops.

The British position at Le Cateau has been described rather confusingly as 'a flattened horseshoe' or a 'tipped up, reversed L'.[41] Smith-Dorrien's line extended for ten miles, east to west; the right was held by 5th Division and the centre by 3rd Division, while on the extreme left, 4th Division adopted a 'refused flank', curling away from the attacker in an attempt to prevent an outflanking manoeuvre. Their three mile-long firing line was far from continuous and for much of the battle the 11th Brigade was Snow's most exposed unit. Wilson's 12th Brigade and two battalions of the 10th Brigade took up position at Wambaix, three quarters of a mile west from Hunter-Weston's force, while the remainder of the 10th stayed behind at Harcourt. Beyond them there remained only the French territorial garrison at Cambrai, six miles away, with General Sordet's rather shadowy cavalry corps in between. The gap of almost a mile separating the 11th Brigade from the left flank of 3rd Division to the east at Caudry was even more serious, and it prompted Snow to request two additional reserve battalions without success.[42]

---

40   Berkeley and Seymour, *Rifle Brigade*, 12.
41   David Ascoli, *The Mons Star* (Edinburgh: Birlinn, 1981) 96; John Terraine, *Mons: the Retreat to Victory* (Barnsely: Pen & Sword, 1991), 131.
42   4th Division B.E.F, 76/79/1, IWM.

The Brigade faced a formidable enemy force, commanded by the accomplished cavalry general, Georg von der Marwitz. This consisted of three *jäger* battalions and dismounted troops from the Second Cavalry Division, equivalent to a further battalion.[43] While both sides appeared evenly matched in terms of manpower, the Germans received more effective support from their mobile horse artillery units and also benefitted from a three-to-one superiority in machine-guns, which were massed to give a concentration of fire.[44] Indeed, the combat power that Hunter-Weston witnessed at Fontaine was a good specimen of the combined arms approach that he had himself promoted as a staff officer.

Soon after 6 a.m., the enemy concentrated very heavy artillery and machine-gun fire on the quarry knoll, with the intention of establishing fire superiority and covering the movement of the infantry. The expected frontal attack did not develop, but while his battalions took comfort that the Germans were pinned down at 'a respectable distance' by rifle fire from the ridge, Hunter-Weston sensed that this was the tactical prelude to a double flanking manoeuvre.[45] With attacks closing up from the northwest along the line of the railway as well as from the northeast, the enemy were able to establish themselves on the outskirts of Fontaine, using machine-guns to deadly effect against the Somersets on the right of the British line. They were forced to retire at around 8 a.m. and regroup at the railway embankment that ran along the valley between Fontaine and Ligny.[46] This set the pattern for the morning, for rather than the static defensive line familiar to the British in colonial warfare, there was constant movement as beleaguered units were ordered in and out of exposed positions, while the Rifle Brigade held the vital centre against repeated German *jäger* assaults.

---

43 Like Mons, Le Cateau has been subject to a thorough revisionist treatment. Zuber argues that the Germans lacked the massive numerical superiority that is often assumed in 'anglophone' historiography: Zuber, *Mons Myth*, 212–13.
44 Anthony Bird, *Gentlemen, We will Stand and Fight: Le Cateau 1914* (Marlborough: Crowood Press, 2008) 96; Zuber, *Mons Myth*, 239.
45 Account [Le Cateau], Hunter-Weston Papers, 6503/39/20, NAM.
46 *OH 1914, (1)*, 168; 1/Somerset Light Infantry War Diary, 26 August, WO 95/1499, TNA.

The absence of divisional arrangements to evacuate the wounded began to tell, while the inadequacy of the brigade's close artillery support was an equally pressing concern.[47] The divisional gunners were still searching for suitable firing positions, and the absence of any heavy artillery battery was particularly problematic; Hunter-Weston was soon forced to request additional support from XXXII Artillery Brigade to divert the attention of the German guns.[48]

Facing an arc of fire, the men displayed incredible powers of endurance. One Boer War veteran compared the battle to 'the whole of the South African campaign rolled into an hour or so'.[49] For some young soldiers, the onslaught from shrapnel and machine-gun fire proved too much to cope with. When the Hampshires began to retire from the firing line north of the railway bridge, Hunter-Weston and his officers led them back personally, explaining to them how essential it was that they maintain their position.[50] He remained a visible presence during the morning, riding around in full view as the Germans systematically traversed the ridge with fire. In the end it was old Solomon who paid the price, when he was shot from under him – the first of eight horses he ultimately lost during the war. As he looked down at Solomon's body, Hunter-Weston reputedly remarked – 'What a glorious death. Bring me my second horse'.[51] Such stories probably grew in the telling, but there was no doubt that he had shown a conspicuous disregard for danger, even if one junior officer of the

47 Wyrall, *Somerset Light Infantry*, 9–10.
48 A. F. Becke, *The Royal Regiment of Artillery at Le Cateau, 26 August 1914* (Woolwich: Royal Artillery Institution, 1919), 38.
49 Wyrall, *Somerset Light Infantry*, 20.
50 Record of the 11th, HW Private War Diary, 48363, BL. His official report noted four occasions where troops in advanced positions retired and who were then either led back or replaced with fresh troops: Account [Le Cateau], Hunter-Weston Papers, 6503/39/20, NAM.
51 Hopkinson, *Spectamur Agendo*, 16. He mourned Solomon to his wife in similar terms. 'A fine ending for a 20-year old hunter, who had seldom in his life been sick and who was one of the most magnificent jumpers that I have put my leg over': HW to GHW 30 August 1914, HW Private War Diary, 48363, BL.

East Lancashires wondered whether his absence from Brigade HQ perhaps actually created more work for his staff.[52]

It was a desperate defensive battle, but 'passive occupation of a position' had no place in the culture of the old army. Mid-morning, Hunter-Weston ordered a counter-attack south of the railway line by the Hampshires to assist 12th brigade on their left, but when they 'came back with some celerity' due to intense artillery fire, he did not press on with the attempt.[53] During a later lull in activity while their Brigadier was visiting the quarry pits, an impromptu conference of his battalion commanders was held at Brigade HQ at which a further counter-attack was mooted. This was sensibly cancelled on his return, as the Germans were seen to have reinforced their line and their artillery fire broke out with renewed intensity.[54]

Having held on to their isolated position for almost ten hours, the situation of 11th Brigade was now critical, as both the 12th Brigade and the 7th Brigade (3rd Division) on the right flank were assumed to be falling back.[55] At around 3 p.m., acting on orders from Divisional HQ, Hunter-Weston prepared to withdraw across the Warnelle Ravine to positions around Ligny village. According to his later account, this was a 'carefully organised retirement', and 'a marvellous experience to be ... under such a shower of steel and iron'.[56]

Not all of his men felt the same way. The Hampshires, who were close at hand and accessible to orders, did manage a steady withdrawal, but his instructions failed to reach other forward companies.[57] The East Lancashires presented an easy target as they moved off en masse contrary to their Brigadier's intentions; despite his attempts to ride among them and

---

52 Hopkinson, *Spectamur Agendo*, 16.
53 Atkinson, *Hampshire Regiment*, 10; Record of the 11th, HW Private War Diary, 48363, BL.
54 Berkeley and Seymour, *Rifle Brigade* 13.
55 In fact, they had counter-attacked and retaken part of the village of Caudry, but due to poor communications Hunter-Weston was unaware of this: *OH 1914, (1)*, 181–2.
56 Record of the 11th, HW Private War Diary, 48363, BL.
57 Private Diary of Lieut.-Col. F. R Hicks, 1/Hampshire Regiment War Diary, WO 95/1495, TNA.

open them out, almost every man was hit or bruised.[58] Artillery cover was lacking in the early part of the climb, but the close support he had requested began to be more effective as the Germans rose from their concealed positions in pursuit and presented the gunners on the Ligny ridge with clear targets. Nevertheless, the Rifle Brigade and those companies left behind in the sunken road suffered heavy losses during their withdrawal; Hunter-Weston himself almost became another casualty as his second horse was shot as he led it up the slope, while Gerald Boyd, his Brigade Major, was wounded by shrapnel as he walked beside him.[59]

Arriving at Ligny, Hunter-Weston's battalions were in some disarray, but he attempted to reform them as much as possible, organising new defensive positions on the north and east of the village. For the next two hours they beat off further attacks from the Germans; finally, at 5 p.m., Snow gave the order to withdraw south towards Malincourt.[60] Having achieved his aim of regrouping, Smith-Dorrien had decided to disengage from the battle. Faced with a dangerous daylight retirement, Hunter-Weston found controlling his brigade to be almost impossible, but he nevertheless attempted to impose order, instructing his men to evacuate in small columns – indeed, his unit was the only one of Snow's brigades to remain in any way collected after the day's fighting.[61]

---

58   1/East Lancashire Regiment War Diary, 26 August 1914, WO 95/1498, TNA; Hopkinson, *Spectamur Agendo*, 15; See also 'Diary of NCO Convalescent', *Essex County Telegraph*, 2 January 1915, which credited his Brigadier's intervention with limiting casualties.

59   Record of the 11th, HW Private War Diary, 48363, BL; Battle of August 26th, 1/Rifle Brigade War Diary, WO95/1496, TNA. He survived to become Major-General Sir Gerald Farrell Boyd, Commandant of the Staff College at Quetta, India.

60   *HW Private War Diary*, 26/8/1914, 48363, BL. There was a rumour that these attacks had been mounted by Prussian Guards, but this remained unconfirmed: Record of the 11th, HW Private War Diary, 48363, BL. Indeed, Zuber's reappraisal suggests instead that no German unit was close enough to have been engaged at Ligny: *Mons Myth*, 225.

61   Wyrall, *Somerset Light Infantry*, 12.

Retreat

Hunter-Weston's sentimental attachment to the 11th Brigade was strengthened by the shared experience of combat. A few days after Le Cateau he wrote to Grace with a curious blend of understatement and emotion: 'The fighting has been interesting, and the brigade seem to be fond of me. I love them, splendid fellows, officers and men.'[62] He did not mention his casualties, but later estimated to Snow that he had lost around 30 officers, and 1,115 men killed, wounded and missing – this amounted to 40 per cent of the total losses incurred by the 4th Division.[63] The action had indeed proved the fighting quality of his soldiers, who had played a pivotal role in blocking an enveloping attack from the northwest that would have been disastrous for II Corps.

After their first encounter with the enemy, the next ten days of retreat called on new reserves of endurance. As he led his force out of Ligny in the fading daylight and drizzling rain, they faced a continuous southwards march of nearly 200 miles. Assuming that the BEF were retiring southwest, the enemy did not mount a vigorous pursuit, and aside from sporadic attacks from cavalry and mobile units, the main dangers were hunger, heat and, above all, fatigue. There were many alarms along the way. Pausing at the village of Nauroy on 27 August, Hunter-Weston was surprised in his bathtub by the news that enemy scouts were approaching from the north and east. Dressing quickly and jumping on his horse, he realised that without artillery his brigade had no option but to resume their retreat as soon as possible.[64] His force then became split as they moved across open country to escape shellfire. He was left with the smaller column of around 700 men, which now began a slog lasting twenty-six hours, covering thirty-five

---

62 HW to GHW, 28 August 1914, HW Private War Diary, 48363, BL.
63 Account [Le Cateau], Hunter-Weston Papers, 6503/39/20, NAM; Extract from the Diary of Private Pattenden, 1/Hampshire Regiment War Diary, WO 95/1495, TNA.
64 Record of the 11th, HW Private War Diary, 48363, BL; Private Diary of Lieut.-Col. F. R. Hicks, 27 August 1914, 1/Hampshire Regiment War Diary, WO 95/1495, TNA.

miles without proper halts or food.⁶⁵ Nevertheless, the men's spirit remained intact and they marched into Ham the next evening whistling and singing.⁶⁶ He was all the more furious to receive an order to discard surplus ammunition and other 'impedimenta' – it was clear that the morale of GHQ was disintegrating faster than it was among the retreating troops. He complained about the 'dampening' effect to his old friend Smith-Dorrien, who promptly countermanded it, much to the anger of Sir John French.⁶⁷

Hunter-Weston's own morale remained unshakable. It was not expected that he should share the same physical discomforts as his men; indeed, Brigade HQ was often in the local chateau, but the retreat was not without its hardships. His kit had disappeared and he had lost many of his personal belongings when Solomon was killed. Fortunately, a kindly curé at his first overnight stop had been able to supply a cardigan and toothbrush, but these were the most basic of consolations for a commander who prided himself on the smartness of his turnout.⁶⁸

It may not have been immediately apparent, but the tide was already beginning to turn. Early on the morning of 28 August, Hunter-Weston rode over to Voyennes, where he found the rest of the brigade concentrated along with the main body of the 4th Division. The next day was the first that they did not set off immediately in the morning, which suggests that they were no longer simply responding to the enemy's movements. Following the divisional route of retreat towards Paris, both brigade columns reunited at Noyon on the Oise canal. As they plodded southwards under the hot sun they were sustained by gifts of bread and apples from French civilians. The brigade now formed the division's advance guard, escorting the guns and transport under the welcome shade of the Forest of Compiegne. Enemy

---

65   HW Private War Diary, 27 August 1914, 48363, BL; Hopkinson, *Spectamur Agendo*, 26.
66   *Essex County Telegraph*, 3 October 1914; 'Account [Le Cateau]', Hunter-Weston Papers, 6503/39/20, NAM.
67   Herbert Smith-Dorrien, *Memories of Forty-Eight Years Service* (London: John Murray, 1925), 416–17.
68   HW to GHW, 26 August 1914, HW Private War Diary, 23 September and 5 October 1914, 48363, BL.

incursions continued but Hunter-Weston was now more confident of his men's ability to resist them. German cavalry attacked near the village of St Sauveur on 1 September, but their attempt was not pressed home with much energy.[69] Scouts continued to follow the column, suggesting that a large force was working round their flank, but the divisional directive was to avoid action unless absolutely necessary.[70] The rest of the march was carried out in comparative security. The first battalions of the 11th Brigade reached Brie-Comte-Robert four days later, exhausted but still a credible combat force. Early on the morning of 6 September they turned northwards to face their pursuers.

Crossing the Aisne

Le Cateau and its aftermath had demonstrated that Hunter-Weston was a confident and effective commander, but it was Battle of the Aisne that won him his reputation as a 'thruster', capable of driving his men on regardless of weariness and risk.[71] Indeed, his dynamic leadership on this occasion marked him out among his colleagues. For Douglas Haig, the use of terrain and the degree of mobility made the Aisne 'the only normal battle in Europe', but historical opinion remains divided in its evaluation of the British performance.[72] The failure to maintain momentum in the counter-offensive was partly a reflection of the fatigue of the BEF, but also hinted at the caution and inexperience of many senior British officers, who allowed

69 *OH 1914, (1)*, 258; HW Private War Diary, 31 August 1914, 48363, BL.
70 Hopkinson, *Spectamur Agendo*, 42.
71 *OH 1914, (1)*, 57.
72 Travers, *Killing Ground*, 88; Murland, *Battle on the Aisne*, 1–10; Terraine, *Retreat to Victory*, 215; Robert Asprey, *The First Battle of the Marne* (New York: Lippincott, 1962), 151; Gardiner, *Trial by Fire*, 74. See also Paul Kendall, *Aisne 1914: The Dawn of Trench Warfare* (Stroud: Spellmount, 2012).

the Germans to withdraw behind formidable defensive positions from which they could not easily be dislodged.

The immediate task was to cross a series of river valleys where the presence of steep ridges and escarpments on the looming northern banks favoured determined rearguard action. Joining the newly formed III Corps, the 4th Division were on the left of the British line as it rotated northeast, with the 11th as the rear brigade. After an initial reaction of disbelief, morale had risen with the news of the advance, but late departures, frequent halts and ignorance of the general military situation soon had a dispiriting effect.[73]

As they marched through the deserted countryside, Hunter-Weston believed that that the enemy were, at last, on the run.[74] The German withdrawal had created significant opportunities, opening up a large gap in the north between their First and Second Armies, which lay directly in the path of the BEF; if this could be exploited, Sir John French believed it might be possible to operate against both flanks while they were engaged elsewhere by the French.[75] Working in two columns of two brigades, commanded by Hunter Weston and 'Fatty' Wilson, III Corps faced fewer obstacles that the rest of the army and arrived on the south bank of the Marne at La Ferté-sous-Jouarre on 8 September. Unfortunately, the leisurely pace of the advance to date meant that the Germans were already well dug in on the other side of the river by then.[76]

The lack of reliable communications as they attempted to push across meant that Hunter-Weston abandoned his horse for a motorcycle.[77] Lieut.-Colonel Delmé-Radcliffe of the 2nd Royal Welch Fusiliers was a rather

---

73 Anonymous account of the 1st Battalion East Lancashire Regiment, Misc 154 (2388), IWM; Wyrall, *Somerset Light Infantry*, 18; Berkeley and Seymour, *Rifle Brigade* 13.
74 HW to GHW, 11 September 1914, HW Private War Diary, 48363, BL.
75 Gardiner, *Trial by Fire*, 79.
76 HW Official War Diary, 8 September 1914, 48355, BL.
77 Niall Barr, 'Command in the Transition from Mobile to Static Warfare, August 1914 to March 1915', in Gary Sheffield and Dan Todman, *Command and Control on the Western Front: The British Army's Experience, 1914–18* (Staplehurst: Spellmont, 2004), 19.

sceptical eyewitness to this dashing leadership style. His unit was providing the left flank-guard to the 19th Brigade, part of Hunter-Weston's column, which had been ordered to advance on the bridges at Ferté:

> I have a vivid recollection of this distinguished officer early in the day's proceedings careering past me on the flapper's perch of a motor bicycle and of thinking how such a means of progression was possible for a British general: it would, even in the last days of the War, have been inconceivable for a Frenchman, or for a German – even in defeat, to get about in such an unseemly manner.[78]

His men were resting by the roadside when the 'peripatetic Brigadier' came along and ordered them to march to a chateau on his map. He continued to pop up repeatedly in different locations over the next few hours with further instructions. One company pushed on northeast, but without maps they had little idea of where they were:

> Within minutes, about 4.00 p.m. a gorgeous General Officer, he of the flapper's perch, burst on our vision. He asked who we were. On my respectfully informing him, he waved his stick and, pointing downhill, exclaimed in the theatrical manner 'Follow me'. He then strode off so rapidly that before one platoon had fallen in he had disappeared – for two years as far as I was concerned.[79]

These accounts were undoubtedly coloured by their narrators' later acquaintance with Hunter-Weston as an eccentric Corps Commander, but having received orders of some description, the men were at least able to advance.

III Corps spent the night on the south bank of the Marne. The pattern was repeated the next morning as they pressed on against a heavy rearguard. German machine-gun fire and snipers on the north bank made the bridges unapproachable.[80] By 3 p.m., Hunter-Weston had impatiently begun collecting a flotilla of boats to make the crossing, but was ordered to delay until the enemy retired. Buttonholing Major C. L. Brereton, commander of 68th Artillery Battery, he insisted on maximum support from

---

78   Dunn, *War the Infantry Knew*, 50–5.
79   Dunn, *War the Infantry Knew*), 50–5.
80   1/East Lancashire Regiment War Diary, 10 September 1914, WO 95/1498, TNA; *OH, 1914 (1)*, 338–9.

'A Brigadier and a Band of Brothers' 99

his six eight-pounder guns for his next attempt to cross in the evening.[81] The dispirited Brereton queried his confident grasp of the situation, but Hunter-Weston clearly understood the need for systematic coordination between artillery and infantry units. Indeed, deficiencies in artillery communications, command organisation and heavy fire support would soon become critical factors which undermined the success of mobile operations on the Aisne.[82]

Poor visibility curtailed Brereton's assistance, but the crossing turned out to be tedious and unopposed. For the next three days the main hardships were traffic congestion, deteriorating weather and limited food supplies – compounded, in the opinion of the Somersets, by faulty brigade staff work.[83] The BEF's pursuit of the enemy was at a leisurely enough pace to allow Hunter-Weston to preside over a remarkable Court Martial at the small village of Chouy on 12 September. During the retreat, two battalion commanders in the 10th Brigade, Mainwaring and Elkington, had attempted to surrender their units to the civil authorities at St Quentin, and were now charged with cowardice and dishonorable conduct. Personally, Hunter-Weston found the men's plight a sad one, but felt that his hands were tied by the 'enormity' of their failure of command.[84] Both were cashiered on the lesser charge, but he confided to Haldane that they would have been shot for cowardice had it not been for the vote of a single panel member.[85] The episode was a stark reminder of the dangers of combat fatigue, and it is probably no coincidence that Lieut.-Colonel Swayne of the Somersets,

81 C. L. Brereton Diary, 9 September 1914, 86/30/1, IWM.
82 Bidwell and Graham, *Fire-Power*, 67.
83 HW Official War Diary, 9 September 1914, 48355, BL; 1/Somerset Light Infantry War Diary, 11 September 1914, WO 95/1499, TNA.
84 HW to GHW, 11 November 1914, HW Private War Diary, 48363, BL. For a full account of the episode, see John Hutton, *August 1914: Surrender at St Quentin* (Barnsley: Pen & Sword, 2010), 150–2.
85 The officer was a 10th Division colleague, Colonel Sir Evelyn Bradford, Haldane Diary, 15 September 1914, Haldane Papers, MS 20248, NLS. Hunter-Weston later campaigned successfully for a pardon for Elkington, who was wounded after enlisting in the French Foreign Legion: HW to J. F. Elkington, 17 July 1916, HW Private War Diary, 48365, BL.

who was 'very run down', received a personal note that morning from his concerned Brigadier advising him to go home on sick leave.[86]

While Hunter-Weston was dispensing justice, his men marched another weary eighteen miles, reaching Septmonts in the evening. Even as they sank into their uncomfortable billets in the gridlocked village, decisions were already being taken which would mean that their rest was short. In a renewed burst of optimism, GHQ committed the army to pushing across the Aisne as soon as possible. At a hasty divisional conference, Hunter-Weston was ordered to seize a crossing at the bridge at Venizel and proceed north of the river; if he secured the bridgehead, he was promised artillery support at daybreak.[87]

Like the night raid at Bloemfontein, this dramatic mission combined hazard and reward, but rather than a band of hand-picked men, this time he had to lead a dejected, hungry brigade, some of them marching in bandages and gym shoes.[88] Whatever the dangers ahead, he believed that the situation was still preferable to making a daylight crossing in full view of the enemy. The Aisne forms a wide loop at Venizel, and any such enterprise was bound to result in heavy casualties as the river was swollen and unfordable, with enemy artillery trained on the few feasible crossing points. The assurance of artillery cover was not of much comfort, since it was highly unlikely that the British guns in their cramped positions on the southern bank would be able to locate and neutralise the German defenders.

The brigade started off towards Venizel at 11 p.m. through sheets of rain and a howling gale. Two junior officers from the Hampshires sent to assess the condition of the bridge had discovered that one of the four charges placed by the enemy had failed to detonate, leaving the central girder that reinforced the concrete roadway still intact. When the officer intended as a guide returned, exhausted, the Brigadier himself led his men

---

86   1/Somerset Light Infantry War Diary, 12 September 1914, WO 95/1499, TNA. He remained with the regiment on home service, commanding the 13th Battalion from 1918–19.
87   An Account of the Actions of the 11th Infantry Brigade on the Night of 12/13 September, Hunter-Weston Papers, 6503/39/2, NAM; *OH 1914, (1)*, 379.
88   Atkinson, *Hampshire Regiment*, 57.

to the bridge, using his military engineering experience to confirm that a crossing could be made safely. His four battalions began to inch their way across in single file, guided by a flash lamp on the north bank. The ammunition carts were unloaded and their contents passed from hand-to-hand. By 3 a.m. the whole brigade had managed to assemble on the north bank.[89]

They had become the first entire British formation to cross the Aisne. It was a remarkable achievement, but Hunter-Weston was determined also to make the crossing secure.[90] Both his options in achieving this were high risk: he could wait and rest his troops then launch an assault on the commanding heights above Bucy-le-Long with artillery support, or he could push his men on in the pitch dark over two miles of water meadows, without any reconnaissance, in an attempt to seize the high ground before dawn. He chose the latter option – the brigade would attack immediately at bayonet point. If the plan was successful this would be a great personal coup, but again his decision reflected the high costs of a daylight assault from the flat ground around the bridge. His formal report on the action set out a detailed scheme of deployment, but the Rifle Brigade recalled that the actual orders they received for the night assault were more basic. Directing his battalion commanders to three 'bumps' on maps that were almost illegible in the wet, he detailed a battalion to each bump and kept a fourth in reserve.[91] Setting off in columns of four, the sudden appearance of his men on the crest of the ridge completely surprised the Germans, who quickly abandoned their outposts and fell back on their main line some hundreds of yards away. By dawn, the 11th Brigade had secured a three-mile front that stretched from the ridges above the village of St Marguerite, west towards Montagne Farm.

The attack had been a complete success and an illustration of how delegation at divisional level could empower an energetic officer to exercise his initiative. At this stage in his career, the flexibility of his orders suggests

---

89 An Account – 12/13 September, Hunter-Weston Papers, 6503/39/20, NAM.
90 They shared the honour of being the first troops with the 4th Division cyclists who had taken the bridge at Missy that morning: *OH 1914, (1)*, 466.
91 Berkeley and Seymour, *Rifle Brigade* 25.

that Hunter-Weston was also willing to allow his subordinates a similar measure of freedom of action. Perhaps somewhat surprisingly, the episode did not find a place in Sir John French's official dispatches, but the image of hundreds of men treading carefully across a single girder was too good to miss for the propagandist histories which quickly multiplied while the war was still in progress.[92] Hunter-Weston's audacity in this action was later praised in Edmonds' *Official History*, which pointedly commented that, had other divisions shown similar enterprise, the fighting at the Aisne 'might have had a different result'.[93] Ultimately, however, such footholds were of limited tactical significance. Not only did the topography of the valley make them difficult to consolidate, but the momentum of the main British advance that could have supported them was quickly lost by delaying it until daylight. As a result, the BEF instead spent the next three days trying unsuccessfully to break through the strengthening German defenses on the Chemin des Dames ridge.

A New Form of Warfare

By the morning of 13 September the tactical weakness of the 11th Brigade's own position was apparent. They were vulnerable to enemy fire and could not break out of their exposed line without substantial artillery support. Indeed, the Brigadier was forced to ride up in person to check an independent attack of the Rifle Brigade on the main German trenches, which he believed would be futile.[94] Far from receiving the support they needed, the guns of 5th Division mistakenly shelled Hunter-Weston's men during the afternoon. Forbidden to take up better positions on the south bank

---

92 J. E. Parrott, *The Children's Story of the War*, vol. 2 (London: Nelson, 1915).
93 *OH 1914, (1)*, 380, 466; for a recent appraisal, see Murland, *Battle on the Aisne*, 8.
94 Berkeley and Seymour, *Rifle Brigade* 26; HW Official War Diary, 13 September 1914, 48355, BL.

'A Brigadier and a Band of Brothers'

for reasons of 'morale', Brereton's 68th Battery had joined the 11th Brigade on the heights, but was hampered by machine-gun fire from the German infantry who were only 800 yards away.[95] When Haldane reinforced Hunter-Weston's men the next day, he found them 'tired and a bit shaken', but still holding on.[96]

The BEF was unable to attack but securely entrenched on their chilly ridge tops; stalemate was already setting in. Heavy shelling continued, but there were no major engagements and the intense tempo of the last month slackened. During the lull, Hunter-Weston even found time to indulge his antiquarian instincts, sketching a wellhead at the fourteenth-century chateau at Bucy-le-Long, which he later adopted as a model for Hunterston.[97]

He also had time to reflect on recent events. Eagerly grasping his new fame, the recent achievements of his brigade hinted at a destiny as a great commander. In his letters to Grace there was now a sense that he was writing with one eye on posterity. This may explain the display of jocular sangfroid with which he sought to reassure her in his first letter after the battle:

> By 200lbs of Lyddite shell [is] history written within 150 yards of me to the west. Shrapnel are bursting behind (south) of me within 100 yards. A great deal of noise, Bang, bang, bang bang. That was the Devil of a noise and confusion! ... shaking the little house in which I have established my HQ, whence I direct the operations of my troops over a biggish front. I am indeed luckily constituted that my bunk is not accelerated by these amusements of the enemy. I am in a safe situation ... but so it is with my men also, at present they are all deeply dug in trenches & unless a shell happened just to land in the trench, which is very unlikely, they are quite safe ...[98]

---

95   HW Private War Diary, 14 September 1914, 48363, BL; Brereton Diary, 86/30/1, IWM.
96   Haldane Diary, 14 September 1914, Haldane Papers, MS 20248, NLS.
97   HW to GHW, 16 September 1914, HW Private War Diary, 48363, BL. The well is still in existence at the front of Hunterston House. His timing was fortuitous; when he visited the site in 1919, he discovered that the Germans had made off with the original.
98   HW to GHW, 15 September 1914, *HW Private War Diary*, 48363, BL. His recollections of the battle were privately published in 1914, *The Battle of the Aisne*, Hunter of Hunterston Papers, NRAS852/4/20; he was also the subject of a hagiographic

In fact, his safety was far from guaranteed; over the next two days Brigade HQ was shelled, with yet another of Hunter-Weston's chargers among the casualties.[99] He moved his base back to a 'really nice villa' at Bucy-le-Long where he could enjoy a southern aspect, fine food and a comfortable bed. His service overseas had taught him to seize whatever amenities were available when he got the chance, and recent experience had confirmed that good health was a commander's most valuable asset. The increased physical distance of Brigade HQ from the front line did not mean that he was out of touch with his troops and their living conditions. Drawing on his RE training, Hunter-Weston's main priority was to secure the defensive line and protect his men from direct artillery fire, replacing their original 'grubbers' with well-prepared entrenchments. Besides the usual network of fire trenches, communication trenches and safe dug-outs, he became an early pioneer of the 'switch' system of defence, ordering the construction of a duplicated trench line from the spur north west of Bucy village to the Aisne, in the hope that if part the front line was captured, this could be quickly linked to the sections still held in order to prevent a decisive breakthrough.[100] His thirst for innovation took other creative forms. The *Official History* personally credits him with originating the practice of naming trenches and posts, a practice which soon became customary on the western front.[101] Meanwhile, the local stalemate provided him with practice in maintaining good inter-allied relations. The French 89th Infantry Brigade under General Trafford was holding the left of the line at the Aisne

---

work by Maj. R. G. Louis, *'The Unconquerable Mind', A Tribute to the General in Command of the 11th Brigade of Infantry*, NRAS852/4/10.

99   HW to GHW, 16 September 1914, HW Private War Diary, 48363, BL.
100 Hopkinson, *Spectamur Agendo*, 63.
101 J. E. Edmonds and C. G. Wynne, *History of the Great War Based on Official Documents by Direction of the Historical Section of the Committee of Imperial Defence: Military Operations in France and Belgium, Winter 1915. Volume I: Battle of Neuve Chapelle: Battles of Ypres* (Macmillan: London, 1927), 5. Peter Chasseaud suggests that the naming process was actually more complex, but confirms that the 11th Brigade took the lead in developing imaginative designations in their sector, believing that clear description was essential where no name existed on the map: *Rat's Alley: Trench Names of the Western Front, 1914–18* (Staplehurst: Spellmount, 2006), 59–60.

and was a formation much given to 'demonstrations', which occasionally led to full-scale assaults.[102] Hunter-Weston's fluent French and his natural good humour greatly assisted his relations with his counterpart, who gave him a cantaloupe melon and confided his antipathy towards unsupported attacks.[103]

Beyond ensuring security, Hunter-Weston's prescription for effective trench warfare was to work his men hard and look after their welfare. He was delighted that they were 'as fit as fleas', with only a third of the number on daily sick parade as there had been at Colchester.[104] They were not permitted to roost in their comfortable dugouts. When not entrenching, patrolling or manning forward observation posts, he required his men to undertake route marches or to climb up and down the ravines at the back of the brigade position. He pushed himself equally hard. Walking round the entire trench line could take seven and a half hours, but he was punctilious in carrying out inspections, sometimes accompanied by distinguished colleagues like Henry Rawlinson, commander of IV Corps.[105] Above all, regular contact with his troops remained important to him on an emotional level, offering reassurance both to himself and the men that the bond of trust between them had not been broken As he wrote home from his dugout above the Aisne: 'The men are so nice to me, and always look happy and smiling when they pass me, even in the most trying circumstances. I love them dearly'.[106]

102 HW Official War Diary, 25, 26, 27, 30 September 1914, 48355, BL.
103 HW to GHW, 23 September and 4 October 1914, HW Private War Diary, 48363, BL.
104 HW to GHW, 23 September and 4 October 1914, HW Private War Diary, 48363, BL; HW Official War Diary, 28 September 1914, 48355, BL.
105 HW to GHW, 16, 23 September 1914, HW Private War Diary, 48363, BL.
106 HW to GHW, 16 September 1914, HW Private War Diary, 48363, BL.

CHAPTER SEVEN

Winter in the Trenches

The September campaign, which began with Hunter-Weston's tour de force on the heights of Bucy-le-Long, ended in frustration. The BEF prepared to quit the Aisne at the beginning of October and begin a transfer to the left of the allied line in Flanders. The rationale involved a complex mix of logistical and political considerations, but a further unspoken motivation at GHQ was the opportunity to return to mobile warfare.[1] The reality was very different. Allied attempts to turn the German flank coincided with a massive enemy offensive which was designed to win the war at a stroke. Rather than advancing, the British were left defending an unprepared and over-extended front out of all proportion to their strength. For Hunter-Weston, the complex, brutal and confused fighting of the First Battle of Ypres and the pernicious stalemate that followed during the winter of 1914–15 marked an important transitional phase in his approach to command.

Promotion and 'Plugstreet'

The 11th Brigade left the Aisne on 7 October, moving off by moonlight to avoid 'dratted airplanes'.[2] Arriving in Flanders five days later, their first impressions of the region were not good. Described rather wistfully in the *Official History* as 'a country of old, decaying towns and prosperous villages',

---

[1] Gardiner, *Trial by Fire*, 111; Ian Beckett, *Ypres: The First Battle, 1914* (Harlow: Pearson, 2006), 19–20.
[2] HW Private War Diary, 7 October 1914, 48363, BL.

its flat, cluttered landscape was very different from the picturesque Aisne.[3] An equally unattractive (if less obvious) feature was the sub-surface water table which carried the constant threat of flooding.

At first, the British advance made impressive progress, with III Corps reaching Armentières and striking out eastwards across the River Lys. Soaked to the skin in a turnip field, the 11th Brigade were initially in reserve, but after switching to the advance guard on 15 October they were able to seize the crossings at Pont de Nieppe and Erquinghem with very little resistance.[4] Initial hopes that an enveloping movement would now sweep round the German right wing were disappointed by the growing strength of the forces opposite the BEF. By the time the brigade returned to the reserve five days later, the advance of III Corps had ground to a standstill on a thinly defended twelve-mile front stretching from the village of Le Gheer, north east of Armentières, to a point due west of Lille. That same day, the enemy counter-offensive opened up all along the British line, falling most heavily on Smith-Dorrien's Corps in the north, but also targeting III Corps, who were hammered by relentless shelling and howitzer fire.

Even though his brigade had been dispersed to shore up other formations, at 3 a.m. on 21 October Hunter-Weston was ordered to reinforce a critical gap on the left flank with his remaining troops.[5] He marched through the night with two of his battalions and a single company of the Essex Regiment and arrived at the front just in time to launch a counter-attack against Le Gheer.[6] The enemy had occupied the village at dawn and, as a result, Major-General Henry de Beauvoir De Lisle's 1st Cavalry Division had already taken heavy casualties. After making his HQ near the divisional artillery at the northwest corner of the Ploegsteert ('Plugstreet') Wood, Hunter-Weston quickly conferred with De Lisle and Lieut.-Colonel

3 *OH, 1914 (1)*, 74–5.
4 HW Private War Diary, 15, 16 October 1914, 48363, BL.
5 *OH, 1914 (1)*, 149; HW Official War Diary, 21 October 1914, 48355, BL.
6 An Account of the Action of the 11th Brigade at Le Gheer on 21 October, 6503/39/20, NAM; HW Private War Diary, 21 October 1914, 48363, BL.

F. G. Anley of 12th Brigade and together they developed a plan of attack.[7] He gave orders to the Somersets to move from the north and along the eastern edge of the wood, firing down on the village with machine guns, while two companies of the East Lancashires were instructed to work their way along the wood's southern edge with fixed bayonets. His decisiveness was rewarded. The village was captured and cleared by 11.27 a.m. and subsequent counter-attacks were decisively repulsed. German losses were estimated to be at least a thousand with 130 taken prisoner, while the 11th Brigade's casualties numbered 17 killed and 69 wounded. As the new battalion commander of the East Lancashires summarised, 'We came off cheap'.[8]

The action was one small episode in the great tidal battle of First Ypres, which saw defensive positions repeatedly taken and retaken in an attempt to keep the enemy away from the Channel Coast. The 11th Brigade now held a fragile line of trenches in the Ploegsteert Wood sector which stretched northwards from the Warnave stream to the River Douve. Pressure peaked at the end of the month, when an entire platoon from the Hampshires was destroyed in a major German assault. Hunter-Weston immediately ordered a bayonet attack after dark to regain the lost trenches, personally led by his aggressive protégé, Major Charles Bertie Prowse.[9] Small, spirited and successful actions of this type brought rapid rewards. Three days after Le Gheer, French wrote to Kitchener recommending Hunter-Weston's promotion for distinguished conduct in the field, alongside Aylmer Haldane and Edward Bulfin (2nd Brigade), as 'officers who have never once failed in the most trying circumstances, and have done great service for their

7   *OH, 1914 (1)*, 149. The involvement of these colleagues was not mentioned in Hunter-Weston's official report.
8   Eight Months Record of Service of 1st Bn., East Lancashire Regiment in Flanders, 28 Sept. 1914–21 May 1915; written by its commanding officer, Lieut.-Col. George Henniker Lawrence, CMG, 21 October 1914, 2006/04/19, NAM; 1/East Lancashire Regiment War Diary, 21–2 October 1914, WO 95/1498.
9   1/Somerset Light Infantry War Diary, 30–31 October 1914, WO 95/1499, TNA; Account of the Fighting at St Yves, 30, 31 Oct. 1914, 6503/39/20, NAM; HW to GHW, 31 October 1914, HW Private War Diary, 48363, BL; *OH, 1914 (1)*, 230. Hunter-Weston successfully recommended Prowse for promotion: *London Gazette*, 1 December 1914.

country'.[10] The rapid advancement of 'young generals' – Hunter-Weston had just turned fifty – reflected the small pool of candidates in possession of suitable operational experience at this stage in the war, but these appointments nevertheless won widespread acclaim, since it was now a commonly held view that 'commands should be held by men in the prime of life, as only they could withstand the strains of modern war'.[11]

Hunter-Weston was thrilled to hear the news from Sir John French, but he explained to his wife, who had promptly sent him three stars for his shoulder straps, that he was not ready to leave his brigade:

> The officers and men are all so nice to me, so evidently genuinely fond of me that it pips me by the heart strings. It is seldom that a British Tommy cheers his officer, but I am constantly cheered as I ride past my dear men. It is wonderful ... You know I was not keen on promotion for promotion's sake. What I wanted was interesting work, and rank and pay ... but this promotion I do appreciate immensely as it came as a complete surprise, for it is not usual to promote in the middle (or rather, I fear, in the beginning) of a campaign.[12]

Despite his protestations, he was an ambitious career soldier, and his need for his men's affection was always tempered by a keen awareness of the opportunities which were likely to arise at divisional level. There seemed little prospect of advancement in the 4th Division, where H. F. M. Wilson had replaced the recently injured Snow, but the loss of Hubert Hamilton, the first divisional commander to be killed in action in the war, created another vacancy – especially as his subordinates in the 3rd Division were reputed to be unfit even for temporary command.[13] Besides, the brigade that Hunter-Weston had taken to war was steadily disappearing. Prolonged fighting had depleted the battalions who had held the line at Le Cateau.

---

10 Sir John French to Lord Kitchener, 24 October 1914. WO 33/713, TNA; he also brought the 'excellent counter-attack' of 31 October to Kitchener's attention: WO 159/13, TNA.
11 *Army and Navy Gazette*, 7 November 1914; Robbins, *British Generalship*, 53–4.
12 HW to GHW, 28 October 1914, HW Private War Diary, 48363, BL.
13 HW to GHW, 25 October 1914, HW Private War Diary, 48363, BL.

Winter in the Trenches

New drafts had come out, including a London Territorial unit, but the lack of experienced officers was already telling.[14]

The face of the war was also changing. Hunter-Weston had a good appreciation of its transnational dynamics: 'We in England are putting up plant and sending managers and paying for large ammunition factories in Japan to supply Russia. The French supplying Serbia & Montenegro. America is supplying Russia & making a fair profit. Germany only has herself for guns rifles and ammunition. But she has vast stores of it & an enormous power of production.'[15] He was also well aware of the local 'log jam', regretting that the lack of conscription had deprived Britain of the sort of mass army that could have tipped the balance of forces on the Western Front.[16] At Ploegsteert, both sides were busy constructing increasingly secure defensive positions. By early November, stalemate had settled in along the line, although costly skirmishes continued. Conditions worsened with the first fall of snow later in the month, with frostbite and dropsy common.[17] Adding to the men's misery, technological bottlenecks had produced ammunition shortages, with the result that enemy bombardments appeared to go unchallenged.

Hunter-Weston admitted to his wife that he was pessimistic about the wider prospects on the Western Front, even allowing himself to express a measure of war weariness:

> how we both wish we could see the end of the war. Its duration no one can foretell for many different factors are unknown that any speculation is useless. On the Western side I do not expect any developments. We are now extended in a continuous line from the sea to the Swiss frontier, and if the Germans after hurling masses of troops at us, where we were very weak and practically unfortified, were unable to break through, I don't think that either side will effect any great progress now we are both strong all along the line.[18]

---

14 They were immediately nicknamed 'the London fatigue party' by the regulars: *A Short History of the London Rifle Brigade* (Aldershot: Gale and Polden, 1916).
15 HW to GHW, 27, 28 December 1914, HW Private War Diary, 48363, BL.
16 HW to GHW, 16 November 1914, HW Private War Diary, 48363, BL.
17 HW Private War Diary, 15, 24 November 1914, 48363, BL.
18 HW to GHW, 23 November 1914, HW Private War Diary, 48363, BL.

His response to these developments was complex. In a defiant display of old army panache, he embarked on a pheasant shoot during a brief lull in operations in late October.[19] Most of the time, though, as a trained staff officer and military engineer, he applied himself to understanding and addressing the new conditions of defensive warfare. With his operational responsibilities reduced by the sedentary condition of his brigade, his restless energy was absorbed in devising more efficient means of waging war. These included prescriptions for improving trench design, as well as a thorough scheme for the training of Territorials on active service.[20]

Beside the technical aspects of war, Hunter-Weston also began to reflect on his changing role as a commander. This was a shared concern among senior colleagues, for in an absence of a clearly articulated doctrine of command, the search for an ideal balance between control and guidance, as Beckett and Corvi observe, allowed a range of interpretations.[21] Hunter-Weston now saw a Brigadier's duties as principally organisational, focussing in particular on the development of good communications from front to rear while maintaining cooperation between neighbouring units. He also had definite views on his own exposure to danger:

> The position of the Brigadier should be such that the orderlies can reach him from all parts of his command with the least possible delay but he should not, in ordinary times, be too close to the firing line. His business is to organize and direct and to see that all that is required by his brigade is got up from the rear. He must also be in such a position that he is within easy touch with Divisional Head Quarters. Of course, there are times when the Brigadier must be close to his troops, but these occasions are rare.[22]

---

19   'A shooting party that we will remember all of our lives': HW to GHW, 28 October 1914, HW Private War Diary, 48363, BL. He was by no means alone in his sporting activities while on active service. The private hare shoot staged by artillery officers at Polygon Wood added to the crossfire on 24 October 1914: Ascoli, *Mons Star*, 210.
20   Scheme for Training a Territorial Division, HW Official War Diary, 48355, BL.
21   Beckett and Corvi, *Haig's Generals*, 5; see also Barr, 'Command', 35–6.
22   Notes on Some of the Duties of a Brigadier when his Troops are in the Trenches, HW Official War Diary, 48355, BL.

Winter in the Trenches 113

The reality was rather different. In his letters to Grace, he emphasised a detached managerial approach, assuring her that 'the general is a long way back at the end of an elaborate system of telephone wires', but in fact, the job of the Brigadier remained a dangerous one; two of his successors as GOC of the 11th Brigade, Julian Hasler and Bertie Prowse, would be killed in action. The Ploegsteert trenches offered few opportunities for heroic leadership, but despite planning and staff work increasingly dominating his days, he was unwilling to abandon his contact with the front line. At a Brigade Conference in November, he took his officers up and down Ploegsteert Wood for four hours, examining the brigade lines and the breastworks of the supporting line, while they 'slipped about in the mud and got well sniped at'.[23] Similarly, Lieut.-Colonel Lawrence's diary recorded almost daily visits to the East Lancashire's trenches at the beginning of 1915, with some full-scale inspections lasting over two hours.[24] This level of engagement helped in monitoring the performance of less experienced officers, but Hunter-Weston also believed that a commander's visibility was instrumental in maintaining morale. His close paternal interest in his men also assumed a very practical form, with his local village back in Ayrshire mobilised to send comforts to the brigade through the medium of his wife.[25] This flair for what Dixon describes as the 'social' aspects of leadership undoubtedly assisted his continuing popularity with his troops, one of whom described him as 'the bravest and cleverest man I know'.[26] His high spirits and indifference to danger marked him out as the sort of

23 Eight Months Record, 21 November 1914, 2006/04/19, NAM.
24 Eight Months Record, 5, 7, 11 January 1915, 2006/04/19, NAM. See also 1/East Lancashire Regiment War Diary, 1 February 1915, WO 95/1498, TNA. Front-line visits also remained frequent among more senior officers: Robbins, *British Generalship*, 79. See also John Bourne, 'British Generals in the First World War', in Gary Sheffield (ed.), *Leadership and Command: The Anglo-American Military Experience Since 1861* (London and Washington: Brassey's, 1997), 101–2.
25 *West Kilbride Parish Magazine*, November 1915.
26 *Dundee Advertiser*, 21 November 1914. The comment was attributed to a Sergeant in the East Lancashires who had been wounded at Armentières. See Norman Dixon, *On the Psychology of Military Incompetence* (London: Pimlico, 1994) 218–19.

'character' that the men appreciated. Corporal Kelson of the Somersets, who had been wounded by shellfire, explained:

> Soon after I was hit General Hunter-Weston came up to me and patted me on the shoulder saying, 'Hard luck, corporal, jolly hard luck. Never mind, you'll get your own back some day' and went off singing ragtime. We soldiers out here know him as the 'ragtime-general' as he's always singing ragtime songs. A fine plucked one he is and there is no such thing as fear about him. He goes about singing ragtime all the while and whenever you see him he always has a cheery smile on his face. 'Never mind', he once said, 'if they (the Germans) won't come for us, then we'll go for them and really give 'em "Alexander's Ragtime Band"'.[27]

For all his concern for his men, Hunter-Weston refused to let their sufferings determine his command decisions. Despite his scepticism over an early end to the deadlock on the Western Front, he remained committed to offensive action wherever possible and became an eager exponent of small-scale attacks to take out troublesome enemy positions. Before 1914, he had embraced the philosophy of the offensive in the abstract, but nothing in his early wartime experience had caused him to reconsider. Above all, he was sustained by the belief in ultimate victory – 'WE can last and stick it out' – while convinced that the war could not be won by defensive action alone.[28] Personal considerations were also at work: Hunter-Weston had been promoted as a thrusting commander, in the company of a distinguished peer group who would be competitors for future promotion, so he had to maintain his reputation for aggression if he wished his career to prosper.[29] But, there was a price. There would be no more 'cheap' victories, and his 'little attacks' would also fuel the continuing attrition of his beloved brigade. Outward 'cheeriness' remained a powerful antidote to self-doubt, but confronting the results of his decision-making at close quarters was still awkward, as he confided in his diary: 'One fine fellow I met, wounded by a bullet in the mouth and covered in blood said, "never

---

27   *Bath Chronicle*, 21 November 1914.
28   HW to GHW, 16 November 1914, HW Private War Diary, 48363, BL.
29   Travers, *Killing Ground*, 12–13.

mind Sir, we'll beat them. Let me shake you by the hand." Grand fellow. Got quite emotional!'.[30]

Yet, like any successful commander, he could not afford a tender conscience. When he wrote to Grace about his preparations for a night-time counter-attack on German positions at St Yves and Le Gheer on 9 November, his self-conscious cultivation of stoicism and disengagement was evident:

> So here I sit, having made out all the plan, waiting to see how the troops that have to carry out the attack will be able to succeed ... An anxious thing to be a general making careful plans, & then once he has committed his troops to the exact spot to assure victory or minimise defeat. Some feel the strain personally, sitting & waiting. I am glad to say that tonight I do not at all. I have organised the affair well, I have taken all precautions to ensure success & minimise defeat. The result is in the Hands of Destiny. I have done my part. Of course sometimes I do feel it. Possibly tonight if something unforeseen transpires, I may feel the excitement that I hope I never show. I always am, I hope, cheery, when, & especially when, things are going wrong; but even so there is a fierce fury in grappling with the difficulty, getting it right, but there are many hellish times ...[31]

The Birdcage

Hunter-Weston had hitherto always been a lucky commander, but his luck was turning. Despite the howitzer bombardment, the attack at St Yves made little progress. His troops in the centre were cut down by a burst of concealed enemy fire, while his left wing completely lost direction.[32] Worse was to come at the 'Birdcage' on 19 December, a fiasco that contained a number of disturbing auguries for his later career. He described the

---

30 HW Private War Diary, 15 December 1914, 48363, BL.
31 HW to GHW, 9 November 1914, HW Private War Diary, 48363, BL.
32 HW Official War Diary, 21 October 1914, 48355, BL; HW Private War Diary, HW to GHW, 10 November 1914, 48363, BL.

enterprise as 'a little attack, not an important affair, but something to tie the Germans to their ground in front of us ...'[33] In fact, it had been planned by III Corps as part of a larger advance to counter the transfer of German troops to the Russian front, but was later scaled down to become a diversion to prevent them from committing reserves against a French offensive at Arras. Hunter-Weston's orders from 4th Division were to mount a daylight attack against the formidable defensive position on the eastern edges of Ploegsteert Wood, and, if possible, to establish a new forward trench line.[34] Foundering through the badly pitted and flooded ground, reconnaissance parties had earlier found the enemy trenches to be weakly held but protected by six feet high wire of considerable strength and thickness – the disturbing feature that had given the position its name.[35] As a result, mattresses were made to throw over the German barbed wire and for days the men practised crossing silently using planks and tripods.

The British bombardment began promptly at 9 a.m., but the lack of accurate observation soon became apparent when the British assembly trenches were almost shelled in error.[36] The divisional guns opened up again for a further hour, firing heavy shells which fell short of the German positions, while the field guns were impeded by the thickness of the wood. As the barrage lifted at precisely 2.30 pm, the attacking companies of the Somersets and the Rifle Brigade emerged.[37] Their advance assumed a farcical aspect as they staggered across in terrible ground conditions, weighed down by their tripods and rabbit-wire mattresses. In his 'Report Centre' at a little farm north of Ploegsteert Wood, Hunter-Weston could do little to intervene as the attack went hopelessly wrong. As his men advanced, a hail of bullets enveloped them from the intact German trenches. The telephone line was breached, and when the British artillery opened up to provide cover,

---

33   HW to GHW, 18 December 1914, HW Private War Diary, 48363, BL.
34   HW Official War Diary, 18, 19 December 1914, 48355, BL.
35   1/Somerset Light Infantry War Diary, 13 December 1914, WO 95/1499, TNA.
36   The officer observing for the 6th Siege Battery was forced to ask the Somersets' HQ for help to distinguish between the British and German trenches: 1/Somerset Light Infantry War Diary, 19 December 1914, WO 95/1499, TNA.
37   Berkeley and Seymour, *Rifle Brigade*, 42.

their 4.5-inch howitzer shells fell among the Somersets, inflicting heavy casualties.[38] Persevering, the survivors got to within twenty yards of their first objective, only to discover that the Germans had already withdrawn to stronger positions in the rear. Meanwhile, on the right, the Rifle Brigade advance had been broken up by mud and shell-holes, as well 'shorts' from their own guns.[39] By 4 p.m., with darkness falling, it was clear that the attack could go no further. Hunter-Weston instructed his battalions to dig in for another attempt the next day, but relented when informed by his officers that the waterlogged ground made even this action impossible.[40] His attack had gained a modest tactical advantage in clearing the enemy from the wood, but it had cost fifty-eight officers and men killed and ninety-eight wounded. His careful assault preparations were unable to compensate for poor intelligence work and inadequate artillery support. His diary entry for the day was uncharacteristically terse in its evaluation – 'Successful on the whole, but many casualties for only a little gain'.[41]

Within days of this bloody episode, the approach of Christmas heralded a wave of fraternisation. The closeness of the opposing trench systems, which had confused the British artillery, now encouraged men from both sides to meet half-way, chatting amicably and exchanging gifts of tobacco.[42] For such a bellicose commander, Hunter-Weston's attitude to this development was remarkably tolerant, but he drew the line when the Germans proposed a formal truce at New Year, being of the opinion that it would take too long to arrange and could be 'a dangerous thing'.[43] He did take advantage of a more informal 'cessation of fire' to walk round the trenches,

38 1/Somerset Light Infantry War Diary, 19 December 1914, WO 95/1499, TNA.
39 Report on Operations of 19th December, 1/Rifle Brigade War Diary, 1914, WO 95/1496, TNA.
40 HW Private War Diary, 20 December 1914, 48363, BL.
41 HW to GHW, 19 December 1914, HW Private War Diary, 48363, BL.
42 The Brigade War Diary records that the enemy were Saxons from the 132nd, 133rd and 134th regiments from Chemnitz: BL 48355. See also Eight Months Record, 25 December 1914, 2006/04/19, NAM; HW to GHW, 27 December 1914, HW Private War Diary, 48363, BL.
43 HW Private War Diary, 21 December 1914, 48363, BL; Eight Months Record, 25 December 1914, 2006/04/19, NAM.

making a careful inspection and wishing every man in the brigade a Happy New Year. Fortified by home-made mince pies and a Hunterston turkey, he had the brigade paraded the next day and told them how proud he was to command them. Walking down the line, he shook each man by the hand, asking them to write home and tell their friends and families how much their general valued their friendship.[44]

Life along the line became very quiet. A wet January gave way to a freezing February. The 11th Brigade's enthusiasm for trench names continued to flourish and ranged from the nostalgic to the ironic. Hunter-Weston was quite content for his own nickname to be used, and 'Hunter Avenue' and 'Bunter Avenue' duly appeared on the trench map, alongside 'Three Huns Farm' and 'Dead Horse Corner'.[45] The trenches themselves required constant maintenance work; the Rifle Brigade estimated that they set out 2,400 yards of wire in the space of a single week as the Germans continued to sap towards them.[46] The monotony of 'situation normal' in the Brigade War Diary was occasionally broken by visits from distinguished guests, including Winston Churchill, whom Hunter-Weston found 'very interesting and pleasant'.[47] Indeed, the Ploegsteert trenches were becoming something of a visitor attraction – one forward post was renamed 'Tourist Peep' – but for the men who lived in them, the sniping and shelling continued, with conditions becoming even more waterlogged and insanitary; the brigade's casualty figures for January totalled 10 officers and 625 other ranks, 491 of them suffering from illness.[48] Hunter-Weston prided himself on his mental and physical toughness, but the strains of winter warfare were beginning to tell. Riding behind the lines to keep fit, he confessed to his wife that he had lost his temper and broken his cane when his grey mare Snowflake misbehaved.[49] His health also suffered from the unrelenting cold and he

44   HW to GHW, 1 January 1915, HW Private War Diary, 48363, BL.
45   Chasseaud, *Rat's Alley*, 62.
46   Rifle Brigade War Diary, 1–7 November 1914, WO 95/1496, TNA.
47   HW Private War Diary, 29 November 1914, 48363, BL.
48   HW Official War Diary, 48355, BL; HW Private War Diary, 15–17 January 1915, 48363, BL.
49   HW to GHW, 11 January 1915, HW Private War Diary, 48363, BL.

developed a chronic throat complaint that troubled him for the rest of the war. He was glad to be granted eight days leave in February. Motoring to Calais, he stayed the night with Sir John French before catching the morning boat for England. Although he was not to know it then, he had left his brigade for the last time.

Already hailed as one of 'the Men of Mark in the War', if Hunter-Weston had been killed during the opening engagements of 1914, instead of one of his unfortunate mounts, he might be regarded today as one of Britain's lost military talents.[50] He had risen to the challenge of commanding a brigade in wartime, deploying a blend of showmanship and paternalism to create build a sense of unit identity which was unusual at that level. The face-to-face and day-to-day nature of the relationship with his officers and men suited him, and the 11th 'Stonewall' Brigade came to be regarded as one of the most aggressive in the BEF. His next command, however, would test his capacity for continued professional growth to the utmost. It would also vindicate his judgement of the wider strategic situation – that this would be a long war, fought on an international scale.

50 *The Windsor Magazine*, February 1915.

CHAPTER EIGHT

'A Second Crimea' – The Road to Gallipoli

The essential purpose of the Dardanelles expedition of 1915 was to deliver a knock-out blow against the Ottoman Empire and thus shorten the war. Nothing else about the campaign was ever that simple. Halfway through his leave, Hunter-Weston received a telegram from Lord Kitchener who wanted to see him immediately. Attending the War Office on 15 February, his old chief briskly informed him that the government was thinking of sending a military force to the Dardanelles to cooperate with the fleet. If the expedition did head east, then Hunter-Weston would take over command of the 29th Division; if not, then its current GOC would take it to France. Either way, he was to give up the 11th Brigade and take command of a newly formed division.[1]

The machinery of promotion had been turning discreetly at the highest levels. Only three days previously, the War Office had requested Sir John French to forward the names of officers of Major-General rank, who had 'a thorough knowledge of French, so as to be able to conduct operations of a detached force of English and French troops combined'.[2] The object of the mission was not specified, but at this stage an allied landing was projected in Salonika with the aim of tempting Greece into the war. Despite being deeply distrustful of such adventures, French speedily forwarded a short-list consisting of Henry Wilson, Hubert Gough and Hunter-Weston. His first choice was Gough, but when Gough declined after taking Sir William Robertson's advice against 'sideshows', French turned to Hunter-Weston as 'the most suitable, as he can be best spared and is available at once.'[3]

[1] Hunter-Weston Private War Diary, Vol. X, 13 Mar.–31 Dec. 1915, Add. MS 48364, British Library. [HW Private War Diary, 48364, BL].
[2] War Office to GHQ France, 12 February 1914, WO 33/713, TNA.
[3] Farrar-Hockley, *Goughie*, 149–50.

'With a Reasonable Chance of Success ...'

Hunter-Weston's acquaintance with the sodden stalemate in Flanders was already drawing him towards an alternative strategy to end the war. He was now presented with a dramatic (if uncertain) role in a mission that had already acquired a new destination. Always a risk taker, the mystique of the Dardanelles was attractive to an ambitious solider who cherished the 'romance of war'. This was, then, a turning point, but not in the way that he imagined. Indeed, in accepting this eye-catching command at a critically early stage in his career, he would seriously compromise his future reputation as a commander. The literature on the Gallipoli campaign is massive and still steadily accumulating, but most contributors agree in their judgement of Hunter-Weston's contribution. In Rhode James's classic study he stands out among a gallery of uninspired commanders as 'in many respects ... a preposterous figure', distinguished by a stubborn commitment to attack and a detached disregard for casualties.[4] In more recent popular narratives such as Les Carlyon's *Gallipoli*, the author's most sarcastic venom is reserved for a general whose 'bushy moustache quivered as he laughed'; who '... threw away troops the way lesser men tossed away socks, all the time bubbling with boisterous good humour'.[5]

Often presented as a tragedy of heroic failure, Gallipoli seems to require a stage villain – a foil for Sir Ian Hamilton's chivalrous, if ineffectual, leadership. Even scrupulously researched analyses, which prioritise systemic failure over individual command mistakes, continue this demonisation by presenting Hunter-Weston as an 'eccentric and traditional' subordinate, exhibiting a 'certain mental and physical detachment from reality' and handicapping Hamilton through his failure to grasp the problems and

---

4   Robert Rhodes James, *Gallipoli* (London: Pimlico, 1999), 210.
5   Les Carlyon, *Gallipoli* (London: Bantam, 2001) 120. See also John Laffin on the 'bovine' Hunter-Weston: *The Agony of Gallipoli* (London: The History Press, 2005), 65.

'A Second Crimea' – The Road to Gallipoli

challenges of the modern battlefield.[6] More recent scholarly accounts have been only marginally kinder. Robin Prior, for instance, strongly condemns the poor planning and decision-making that blighted Hunter-Weston's handling of the initial landings and subsequent set-piece battles, but admits that there was perhaps 'a little more to him'. He identifies, for example, a certain capacity for tactical analysis and development, resulting in some small-scale successes, which while 'not masterpieces of military art', began to grope towards alternative ways of gaining ground at a reduced cost.[7] Peter Hart also offers a nuanced analysis which stresses the paradoxes of Hunter-Weston's command, observing that the qualities of drive and determination he had displayed in his earlier career were ill-suited to a hopeless military situation. His performance combined 'piercing insight' with serious errors of judgement, but ultimately, Hart argues, the responsibility for the costly disasters that befell the expedition were not Hunter-Weston's alone, but instead lies with the man in overall command – General Sir Ian Hamilton.[8]

The sustained critique neglects that while every senior officer in early 1915 was trying to make sense of new methods of combat, Hunter-Weston faced a combination of exceptional challenges at Gallipoli. The first was simply his lack of experience. Having commanded a brigade in France for six months, he was now entrusted with executive command of the first opposed amphibious landings in modern warfare. Nevertheless, he was determined to approach his new task 'scientifically', through a rigorous application of the tactical principles had had studied as a staff officer. Here, war was stripped down to its essentials: victory in combat came from defeating the enemy's field army by concentrating superior resources at a decisive point; high morale, a fighting spirit and a willingness to accept

---

[6] Tim Travers, *Gallipoli 1915* (Stroud: Tempus, 2003), 104; and his 'Command and Leadership Styles in the British Army: the 1915 Gallipoli Model', *Journal of Contemporary History* 29 (1994), 411.
[7] Robin Prior, *Gallipoli: The End of the Myth* (New Haven: Yale University Press, 2009), 245–6.
[8] Peter Hart, *Gallipoli* (Oxford: Oxford University Press, 2013), 273–4.

casualties were essential in this enterprise, as was determined leadership.[9] His attempts to apply these long-established axioms explain many of his later command decisions, even though the real nature of the warfare at Gallipoli often negated them.

Second, Hunter-Weston had become part of a chaotic military adventure, in which muddle and improvisation made it very difficult for any commander to shine. There were immediate warning signs after his interview with Kitchener, when 'his' division became a pawn in War Council power play over the future direction of British strategy.[10] Indeed, the twists and turns of its deployment over the next three weeks suggested that the expedition itself had become a dependent variable whose fate would be determined by powerful external drivers. The ambitious plan for a purely naval attack to force a passage through the narrow Dardanelles straits and steam on to Constantinople evolved after an initial bombardment of the Turkish defences in November 1914. The strategic objectives of this dramatic operation were to support Russia, take Turkey out of the war and rally the Balkan states behind the allies.

By the time the War Council met on 16 February 1915, Admiralty opinion had drifted towards the need for a military presence to assist the fleet. Indeed, Winston Churchill had already ordered that two battalions from the Royal Naval Division (RND) were to be made available. The Council approved the despatch of the 29th Division to the Aegean, where it was to be joined by Australian and New Zealand Army Corps (Anzac) units who were still training in Egypt. At this stage it was far from clear what these troops would actually do beyond garrison duty or small-scale landing parties, but full-scale combined operations to invade the Gallipoli peninsula were certainly still not envisaged. Anxious to maintain the momentum,

---

9   Hunter-Weston, Evidence to Dardanelles Commission, 12 February 1917, Hamilton Papers, 8/2/50, LHCMA.
10   The genesis of the campaign is extensively covered by the historiography. See for example, Prior, *Gallipoli*, 1–71; Travers, *Gallipoli*, 20–36. Also, C. F. Aspinall-Oglander, *History of the Great War based on official documents by direction of the Historical Section of the Committee of Imperial Defence: Military Operations, Gallipoli. Volume I: Inception of the Campaign to May 1915* (London: William Heinemann, 1929), 108–9 [*OHG (1)*].

Churchill sent Kitchener a typically imperious missive on 20 February lobbying him to appoint Hunter-Weston, 'or someone equally competent', to take command of the troops who were now intended to concentrate in the Dardanelles vicinity.[11] Far from complying, Kitchener had in fact already decided the previous day, just as the naval bombardment at the Dardanelles was beginning, not to send the division after all, preferring instead to wait until the general strategic situation became clearer. Only after a series of Russian victories were reported in the Carpathians in March did he release it. Still officially 'on loan' from the Western Front, and without its normal 10 per cent reinforcement draft, it joined an allied expeditionary force that had swollen to around 80,000 men under a newly appointed commander, Ian Hamilton. The aims of the mission remained poorly articulated, but the prospect of a major land campaign was drawing closer. Crucially for the fate of Hunter-Weston and his men, diplomatic expediency had supplanted military planning, leaving Hamilton's 'Mediterranean Expeditionary Force' (MEF) singularly ill-equipped for such an audacious enterprise.

After kicking his heels as Sub-Inspector of the New Armies, on 10 March Hunter-Weston was ordered to take command of the 29th Division as soon as possible. The next week was busy with meetings at the War Office, where he tried to get prior intelligence for his mission. He had an uplifting chat with Churchill on the general situation in the Dardanelles, but came away empty-handed when he tried to glean more detailed information from Sir James Wolfe-Murray, Chief of the Imperial General Staff.[12] He was therefore given neither the 1906 Committee of Imperial Defence paper warning against combined operations at Gallipoli, nor the equally sceptical appreciation from Colonel Maucorps, the former French Military attaché at Constantinople, which had been telegraphed to Kitchener on

---

11   W. S. Churchill to Lord Kitchener, 20 February 1915, Sir Winston Churchill Papers, CHAR 12/47/86, Churchill Archives Centre, Churchill College, Cambridge (CCC); also unsent minute from W. S. Churchill to Lord Kitchener, 22 February 1915, CHAR 45/124.
12   HW Private War Diary, 11, 12 March 1915, 48364, BL. Wolfe-Murray's reticence was hardly surprising, as he had been largely excluded from the planning process; see *OHG(1)*, 72.

26 February.[13] At the same time, he was left in no doubt about the hopes that had been invested in the campaign. Summoned to an interview at Buckingham Palace on 15 March, he was asked by the King to write confidentially to him through his Assistant Secretary, Clive Wigram.[14]

His last days in England were spent with his new troops. Drawn from regular battalions from stations across the empire, the 29th Division was the last that the old army had to give.[15] The formation assembled in Warwickshire in January under the command of Major-General Frederick Shaw, a popular and distinguished soldier, who been able to hand-pick his staff. He was now 'sick' to give it up, and the sudden advent of Hunter-Weston in his Rolls Royce, with his wife at his side, seemed 'extraordinary and inexplicable' to his officers.[16] Gossip over his selection had clearly been circulating, as Brigadier William Marshall, an old friend of Shaw, sniped that his only qualification for command was his fluent French.[17]

---

13 Hunter-Weston, Evidence to Dardanelles Commission, 12 February 1917, Hamilton Papers, 8/2/50, LHCMA; *Defeat at Gallipoli: the Dardanelles Commission Part II, 1915–16* (London: The Stationery Office, 2000), 12–13.

14 HW Private War Diary, 10–16 March 1915, 48364, BL. The peninsula was packed with the King's correspondents, including Hamilton, Birdwood, Major-General Alexander Godley, the Earl of Granard and Lord Lovat: Ian Beckett, 'King George V and his Generals', in Matthew Hughes and Matthew Seligman, eds, *Leadership in Conflict, 1914–18* (Barnsley: Pen & Sword, 2000), 247–64.

15 The 29th Division had originally been intended as one of four divisions to be used in operations at Zeebrugge. It was configured as follows: 86th Infantry Brigade – 2/Royal Fusiliers (Calcutta), 1/Lancashire Fusiliers (Karachi), 1/Royal Munster Fusiliers (Rangoon); 1/Royal Dublin Fusiliers (Madras); 87th Infantry Brigade – 2/South Wales Borderers (Tientsin), 1/King's Own Scottish Borderers (Lucknow), 1/Royal Inniskilling Fusiliers (Trimulgherry), 1/Border Regiment, (Maymo); 88th Infantry Brigade – 4/Worcestershire Regiment (Burma), 2/Hampshire Regiment (Mhow), 1/Essex Regiment (Mauritius), 1/5 Royal Scots (the only Territorial Battalion). See *Midland Daily Telegraph*, 19 August 1932.

16 HW Private War Diary, 11 March 1915, 48364, BL; C. A. Milward Diary, 20 January 1915, 6510/143/4, NAM.

17 William Marshall, *Memories of Four Fronts* (London: Edward Benn Ltd, 1929), 41. In one of the more extreme examples of giving a general a bad name, Samuels

'A Second Crimea' – The Road to Gallipoli

After this inauspicious start, Hunter-Weston and his division travelled to Avonmouth for embarkation, where motor lorries labelled 'Cheap Trip to the Dardanelles' suggested that security was not being taken too seriously.[18] After a final tea with Grace, he sailed out on the evening of 17 March aboard the Cunard liner *Andania*. The journey time gave him an opportunity to get to know his officers, but as they neared Gibraltar they heard the crushing news by wireless that three allied warships had been sunk as they blasted the Turkish forts along The Narrows.[19] These losses finally convinced the commander of the allied fleet, Admiral Sir John De Robeck, that combined action with the army had become essential. At a critical meeting with Hamilton on 22 March, the respective roles of the army and navy were reversed, with the operation increasingly assuming the character of a predominantly military campaign with naval support.

Hunter-Weston was still unaware of this fundamental shift in his mission when he arrived at a dull and rainy Malta on 25 March in uncharacteristically low spirits. He had already begun to worry about whether forcing the Dardanelles was 'a feasible operation', hinting to his wife that he would not be surprised if the expedition returned home again.[20] The limited intelligence he received the next day from Rear-Admiral Arthur Limpus, the former head of the British Naval Mission to Turkey, however, confirmed his worst fears. The admiral had originally advised Churchill against the fleet bombardment in November, and now warned Hunter-Weston that the Turks had made the most of the subsequent months to build up their defences on the peninsula.[21] Asked by Hamilton for an appreciation of the situation, Hunter-Weston finished his task at 3 a.m. on the morning of 28 March. The result has been interpreted as a 'safety outlet' in case of failure,

---

    mistakenly suggests that Hunter-Weston spent the six months before the Gallipoli landings mostly training his division: *Command or Control?*, 50.
18 H. F. Stacke, *The Worcester Regiment in the Great War* (Kidderminster: G. T. Cheshire & Sons, 1928).
19 HW Private War Diary, 17, 21 March 1915, 48364, BL.
20 HW to GHW, 24 March 1915, HW Private War Diary, 48364, BL.
21 HW Private War Diary, 25 March 1915, 48364, BL.

but coming from a well-schooled soldier, it was also a strikingly prescient analysis of the issues which dominated the Gallipoli campaign.[22]

Hunter-Weston did not challenge the dubious propositions underpinning the enterprise itself, which were that that the Turkish regime would fall along with Constantinople, in turn encouraging the Balkan states to form a cohesive allied block. Indeed, he pronounced that, 'with a reasonable chance of success … the forcing of the Dardanelles should be undertaken whatever the cost'.[23] However, the rest of his appreciation was firmly grounded both in military logic and his recent experience of modern warfare. For example, he was under no illusion over the scale of the task, which would involve a deliberate advance to seize the Gallipoli peninsula, as well as operations on the Asiatic coast. The 'gross total' of men currently available for the attack stood at 80,000, but the landings themselves would require a larger force, a necessity that would have to be put in place before operations began. Nor would it be an easy task to destroy the Turkish armament protecting the channel on both sides, as his experience in France and Flanders had shown that well-concealed guns and howitzers could not be easily knocked out.

Although he later admitted that he had over-estimated the Turks' ability to bring out heavy moveable armament, the problem remained that they had been given sufficient time to turn the peninsula into an 'entrenched camp'.[24] The intelligence received at Malta suggested that the south end near Cape Helles offered the best chance of success. The most important enemy position ran across the peninsula via the Achi Baba Ridge to a mile north of Krithia village. By attacking from this direction, with the support of fleet guns, they might unlock the Kilid Bahr plateau, taking the Turkish positions in reverse. The disadvantages of this location were the lack of any

22   Travers, *Gallipoli*, 47.
23   Note with regards to the opinion of Major-General Hunter-Weston, as to the best utilisation of our forces in the Eastern Mediterranean, March 1915, HW Private War Diary, 28 March 1915, 48364, BL. This is the full appreciation, including later annotations completed in January 1915.
24   Note with regards to the opinion of Major-General Hunter-Weston, HW Private War Diary, 28 March 1915, 48364, BL.

sheltered bay and also that the narrowness of the peninsula itself left 'no scope for manoeuvre'.

The full extent of Hunter-Weston's pessimism was reserved for the 'probable further course of operations':

> Throughout this war none of the combatants has ever succeeded in breaking quickly through even indifferent entrenchments. The usual result has been stalemate. Success has only been attained after long and careful preparation and after the expenditure of an enormous amount of High Explosive Gun ammunition both from quickfirers and howitzers. We are very short of gun ammunition and are particularly short of High Explosive Shell. There appears therefore every prospect of getting tied up on an extended line across the Peninsula, in front of the Turkish Kilid Bahr plateau trenches – a second Crimea ... We shall have a most precarious and insufficient landing place and shall be entirely cut off if stormy weather intervenes.

He concluded in a similar vein:

> if the Expedition had been carefully and secretly prepared in England, France and Egypt; naval and military details of organization and equipment for disembarkation carefully worked out by the General Staff and Naval War Staff, and if no bombardment or other warning given ... the capture of the Gallipoli Peninsula and the forcing of Dardanelles would have been a perfectly feasible operation of war and would almost certainly [have] been successful ... but if the views expressed in this paper be sound there is not at this period a reasonable chance of success ... The return of the Expedition when it has gone so far will cause discontent, much talk, and some laughter ... It will be a heavy blow to all us soldiers; and will need great moral courage on the part of the Commander and the Government. But it will not do irreparable harm to our cause, whereas to attempt a landing and then fail to secure a passage through the Dardanelles would be a disaster to the Empire.[25]

Upon arriving at Alexandria, Hunter-Weston rushed to the Savoy Hotel to give his appreciation of the situation to Hamilton's Chief of Staff, Major-General Walter Braithwaite.[26] He was far from alone in his reservations. Both Lieutenant-General Sir William Birdwood, commander of the Anzac

---

25 Note with regards to the opinion of Major-General Hunter-Weston, HW Private War Diary, 28 March 1915, 48364, BL.
26 Hamilton, *Gallipoli Diary (1)*, 62.

contingent, and Major-General Archibald Paris of the RND had expressed doubts about the prospects of success, while General Albert d'Amade, commander of the French expeditionary contingent, 'a clever and charming man', had already pressed for a postponement.[27] A 'startled' Hamilton railed privately to Kitchener over his colleagues' defeatism, but admitted that Hunter-Weston's conclusion had depressed him very much, as he valued his professional opinion.[28]

Hunter-Weston's preferred option was to wait until sufficient divisions could be equipped, and then to offer the troops and a payment of £50 million to Bulgaria to assure them of rapid victory over the Turks.[29] However, the time for new strategic initiatives had passed. Hamilton explained that as the Cabinet had decided on the operation, it was now for him as Commander-in-Chief to carry it out – and, indeed, he was confident of success. The army's rigid authority structure thereby swung into place. After placing his concerns before his superior, there was nothing left for Hunter-Weston to do 'other than to loyally accept whatever plan he decided on and do my utmost to bring his plan to a successful issue'.[30] Although he would experience some heady bursts of optimism in the weeks to come, his basic lack of confidence in the mission did not leave him, so 'doing [his] duty as a man of action & as a subordinate leader' would not be easy.[31]

---

27 HW Private War Diary, 30 March 1915, 48364, BL; Randolph Churchill and Martin Gilbert, *Winston S. Churchill: 1914–16, the Challenge of War. Companion (London: Heineman, 1972)*, 766. For the Paris appreciation, see Hamilton Papers, 17/7/31, LHCMA.
28 Hamilton, *Gallipoli Diary (1)*, 91; Hamilton to Kitchener, 3 April 1915, Hamilton Papers, 5/1, LHCMA.
29 His idea was taken up by Sir Thomas Cunninghame, the British military attaché in Athens, who discussed it with the *Entente* ministers there.
30 Note with regards to the opinion of Major-General Hunter-Weston, HW Private War Diary, 48364, BL.
31 HW to GHW, 7, 8 April 1915, HW Private War Diary, 48364, BL.

'A Second Crimea' – The Road to Gallipoli   131

Planning the Landings

Hunter-Weston's reputation had preceded him at Alexandria. Captain Orlo Williams, Hamilton's Chief Cipher Officer, recorded in his diary that 'Hunter-Weston whom all call a thruster and who has done very well in France, is a vivacious, loud voiced man with a lot to say: hook nose, large moustache and wide mouth and bushy eyebrows'.[32] The GOC 29th Division and his staff settled into the deserted Hotel Excelsior but were soon paying the price for the haphazard origins of the expedition. Their hurried departure, coupled with the lack of logistical planning for a forced landing, meant that all their ships had to be completely unloaded and reloaded before setting off for the Dardanelles.[33] Relations with GHQ also became fraught, as Braithwaite denied Hunter-Weston the same autonomy as Birdwood and d'Amade in planning for the disembarkation of his men.[34] Despite being classmates at Staff College, the two men were not destined to work harmoniously together, nor did Hunter-Weston's attempts to glean information from junior GHQ staff improve their relationship.[35] In contrast, he was drawing closer to Hamilton, who later reported a 'transformation' in his attitude, believing him to be 'more sanguine than myself'.[36] In private though, he admitted to his wife that despite his subordinate's 'truly great qualities as a Commander', he remained 'grasping & tiresome & talkative in ordinary life'.[37]

32 Orlo Williams Diary, 30 April 1915, 69/78/1, IWM.
33 *OHG (1)*, 117; HW to GHW, 5 April 1915, HW Private War Diary, 48364, BL. See Divisional Orders by Maj.-General A. G. Hunter-Weston, 6 April 1915, 87th Brigade War Diary, WO 95/4312, TNA.
34 HW Private War Diary, 31 March 1915, 48364, BL; *OHG (1)*, 116. See also Hunter-Weston Official War Diary (29th Division/VIII Corps) Vol. II, Jan.–July 1915: 1–3 April 1915, Add. MS 48356, British Library [HW Official War Diary, 48356, BL].
35 James, *Gallipoli*, 82. As a substantive Major-General, he was senior to Braithwaite, whose rank was temporary.
36 Hamilton, *Gallipoli Diary (1)*, 103.
37 HW to GHW, 15 April 1915, HW Private War Diary, 48364, BL; I. Hamilton to J. Hamilton, 3 May 1915, Hamilton Papers, 7/1/4, LHCMA.

Meanwhile at Alexandria, Hunter-Weston found more to worry him. He assessed the Australians as impressive raw material, 'good fighters, good physique, intelligent looking & ... plenty of grit', but this was more than could be said for the 'weak and ill-trained' RND and the French force, 'half of which were niggers'.[38] The regulars of the 29th Division were of course 'magnificent' but, unlike his old brigade, they lacked combat experience. Billeted separately in England and employed on heavy fatigues in Egypt, there had been scant opportunity for training at divisional or even brigade level. Leadership was another concern, as some of his battalion commanders appeared too old to cope with the conditions of a tough campaign.[39] Indeed, although he publically cited the quality of the *division de luxe* as a factor behind his growing enthusiasm, he admitted to Wigram that it was not the 'well-oiled machine' that the 4th Division had been.[40] Three weeks in camp might have rectified this, but instead Hunter-Weston had to set off for Mudros, where the invasion fleet was mustering. Arriving on 12 April, he demanded to be rowed to the GHQ ship, *Arcadian*, where planning had been continuing in his absence.

Hamilton's original instinct had been for a hammer blow through landing his whole force at a single location, but the element of tactical surprise had already been lost and the Gallipoli peninsula was an unusually cramped area for military operations. The alternative plan developed by Braithwaite and his staff, and approved by Hamilton on 23 March, envisaged a landing by the Anzac force north of Gaba Tepe on the Aegean coastline, while the main attack would throw the weight of the 29th Division against the tip of the peninsula at Cape Helles. Its objective was to drive six miles northwards to Achi Baba Ridge, which had been singled out in Hunter-Weston's appreciation. After discussions with the joint naval and military staffs, the plan continued to evolve. There would be five landings at Helles at Beaches X, W, V, S and Y, carried out in four phases, with a view to confusing the Turks and forcing them to expose their reserves.

38   HW to GHW, 8 April 1915, HW Private War Diary, 48364, BL.
39   HW Private War Diary, 6 April 1915, 48364, BL.
40   HW to C. Wigram, 22 April 1915, HW Private War Diary, 48364, BL.

X Beach was on the west coast, about three quarters of a mile north of Cape Tekke; W was situated between Cape Tekke and Cape Helles; V lay a mile further along the coast, bounded by the ruined castle of Sedd-el-Bahr to the east; S and Y were intended as additional flanking beaches, the former lying beyond V Beach at the eastern extremity of Morto Bay, while Y Beach was situated about a mile west of Krithia village on the Aegean side of the peninsula. Even though the multi-pronged attack would inevitably place their own rudimentary communication systems under strain, it was hoped that the combined momentum would cancel out difficulties encountered on any one of the beaches.

It was a complex plan – the level of precision reminded d'Amade of a ceremonial parade at Whitehall – yet in certain key respects it remained crucially vague.[41] The ultimate objectives of the Kilid Bahr and Narrows defences were perhaps too obvious to be spelled out, but the more immediate instructions for the main attack at Helles – on which the whole success of Hamilton's enterprise depended – were also left unclear. The roles of the landings at V and W Beaches, where most troops would be concentrated, were not fully explained, nor were those of the flanking beaches' landings, even though Y Beach had been Hamilton's idea to exploit a poorly defended Turkish position. Rather than make contingency plans for an attack on the enemy's positions in the rear if the main assaults failed, the progress of these subsidiary landings remained dependent on progress from the south.

Hunter-Weston accepted this broad outline, but making use of his natural inclination to verbosity that so irritated Hamilton, he was determined to put his stamp on the specific arrangements for the 29th Division landings. A major issue was how to reduce the time during which the troops would be exposed in boats during their final approach. He protested strongly against the night landing favoured by Hamilton and Birdwood, arguing that he would prefer to attack at dawn and 'face the losses the men in boats must suffer from aimed fire', rather than risk the dangers of

---

41   *OHG (1)*, 218; Prior, *Gallipoli*, 85–6.

darkness and an unknown terrain.[42] Some of his Brigadiers later expressed their doubts about this, but he was probably correct in his view. He had nothing against night operations in principle, but he knew from experience that they had to be tightly controlled. He also had the support of his naval colleagues, since the strong currents and the danger of uncharted rocks would make it unlikely that the tows would reach the beaches in the dark.[43] Hamilton eventually gave way as Hunter-Weston was 'executively responsible'; it was agreed that warships would take the advance troops close in to the main beaches before transferring them to the landing flotilla as soon as possible after dawn.[44]

A dawn attack would allow a preparatory bombardment, but dependence on naval artillery brought its own problems. Hunter-Weston had already made his views known that the flat trajectory and armour-piercing design of the ships' guns would limit the support that they could offer.[45] The normal challenges of fire control would also be magnified in attempting to coordinate a bombardment of shore-based targets – indeed, his naval colleagues openly doubted their ability to provide indirect fire.[46] It was just as well that congenial relationships had quickly developed between the respective commanders; on first acquaintance at least, his bluff naval counterpart, 'Rozy' Wemyss had seemed 'a capital fellow'.[47] Nevertheless,

---

42 HW Private War Diary, 14 April 1915, 48364, BL. Birdwood suggests that since Hunter-Weston had decided that he must land after daybreak, he felt that if he landed further up the coast before the 29th Division, he might succeed in drawing Turkish troops away from Helles: *Khaki and Gown: an Autobiography* (London: Ward Lock, 1942), 256. However, Hamilton's diary gives no indication of this altruism: *Gallipoli Diary (1)*.

43 Admiral Rosslyn Wemyss, *The Navy in the Dardanelles Campaign* (London: Hodder Stoughton, 1924), *OHG (1)*, 140; See Marshall, *Four Fronts*, 61.

44 *Gallipoli Diary (1)*, 108.

45 Note with regards to the opinion of Major-General Hunter-Weston, HW Private War Diary, 28 April 1915, 48364, BL.

46 Orlo Williams Diary, 21 March 1915, 69/78/1, IWM; Major-General Sir Steuart Hare Diary, 18 April 1915, 66/85/1, IWM.

47 HW to GHW, 12 April 1915, HW Private War Diary, 48364, BL. In his memoirs, Wemyss hailed him 'a gallant soldier': *Navy in the Dardanelles Campaign*, 54. Their friendship was not destined to survive: (See Chapter Twelve).

a formalised understanding regarding the nature and capabilities of naval support was needed between all parties. Hunter-Weston's note on 17 April to Rear-Admiral Stuart Nicholson, whose First Squadron would cover the Helles landings, began to establish a set of guiding principles. The most important was the need for 'a great concentration of effective gun-fire in order to silence guns or howitzers, clear wire entanglements, kill the enemy in trenches and prevent reinforcements'.[48] Careful air reconnaissance and a pre-arranged communication system were also deemed vital, as well as the placing of ships so that their gun trajectories could reach their objectives. A joint memorandum on artillery cooperation followed two days later, drawn up by Hunter-Weston's GSO2, Lieut.-Colonel Harold Street, in conjunction with Captain C. Maxwell-Lefroy of the squadron's second flagship HMS *Swiftsure* and Flag Commander Alexander Ramsay of the HMS *Queen Elizabeth*.[49] The first action of the ships was to be to bombard the beaches in order to demolish all defences, batteries and buildings. This would commence simultaneously with the surprise landing on Y Beach, which would not require any artillery support. When the troops had landed on the main beaches, the fire of the ships would shift to the reverse slopes, moving northwards with increasing intensity as forward movement progressed. Artillery observation officers were to land with the leading troops and signalling stations were to be established on the beaches as soon as possible, supplemented by aeroplanes using wireless communication.

These painstaking arrangements were promptly circulated to all ships and the relevant army officers, but the underlying and obviously essential aim of effective inter-service cooperation was not achieved. At a naval conference on 21 April, with Wemyss in the chair, the emphasis shifted to the bombardment of the coastal ridges during the landing rather than the beaches and approaches, leaving the final decision on the provision of

48 Note from Aylmer Hunter-Weston to Rear-Admiral Stuart Nicholson, commanding the squadron covering 29th Division landing, 17 April 1915, HW Private War Diary, 48364, BL.
49 Memorandum of Artillery Cooperation between HM Ships and 29th Division, 19 April 1915, HW Private War Diary, 48356, BL.

close-in fire support to individual captains.[50] Despite Hunter-Weston's best efforts, the naval guns consequently failed to offer a protective arm for his men when they most needed it.

With packed MEF transports arriving on a daily basis, Mudros now housed an armada of over 200 ships. Hunter-Weston was not immune to the romance of the setting, but the daily round of shipboard conferences and coastline inspections left little time for lyricism. After inspecting air reconnaissance results, he took his seasick staff on a cruise on the fast turbine cruiser, HMS *Dartmouth*, steaming round Cape Helles and up the western coast.[51] Turkish forces in the region of the peninsula were estimated to number upwards of 40,000 soldiers by this point, with a further 20,000 on the Asiatic side of the straits. Unlike the British, many of them were seasoned troops with recent combat experience. Well trained and highly motivated, their morale and self-confidence had grown following the failure of the British naval onslaught the previous month.[52] On this trip there was no sign of activity apart from some smoke from camps behind the spur of Achi Baba, but heavy entrenchments and extensive wire were all too visible in the south.[53]

Hunter-Weston returned from his trip in apparently boisterous spirits. The gossip circulating around the division was that while Hamilton was 'anxious over this job ... Hunter-Weston ... is full of pluck and confidence'.[54] In truth, this was far from the case. He normally tried to shield Grace from worry, but in a highly unusual step he now assured her that if anything happened to him, 'in the way of wounds or death', he had arranged that she should be informed by wire. Meanwhile, he took the precaution of practising his shooting with an automatic pistol, while thoroughly depressing

---

50 H. C. Lockyer, *Gallipoli, Cape Helles, April 1915. The Tragedy of 'The Battle of the Beaches'. Together with the proceedings of HMS Implacable* (n.p., 1936).
51 Hare Diary, 14 April 1915, 66/85/1, IWM.
52 Edward Erickson, *Gallipoli: The Ottoman Campaign* (Barnsley: Pen & Sword, 2010), 29, 35–6.
53 HW Private Diary, 14 April 1915, 48364, BL; Marshall, *Four Fronts*, 51.
54 John Graham Gillam, *Gallipoli Diary* (London: Allen & Unwin, 1918), 30.

'A Second Crimea' – The Road to Gallipoli

his staff by telling them that they must go ashore separately because 'some of the boats are certain to be hit'.[55]

As he had feared, the strain was beginning to tell on his officers. Brigadier Steuart Hare was forced to report one of his subordinates who 'was going off his head or having a nervous breakdown'; after talking to the man for half an hour, Hunter-Weston persuaded him to request sick leave.[56] A passionate believer that units should reflect the fighting spirit of their commander, his own confidence could not be seen to falter. Nevertheless, in preparing his men for the daunting enterprise that lay before them, he could not quite put the nightmare of open boats raked by fire out of his mind. Unable to deliver a face-to-face address, his answer was a 'Personal Note' issued to each man. While it lacked Hamilton's terminal eloquence, he believed that it would 'enthuse' them all.[57] It was certainly a remarkable outpouring on the eve of a battle:

> Personal Note
>
> The eyes of the world are upon us and your deeds will live in history.
>
> To us now is given an opportunity of avenging our friends and relatives who have fallen in France and Flanders.
>
> We also must be prepared to suffer hardships, privations, thirst and heavy losses, by bullets, by shells, by mines, by drowning. But if each man feels as is true, that on him individually, however, small or however great his task, rests the success or failure of the Expedition, and therefore the honour of the Empire and the welfare of his own folk at home, we are certain to win through to a glorious victory.
>
> In Nelson's time it was England, now it is the whole British Empire, which expects that each man of us will do our duty.
>
> A. H. W.

---

55 HW to GHW, 15 April 1915, HW Private War Diary, 48364, BL; Milward Diary, 10 April 1915, 6510/143/4, NAM.
56 Hare Diary, 20 April 1915, 66/85/1, IWM; Oswin Creighton, *With the 29th Division in Gallipoli: A Chaplain's Experiences* (London: Longmans, 1916).
57 HW Private War Diary, 16 April 1915, 48364, BL. He was extremely proud of his note and was delighted to discover that the men had retained and circulated copies.

At first sight, 'Hunter-Weston's insurance policy', as it became known, appears to be an example of the grandiloquence for which he would become famous. It did, however, have a gravely serious intent. He wished to inspire his men with faith in their destiny, while awakening them to the realities of modern combat. Unfortunately, this intended balance was rather lost in communication. Possessing great physical courage himself, he found it difficult to appreciate the fears of those who were less brave or confident. In the 86th Brigade, for example, the eyes of the men were already wide open to prospect of heavy casualties on landing, but following his 'cheery' message, their chaplain commented that 'slaughter seems to be inevitable'.[58] Aspinall-Oglander suggests that the note may even have prompted some of the men's hesitation to press forwards on the first day of battle. Realistically, the shock of close combat and extensive officer casualties are more likely explanations, but the incorporation of Marshall's anecdote of a soldier mistaking a dead tortoise for one of Hunter-Weston's 'mines' provides one of the few humorous interludes in the *Official History*.[59]

At another joint planning conference on 19 April – 'after a lot of talk, esp. from Hunter Bunter' – further alterations were made to the plan.[60] These were reflected in the orders issued to the 29th Division the next day. Hunter-Weston already knew where his troops would land and how they would be deployed on his five target beaches. He had twelve and a quarter battalions available to him, including two from the RND, of which seven and quarter were allotted to the covering force and five to the main body of the invasion. As prescribed in the *Manual of Combined Naval and Military Operations* (1913), the covering force had to be of sufficient size to allow the main force to land without serious interference from enemy fire. Commanded by Brigadier Hare and largely comprising units from the 86th Brigade, this body would have to disembark from eighteen open tows

---

58 Creighton, *With the 29th Division*, 43; the 1/Dublin Fusiliers were also aware that they would have to fight their way through large wire entanglements on V beach: George Davidson, *The Incomparable 29th and the River Clyde* (Aberdeen: Bissett, 1919), 39–41.
59 *OHG (1)*, 254; Marshall, *Four Fronts*, 254.
60 Orlo Williams Diary, 20 April 1915, 69/78/1, IWM.

at X, V and W Beaches following a half-hour naval bombardment timed to begin at 5 a.m. The troops at S beach, three companies of the 2/South Wales Borderers (SWB), were to be ready to disembark from trawlers at the same moment. The Y Beach attack would precede this, involving over 2,000 men from the 1/King's Own Scottish Borderers (KOSB), SWB and Royal Marines, who would be landed directly in trawlers before daybreak, using the advantage of surprise to storm up the cliffs. As soon as the first tows arrived at V Beach, the *River Clyde* – the 'wooden horse' as Hunter-Weston named it – was to be run aground with a further 2,000 troops, and after 45 minutes, the rest of the covering force would land in the second journey for the tows. It was hoped that the covering force would all be ashore by 7 a.m., with the landing of the main body commencing around 8.30 a.m. He shared executive command of the landings with Wemyss, whose flagship, the sleek four-funnelled cruiser HMS *Euryalus*, was to become a joint headquarters anchored off W Beach, while Hamilton patrolled the landing sites on the *Queen Elizabeth*.

The plan specified that key battles would be fought on the narrow landing beaches, but Hunter-Weston's updated orders made clear that the ultimate goal in throwing his force ashore was the Kilid Bahr plateau.[61] Reaching this would involve a rush on the Krithia–Achi Baba position from the south, and although the precise timeframe was left unspecified, the attack was now divided into five phases. As in Braithwaite's original design, the immediate task was to capture the commanding features of Hills 141, 138 and 114, which would help secure the beaches. Hare was then directed to gain a diagonal line right across the peninsula from the hilly ground east of ruined fortress at V Beach, joining on the left with the force at Y Beach. He had originally been in command of the entire covering force, but it was later agreed that it would be impossible to control the distant landings at Y and S, which were put directly under Divisional HQ.[62] In another addition to the GHQ plan, unified command was then to be restored under

---

[61] Enclosure to 29th Division, Operational Order No. 1, HW Official War Diary, 48356, BL.
[62] *OHG (1)*, 202.

Hunter-Weston, who would come ashore to lead a new advance, capturing a line stretching from Eski Hisarlik Point, on the east of Morto Bay, to Hill 472 (Yazy Tepe), and from there to the sea. Brigadier Henry Napier would be thrown in with three battalions from the 88th Brigade on the right from V Beach, while Marshall, who was landing at X Beach with the remainder of the 87th Brigade, would command the divisional reserve. Achi Baba and the spur running south of it were to be taken from this position, with the 87th Brigade reincorporating its detached battalions and moving through the 88th. However, rather than halting at the defensive point near Tener Chift Knoll, which GHQ had assigned as the rightwards boundary of the advance, Hunter-Weston now set his division the target of gaining all the high ground running due east of Achi Baba to the Dardanelles.

His staff officers, who included another Staff College contemporary, Lieut.-Colonel Owen Wolley Dod (GSO1), were far from convinced that all these objectives could be achieved on the first day of battle, but although they found his plans to be 'over-sanguine', they did not feel confident in expressing their views.[63] His inherited team had evidently failed to bond with their new commander, who was proving a hard taskmaster. Whereas Major-General Shaw had been 'charming and entertaining', Hunter-Weston's 'horribly active brain' left Captain Clement Milward, the Divisional Intelligence Officer, feeling 'like a bit of chewed string'.[64]

Hunter-Weston's sudden surge of confidence seems curious. Focussing on the distant horizons of Achi Baba may have helped to distract him from the carnage he expected on the beaches, but important tactical considerations were also at work. If the landings did succeed, rapid movement inland from the cramped beaches was essential to maintain the tempo of the offensive and to prevent the enemy from massing and regaining the initiative. The likely alternative, as his appreciation had argued, was an extended stalemate across the peninsula, or the containment of his force in a precarious landing zone that could be cut off in bad weather. His new objective was also consistent with what he considered to be the essential

---

[63] Milward Diary, 24 April 1915, 6510/143/4, NAM.
[64] C. A. Milward, Diary, 10, 11 April 1915 [expanded typescript], CAB 45/259, TNA.

purpose of his mission: providing assistance to the naval attack, since the capture of the lesser summit of Tenkir Tepe, east of Achi Baba, offered a more valuable observation point across the Narrows than the main ridge.[65]

This eagerness to thrust northwards may explain Hunter-Weston's failure to address the role of the flanking beaches. Although his appreciation had noted that Turkish positions in the south might be taken in reverse as per the GHQ plan, he did not seriously consider the alternative possibilities these landings offered, far less devise the sort of imaginative 'pincer movement' of a type envisaged by later commentators. Instead, their value was seen to lie in assisting the main operations by drawing off enemy reserves, and in boosting the main advance when it drew level with them. In contrast, their danger lay in dispersing and weakening this central thrust from the outset. Following tactical orthodoxy, Hunter-Weston believed that the enemy could best be defeated by a general engagement across the south of the peninsula, followed by the delivery of a concentrated blow on the decisive Achi Baba position. A 'first rush' assault here – under his own vigorous leadership – would sow panic among the Turks and allow the landings to be properly consolidated, while helping the Anzacs push from the northwest. It would also give him a favourable position for 'attacking the real crux of the matter' – the Kilid Bahr Plateau. As this location was likely to be fully entrenched and wired, nothing less than a full force attack from the south would be likely to be enough to achieve a breakthrough.[66]

Hunter-Weston's relative inexperience at divisional level, combined with an absence of attention to detail among his staff, may have been responsible for the causal transmission of these orders to his subordinate commanders. He appeared 'very excited' as he set out to explain his intentions at

---

65 *OHG (1)*, 220–1; Hunter-Weston, Evidence to Dardanelles Commission, 12 February 1917, Hamilton Papers, 8/2/50, LHCMA. The summit of Achi Baba did not offer the observation that was claimed for it during the campaign. On a later visit, Keyes called it a 'gigantic fraud', James, *Gallipoli*: 75.
66 Hunter-Weston, Evidence to Dardanelles Commission, 12 February 1917, Hamilton Papers, 8/2/50, LHCMA.

a Divisional Conference on board the *Andania* on 21 April.[67] The Brigadiers and all unit commanders were supposed to be present, but the absence through illness of Lieut.-Colonel Archibald Koe, whose KOSB battalion were to land at Y Beach, seems to have passed unnoticed.[68] Consequently, the command structure for this landing became thoroughly confused in the actual course of events. Hunter-Weston personally informed Lieut.-Colonel Geoffrey Matthews, who commanded the Plymouth Battalion, Royal Marine Light Infantry, that he would be the senior officer, despite his unit having a lesser role, but written confirmation of this arrangement was not circulated. Matthews had been with Hunter-Weston when Y Beach was chosen as a landing site and had been asked for his opinion on its suitability at that time. His familiarity with the location may explain why Hunter-Weston only felt the need to give him vague verbal instructions about his objectives, which were to advance a little inland, capture a Turkish gun, and wait until the 87th Brigade arrived.[69] He was also to make 'contact' with the troops disembarking at X beach, although Matthews failed to query whether this was to be visual or physical in nature. Such informality might have been acceptable when briefing battalion commanders in France, but it created serious problems in complex mobile amphibious operations, where, as Till suggests, subordinates needed to know the commander's 'intent' with precision and certainty before they could make best use of delegated command.[70]

Poor weather led to a postponement of the landings, but on 23 April orders were issued to commence operations. In his private correspondence to Kitchener, Hamilton could not help contrasting his two commanders:

---

67   Milward Diary, 23 April 1915, 6510/143/4, NAM; G. E. Matthews Evidence to the Dardanelles Commission, 16 February 17, CAB 19/33, TNA. See also his operational report, 27 April 1915, in the RND War Diary, WO 95/4290, TNA.

68   Both his private diary and the 29th Division War Diary suggest that all unit commanders were present.

69   Matthews Evidence to the Dardanelles Commission, CAB 19/33, TNA; *OH1*, 203.

70   Geoffrey Till, 'The Gallipoli Campaign: Command Performances' in Sheffield and Till, eds, *The Challenges of High Command. The British Experience* (London: Palgrave, 2003), 27.

'A Second Crimea' – The Road to Gallipoli

Birdwood was 'absolutely confident' and his only worry was that his enthusiasm might cause him to bear away northwards, while Hunter-Weston was 'more inclined to see the barbed wire and machine guns, but ... is one of those who will be venturesome to a fault once the flag drops'.[71] In fact, the work of detailed planning seems to have acted as a balm on Hunter-Weston's worst fears. Dutifully writing to Wigram on the eve of his departure from Mudros, the 'second Crimea' had given way to the 'Great Adventure'.[72] At his last Divisional Conference aboard the *Andania* on 22 April, Hunter-Weston treated his senior officers to a lengthy lecture, in which he argued that the '*moral*' as well as material effect of the preliminary naval bombardment would astonish the world – and particularly, of course, the Turks – to such an extent that their resistance would be paralysed. The message, recalled the sceptical Marshall, implied that they would probably not see much of the enemy before they reached Constantinople.[73] The next day he transferred his HQ to the *Andania*, and as the transports of the 29th Division slipped out of the harbour to the sound of cheering and martial music, the atmosphere of exhilaration grew even more infectious.

Arriving off Tenedos on the morning of 24 April, Hunter-Weston and Wolley Dod boarded a pinnace for the *Euryalus*. Captain Milward watched with some amusement as his GOC almost fell into the water from the dancing boat.[74] It was an awful crossing and there was a strong possibility that the landings would have to be postponed again, but in the afternoon the wind suddenly dropped and the sea became calm; by 4 p.m. the troops began transferring to the trawlers and warships that would take them to the beaches. Hunter-Weston had seemed 'highly strung' to his staff during the day, but by the time the ship weighed anchor that evening he had regained his composure – at least in his correspondence with Grace. Describing to her the sombre and beautiful scene at sunset as the *Queen Elizabeth* steamed off to take up her station, he wrote: 'I have no

---

71   I. Hamilton to Lord Kitchener, 23 April 1915, PRO 30/57/61, TNA.
72   HW Private War Diary: HW to C. Wigram, 22 April 1915; HW to GHW, 23 April 1915, 48364, BL.
73   Marshall, *Four Fronts*, 254.
74   Milward Diary 24 April 1915, 6510/143/4, NAM.

anxieties, no troubled fears as to tomorrow. My mind is absolutely at rest. I have done my part, I have issued & explained my orders, I have "enthused" my officers & men. The rest is in God's hands, & I go to sleep now with my mind at rest ...'[75]

---

75 HW to GHW, 24 April 1915, HW Private War Diary, 48364, BL.

1. Already in the saddle – Aylmer on his pet donkey Johnie at Hunterston. The family servants look on fondly. (West Kilbride Museum)

2. Grace Strang Steel, Lady Hunter-Weston. 'Dear Grace' was a constant correspondent during the Great War. (West Kilbride Museum)

3. 'There are many hellish times ... ': Hunter-Weston (left) at St Yves, the scene of his failed counter-attack in November 1914. (IWM: Q 56686)

4. 11th Brigade troops (London Rifle Brigade) fraternise with their Saxon opponents at Ploegsteert during the Christmas ceasefire, 1914. (IWM: Q 11745)

5. Hunter-Weston pictured outside his Gallipoli dugout with Harold Street and Cyril Macmullen. (IWM: Q 13307)

6. 'Nobody's children': 52nd Division Bathing Parade, Gallipoli. (IWM: Q 13386)

7. Major-General Henry de Beauvoir De Lisle, KCB, DSO – a trusted colleague at Gallipoli and on the Western Front. (IWM: HU 94721)

8. Hunter-Weston and VIII Corps staff at Chateau Marieux, 24 June 1916 (IWM: Q 736)

9. The Corps Commander shows the way! Hunter-Weston and a rather apprehensive Reginald Pinney during the visit of Prime Minister Clemenceau at Cassel, April 1918. (IWM Q 6544)

10. Local MP – the Hunter-Weston Masonic Bowling Trophy, which he donated to Lodge Royal Arch West Kilbride No. 314 in 1927. Hunter-Weston is standing third from left. (West Kilbride Museum)

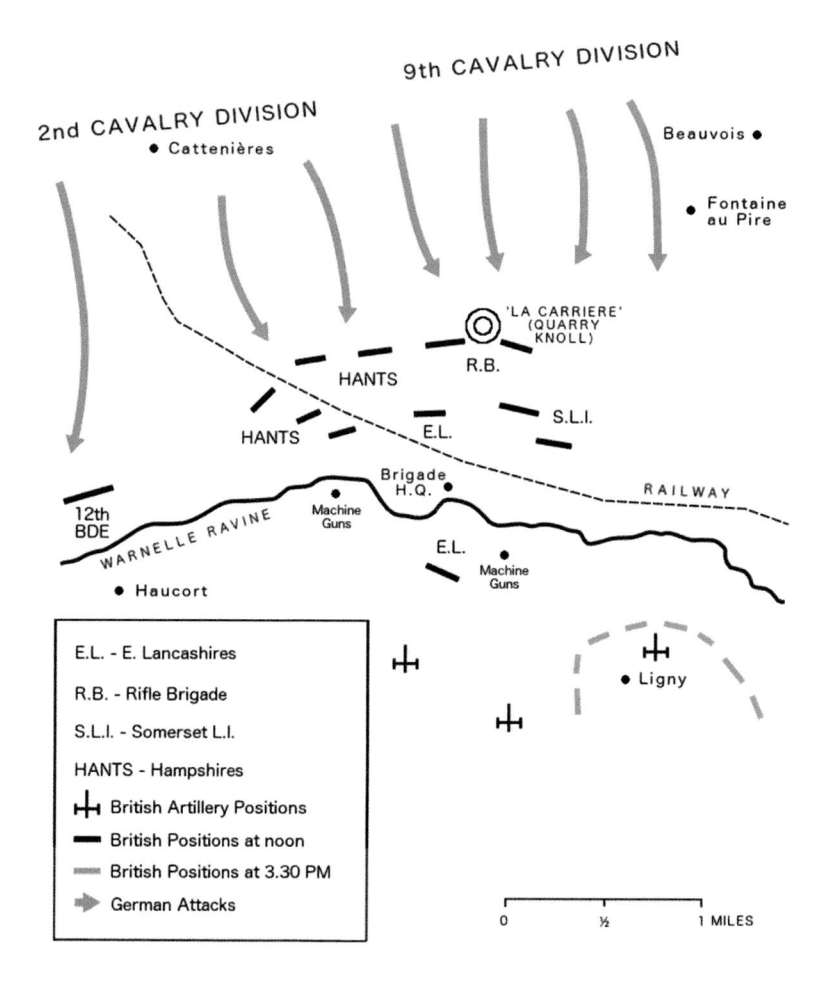

Map 1. 11th Brigade at Le Cateau, 26 August 1914.

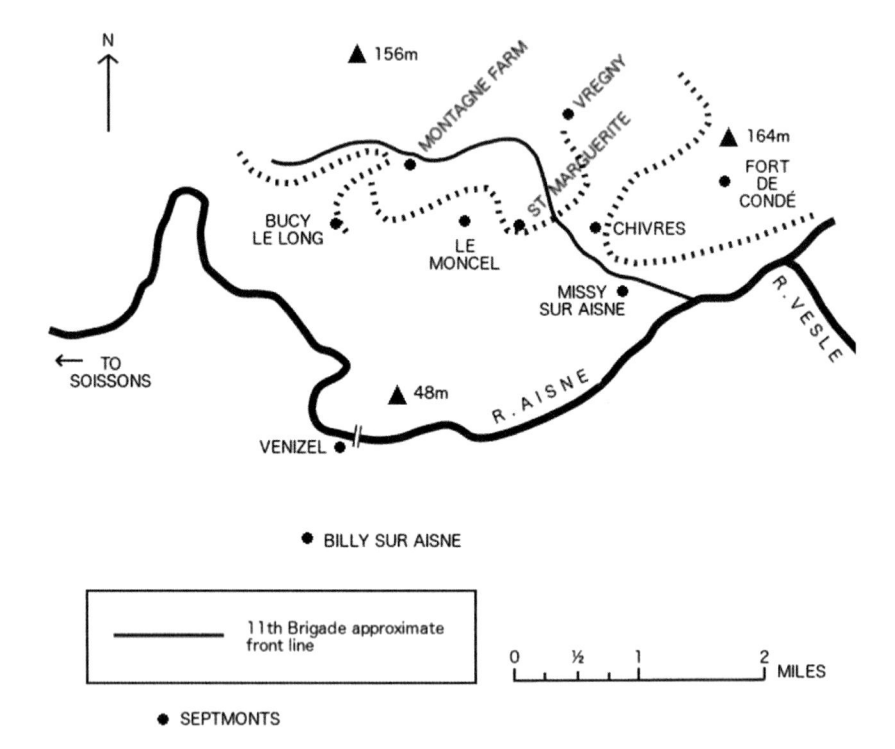

Map 2. Operations on the Aisne, 12 September–7 October 1914.

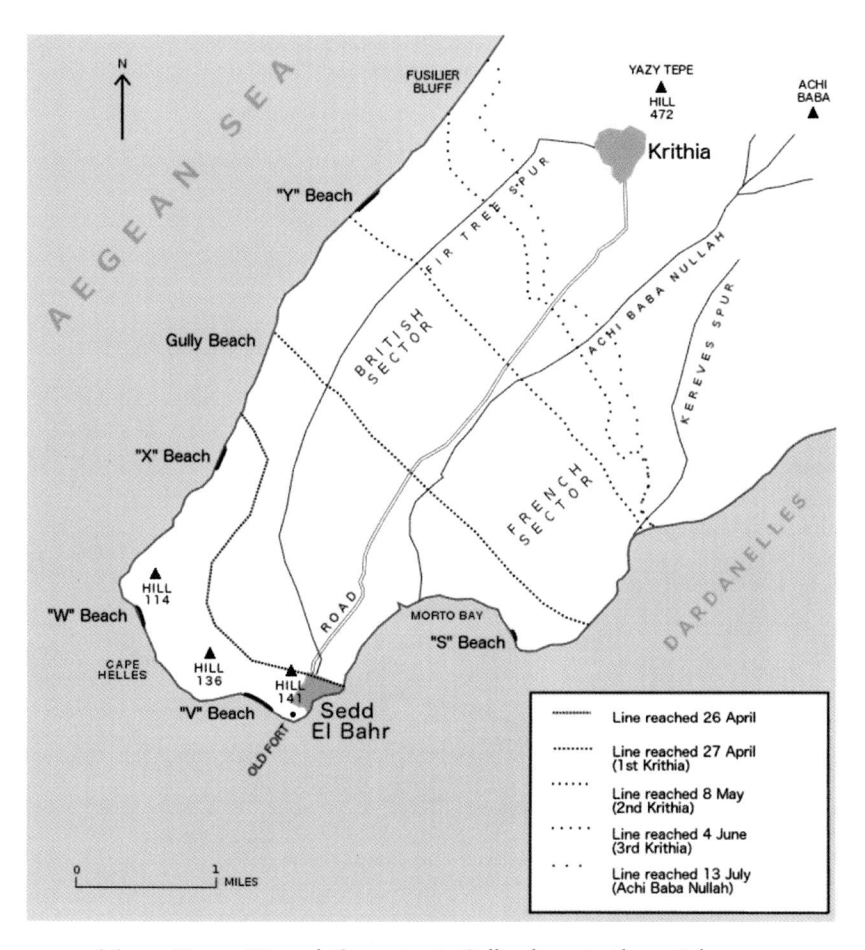

Map 3. Hunter-Weston's Campaign in Gallipoli, 25 April to 13 July 1915.

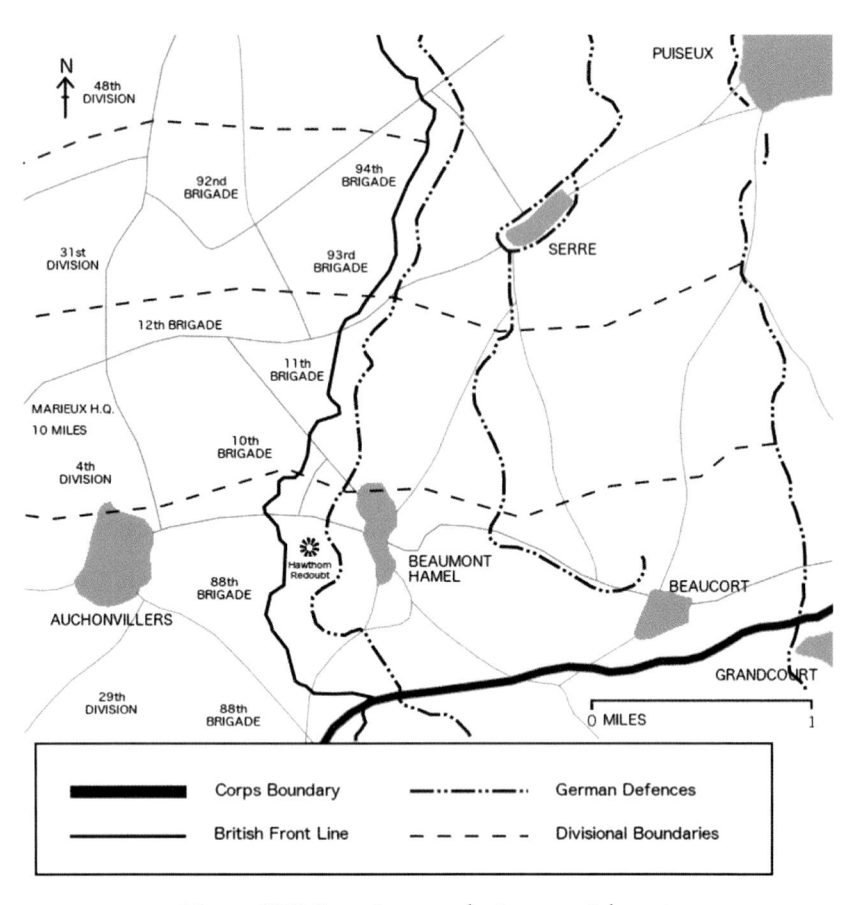

Map 4. VIII Corps Sector at the Somme, 1 July 1916.

CHAPTER NINE

Achieving the Impossible – The Beaches and Beyond

There was to be no triumphant charge up Achi Baba. Instead, the unassuming ridge remained a recurring image in Hunter-Weston's scrapbook, seeming to edge a little further away in each photograph. During the first desperate weeks of the campaign, he launched a series of brutal, slogging attacks that barely had any effect on the enemy's defensive superiority. Having lost any hope of surprise, both the magnitude of the challenge facing the expedition and the risks of failure continued to grow rapidly. Many of the decisions that Hunter-Weston made during the initial phase of the fighting at Gallipoli may have been wrong or poorly judged, but none of them was easy.

The View from the Bridge

The landings made at Helles on 25 April were fought as separate battles, but together they removed any hope of a swift and decisive resolution to the campaign. Reports of enemy activity were already reaching the Turkish III Corps HQ as the *Euryalus* sailed within sight of Cape Tekke at 3 a.m.[1] Two hours later, the KOSBs and Royal Marines were able to struggle up the cliffs at Y Beach unopposed. Lieut.-Colonel Matthews, who persisted in viewing the landing as a 'demonstration', sent out scouts, but otherwise he spent the morning awaiting further orders.[2] The SWBs also easily achieved

---

1   Godfrey, II, 4: 81/496, IWM; Erickson, *Gallipoli*, 69.
2   Matthews, Evidence to the Dardanelles Commission, CAB 19/33, TNA.

the other flank assault at S Beach on the eastern edge of Morto Bay; the shortage of boats meant that this was a small-scale landing, but Hunter-Weston had attached great importance to it, as success here would assist by suppressing enemy fire on his right flank at V Beach.[3] It had been scheduled to begin at 5.30 a.m., but was almost called off because the slow-moving trawlers were late arriving due to the strength of the tide. Fortunately for their occupants, the signal to divert to V Beach did not get through. At 7.30 a.m., they were able to storm ashore with minimal casualties; Lieut.-Colonel Hugh Casson fully secured the position an hour later, then settled down to await the main advance from the south.[4]

The 2/Royal Fusiliers at X Beach also had a share of the limited luck available that morning. After taking the narrow strip of sand, their objective was to seize Hill 114 and secure the left flank of the advance from W Beach. Supported by destructive fire from HMS *Implacable*, which had followed Hunter-Weston's guidelines for a beach bombardment, their efforts progressed well and by 6.30 a.m. the leading companies had reached the top of the cliff.[5] The enemy reacted quickly and their resistance grew as the British pushed towards their objective, but the advance pressed on until the summit was taken at 11 a.m.. The divisional reserve under Marshall had begun to land two hours before, putting 2,500 men behind the enemy redoubts that threatened the landings at W and V Beaches.

At W Beach, the dip in the hills became visible as dawn broke. As the *Euryalus* made its final adjustments to take up position, Hunter-Weston and his staff climbed up to the crowded compass platform on the upper bridge to observe the progress of the naval bombardment.[6] The thundering of gunfire from three directions had already alerted attackers and defenders alike that the main landings were imminent. Shortly before 6 a.m., the signal was given for the tows to begin their journey to the remaining beaches. Facing Hunter-Weston's men at the tip of the peninsula was

3   Wemyss, *Navy in the Dardanelles Campaign*, 67.
4   HW Private War Diary, 25 April 1915, 48364, BL; HW Official War Diary, 25 April 1915, 48356, BL.
5   Lockyer, *Gallipoli*, 15; 87th Brigade War Diary, 25 April 1915, WO 4311, TNA.
6   Godfrey, II, 4: 81/496, IWM; Milward Diary, 25 April 1915, 6510/143/4, NAM.

the fully manned and trained 26th Infantry Regiment (9th Division). Its companies were thinly distributed in strongpoints among the low hills overlooking X, W, and V Beaches, with a strong mobile reserve from the 19th Division shielded to the rear.[7] The day was marked by an overestimation of the enemy's strength, but the deliberately light screening of troops also meant that the Turks lacked the concentrated strength required to throw the invaders off Cape Helles.

Rear-Admiral Wemyss and Hunter-Weston trained their binoculars on the landings at W Beach as the 1/Lancashire Fusiliers launched their frontal assault on the enemy's network of defensive strongpoints.[8] Heavy machine-guns opened up as soon as the leading tows came into range, while 200 riflemen held their fire until the British were just forty yards from the shore. Naval support was desperately needed but the guns of the *Euraylus* and *Swiftsure* had failed to subdue the shore defences, lifting their fire ten minutes before the boats reached the shore and switching to pound battery positions beyond the costal ridges.[9] The main attack faltered at the water's edge, although Brigadier Hare was able to establish a vital foothold on the northern flank of the bay before being severely wounded. Watching with emotions veering from 'wild hope' to 'sickening horror', Wemyss and Hunter-Weston saw the boats disappear into the smoke of the bombardment.[10] When the empty boats re-emerged half an hour later, their first reaction was 'My God. They haven't got through'.[11] There already appeared to be a row of dead men along the beach, but soon ten soldiers stood up and calmly climbed over the barbed wire; two got across and lay in the sand hills beyond, but the rest fell on top of the wire and remained there. Elsewhere, the 'corpses' were only men's packs, and as the mist began to lift, Wemyss and Hunter-Weston could see that half of the force had in fact reached the base of the sandy cliffs at the back of the beach. By 7.30 a.m.,

7   Erikson, *Gallipoli*, 69.
8   Godfrey, II, 4: 81/496, IWM; Wemyss, *Navy in the Dardanelles Campaign*, 72.
9   Lockyer, *Gallipoli*, 15; Archibald Paris to Mrs C. Pilkington, 5 May 1915, DS/MISC/57, IWM.
10 Milward Diary, 25 April 1915: 6510/143/4, NAM.
11 Godfrey, II, 5: 81/496, IWM.

the Lancashires had managed to establish a thin perimeter line and were moving northwards to link up with X Beach, although their casualties were too severe to allow them to stretch out to V Beach on the right.

It was V Beach that should have provided the vital link in Hunter-Weston's plan to create a continuous line of advance across the tip of Cape Helles, but attacking this natural amphitheatre proved the bloodiest task that morning. The tows containing the first wave from the 1/Royal Dublin Fusiliers were delayed for over an hour by the tide, disrupting the planned naval bombardment.[12] As they began to approach at 6.30 a.m., the Turks opened fire at a range of under 400 yards with machine-guns and light artillery. The defenders were puzzled at first to see the steamship *River Clyde* among the smaller craft, but once they grasped its significance it too became a magnet for determined fire. Accurate naval gunnery might have provided a much-needed counterbalance, but HMS *Albion* and HMS *Cornwallis* were anchored too far out to be able to identify targets. Few survived the slaughter on the boats and the beaches. By 9 a.m., around 200 survivors were left sheltering behind a sand ridge, unable to move from that position. This was the limit of the first day's advance.

If Hunter-Weston had been a confused spectator at W Beach, he was completely cut off from the disaster along the coast. The two-way flow of information that he knew would be required in directing amphibious operations failed almost immediately, largely due to the high number of officer casualties ashore.[13] Most of the orders issued by Divisional HQ that day were in his own handwriting, but a number never reached their intended recipients. Conditions on his floating HQ were also far from ideal. Harold Street was forced to set up his office in the ship's charthouse, which was only twenty feet away from 9.2 gun turret firing every five minutes: 'whenever it went off it made chaos of divisional signals and reports which were laid in neat rows on the chart table'. Watching the divisional general and his staff at work, it was hardly surprising that Lieutenant John

12 HW Private War Diary, 25 April 1915, 48364, BL.
13 Milward Diary, 25 April 1915: CAB 45/259, TNA; *OHG (1)*, 206; Memorandum of Artillery Cooperation, 19 April 1915, HW Official War Diary, 48356, BL.

Godfrey RN observed the army chain of command to be 'fragile and at times impalpable'.[14]

The inward flow of information was equally unreliable. At 7.50 a.m., Hunter-Weston received an erroneous report from HMS *Lord Nelson* that his troops had successfully landed Sedd-el-Bahr village to the east of V Beach.[15] This was used as a basis for his decision to send in units from the main force, led by Brigadier Napier and his 88th Brigade HQ, in the hope that that a successful assault on the beach's western defences would assist the troops on W Beach to advance inland. The attempt was futile, as Napier was killed before he even landed. Where Hunter-Weston was able to directly observe events, he could at least attempt to intervene, sensibly diverting the 1/Essex to W Beach around 9.20 a.m.[16] But, in lacking any reliable means of communication, he also lacked the means of command. The idea that he should have investigated the situation at V Beach personally, 'only five minutes steaming away', fails to appreciate his situation aboard the *Euryalus*.[17] Not only did her deep draft prevent her from getting close to the shore, but her role as an 'attendant ship', responsible for transport and the evacuation of the wounded, tied her firmly to her station. Godfrey's idea of 'a sloop, destroyer or small cruiser' as a command centre was a sensible one – it would certainly have suited Hunter-Weston's restless instincts – but at Gallipoli, most of the best suggestions were made after the event.[18]

Cruising along the coast aboard the *Queen Elizabeth*, Hamilton took advantage of his own superior mobility to stop further reinforcements at V Beach. More controversially, he also signalled to Hunter-Weston at 9.15 a.m. that he might wish instead to divert troops to Y Beach; when the latter had not replied after forty-five minutes, he repeated the signal, using Lord Roberts' old ruse of ordering him to acknowledge receipt.[19] Still believing that V Beach was only 'hung up', Hunter-Weston replied

14   Godfrey, II, 8: 81/496, IWM.
15   HW Official War Diary, 25 April 1915, 48356, BL.
16   HW Official War Diary, 25 April 1915, 48356, BL.
17   James, *Gallipoli*, 122; Prior, *Gallipoli*, 104.
18   Godfrey, II, 5: 81/496, IWM.
19   Hamilton, *Gallipoli Diary (1)*, 133; HW Official War Diary, 25 April 1915: 48356, BL.

at 10.35 a.m., rejecting this invitation. For years afterwards, Commodore Roger Keyes, who had initially suggested the switch, 'cursed his blindness' without realising that Hunter-Weston's decision was based on advice from naval colleagues who believed that it would impede the landing of artillery and reinforcements elsewhere.[20] After consulting with Wemyss, Hunter-Weston realised that he could not afford the delay, while believing that his original idea of transferring troops to W Beach would be less disruptive.[21] The strict military protocol that had bound him to support Hamilton's policy regardless of his doubts now operated in reverse; Hamilton later suggested in his published diary that he had accepted Hunter-Weston's refusal with some regret, but was advised by Braithwaite that it was highly unusual for a Commander-in-Chief to 'barge into' his subordinate commander's decision-making.[22]

Hunter-Weston's disconnection from the wider battlefield had increased by late morning. Taking advantage of a lull in the battle at W Beach, he insisted that his staff officers should go to lie down an hour at a time.[23] Enemy resistance on the beach had begun to subside, but despite outnumbering the enemy by six to one, there seemed little impetus for capturing the redoubt on Hill 138, which continued to block progress inland. In response to a request to fill the command vacuum ashore, Hunter-Weston was forced to despatch Wolley Dod around noon, giving him the authority to issue orders in his name.[24] Shortly afterwards, the full extent of the crisis at V Beach became clear. A delayed signal from 86th Brigade arrived at around 1 p.m., noting the plight of the pinned-down survivors and suggesting an alternative landing site, but it came too late to divert the reinforcements which had already been sent to W Beach.[25]

Hunter-Weston had been badgering Wemyss to speed up the disembarkation of the main force, as every minute that passed put Achi Baba

20 Sir Roger Keyes, *The Fight for Gallipoli* (London: Eyre and Spottiswood, 1941), 123–4.
21 Wemyss, *Navy at Dardanelles*, 83.
22 Hamilton, *Gallipoli Diary (1)*, 133.
23 Milward Diary, 25 April 1915, 6510/143/4, NAM.
24 HW Private War Diary, 25 April 1915, 48364, BL; *OHG (1)*, 246.
25 HW Official War Diary, 25 April 1915, 48356, BL.

Achieving the Impossible – The Beaches and Beyond

further out of reach.[26] Now, the delay in capturing Hill 138 and the failure at V Beach meant that it was impossible to capture even his second-stage targets. Control of the battle was slipping away. Instinctively, he wanted to land at V Beach and lead the advance himself. As a Brigadier, he had in the past been able to intervene personally and influence battlefield outcomes, but this method of command was quite impossible for a divisional commander – if he had attempted to do so, he would almost certainly have shared Napier's fate. His staff managed to dissuade him, pointing out that with the large numbers of troops now landed at W Beach they could afford almost to ignore the Sedd-el-Bahr position by attacking the enemy defences there from the west.[27]

Hunter-Weston therefore reverted to a more orthodox directive approach. Seeking to regain the initiative, his attention focused upon X Beach and Hill 114, where an earlier counter-attack had been beaten off and where the situation had remained unchanged since 11.30 a.m. Tactically, the position had great potential for outflanking the enemy defences across the tip of the peninsula; a situation of which the Turks were well aware. He sent a signal to Marshall at 2.15 p.m. requesting him to keep in contact with the troops at Y Beach to his left and asking if he could attack Hill 138 from the north – in effect releasing the divisional reserve. This order did not get through. Having established a bridgehead of some 800 yards around, Marshall was unwilling to split the reserve or to commit it on his own initiative; he later suggested that X Beach, once secured, might have become the main landing site if the other landings failed.[28] Fortunately, the enfilading movement from W Beach westwards was now underway. A combined attack by the Essex and 4/Worcester battalions led by Wolley Dod succeeded in taking Hill 138 around 3 p.m., followed an hour later by the capture of Guezji Baba, an even higher summit which had been unmarked on British maps. The news that Hill 138 had fallen took almost

26 Wemyss, *Navy at Dardanelles*, 88.
27 Milward Diary, 25 April 1915, 6510/143/4, NAM.
28 HW Official War Diary, 25 April 1915, 48356, BL; 87th Brigade War Diary, 25 April 1915, WO 4311, TNA; Marshall, *Four Fronts*, 58.

two hours to reach Hunter-Weston, who replied at 6.12 p.m. that the position should be consolidated, with one detachment attacking the enemy trenches overlooking V beach from behind and the remainder pushing on to take Hill 141 above the beach. Then, showing rather less situational awareness, he also signalled to the *River Clyde* that the attack should be supported from that direction.[29] Again, both these messages went astray.

In fact, the situation at V Beach, where Lieut.-Colonel H. E. Tizard of the 1/Royal Munster Fusiliers had taken command, was still precarious. The attacks on Turkish defences from the west had continued with little effect, despite the support of another naval bombardment. Hunter-Weston was desperate to press on. Just before midnight, he sent another of his staff officers, Captain Garth Walford, ashore with orders to advance immediately to seize Hill 141. Although parties of Tizard's men began to inch out of the *River Clyde* as dusk fell, it was clear to those on the spot that no movement would be possible until the next morning.[30]

In contrast to the drama of the main beaches, the landings at S and Y Beaches had followed a more languid course. From their vantage point above S Beach, Lieut.-Colonel Casson's men could observe the struggling assault at Sedd-el-Bahr. Despite the significance that Hunter-Weston had attached to their position, he had given them no instructions as to what to do in this eventuality. The invaders were subjected to sporadic howitzer fire from the Turkish artillery batteries during the afternoon, but their casualties were slight. Conscious of their exposed position, Hunter-Weston briefly updated Casson on the general situation and endorsed his defensive stance.[31]

The force at Y Beach was even more cut off from developments. Milward's vague mention of a landing 'far away, about four miles from Helles, opposite Krithia', probably summed up the views of 29th Division HQ, who had never been convinced of the arguments for the detaching of nearly one sixth of the infantry for an enterprise which was so clearly

29   HW Official War Diary, 25 April 1915, 48356, BL.
30   H. E. Tizard Report in G. B. Stoney Papers, 76/107/1, IWM; *OHG (1)*, 248–9.
31   87th Brigade War Diary, 25 April 1915, WO 4311, TNA.

separated from the main landing sites.[32] It is also revealing that in his recording of the various beaches later in his diary, Hunter-Weston mentioned only V, W and X, omitting both of the flank landings.[33] He heard nothing directly from Matthews' force all morning – and, indeed, there was little to report. Still assuming that he was in command, Lieut.-Colonel Koe had signalled X Beach at 11.45 a.m. to ask whether he should remain in position or join up with troops further south. This was immediately forwarded to the *Euryalus*; the report of their landing, along with the news that they had not yet made contact with X Beach, was repeated an hour later.[34] The 'fog of war' now descended, as a later signal from 86th Brigade HQ (received at 3 p.m.) gave the false impression that a connection between the beaches had been established. As the force at Y Beach was not in a position to influence the struggle at the tip of the peninsula, there seemed little urgency in confirming this information or in issuing new orders. In fact, by this point Matthews had pulled his force back from the high ground beyond the cliffs. They were now perched back on the crest of the cliff ridge, where there still had been no serious attempt to dig in. As a result, his men's introduction to combat was sudden and ferocious. Late in the afternoon, Turkish reinforcements began to arrive from the central reserve. They made their first concerted attack around 5.30 p.m., which was only driven off by the guns of HMS *Sapphire*.[35] Marshall at X Beach heard the firing and contacted Divisional HQ for instructions, but was told to consolidate and wait until the general advance resumed the next morning; cutting himself a bed of lavender, he slept soundly under his warm Burberry.[36]

It was not until 9 p.m. that Hunter-Weston finally came aboard the *Queen Elizabeth* to take a glass of wine with de Robeck, Hamilton and Braithwaite, all of whom were 'elated' by the 29th Division's feats.[37] Years

32 Milward Diary, 25 April 1915, CAB 45/259, TNA; H. E. Street, Evidence to the Dardanelles Commission, CAB 19/31, TNA.
33 HW Private War Diary, 26 April 1915, 48364, BL.
34 HW Official War Diary, 25 April 1915, 48356, BL.
35 Matthews' Report, 27 April 1915, WO 95/4290, TNA.
36 HW Official War Diary, 25 April 1915, BL 4835; Marshall, *Four Fronts*, 59.
37 Milward Diary, 25 April 1915, 6510/143/4, NAM.

of writing reports on military operations had taught him how to put the most positive construction on events. Despite the mixed fortunes of the day, he gave his audience the good news they wanted to hear, telling his story 'breathlessly'. When Hamilton enquired about Y Beach, he replied that his last message was that they were hard-pressed, but, 'as he had heard nothing more since then he assumed they were all right ...'[38]

Despite frantic firing heard during the night along the various beach perimeters, there seemed to be nothing substantial for Hunter-Weston to worry about.[39] Back at Y Beach, however, darkness had brought a rapidly deteriorating situation. Successive waves of attacks battered Matthew's fragile position without the navy being in a position to provide support. From midnight onwards, he began to send a series of increasingly desperate signals to Divisional HQ, requesting reinforcements and ammunition. He received no reply or acknowledgement in response.[40] No help from could be expected from their neighbours until the remaining enemy strongholds were cleared. Hunter-Weston did signal the *Implacable* to send ammunition, but despatching reinforcements was a more difficult proposition, as his priority remained to secure a landing on V Beach as a springboard for his drive northwards.

The situation at daybreak on 26 April was still highly confused. Hunter-Weston had already asked Hamilton for three French battalions to be landed at W Beach to assist an attack of V Beach from the west. This crossed a message from GHQ offering a whole French brigade as reinforcements, but when Hamilton suddenly became aware of the seriousness of the situation at Y Beach, he instead ordered the troops to be landed at X Beach, where they could march to Matthew's assistance. This message was not relayed to Matthews from Divisional HQ – indeed, the staff did not bring it to Hunter-Weston's attention for a further two hours.[41] By then, it was too late. By 9 a.m., Hamilton could see for himself that a full-scale evacuation

---

38   Hamilton, *Gallipoli Diary (1)*, 153; Keyes, *Fight for Gallipoli*, 124.
39   Milward Diary, 25 April 1915, 6510/143/4, NAM.
40   HW Official War Diary, 25 April 1915, 48356, BL.
41   *OHG (1)*, 214.

Achieving the Impossible – The Beaches and Beyond

down the cliffs at Y Beach was underway, but he did not intervene, wrongly assuming that Hunter-Weston had sanctioned it.[42]

There is probably no aspect of Hunter-Weston's conduct with regard to the landings which has attracted more criticism than this episode. Cecil Aspinall-Oglander's *Official History* led the attack, condemning his 'apparent lack of interest' in the fortunes of Matthews' force, and arguing that exploitation of the bridgehead would have helped to short-circuit the ensuing slaughter on the beaches, bringing the 29th Division a 'decisive victory'.[43] It may be, as Macleod suggests, that as a staff officer at Gallipoli the author found it easier to criticise field commanders like Hunter-Weston for failing to implement otherwise 'viable' GHQ plans than to query the plans themselves.[44] However, there is no doubt that serious operational errors were made in this case. Neither Matthews nor Koe, who was fatally wounded in the action, had been particularly enterprising – Hunter-Weston's own night attack at the Aisne had proved how a subordinate commander could seize the initiative and influence events.[45] But, Hunter-Weston was personally culpable on two counts. The first was his failure to ensure that his HQ was in contact with Y Beach. This compounded Matthews' isolation by leaving him without any orders or situational reports for over twenty-four hours. The second problem was the vagueness of the original verbal instructions issued by him. Given Matthews' recent combat experience, this oversight may have been significant. In early March, he had led a demolition party landing at Kum Kale, which had to be abandoned in the face of strong opposition.[46] Being used to raids and 'cutting out' expeditions of this type,

---

42   G. P. Dawnay to C. Dawnay, 29 April 1915, Dawnay Papers, 69/21/1, IWM. HW Private War Diary, 25 April 1915, 48364, BL.
43   *OHG (1)*, 214–15, 221.
44   Jenny Macleod, *Reconsidering Gallipoli* (Manchester: Manchester University Press, 2004), 85.
45   Milward blamed 'the Col of the KOSBs [who] had misinterpreted orders and forbidden men to entrench': Milward Diary, 25 April 1915, 6510/143/4, NAM.
46   *OHG (1)*, 82.

a set of clear objectives were vital to underline that Y Beach would function as a full-scale landing intended to anchor the main advance.[47]

Beyond this, it is more difficult to apportion individual blame for the failure to grasp the full potential of Y Beach – or indeed the other flanking positions. The original GHQ plan had apparently been unsure itself of how best to use these beaches, or of how to respond generally in the event of unexpected developments in the main landings. A larger floating reserve, for example, might have given greater flexibility to exploit success. While Hunter-Weston shares some of the responsibility for the rather linear approach to planning, it seems unfair to condemn him for neglecting to exploit opportunities which arose in the midst of battle that were never collectively identified around the conference table of the *Queen Elizabeth*. Already, a personalised command style was developing on the campaign. Y Beach had been Hamilton's pet project, but it seems that the Commander-in-Chief had been no more effective in communicating his intentions than Hunter-Weston had been in briefing the unfortunate Matthews.

Did the failure to support Y Beach really matter? As their response suggests, the Turks certainly grasped its tactical value.[48] Matthews himself believed that he could have done more with reinforcements and extra ammunition, but it is difficult to see how additional troops could have helped the situation in the absence of determined and proactive leadership.[49] Indeed, Prior is probably correct when he dismisses claims of missed opportunities in this instance as 'a mixture of fantasy and hindsight'.[50] Not all of Aspinall-Oglander's contemporaries shared his assessment of

---

47   I. Hamilton to C. F. Aspinall, 12 March 1918, Hamilton Papers, 8/1/4, LHCMA. Basil Liddell Hart attempted to deflect the criticism of Matthews, feeling that he had been 'let down by his divisional commander', and that Hunter-Weston's failure to respond to his messages was 'the main cause of the disaster': B. Liddell Hart to C. F. Aspinall, 10 January 1930, Liddell Hart Papers, 1/23, LHCMA. See also Douglas Jerrold, *The Royal Naval Division* (London: Hutchinson, 1923), 84.
48   Hans Kannengiesser, *The Campaign in Gallipoli* (London: Hutchinson, 1927), 106; Erickson, *Gallipoli*, 75.
49   Matthews, Evidence to the Dardanelles Commission, CAB 19/33, TNA.
50   Prior, *Gallipoli*, 98.

Achieving the Impossible – The Beaches and Beyond 157

the beach's significance. Street (albeit commenting as an interested party) phlegmatically insisted that the failure to retain it could 'hardly be held to be more than the ordinary fortune of war of this description'.[51] Although Hamilton initially felt the next stage of the advance would have been 'a promenade' if Y Beach had been held, he too remained unconvinced that the evacuation had had a decisive impact on the future course of events.[52] He raised the issue with Hunter-Weston a few days later, but concluded that 'least said, soonest mended'.[53] What had happened certainly did not cloud their working relationship – indeed, after the war they swapped views quite merrily on the issue. Criticised in the *Official History* for not intervening more forcefully, Hamilton transferred blame squarely onto Matthews, who, 'being a Marine ... considered it the right thing to do to get back on his ship on the first opportunity', but as usual, Hunter-Weston loftily closed the discussion: '... even if there had been a certain lack of tenacity, the circumstances of the fighting at Y beach made criticism ungenerous as well as useless. I neither by word or action cast blame either on Marine or KOSB'.[54]

Some compensation for this fiasco came in the form of the progress being made in securing V Beach, where Walford and his staff colleagues had taken over effective control from Tizard. Just after noon on 26 April, Milward rushed down to the General's cabin to tell him that Sedd-el-Bahr village had been cleared.[55] The capture of Hill 141 followed a few hours later. By 3 p.m., the 29th Division at last held a continuous line across the tip of the peninsula.

---

51 Street, Evidence to the Dardanelles Commission, CAB 19/31, TNA.
52 Hamilton, *Gallipoli Diary (1)*, 170.
53 Hamilton, *Gallipoli Diary (1)*, 181. There is no evidence that Hunter-Weston deliberately falsified his account of events as Travers suggests. Aspinall's evidence to the Dardanelles Commission [29 January 1917], which focuses on the order for re-embarkation, does not support this interpretation: Hamilton Papers, 8/2/4, LHCMA.
54 I. Hamilton to HW, 29 March 1923; HW to I. Hamilton, 18 April 1923, Hamilton Papers, 13/11, LHCMA. Matthews was later promoted to Brigadier, but died of wounds sustained in April 1917.
55 Milward Diary, 25 April 1915, CAB 45/259, TNA.

Despite lacking an adequate system for communicating orders and information, Hunter-Weston had ultimately managed to land some 17,000 men on the three main beaches in over twenty-four hours. This was an unprecedented feat of amphibious warfare, and if his first day objectives had not been so unrealistic, the achievement that was reached might have been better recognised. Further west, the Anzac forces had experienced similar confusion as they tried to force their way inland, but here, too, a bridgehead had been established in the face of strong Turkish counter-attacks. The temporary French landing at Kum Kale had also been successful and d'Amade's troops were already re-embarking to take up their place at the right of the line at Helles. Meanwhile, the remnants of the Turkish defending battalions, who had suffered around 1,000 casualties, were making a deliberate withdrawal towards their second defensive line. This ran roughly northwest and southeast in front of Krithia village, from a point a few hundred yards beyond Y Beach, across to the high ground west of Kereves Dere. For Hunter-Weston, the exhaustion of his men and the failure of the French transports to arrive meant that 26 April would become a day of consolidation rather than one of pursuit. Fears of a Turkish counter-attack lent a typically melodramatic flourish to his message to his troops – 'Every man will die at his post rather than retire'. Writing his report to Hamilton at midnight, he pronounced the results of the previous day's fighting as 'satisfactory' and promised that despite the thinness of his line and the tiredness of his men, he would be ready to push forward the next day.[56] As a mark of this determination, he summoned Tizard on board the *Euryalus* and removed him from command for his failure to press home the advance at V beach.[57]

---

56 HW Official War Diary, 25 April 1915, 48356, BL.
57 Tizard Report, 7301, IWM.

'Half of our Difficulties are Over'

The continued depletion of his division and the slow arrival of his French reinforcements convinced Hunter-Weston that the assault on Achi Baba would have to be postponed for a further twenty-four hours. As the French troops would be under his tactical command until d'Amade established his HQ, he also decided to remain on board the *Euryalus* for another day, placing Marshall in temporary command ashore.[58] Orders were issued for a movement across the peninsula to begin at 4 p.m., bringing his force into line for battle the next day. Pivoting on the extreme left at X Beach, the advance crawled forward for up to two miles without encountering any significant opposition. By early evening, the French had joined up with the British on the right, but on the left the flank company of the 87th Brigade remained in its original trenches near the coast, creating a difficult bend near the centre of the British assault line.

While Travers argues that Hunter-Weston's failure to maintain the tempo of the offensive on the 27 April was a missed opportunity, it should also be borne in mind that further Turkish reinforcements were already on their way. The first battalion had arrived at noon, followed by an entire regiment of 3,000 experienced and well-trained men, who relieved their exhausted colleagues and took up position on the west of the peninsula.[59] Coming from an aggressive commander, Hunter-Weston's assessment of what his men could realistically achieve should be taken seriously. However, Travers is on firmer ground when he suggests that Hunter-Weston's gaze had been fixed on the success of the landings rather than on what was to happen next. This was an understandable reaction and was shared by Hamilton down to the ordinary soldier. In Hunter-Weston's case the fact that his men had actually managed to get ashore offered an immediate emotional release, as well as appearing to be a talisman which could protect him against future disappointments. Foreboding was replaced with elation.

---

58 *OHG (1)*, 282.
59 Travers, *Gallipoli*, 93; Erickson, *Gallipoli*, 78–9.

Whatever the future held, this historic victory could not be erased. The human qualities of 'heroism and endurance' had overcome the worst that modern industrialised warfare could throw at his men:

> The 29th Division has fought gloriously. It has achieved the impossible. It has landed on the beaches, covered with wire entanglements, flanked with machine guns & pom-poms and dominated by trenches, filled with the enemy's riflemen. Whole boatloads of officers, soldiers and sailors were wiped out; men were mown down by machine guns and lay in a row along the front of the wire entanglements, but the rest pressed on ...[60]

His first letter to Grace after the landings had a similar tone and outlook. From 'a four to one chance' against success, the odds had now turned in their favour:

> We have a very tough job before us, but ½ of our difficulties are over now we are landed. When we get the strong covering position in the ACHI BABA range of hills 6 miles from CAPE HELLES, ¾ of our difficulties will be over and the remaining quarter, though still very difficult, will have very strong chances in its favour. ACHI BABA will, I fear, take some time to gain; but after what we have done, I am sure we shall do it.[61]

His calculations neglected one vital factor. The landings cost him at least a fifth of his force; indeed, in a later estimate, he placed the figure as high as a third.[62] He had lost so many men that it was doubtful whether or not he could advance rapidly enough, and yet speed was essential. If the Turks were given time to breathe, it could only mean a long, drawn-out struggle, sucking in many more troops. Milward grasped the truth only too clearly – 'From the start the whole show was a toss-up'.[63]

The sense of urgency was fuelled by reports on the evening of 27 April that further enemy troops were crossing the Narrows.[64] That night brought

60 HW to C. Wigram, 6 May 1915, 6503/39/21, NAM.
61 HW to GHW, 27 April 1915, HW Private War Diary, 48364, BL.
62 Prior, *Gallipoli*, 108; HW to GHW, 6 May 1915, HW Private War Diary, 48364, BL.
63 Milward Diary, 25 April 1915, 6510/143/4, NAM.
64 Hamilton, *Gallipoli Diary, (1)*, 163.

little rest for Hunter-Weston and his staff, who were busy drawing up the plan for the next day's advance. Unfortunately, their work was handicapped by their failure to undertake a thorough reconnaissance. As a result, the divisional orders which were issued at 10 p.m. ran to only half a page of text.[65] Brevity, however, did not imply simplicity. Rather than Achi Baba, Hunter-Weston had instead realistically set a line along the Krithia road running north to Yazy Tepe as his objective. Hoping to keep the Turks guessing, he intended this action as the jumping off point for a final assault on the ridge from the west, rather than a more a direct frontal attack from the south. This would involve throwing forward his left and centre in a complex right-wheeling movement. On the left, the 87th Brigade were to advance five miles northwards to capture Sari Tepe on the Aegean Coast and Hill 472 at the end of Gully Ravine. In the centre, the 88th Brigade, with the 86th in reserve, were to seize Krithia and take up a line running north to south on the east of the village. The French on the right were to join up with them, forming the pivot of the action. The allied front was therefore to be extended by three and a half miles and to undergo a complete change of direction in front of the enemy, with the 88th Brigade and the French making a 90-degree turn to form a north-south line. The men's understanding of their task was not helped by the late communication of orders, which took till dawn to reach the battalions.[66]

This display of tactical sophistication has since been condemned as unsuited to tired soldiers operating on unfamiliar terrain (as was the case at Gallipoli). There is some justice in this viewpoint. Street, who was now acting as the division's senior staff officer, expressed the opinion that the decision to attack with worn-out brigades was a 'bold' one, but Hunter-Weston believed that he fully appreciated the risk, which had paid off in

---

65 *History of the Great War based on official documents by direction of the Historical Section of the Committee of Imperial Defence. Military Operations. Gallipoli. Volume I: Inception of the Campaign to May 1915. Appendices* compiled by Brigadier-General C. F. Aspinall-Oglander (London: William Heinemann, 1929) [*OHG (1)* app.], 60.
66 *OHG (1)*, 287. See, for example, 88th Brigade War Diary, 28 April 1915, WO 95/4311, TNA.

the past.[67] The condition of his men was not his only problem. It is significant that his orders for the coming battle made no reference to artillery support. The unloading of the division's guns and ammunition was still incomplete, and in the absence of accurate intelligence regarding the enemy's positions it was doubtful that the navy guns could fill the gap. Moreover, although he was delighted that his command responsibilities had rapidly grown and now covered 5,000 French troops and an RND battalion, this brought its own operational challenges, as the units had not worked together or been trained for cross-attachment. Indeed, telephone communication had not even been established between them, so when the French commander, General Vandenberg, decided to substitute his own plan for Hunter-Weston's, the neighbouring 88th Brigade were not informed.[68] Further, the extra manpower did not compensate for earlier casualties, which had fallen heaviest on the 86th Brigade where some battalions had been reduced to half their fighting effectiveness. The loss of senior officers across the division was a further concern, with only one Brigadier and three of the original battalion commanders still remaining on duty.[69]

Facing Hunter-Weston's hastily assembled force was the Turkish 9th Division, reorganised under Colonel Halil Sami Bey. His ten battalions had already regained some equilibrium and were busy preparing defensive positions to cover the approaches to Krithia. Hamilton's intelligence was proved correct and a fresh regiment and two further battalions had begun to arrive from first light; following Turkish army practice, these mixed reinforcements were absorbed into a unified command structure in order to aid cohesion. The division's limited artillery, controlled from Achi Baba, had also been reinforced and centralised into two groups to support the eastern and western wings of the Turkish line, thus enabling a critical mass of firepower to be assembled when required.[70]

---

67 Street, Evidence to the Dardanelles Commission, CAB 19/31, TNA.
68 HW to GHW, 27, 29 April 1915, HW Private War Diary, 48364, BL; Erickson, *Gallipoli*, 80; Milward Diary, 28 April 1915, CAB 45/259, TNA.
69 *OHG (1)*, 284.
70 Erickson, *Gallipoli*, 78–81.

The delayed allied advance began at 8 a.m. on 28 April. Hamilton had sanctioned a daylight attack, counselling Hunter-Weston to start as late as possible so that the men could be rested and good light could be provided for the naval artillery.[71] The preliminary bombardment was meagre. Major Douglas Forman, who commanded B Battery of 15th Brigade Royal Horse Artillery, brought his three guns to bear, but could only use two simultaneously during the day, as he had to ration his ammunition.[72] Nevertheless, the infantry progressed well at first, especially on the left where the 87th Brigade tramped steadily along either side of Gully Ravine. When Hunter-Weston arrived ashore at 9.15 a.m., the capture of Krithia seemed achievable.[73] Despite establishing his HQ at Hill 138, he did not attempt to intervene personally, but instead instructed Marshall to superintend the advance, hoping to provide the sort of proximate command that had been missing on the beaches. However, the experiment was doomed to failure, as without a fixed HQ or even a telephone line, Marshall was no better placed to impose his will across a two-mile front than Hunter-Weston.[74]

Marshall saw himself as 'a sort of battle policeman', but by the time he reached the front line at around 11.30 a.m., the tempo of the attack was failing.[75] As the skirmishing line of the 88th Brigade confronted the interlocking Turkish forward posts half a mile ahead of the main defensive line, Hunter-Weston's sophisticated arc of advance gave way to a series of independent battles that were fought at company level. The Turkish line almost cracked in the centre, but British cohesion ebbed away just as reinforcements were brought up to exploit this. On the left, the Turks had positioned themselves in the deep gullies that separated the attackers and left the allied forces without flank protection; on the right, the independent French attempt to seize the enemy positions at the Kereves Dere ravine quickly foundered under punishing fire from concealed artillery.

---

71 HW Official War Diary, 27 April 1915, 48356, BL.
72 D. E. Forman, Evidence to the Dardanelles Commission, CAB 33/29, TNA.
73 HW Official War Diary, 28 April 1915, 48356, BL.
74 HW Private War Diary, 28 April 1915, 48364, BL; *OHG (1)*, 289.
75 Marshall, *Four Fronts*, 61.

In the belief that only his men's exhaustion was delaying the advance, Marshall threw in the weakened 86th Brigade at around noon with orders to carry forward the line and take Krithia. The 87th also attempted to resume the attack at Gully Ravine around 1 p.m., but suffered grievous casualties in so doing. Meanwhile, the 86th Brigade attack, made by two unsupported battalions, made little progress; when the French fell back at 3.15 p.m. after another counter-attack, the 88th Brigade's companies also began to withdraw. This sealed the issue. At around 5 p.m., Marshall reported to Divisional HQ that brigades and battalions were 'very mixed up and the men are thoroughly done'; Hunter-Weston responded to concerned enquiries from GHQ by assuring Hamilton that there had been 'local successes and local reverses', but that there was no prospect of a further advance.[76] By nightfall the allied troops had dug in, with the 86th and 88th brigades back on their original start line; the 29th Division's casualties numbered around 2,000, including a high percentage of officers, while the French had lost around a fifth of their strength.[77]

Rhodes James has hailed the First Battle of Krithia as 'one of the decisive battles of modern history', but on a more modest level it can also be described as ending the 'battle of the beaches'.[78] Hunter-Weston's haste was understandable, but a poorly supported attack against concealed enemy positions stood little chance of success. In explaining his failure, he sidestepped issues of planning and tactics, claiming that he simply 'had not enough weight to get through'.[79] Street, who believed that 28 April was the nearest that that they came to victory in the campaign, also argued that the lack of sufficient numbers of fresh troops to throw in at the right moment was decisive.[80] The implication that battlefield success automatically followed resources was an early variant of what Travers terms the

---

76 HW Official War Diary, 27 April 1915, 48356, BL.
77 *OHG (1)*, 294.
78 Rhode James, *Gallipoli*, 141; Nigel Steel and Peter Hart, *Defeat at Gallipoli* (London: Macmillan, 1994), 129.
79 HW to GHW, 29 April 1915, HW Private War Diary, 48364, BL.
80 HW to GHW, 29 April 1915, HW Private War Diary, 48364, BL. Street, Evidence to the Dardanelles Commission, CAB 19/31, TNA.

'more and more' concept, which became as common at Gallipoli as it did on the Western Front.[81] There was no denying that the campaign had been deficient in manpower from the outset, but it was unclear exactly what level of resources would have been 'sufficient' to alter the outcome. Hunter-Weston told a sceptical Hamilton before the battle that he would rather have a normal reinforcement draft of 1,200 men than two fresh battalions, while Street argued in the immediate aftermath that 'with one more brigade' Achi Baba would have been in allied hands.[82] By the time the Dardanelles Commission met two years later, both seemed to agree that an extra division might have turned the tide.[83] Even this hypothesis is, however, doubtful. The sheer weight of numbers might have prevailed as they did at the landings, but given the limited reconnaissance, inadequate fire support and poor inter-allied cooperation, losses would have been severe in taking this approach. Cramming additional troops onto the peninsula would also have worsened the logistical crisis and with a further three Turkish divisions on their way south, the most likely outcome would have been an eventual stalemate on the Kilid Bahr plateau.

Reliance on the resources argument at the time to explain the allied failure at Krithia also diverted attention from the tactical capability of their enemy, who had again reacted quickly and effectively to developing situations during the day, with commanders frequently using their own initiative. Having studied the Balkan Wars as a staff officer, Hunter-Weston was less likely to underrate his opponents than many of his colleagues, but his favourite nostrum, that he faced 'German brains and Turkish hands', failed to recognise that German command assistance and the accumulation of men and materials were not the only factors behind the enemy's combat power.[84] The Turkish army also benefited from well-coordinated planning

---

81 Travers, 'Command and Leadership Styles', 430–1.
82 Hamilton, *Gallipoli Diary (1)*, 164; I. Hamilton to J. Hamilton, 29 April 1915, Hamilton Papers, 7/1/4, LHCMA.
83 Street, Evidence to the Dardanelles Commission, CAB 19/31, TNA; Hunter-Weston, Evidence to Dardanelles Commission, Hamilton Papers, 8/2/50, LHCMA.
84 HW to C. Wigram, 22 April 1915, HW Private War Diary, 48364, BL; Hunter-Weston, Evidence to Dardanelles Commission, Hamilton Papers, 8/2/50, LHCMA.

and reporting systems and a cohesive command structure which allowed commanders to calculate risks and take decisions with greater accuracy than Hunter-Weston. In other words, he was already being out-thought as well as out-fought.

Second Attempt

Hunter-Weston was a 'front row, dress circle' onlooker on 28 April, fielding alarmist messages with phlegmatic detachment.[85] His display of confidence in the aftermath was just as important as his coolness, as the next few days were some of most anxious that the allies would spend on the peninsula. With shocked troops clinging on to a position barely three miles deep, the need for rest and reorganisation had become urgent.[86]

Conditions at Gallipoli were tough even for senior commanders. Hunter-Weston and his staff had arrived ashore in the clothes in which they stood up, with one change of underwear.[87] The shortage of water made washing impossible and he confessed to Grace that he was 'burnt and dirty' after a week of campaigning.[88] He chose a spot on the reverse slope of Hill 138 as his HQ, which was soon renamed 'Hunter-Weston Hill'. Visiting from his own tin shack at Imbros, Hamilton found it 'a strange abode for a boss'; the views over the Gulf of Xeros were breath-taking, with the humped back of Achi Baba visible over the nearby fields and woods,

---

85 Milward Diary, 28 April 1915, 6510/143/4, NAM.
86 Street, Evidence to the Dardanelles Commission, CAB 19/31, TNA.
87 HW to GHW, 6 May 1915, HW Private War Diary, 48364, BL; Captain Stair Gillon, *The Story of the 29th Division: A Record of Gallant Deeds* (London: Thomas Nelson, 1925) 138.
88 Gillon, *Story of the 29th Division*, 138; HW Private War Diary, HW to GHW, 6 May 1915, 48364, BL.

but the accommodation itself consisted of holes dug into the hillside and little tents which were freezing cold at night.[89]

The immediate process of consolidation was successful enough to withstand the inevitable Turkish counter-attacks, which began during the night of 1 May. The blow fell heaviest on the French sector on the right, but a worried Hunter-Weston was reluctant to send reinforcements, and the direct intervention of GHQ was required before the Anson Battalion of the RND was detached to assist. As the position stabilised the next morning, the allies mounted a hopeless assault which was easily repelled by the Turks without any significant ground being gained. This operation was not, as Prior implies, inspired by Hunter-Weston but, rather, it was driven by d'Amade, who had gained the approval of Hamilton for the 29th Division to conform to the movement of the French.[90] 'It would have melted a heart of stone', Hunter-Weston later told Hamilton, 'to see how tired our men looked in the grey of morning, when [his] order came to hand urging them to counter-attack and pursue'.[91] Anglo-French relationships became increasingly strained as Hunter-Weston attempted to retrieve his 'loaned' troops. Hamilton's direct arbitration was necessary, but a soothing letter from GOC 29th Division to the Commander of the *Corps Expéditionnaire d'Orient* also helped settle to the 'little misunderstanding' fairly amicably.[92]

The Turkish attacks had diverted preparations for resuming the attempt on Achi Baba, but the continuing defensive build-up along the ridge made this advance as vital as ever. Prodded on by Kitchener, Hamilton was determined to begin it on 6 May, switching resources from the Anzac sector where the situation had stabilised. For Hunter-Weston, renewing the offensive meant maintaining the local 'dominance' that he believed he had established, but he also admitted that 'By Jove it is a hard task.'[93] Adversity had brought him closer to Hamilton, in a far from obvious partnership. The

89 Hamilton, *Gallipoli Diary (1)*, 177; Milward Diary, 28 April 1915, 6510/143/4, NAM.
90 *OHG (1)*, 319; Hamilton *Gallipoli Diary (1)*, 189; HW War Diary, 2 May 1915, 48364, BL.
91 Hamilton, *Gallipoli Diary (1)*, 190.
92 HW Private War Diary, 4 May 1915, 48364, BL.
93 HW to GHW, 6 May 1915, HW Private War Diary, 48364, BL.

hearty, athletic Hunter-Weston contrasted with Hamilton's artistic interests and liberal sensibilities. Even in physical terms, the two differed quite markedly, one bristling and hawk-like and the other resembling a frail and elegant wading bird. Although his verbosity was still an irritant, Hunter-Weston's loyalty and boundless reserves of confidence were beginning to win over his commander-in-chief, who rewarded him with increasing responsibility and autonomy.

Hunter-Weston estimated that the First Battle of Krithia had cost him a further sixth of his division's strength, but the troops placed under him for tactical purposes now began to increase in numbers ahead of the next offensive.[94] The 29th Division, reduced to two brigades, was augmented by the Territorials of the 125th Brigade. Arriving on 5 May, these were first reinforcements from 42nd (East Lancashire) Division, which had been recently prised from Sir John Maxwell's command in Egypt. Also attached was Brigadier Herbert Cox's 29th Indian Brigade (except its Muslim companies) which had landed on 1 May. In addition, Hunter-Weston had a 'Composite Division' commanded by Major-General Paris at his disposal, comprising the remaining RND battalions and the two Anzac battalions that Hamilton had sent south. All the available artillery, including Anzac reinforcements, was placed under the orders of his Divisional HQ. In all, this brought the force under his command to a total of 25,000 men.[95]

For his part, Hunter-Weston luxuriated in his commander's approval. As he explained to his wife:

> Sir Ian Hamilton has left things here pretty much to me. He is evidently very pleased with my handling of affairs. He wrote to K to say that throughout all this heavy fighting I have displayed all the qualities of a great commander [he actually wrote 'great qualities as a commander']. He also warned me not to get under fire for he considered me to be of more value than a whole brigade (4,000 men).[96]

---

94   HW to GHW, 6 May 1915, HW Private War Diary, 48364, BL.
95   *OHG (1)*, 322–3.
96   HW to GHW, 6 May 1915, HW Private War Diary, 48364, BL.

Achieving the Impossible – The Beaches and Beyond 169

There were only two days left in which to plan the offensive. GHQ orders were issued at 1.45 p.m. on 5 May; the object of the attack was to capture of the enemy's main position on Achi Baba. Again, the principal advance was to sweep from the west and southwest, involving a complex right-wheeling movement. The French were to advance about a mile to their front, capturing the Kereves Dere ravine. Once this position was secured, the 29th Division, who formed the backbone of the attack, were to use the French left flank as a pivot point, turning 90 degrees to capture Krithia; assisted by a subsidiary French attack against a spur to the southeast, they were then to press on and take the Achi Baba position.[97] Since Hunter-Weston and his staff believed that their first attempt had almost succeeded, there seemed little point in adopting a radically different battle plan. Divisional orders now ran to four pages, which were distributed to brigades at 4 a.m. on the morning of the battle.[98] Their length and detail was hardly surprising given the intricacy of the plan and the size and complexity of the attacking force involved. Indeed, they covered only the first two phases of the battle – effectively renewing the objectives of 'First Krithia' – with instructions for the third 'pursuit' phase, the final advance on Achi Baba, to be issued only if progress to that point had been satisfactory. The first phase planned to take the division to a line about one mile from Krithia; the newly arrived 125th Brigade was given the simplest objective of advancing with the 88th Brigade along Gully Ravine on the left. The second phase featured the dramatic rightwards pivot by the 88th Brigade, which was to halt east of Krithia village, while the Territorials were ordered to continue to push forwards to seize the high ground at Hill 472, extending along a two mile frontage to link up with the 88th. The Indian Brigade and the 87th Brigade were to be kept in hand for the final assault on Achi Baba, while the Composite Division, which formed the GHQ reserve, was also put at Hunter-Weston's disposal.

The plan's success depended on a high degree of coordination between the new attacking units, but the risks involved were depressingly familiar.

97 *OHG (1)* app., 62–5.
98 HW Official War Diary, 6 May 1915, 48356, BL.

Despite his reinforcements, Hunter-Weston was still planning to attack with tired troops. The intelligence situation had also failed to show any improvement during the previous week. Enemy strength was estimated at 20,000, but modern Turkish accounts suggest that there were perhaps only half that number, supported by twenty-four machine-guns and forty artillery pieces.[99] Not only did the allies remain unsure as to where the main defensive positions were, they had also failed to locate the enemy's outpost line with its carefully deployed machine-guns. It was, however, the ammunition situation that most concerned Hamilton and Hunter-Weston – in a classic Hamiltonian turn of phrase, there was a want of 'pebbles for the Goliath of Achi Baba'. The basic artillery plan, drawn up by Hunter-Weston's old schoolmate, Brigadier R. W. Breeks, divided the available guns into four groups to cover each sector of the attack.[100] But, even if they had known where to shoot, they did not have enough ammunition to do so effectively. Although the number of shore-based guns had increased to include a handful of heavy howitzers, the shortage of shells had worsened, with half of the allotted supply already fired away.[101] The naval guns which were also in place to support the attack faced a similar shortage as their stocks were being conserved for the task of forcing the straits and bombarding Constantinople.

Hunter-Weston could not resist unfavourably comparing the present situation with Flanders, where 'they would never attack with empty limbers behind them', but Hamilton reminded him that time was of the essence. On the Western Front they could afford to wait, but at Gallipoli the Turks would only become twice as strong and their trenches twice as deep if they were given yet more time to prepare. Hunter-Weston accepted Hamilton's logic. While in later battles on the peninsula his infantry attacked as accessories to rudimentary fire tactics, here his men functioned as substitutes for firepower. Aware of the hazards, Hamilton counselled crossing the danger zone before daybreak to get close to the enemy, but Hunter-Weston

99 Erickson, *Gallipoli*, 100.
100 *OHG (1)* app., 68.
101 *OHG (1)*, 325.

disagreed, fearing a loss of control of the situation as so many company officers had recently become casualties. His views on the dangers of night operations had some foundation – the recent Turkish attacks had cost around 2,000 men without attaining their objectives – but the minor tactics he offered as an alternative lacked the sophistication of his battle plan. Hamilton reported that: 'Hard up as we are for shell he thinks it best to blaze it away freely before closing and to trust our bayonets when we get in.'[102]

From his elevated HQ, Hunter-Weston watched as the Second Battle of Krithia opened at 10.30 a.m. on 6 May with a slow and notably meagre bombardment from the precious heavy howitzers. Telephone systems were at last in place, though, and each of the brigades were instructed to send in hourly progress reports.[103] Hunter-Weston's direction of this battle illustrated how completely he had come to embrace a managerial model of command. The improvement in communications encouraged him to persevere with using Marshall to coordinate the 29th Division's advance, while also commanding his own brigade. While Hamilton later described the role of the commander as 'a sort of mental crucifixion', it was not Hunter-Weston's style to wallow in tortured introspection. He passed the time during the battle writing to Grace on a little card table, 'in the same frame of mind as if I were writing to you from some hotel in England'.[104] However, he reserved his fullest description of modern generalship for Wigram, in the hope that the King would appreciate 'a note written in the midst of an action':

> My orders have been issued, the troops are in motion, the guns on sea and on land are mingling their reports with the continuous rattling of the musketry, and for the General at the end of the net of telephone wires there remains nothing to do but to await developments. My job is temporarily suspended until a difficulty arises or a new situation to be dealt with. Now is the time for detachment, for a health body and a calm & confident mind, which can cast off all anxiety till the time comes to act again.[105]

102 Hamilton, *Gallipoli Diary (1)*, 201.
103 HW Official War Diary, 25 April 1915, 48356, BL.
104 HW to GHW, 6 May 1915, HW Private War Diary, 48364, BL.
105 HW to C. Wigram, 6 May 1915, Hunter-Weston Papers, 6503/39/21, NAM.

The next three days witnessed a series of repetitive attacks of diminishing power which left the allies half a mile short of their Phase One objective. On the first day, the bombardment had shaken the defenders but was unable to suppress their fire.[106] On the left, the 88th Brigade moved off slowly and was pinned down in front of the Turkish advance posts after a few hundred yards.[107] A renewed effort in the afternoon pushed the line on a little further, but it soon ground to a halt again. The Lancashire Territorials suffered a similar fate, beginning late and punished throughout most of the day by Turkish machine-guns. On the right, the French advance was also partly delayed, but the *Brigade Metropolitaine* managed to gain the high ground at the mouth of Kereves Dere before being halted by heavy fire, while the *Brigade Coloniale* attack also quickly lost its momentum. The first reports at Divisional HQ had suggested that most of the day's targets had been largely achieved, but in reality only modest local successes were made, with an average of some 400 yards of ground gained along the length of the line. Hunter-Weston's ability to accentuate the positive was tested, but won out in the end. He recorded in his diary that progress was 'not great', but that 'no great change of position was intended'.[108]

He was determined to continue the offensive, asking Cox to send out his Gurkha scouts to reconnoitre the ground once the fighting had stopped.[109] Phases One and Two were now collapsed together, with the 29th Division ordered to proceed straight to its second objective of wheeling to capture Krithia.[110] Hunter-Weston spent the morning telephoning his Brigadiers and sending messages of encouragement.[111] Another ineffectual barrage began at 9.45 a.m., supplemented with naval guns, but their flat trajectory and the saucer-shaped terrain left little scope for close support. The renewed attacks of the 88th and 125th Brigades stalled under heavy machine-gun fire. Limited advances were made during the afternoon by

106 Kannengiesser, *Campaign in Gallipoli*, 138–4.
107 88th Brigade War Diary, 6 May 1915, WO 4312, TNA.
108 HW Private War Diary, 6 May 1915 48364, BL.
109 HW Official War Diary, 25 April 1915, 48356, BL.
110 *OHG (1)* app., 71.
111 HW Private War Diary, 7 May 1915, 48364, BL; *OHG (1)*, 338.

individual units, but lacking support, they were forced back to their start lines. Determined to avoid another night of stalemate, Hunter-Weston intervened at 3.30 p.m., ordering a renewed fifteen-minute bombardment and throwing forward the 87th and 88th Brigades on the left, with the New Zealand and Indian Brigades in support.[112] A few hundred yards were gained in places, but the enemy machine-guns again prevented the attackers from even approaching the Turkish forward line.

The third day of the battle was a microcosm of the whole Gallipoli campaign. Artillery ammunition was almost exhausted and the chances of further gains seemed minimal. Yet, Hamilton's 'time problem' also still remained. Some ground had at least been won: would not one final assault break the Turks? And, if they did not go forwards, might not the enemy be encouraged to renew its counter-attacks and drive them into the sea? While forward units had been badly mauled, casualties as a whole had not been severe enough to impair the overall combat effectiveness of the allied force – and besides, there still remained three fresh brigades to be thrown into the battle. The shared commitment of the senior allied commanders to offensive action was also mutually reinforcing. When GHQ issued orders at 10.45 p.m. for a renewal of the battle, Hunter-Weston did not demur.[113] Working through the night, his detailed orders for a general advance were issued only two hours before it was due to begin. The 29th Division were ordered to spearhead the assault, reinforced by the New Zealand Brigade, whose role had grown after the Territorials were withdrawn. D'Amade was similarly energised, although his orders from GHQ were mainly limited to consolidation while pushing his right flank across the Kereves Dere.

After a fifteen-minute barrage from ship and shore artillery, the New Zealanders steadily moved off at 10.30 a.m. but were halted by the same shrapnel and machine-gun fire that had prevented progress for the past two days. By the afternoon, it was clear that the British attack had completely collapsed, as had the French attempt on the right. After receiving reports from his forward units, Hunter-Weston was already organising a further

112   HW Private War Diary, 7 May 14, 48364, BL.
113   HW Official War Diary, 6 May 1915, 48356, BL.

attack when Hamilton, who had come ashore to supervise operations, ordered a general advance at the bayonet point all along the allied line. This fresh attack began at 5.30 p.m., with the gunners instructed to pour their reserves into the preliminary barrage, which was the heaviest yet seen on the peninsula. Hunter-Weston's diary noted the 'perfect cooperation of artillery and infantry', but this effort was largely wasted given the lack of information on their targets.[114] Lieutenant Godfrey, who was a spectator, could not help contrasting the approach of the different allies.[115] On the right, the French tried to advance with drums, flags and bugles, but failed. On the left, the 87th Brigade and the New Zealanders moved more cautiously through very jagged country, managing some piecemeal gains of around 200 yards, but these could not be reinforced. In one of the most poignant moments of a bad battle, the 2nd Australian Brigade, who had been in reserve only minutes before, charged across open ground and were brought down by converging fire from both flanks.

This last dramatic effort brought the Second Battle of Krithia to an end. The action had cost the allies 6,500 casualties, amounting to almost 30 per cent of those engaged.[116] At no time had the Turkish positions been seriously threatened. Ironically, the advance had helped the enemy to consolidate their defensive line by preventing their own planned frontal attacks. The next few weeks brought a brief respite for the 29th Division, who were at last withdrawn from the trenches. Turkish shelling and sniping was incessant, but now that they were given some time to consider their surroundings, they realised the beauty and strangeness of the peninsula, with its thyme-covered hills and frog-filled gullies. As one survivor of V beach commented, 'so far as soldiering goes, it could not be nicer' – apart, of course, from the Turks and the war.[117]

During the pause in offensive operations, Hunter-Weston was punctilious in observing the military courtesies that traditionally recognised

114 HW Private War Diary, 8 May 1915, 48364, BL.
115 Godfrey, II, 19: 8/496, IWM.
116 *OHG (1)*, 347.
117 G. B. Stoney to T. R. Stoney, 27 May 1915, G. B. Stoney Papers, 76/107/1, IWM.

Achieving the Impossible – The Beaches and Beyond 175

sacrifice and achievement. Still eager for his men's affection, he was delighted when the 29th Division responded to his laudatory address with a hearty cheer.[118] In private, however, cynicism was already spreading among the ranks. Private Lambert of the 88th Field Ambulance dismissed Hunter-Weston's kind words to his unit as 'a lot of eyewash', while Captain Guy Geddes felt that his praise for the Munster Fusiliers seemed to be 'all ego & to varnish over trouble'.[119] The psychological pressure on the senior officers was also increasing. Following the departure of a 'very jumpy' d'Amade in the middle of May, Hunter-Weston was forced to deal with the case of his friend Breeks, 'an excellent officer', who left the peninsula on sick leave at the end of the month.[120]

The second failed attempt at Krithia not only marked the end of Hunter-Weston's immediate gamble, but also resolved the 'toss-up' at the heart of the campaign – the risky attempt to seize the peninsula with a small, indifferently equipped force. Summing up the contradiction at the heart of his command, he wrote: 'As a man I rejoice in this enterprise, though as a strategist and a general, I cannot approve it'.[121] This combination of personal enthusiasm and professional pessimism was a useful asset for a commander, but in Hunter-Weston's case, the delicate balance between the two had already been disturbed. He had started the campaign with a better grasp of the strategic situation than that held by Hamilton, but the determination that made him an aggressive and self-confident leader also prevented him from admitting the implications of his current predicament. On 15 May, Hamilton came ashore to consult him on what policy the War Office should be advised to pursue with regard to the operations at Gallipoli.[122] Evacuation was not an option for Hunter-Weston, who

---

118 HW Private War Diary, 12 May 1915, 48364, BL.
119 S. L. Lambert Papers, 01/21/1, IWM; Geddes Diary, 15 May 1915, G. W. Geddes Papers, 09/81/1, IWM.
120 HW to GHW, 15, 21 May 1915; HW Private War Diary, 48364, BL; HW to I. Hamilton, 29 May 1915, Hamilton Papers, 7/2/2, LHCMA.
121 HW to GHW, 6 May 1915, HW Private War Diary, 48364, BL. The aphorism pleased him sufficiently to repeat it later to Marshall: *Four Fronts*, 85.
122 HW Private War Diary, 15 May 1915, 48364, BL.

believed it impossible to get more than a few men away, but neither did he favour intensifying the operations at Helles.[123] He suggested that the 29th Division be withdrawn to Lemnos to rest and refit, but that no more troops should be landed except for reinforcements of existing units. His alternative proposal was a fresh start that would deliver the original objectives of the campaign, but avoid its current deadlock. In an ambitious variant of the 'more and more' concept, he strongly advised that six New Army divisions should be landed at Enos, on the western coast of Thrace, to seize the neck of the isthmus at Bulair and drive straight to Constantinople. It was imaginative but unrealistic, as the navy could no longer support any landing force due to the presence of German submarines in the area.[124] Besides, Hamilton's mind was already turning towards the possibility of a breakout from Anzac, which would require the capture of Achi Baba to secure the position in the south. Hunter-Weston had originally requested two fresh divisions, organised as a corps, but replied to Kitchener on 17 May with his customary blend of optimism and equivocation that four divisions would be required if he was to proceed unassisted, but that the situation was daily improving and he was doing all that he could 'with the force at my disposal'.[125] For the moment, reinforcements would continue to arrive in a piecemeal manner, without any resolution to the ammunition crisis.

Hunter-Weston was now thoroughly enmeshed in a failing campaign, but as he explained to Wigram, there was nothing else for it: 'We have a difficult task no doubt, but still a simple task; we can only push straight forward'.[126]

---

123 HW Official War Diary, 11 July 1915, 48356, BL.
124 C. F. Aspinall-Oglander, *History of the Great War Based on Official Documents by Direction of the Historical Section of the Committee of Imperial Defence: Military Operations, Gallipoli. Volume II: May 1915 to the Evacuation* (London: William Heinemann, 1932), 67–8 [*OHG (2)*].
125 I. Hamilton to Lord Kitchener, 17 May 1915, Dawnay Papers, 69/21/1, IWM.
126 HW to C. Wigram, 8 June 1915, Hunter-Weston Papers, 6503/39/21, NAM.

CHAPTER TEN

A Dealer in Hope – The Last Battles

Unsuccessful generals attract few admirers. Amid the flyblown ineptitude that came to symbolise the Gallipoli campaign, Hunter-Weston is often presented as a pitiless driver of events; the man who exhausted and 'broke' the Helles army.[1] Many senior Great War commanders would suffer the erosion of their reputations after the war, but in his case the damage began while the fighting was still underway. His public persona, as well as his command decisions, fuelled this process. He was aware that he faced an able opponent, who had the advantage of superior communications by land and sea. For an advocate of the psychological battlefield, this was a painful realisation. The threat of being driven off the peninsula convinced him of two things: that a bold offensive strategy was the only viable route to survival; and that the public face of his command must be one of inspiring optimism. However, Hunter-Weston's ebullient stance, which had served as 'quite a good tonic' at the outset of the expedition, appeared increasingly out of touch as his assault on Achi Baba continued to falter.[2]

Third Attempt

After less than month on the peninsula, Hunter-Weston was promoted to Corps Commander and temporary Lieutenant-General, formally recognising the authority that he had already accumulated. He was delighted to be

---

1 James, *Gallipoli*, 234.
2 Hamilton, *Gallipoli Diary (1)*, 137.

'"a big bug" & yet feeling so entirely unlike a big bug & feeling thoroughly capable of filing the position ..."[3] This level of self-regard was not unusual, but he was also relieved that there would be no dispiriting demotion as had happened after the South African War. He wrote to Grace:

> Isn't it quaint being a Lieutenant General and an army Corps Commander? ... It hasn't taken long to go from Brigadier General and Major General to Lieut. General! No chance of reverting to the command of a brigade or even a Division at Colchester now! So you can leave Abbey House with sentimental regret only, but with a quiet mind, knowing that I could never go there now after the war ...[4]

He was grateful for the support of his 'brother Sapper', Lord Kitchener, but his promotion had, in fact, breached the normal rules of seniority and would therefore add fuel to the already combustible relations among senior officers on the peninsula.[5] For the moment, it helped that Major-General William Douglas, over whose head he had been appointed, was 'a nice little man', who expressed 'every confidence' in his new Corps Commander.[6] Another favourable factor was that he could build his own team around him. While ADCs such as Lord Archibald Montgomerie were selected for their social cachet, he ensured that his staff officers were committed professionals.[7] Both 'Cyril' Norman Macmullen (GSO2) and Claude Moore (GSO3) would go on to pursue distinguished military careers, but his closest and most controversial associate was Harold Street, 'the best of all the 29th Division staff', who became his chief staff officer.[8] Sometimes portrayed as the evil genius behind Hunter-Weston, Street was a forceful, hard-working

---

3   HW to GHW, 31 May 1915, HW Private War Diary, 48364, BL.
4   HW to GHW, 28 May 1915, HW Private War Diary, 48364, BL.
5   HW to Lord Kitchener, 31 May 1915, PRO 30/57/61, TNA.
6   HW to GHW, 31 May 1915, HW Private War Diary, 48364, BL.
7   Archibald Seton Montgomerie was heir to the 15th Earl of Eglinton: HW to I. Hamilton, 22 July 1915, Hamilton Papers, 7/1/24, LHCMA.
8   HW to GHW, 31 May 1915, HW Private War Diary, 48364, BL. Hunter-Weston did not forget Wolley Dod, whom he had strongly recommended to command the reformed 86th Brigade: GHQ War Diary, 5 June 1915: WO 95/4264, TNA. For Macmullen, see Robbins, *British Generalship*, 107–8.

and single-minded officer with considerable technical ability. As an artillery officer, he had been critical of the Navy's initial performance, but subsequently worked closely with them to improve gunnery cooperation.[9]

From the outset, Hunter-Weston was determined that VIII Corps would be more than an administrative post box. Although he was tactful in dealing with Douglas, he made no concessions in imposing his authority on subordinate commanders, establishing direct reporting lines to Corps HQ rather than GHQ.[10] He began by driving his senior officers as hard as his troops in striving to standardise training, intelligence gathering and administrative procedures, while keeping an eagle eye open for any instances of deviation and 'slacking', which he considered an abomination.[11] His eagerness for cohesion was understandable given the situation at Helles in late May. The enemy had continued to grow in strength, to the point that the allies were now facing a total Turkish force of around 15,600 men, with a further 18,500 in close reserve, as well as twenty-five batteries of artillery.[12] The Turkish battalions were well dug-in along a continuous line from east to west, with their counter-attack plans prepared and rehearsed. Meanwhile, conditions in the allied sector had become noxious and depressing. German submarine activities had increased, and the departure of the Royal Navy's battleships and transports from the coast seemed to signal that the army was now alone in its mission.[13]

It gave Hunter-Weston little satisfaction that the stalemate he had predicted had become a reality. Although he seemed optimistic that a general attack could be quickly resumed after the Second Battle of Krithia, his private summary was rather different – 'Our progress ... must remain

---

[9] Keyes, *Fight for Gallipoli*, 170. Street was killed at Ypres in 1917; for a penetrating portrait of him, see Mackenzie, *Gallipoli Memories*, 157–8.
[10] HW Official War Diary, 29 May 1915, 48356, BL.
[11] 42nd Division were typically reprimanded for circulating reports without going through Corps HQ: HW Official War Diary, 10 June 1915, 48356, BL; see also Hunter-Weston, Evidence to Dardanelles Commission, Hamilton Papers, 8/2/50, LHCMA.
[12] Erickson, *Gallipoli*, 109.
[13] HW to C. Wigram, 8 June 1915, Hunter-Weston Papers, 6503/39/21, NAM.

painfully slow; but not I hope quite so slow as in Flanders.[14] Allied hopes of a general attack only revived at the end of May. The return to an aggressive stance has been interpreted as the product of Hunter-Weston's dominance at GHQ, if not his active 'misleading' of Hamilton through 'over-optimistic' reports.[15] In reality, the dynamics were rather more complex. The new Corps Commander remained firmly committed to achieving a decisive breakthrough, thereby removing any further awkward comparisons with the Western Front. He was also buoyed up by the growing forces at his disposal. Over the previous weeks, the 29th Division had received 3,000 reinforcements and the RND presence had expanded to twelve battalions. The 42nd Division was now up to full strength, and the 52nd (Lowland) Division was also on its way.[16] Canvassing plans with him, Hamilton felt 'refreshed', but Hunter-Weston was not the only advocate for a renewed advance.[17] Another key contributor was the new French GOC, General Henri Gouraud. Arriving fresh from the Western Front, he was a forceful personality who brought new heart to the French contingent. Over a splendid dinner featuring *Sardines à la Gallipoli, Crêpes Achi Baba* and *Croutes Sedd-el-Bahr*, he and Hunter-Weston began to form a close personal and professional bond.[18] Together viewing the capture of Achi Baba as a military necessity, they also agreed on tactics, with Gouraud favouring the pivot approach.[19] As usual, the final goad to action came from Kitchener, who telegraphed Hamilton on 19 May and asked him to do his utmost 'to bring the present unfortunate state of affairs in the Dardanelles to as early a conclusion as possible.'[20]

The final decision to resume the offensive was taken at a GHQ conference aboard the *Arcadian* on 31 May. Most of the details were subsequently hammered out at corps level. The two allied commanders pooled their

14   HW to GHW, 23 May 1915, HW Private War Diary, 48364, BL.
15   *OHG (2)*, 32, 41; James, *Gallipoli*, 210–11.
16   HW Private War Diary, 1 June 1915, 48364, BL.
17   Hamilton, *Gallipoli Diary (1)*, 254.
18   HW to GHW, 28 May 1915, HW Private War Diary, 48364, BL.
19   HW Private War Diary, 23 May 1915, 48364, BL; *OHG (2)*, 34.
20   Hamilton, *Gallipoli Diary (1)*, 236.

A Dealer in Hope – The Last Battles 181

trench warfare experience, attempting to adapt their scheme to meet the new conditions on the Helles front. The date of the general action was set for 4 June. Haste had led to failure at the First and Second Battles of Krithia, but there was now time to minimise the risks of an all-out attack. Street and Hunter-Weston had previously reconnoitred the coast at Y Beach in search of landing sites for a new approach on Hill 472 to turn the enemy flank, but plans for any fresh landing were quickly ruled out.[21] Instead, the focus was on limiting the distance between VIII Corps' existing line and the Turkish defensive positions through a series of night-time sapping operations and small-scale advances.

Intelligence gathering intensified, telephonic communications were checked and detailed trench maps and assault schedules were drawn up. The supply of munitions still presented the toughest challenge. With only three days to go until the offensive, Hunter-Weston protested to GHQ that no HE reserves existed at Imbos for his howitzers or 18 pounders; artillery ammunition was therefore carefully husbanded, with the daily expenditure per battery limited to less than ten rounds.[22] The training of his troops was also prioritised. The 125th brigade had been 'blooded' on 6 May, but had soon become demoralised.[23] His previous experience of Territorial units had convinced him that such young soldiers were good raw material, but lacked combat experience. One of his first acts as Corps Commander had therefore been to insist that regular officers were placed as mentors among the 42nd Division.[24] Marshall, who was personally despatched to instruct Brigadier Noel Lee of the 127th Manchester Brigade, bridled at this 'unpleasant' duty, but it was a sensible precaution; the brigade was to have a substantial role in the new attack, and not all senior Territorial officers were of Lee's quality.[25]

---

21 HW Private War Diary, 16 May 1915, 48364, BL.
22 HW Official War Diary, 1 June 1915, 48356, BL; Forman, Evidence to the Dardanelles Commission, CAB 193/29, TNA.
23 HW Private War Diary, 6 May 1915, 48364, BL; Marshall, *Four Fronts*, 62.
24 HW Private War Diary, 24 May 1915, 48364, BL.
25 Marshall, *Four Fronts*, 77–9. One of the division's other brigades was later considered so 'dangerously bad' that it was divided up for the purposes of retraining:

The plan which was ultimately devised by Hunter-Weston and Gouraud sacrificed depth for a broad forward movement. The two French Divisions were to make a concentrated assault on the high ground overlooking Kereves Dere; on their left, the RND and 42nd Division were originally to be asked to take the Turkish forward positions by attacking on a front of over 2,000 yards, but Corps HQ subsequently extended their objectives to include the enemy support line, which lay on higher ground to the rear; meanwhile, the 29th Division were ordered to capture three lines of trenches on either side of Gully Ravine, the most ambitious target of the day. The plan was systematic and single-minded in approach, but it also attempted to build in measures to exploit success, including Hunter-Weston's favourite 90-degree pivot to take Krithia. The allies had a combined total of 24,000 troops at their disposal for the attack, with a reserve of 10,000 scattered through the southern end of the peninsula. Their assault troops were organised in two waves, followed by 'mopping-up' parties; the plan even included the novelty of armoured cars, which were to force their way along the Krinthia road.[26]

Hunter-Weston was joined at Helles by a new artillery commander, the 'very young and very lucky' Brigadier Hugh Simpson-Baikie, who had been specially requested by Hamilton.[27] However, the new team still had much to learn about the tactics of close artillery support. Special artillery arrangements were also devolved to the corps, but Hunter-Weston's attempts at innovation were sensibly brushed aside by Braithwaite. He had proposed a 6 p.m. attack to allow pursuit of the enemy, while denying time for counter-attacks, and also suggested that the naval artillery should fall silent five minutes before the advance, with the other guns shifting to targets in the rear two minutes before zero hour. With only limited faith in the accuracy of the guns, he argued that this would act as a warning to

---

Hunter-Weston, Evidence to Dardanelles Commission, Hamilton Papers, 8/2/50, LHCMA; HW to W. Braithwaite, 25 June 1915, Hamilton Papers 7/1/21, LHCMA.
26   Hunter-Weston asked for a further four of these to be landed: GHQ War Diary, 1 June 1915, WO 95/4264.
27   Milward Diary, 30 May to 2 June 1915, 6510/143/4, NAM; I. Hamilton to J. Hamilton, 13 March 1915, Simpson-Baikie Papers, GB99, LHCMA.

A Dealer in Hope – The Last Battles 183

the infantry to 'get ready', ensuring that there would be no hesitation in rushing forward at the exact hour of the assault.[28] The cessation of naval fire was approved by GHQ, but the evening assault and the barrage lift were vetoed on the grounds that the latter would signal to the enemy that the attack was about to begin while denying artillery cover at the most crucial stage of the action.[29] Instead, the four-hour bombardment was timed for noon, with a ten-minute pause at 11.20 a.m., designed to encourage the Turks to rush into their trenches and expose their artillery positions, at which point the allied guns were planned to blast them to destruction. Guns and ammunition were limited, but in addition to navy firepower, the two British howitzer batteries and seventy other artillery pieces would be supplemented by six French 75mm batteries, whose fire-rate and HE shell were considered perfect for high-speed demoralisation.

It was hoped that two ingredients would lead to victory on 4 June – a powerful and accurate barrage and interlocking success along the line of attack. From his new observation dugout on Hill 138, Hunter-Weston and his staff watched the guns open up all along the line, 'a wonderful sight', but as the first line of infantry dashed out of their trenches, they were obscured by smoke and dust – only the bayonets of the Lancashire Territorials could be seen on the right advancing along the road, while a number of the armoured cars were already being held up by barricades.[30] For all its fury, the bombardment was unimpressive by Western Front standards and its results were patchy.[31] The Third Battle of Krithia would follow the usual pattern: a hopeful morning followed by a frustrating afternoon. For the French, things immediately began to go wrong, as the opposing trenches in their sector were too close to allow adequate covering fire. Raked by rifles and machine-guns, their assault battalions suffered 2,000 casualties

---

28 Hunter-Weston Memorandum, 29 June 1915, GHQ War Diary, 95/4264, TNA.
29 W. Braithwaite to HW, 29 May 1915, GHQ War Diary, 95/4264, TNA.
30 HW Private War Diary, 24 May 1915, 48364, BL; Milward Diary, 4 June 1915, 6510/143/4, NAM.
31 Forman, Evidence to the Dardanelles Commission, CAB 19/29, NRA; Simpson-Baikie, manuscript notes on artillery situation at Helles, Hamilton Papers, 7/10/2, LHCMA.

in a few minutes, ending their participation in the battle almost as soon as it had started. In contrast, the advance on the RND front started well, as here the French 75s had been able to demolish the shallow enemy forward positions. The 2nd Naval Brigade were able to take their first objective, but by the time the Collingwood Battalion moved up in extended order to attack the support line, the full effects of the French collapse to the right were beginning to be felt. Exposed to deadly fire from this flank, the battalion simply ceased to exist. Their RND colleagues pushed on to gain their second objective, but continued pressure from the right drove them back to their original starting point. In less than forty-five minutes, then, the division had lost sixty officers and over 1,000 men.[32] Elsewhere, in the centre of the advance where the howitzer barrage had been focussed, impressive gains had been made and maintained. By 12.42 p.m., the 42nd Division reported that their second attacking line had gone past their second objective, assisted by three of the armoured cars.[33] To their left, the KOSBs were swept by unsuppressed machine-gun fire as they tried to advance, but elsewhere the 88th Brigade achieved strong local successes, with some advanced units penetrating the Turkish defence system and able to dig in just 500 yards south of Krithia. These gains were balanced by the complete failure of the Indian Brigade's attack on the left flank, where a shrapnel barrage had been considered sufficient to deal with the trenches on Gully Spur. Again, the assault battalions were driven back to their start lines with heavy casualties.

The information coming from the battlefield that afternoon was the most accurate and complete of the campaign to date, but this did not simplify the problems facing Hunter-Weston and Gouraud. How many of their reserve battalions should they commit, and where? Should they exploit the gains in the centre, or regain the momentum on the flanks? Their opportunities for risk-taking were limited as their reserves were too precious to be committed en masse in one last throw. Instead, Hunter-Weston fed

32 Major-General Paris, Report on Operations on 4th June, 6 June 1915: RND War Diary, WO 95/4290, TNA.
33 HW Official War Diary, 4 June 1915, 48356, BL.

A Dealer in Hope – The Last Battles

in individual units at various points during the afternoon in the hope of pressing home the advances on the flanks. On the right, three battalions from the 1st Naval Brigade were released in turn for a joint attack with the French, but when Gouraud admitted at 5 p.m. that his men were in no condition to renew the offensive, Hunter-Weston was forced to cancel his orders, instead instructing the Hawke battalion to extend in order to make contact with the flank of the 42nd Division which had been badly exposed by the collapse of the RND.[34] Similarly, three battalions from Corps Reserve were despatched to the Indian Brigade and 88th Brigade sectors, but no further progress was possible along Gully Spur. The Territorials held on for the moment, but after facing counter-attacks on three sides for over an hour, they were forced to withdraw to only 500 yards from their original starting line. This represented the maximum gain of the day, in a battle that had cost 4,500 casualties from a total of 16,000 VIII Corps troops who had been engaged.[35]

The decision to reinforce the flank attacks was consistent the battle's original aim of engaging the enemy along a broad front. Pushing ahead in the centre risked damaging enfilading fire, as the Collingwood experience demonstrated only too clearly. Hunter-Weston's approach might have lacked flexibility, but few Western Front generals in 1915 would have done much differently.[36] Prior is quite correct to identify that the central flaw in his decision-making was his continued conviction that infantry attacks could redeem artillery failure.[37] On a broader level, it is more debatable whether advancing to capture Krithia would have had turned the sagging fortunes of the allied campaign. This action might have helped to roll up the rest of the Turkish line, but as the main Turkish reserves were not yet committed, this is unlikely. Indeed, the vicious and persistent counter-attacks launched over the next two days suggest that Hunter-Weston would have been pursuing anything but a beaten enemy.[38]

---

34   *OHG (2)*, 51–2.
35   *OHG (2)*, 53.
36   Robbins, *British Generalship*, 29–30.
37   Prior, *Gallipoli*, 152.
38   Erickson, *Gallipoli*, 110; Steele and Hart, *Defeat at Gallipoli*, 198.

For once, he admitted disappointment at the outcome of his 'big fight'. Unusually for one who was usually liberal in praise for his troops, he turned some of the blame on the RND who, 'being ill trained and their officers being killed ... did not know how to hold on to the trenches they had gained'.[39] More importantly, the battle confirmed his view of artillery as the key determinant of battlefield success. Given that HE ammunition was critically lacking, he realised that he must not be 'over-sanguine' in his expectations of what could be gained from future attacks, reverting to his earlier view that the campaign would be 'a long slow job'.[40] These perspectives were anchored in his more general pessimism that the war in Europe could only be won by a 'gradual attrition', for which 'more men, more big guns, especially more ammunition' were needed.[41]

It was against this background that a new tactical formula was generated by the Hunter-Weston and Gouraud partnership, with, 'every effort being directed towards gaining ground, killing Turks, or both'.[42] During June, they began to plan a series of small-scale operations aimed at seizing favourable tactical positions; planning continued after the seriously wounded Gouraud was replaced by General Maurice Bailloud in early July. The targets were the trench networks crowning the high ground on each flank, where previous attacks had failed. Two independent assaults were to be launched, with the possibility of a third to bring the centre into line. These actions were to be shaped by the limited resources available, with the central idea of concentrating massed artillery on a narrow front and forcing the Turks to launch costly counter-attacks in an effort to gain lost ground – essentially, this was a version of the 'bite and hold' approach pioneered earlier that spring on the Western Front. Some commentators have found it difficult to credit Hunter-Weston with any capacity for innovation, but in fact, this was a genuinely pragmatic response to a critical situation.[43] As

39 HW to GHW, 8 June 1915, HW Private War Diary, 48364, BL.
40 HW to GHW, 5 June 1915, HW Private War Diary, 48364, BL.
41 HW to GHW, 11 June 1915, HW Private War Diary, 48364, BL.
42 C. Macmullen to GOCs Divisions, 9 July 1915, HW Official War Diary, 48356, BL.
43 Travers credits Hamilton with this evolution to 'rational' thinking, drawing on inspiration from Birdwood: *Gallipoli*, 104–5. For his part, Marshall suggests that

A Dealer in Hope – The Last Battles

he later explained, the scope of every operation had to be carefully crafted through careful calculations of artillery and manpower:

> It was a very pretty, a very difficult and a very interesting problem in each attack to determine how much length of trench could be attacked with the ammunition available and the men available. On each occasion the attack was made with the full amount that could be done with the means at our command, and leaving the reserves of men and ammunition at a very low amount.[44]

By forcing the Turks to give ground and readdressing the balance of casualties, these attacks offered a new method for prosecuting the offensive in the south. They promised 'good progress without inordinate loss', but ironically for Hunter-Weston, they also cemented the charges of callousness and incompetence that were beginning to dog his reputation.[45]

Death and Glory

The ferocious criticism directed at senior officers was a symptom of the weariness and disillusionment that had come to dominate the battered army at Helles. Under constant shellfire by day and obliged to work all night on fatigue parties, any lingering Homeric pretensions for the Gallipoli expedition were dispelled by the news that preparations were being made to withstand Turkish gas attacks.[46] The campaign that had begun as an alternative to the Western Front had now begun to follow the same pitiless

---

    he personally tried to persuade Hunter-Weston to adopt 'bite and hold' tactics after the Third Battle of Krithia, apparently with no success: *Four Fronts*, 87.
44 Hunter-Weston, Evidence to Dardanelles Commission, Hamilton Papers, 8/2/50, LHCMA.
45 *OHG (2)*, 73.
46 HW to C. Wigram, 8 June 1915, Hunter-Weston Papers, 6503/39/21, NAM. See Yigal Sheffy, 'The Chemical Dimension of the Gallipoli Campaign: Introducing Chemical Warfare to the Middle East', *War in History* 12/3 (2005), 278–317.

and relentless logic. Lieutenant Douglas Talbot of the Lancashire Fusiliers, who had once found the enterprise 'so toppingly original', finally grasped the scale of casualties when going through the 'killed bag', signing off mail intended for dead colleagues – 'Why must we throw so many noble lives away as if they were dirt?'.[47]

Hunter-Weston had joined the MEF with the reputation of being 'more popular with men than officers'.[48] While many ordinary soldiers may have preferred to believe the best of the lofty figures on whom their lives depended, the officer corps at Gallipoli was rather more critical. Drawing on a varied cross section of men from civilian life, it was a particularly vocal and articulate body, including a number of serving members of parliament.[49] Shortly before he was killed in action in August, Captain Harold Cawley MP wrote to his father. The analysis that he offered of a bloody, mishandled campaign was becoming common currency on the peninsula:

> The curse of the whole show had been the absurd optimism of the chief generals, particularly Ian Hamilton and Hunter-Weston, and the way they have under-rated their opponents. The first force here was ludicrously inadequate ... the landing was a magnificent feat of arms, thought the planning was nothing to boast about. Then after the landing the men were hurled forwards time after time to the attack ... There was an attack almost every day for a fortnight and at the end of that time there was not much of the 29th Division left.[50]

According to Captain Cawley, Hamilton was 'a popinjay and no soldier', and he reserved his worst venom for his commanding officer, Major-General Douglas – 'the most contemptible man I have ever met'. Hunter-Weston did not escape either; in Cawley's view, '[he] was a breezy optimist, a fighting man and keen, but he poured out his men's blood like water without turning a hair and did not make a success of it'.

Hunter-Weston's limitations were not only rehearsed in private. War correspondents had become a powerful group at Gallipoli, and among

47   A. D. Talbot to D. Turle, 24 May 1915, 13493, IWM.
48   Orlo Williams Diary, 15 April 1915, 69/78/1, IWM.
49   Archibald Paris to Mrs C. Pilkington, 10 April 1915, DS/MISC/57, IWM.
50   H. T. Cawley to F. Cawley, n.d., GB 0099, LHCMA.

them, the charismatic British journalist Ellis Ashmead-Bartlett stood out as one of the campaign's most trenchant critics. After the Third Battle of Krithia, he became a conduit for every form of gossip among the MEF, some of it later featuring in his testimony at the Dardanelles Commission. Some of his most compelling 'evidence' came from Lieut.-Colonel Leslie Orme Wilson MP, who commanded the Hawke Battalion of the RND. Although his battalion had not actually taken part in the initial assault on 4 June, Wilson gave what had become the accepted version of events among his colleagues: 'He declared that none of Hunter Weston's orders were ever intelligible and always had to be changed or modified, or ignored. He could never give a definite objective for an attack but would end up every order with "Go as far as you can and then entrench". He described the battle of June 4th as a cold-blooded massacre'.[51]

It is difficult to know how far Hunter-Weston aware of this growing criticism; he certainly offered no acknowledgement of it in his diary or personal correspondence. Nor is it likely that his staff drew it to his attention; Street later insisted that relations between Corps HQ and the fighting troops 'were always what is best expressed perhaps by the term "a happy family"'.[52] However, the generally corrosive effect of life at Gallipoli was more difficult to ignore. Hunter-Weston assured Wigram for the King's benefit that his men were 'cheery as sand boys', but his correspondence also revealed a more fatalistic grasp of the campaign's impact on morale and wellbeing:

> The ding-dong fighting & constant exposure to fire day and night has an effect on most men's nerves ... Lack of sleep is the most serious cause of trouble. Insomnia is a fatal enemy. The interaction of mind and body is interesting. When men get really physically exhausted to near the limit of human endeavour almost every man's mind & strength will go & some become gibbering idiots ... On the other hand there are men with such force of will and character that though they are physically exhausted to that degree that it is impossible for folk in time of peace ever to imagine, yet by

---

51 Ashmead-Bartlett, Evidence to the Dardanelles Commission, Hamilton Papers, 8/2/6, LHCMA.
52 Street, Evidence to Dardanelles Commission, CAB 19/31, TNA.

their force of character they can keep going ... Such men are worth much to their country & and fortunately we have many, though alas most of them get killed off.[53]

Hunter-Weston had always fully embraced the Napoleonic maxim that a leader should be a 'dealer in hope'. In other words, in a critical situation it was vital to display confidence, whether genuine or not. Although he could no longer intervene directly on the battlefield, his heroic command style survived in his attempts to inspire by example. Searching for honour and nobility in the charnel house of Gallipoli, he was anxious to reward examples of individual gallantry. Douglas Talbot and his officer colleagues, for example, were invited to spend the evening at Hunter-Weston's HQ, where he told them that 'every man should have a VC, if they had their rights'.[54] There were fewer opportunities for personal contact with his men, but he remained energetic in visiting the trenches and addressing units who had been withdrawn to the rest areas.[55] His uplifting remarks, calculated to build morale, were often reported in local newspapers, in which the idioms of heroic warfare – 'glorious victories' and 'bayonets gleaming in the moonlight' – struck an inspiring note for home front audiences.[56] Back at Helles, the gap between rhetoric and reality was more obvious. Here, when Corps Orders declared that 'every life has been given for our Country, and our continued progress is a witness that they have not been given in vain', bemused scepticism was the response.[57] Hunter-Weston also made the mistake of exposing Ashmead-Bartlett to his personal brand of bracing cheeriness. He welcomed the journalist to his HQ on a number of occasions, unreservedly discussing his hopes for taking Achi Baba and begging him to encourage the troops by talking to them when he went

---

53 HW to C. Wigram, 8 June 1915, Hunter-Weston Papers, 6503/39/21, NAM.
54 A. D. Talbot to D. Turle, 27 May 1915, 13493, IWM. For the Corps Commander's determination to ride to the firing line to personally present the DSO to Lieut.-Colonel J. T. R. Wilson of the 5/Royal Scots, see Mackenzie, *Gallipoli Memories*, 159.
55 HW Private War Diary, 14, 16 June 1915, 48364, BL.
56 *Aberdeen Free Press*, 9 June 1915; *Daily News*, 11 June 1915; *Irish News*, 11 June 1915; *Ardrossan and Saltcoats Herald*, 9 July 1915.
57 Army Corps Order No. 10, 5 July 1915, HW Official War Diary, 48356, BL.

round the front lines. Characteristically, the journalist told him he would do his best, although it was 'not easy to look very gay, with hundreds of shells and thousands of bullets jeopardising one's existence morning, noon and night'.[58] Restrained by a fear of libel, his published verdict was of 'a most charming man to meet', who was 'invariably unhappy in his prognostications', but in his private diary (which did not remain very private), the journalist branded Hunter-Weston as the 'giggling butcher' and as 'a perfectly incompetent commander', who threw away lives 'in the most wicked and reckless manner'.[59]

It is indeed Hunter-Weston's attitude to casualties at Gallipoli that has done most to secure his notoriety as 'the Butcher of Helles'. There are two related accusations. The first is that he inflicted unnecessary casualties; the second is that his attitude towards them was one of callous indifference. He was hardly alone among the British military establishment in subscribing to the doctrine of offensive action while believing that modern firepower made heavy losses inevitable.[60] At Gallipoli, the lack of artillery support made crossing the fire zone particularly deadly, but in his set piece battles Hunter-Weston calculated 'acceptable casualties' by balancing the greater losses that might result if the Turks were not driven from their positions. The renewal of failed frontal attacks at Second Krithia was one of the bloodiest demonstrations of this grim method of arithmetic. His new 'bite and hold' approach may have involved a recalibration of the relationship between firepower and infantry support, but the battles of June and July were driven by the same reasoning. He believed that the expedition was still finely balanced between success and failure. Victory was only possible if the government were willing to commit sufficient reinforcements and munitions, while his depleted and demoralised troops could easily be entirely swept off the peninsula if the enemy was able to punch through two or three miles. His fears were not unrealistic. Despite heavy losses and

---

58 Ellis Ashmead-Bartlett, *The Uncensored Dardanelles* (London: Hutchinson, 1920), 138.
59 Ashmead-Bartlett Diary, 24 July 1915, Mitchell Library, State Library of New South Wales: (http://acms.sl.nsw.gov.au/_transcript/2014/D24757/a6833.html).
60 Senior, *Lieutenant General Sir Richard Hacking*, 246–7.

similar deficiencies in artillery and munitions, the Turks remained equally committed to the spirit of the offensive. After reorganising their forces in mid-June, they continued to apply pressure by pounding the slender beachheads with their medium and heavy artillery by day and undertaking trench raids by night.[61]

Even if the tactical situation was unfavourable, Hunter-Weston argued that they simply could not afford to be quiescent. As he explained to the Dardanelles Commission: 'when people who know very little about it say "frontal attacks are dangerous and lose life", you have to say to them: "that depends on the circumstances" if you do not attack you will be attacked; if you do not keep up the morale of your men by the offensive you will certainly be defeated.'[62] The difficulty with this argument, however genuinely it was held, is that rather than raising morale, such attacks often appeared fruitless to the men on the spot.[63] Even from his vantage point at GHQ, Captain Jack Churchill fully realised this. Despite being an admirer of Hunter-Weston, he wrote resignedly to his brother Winston in early July: 'These continued frontal attacks are terrible and I fear that the Generals will be called butchers by the troops. H. W. [Hunter-Weston] already has that reputation with the 29th ... I suppose it cannot be helped.'[64]

Continuing the offensive also placed further strain on Hunter-Weston's relationships with his divisional and brigade commanders, a group who had already become increasingly irritated by his intrusive and censorious command style. His frustration with their equivocation shaped the description he offered Hamilton of his ideal commander – one who could push on unceasingly, 'without any regard to the yelping of subordinate commanders for reinforcements and to their cry that men are dead with fatigue'.[65]

As Corps Commander, the pressure involved in sending men to kill and be killed was enormous. However, the desensitisation process that

61 *OHG (2)*, 78.
62 Hunter-Weston, Evidence to Dardanelles Commission, Hamilton Papers, 8/2/50, LHCMA.
63 Creighton, *With the 29th Division*, 117.
64 Churchill and Gilbert, *Churchill: 1914–16. Companion*, 1073.
65 HW to I. Hamilton, 11 August 1915, Hamilton Papers, 7/1/33, KGL.

A Dealer in Hope – The Last Battles

enabled him to take difficult decisions had already begun in France, where the process of attrition had destroyed his brigade. This experience became an important reference point in his coming to terms with the scale of casualties at Gallipoli. He wrote to his wife after the Second Battle of Krithia:

> the survivors; viz of the infantry 90 officers and 4891 other ranks, out of 312 officers and 12000 other ranks. That is all I have left; much less than ⅓ of my infantry officers & only a little more than a third of my infantry NCOs and men. A heavy toll; but no heavier than that paid my beloved 11th Infantry Brigade; of them, I lost 5000 out of 4000, about 1⅓ times as much as my original strength. But that was over a much longer time. In the one day's landing and subsequent fighting for 24 hours I lost nearly half my infantry. Glorious fellows ...[66]

Deeply sentimental about his soldiers, command of a larger formation at Gallipoli may also have helped to shield Hunter-Weston from the consequences of his orders, as casualties became the comfortingly abstract 'glorious fellows'. Other senior commanders, such as Sir John French, were never able to develop this level of personal detachment when ordering attacks with limited fire support, but in the challenging context of the peninsula Hunter-Weston believed that such diffidence was dangerous.[67] As a result, a willingness to attack at all costs, regardless of likely casualties, became a part of his leadership style which sat uncomfortably with his joviality and paternalism in person. Above all, his defiant eagerness to expound these views created the image of a general who had sacrificed his humanity in the pursuit of victory. One familiar anecdote from Marshall's memoirs is an exchange in the run up to the Third Battle of Krithia. Marshall was still mentoring Lee's brigade and was reluctant to have them sap forward into an exposed position close to the enemy trenches. Hunter-Weston insisted that he follow orders, and when the operation succeeded, came up personally to congratulate the brigade. Marshall takes up the story – 'He said: "There you are! You see the thing has been done with no casualties." I gently murmured "Fifty" to which he retorted: "Well, that's nothing, it

---

66   HW to GHW, 15 May 1915, HW Private War Diary, 48364, BL.
67   Holmes, *Little Field Marshal*, 278.

would have been worth doing if you had five hundred".[68] Given that object of the operation was to reduce losses in the main assault the next day, such ruthless posturing was quite unwise and unnecessary.

Marshall was no friend of Hunter-Weston, but it was the Corps Commander's performance in the presence of a much more sympathetic listener, the novelist Compton Mackenzie, that did him even greater long-term damage. Attached to GHQ, the urbane 'Monty' was sent by Hamilton to VIII Corps HQ in June to help compile intelligence reports. As with Marshall's account, his narrative was retrospective in that it was written once Hunter-Weston's sanguinary reputation had already become established. As an enthusiastic amateur, the bubbling, singing, booming Corps Commander, the apparent epitome of a 'real soldier', fascinated him. He found his HQ a paradox. Hunter-Weston was concerned for his comforts; champagne was freely available and the food in the mess tent was far superior to camp rations (indeed, one happy product of his friendly relationship with Gouraud had been the chance to employ a French chef).[69] But far from the cosy, insulated image of high command, there was no escape from the masses of flies or the heavy shelling that tortured the rest of the army. Prior to Mackenzie's arrival at Hunter-Weston Hill, a new dug-out had been excavated for the general's mess for when the bombardments became too fierce. When Hunter-Weston's orderly brought in a small spent shell, he was on hand to capture the general's remarkable table talk:

> 'Hullo, hullo!' shouted Hunter-Bunter at the top of his voice. 'What's this little woofer? What a nice little chap. How did he get in?'
> 'Came in through the side, sir' the orderly replied indignantly, pointing to the narrow slit below the roof that let in the light.
> 'How jolly! Dear little chap! Came to give us a house warming. What is there for lunch? Ham! Beef! Capital!'[70]

68   Marshall, *Four Fronts*, 189.
69   HW Private War Diary, 9 June 1915, 48364, BL. After enduring bully beef for three months, Dr George Davidson, RAMC 89th Field Ambulance, was entranced by his visit to VIII Corps HQ where he was treated to cocktails made by Hunter-Weston's ADC: *The Incomparable 29th*, 128.
70   *Gallipoli Memories*, 159. See HW Private War Diary, 23 June 1915, 48364, BL.

A Dealer in Hope – The Last Battles   195

His boisterous good humour was less in evidence during a visit by Major-General Paris. Hunter-Weston enthusiastically briefed him on a successful action that had recently taken place:

> 'Many casualties?' asked General Paris in a voice that could not hide the bitterness he felt over the losses of his own splendid Division. And as I think of General Hunter-Weston's reply I fancy I see a falcon strike angrily at some grizzled trusty old dog.
> 'Casualties?' he cried eyes flashing, aquiline nose quivering. 'What do I care for casualties?'
> The other rose from his chair.
> 'I must be getting back,' he growled.
> 'You'll stay to tea?'
> 'No, thanks.'[71]

Returning to the peninsula on a commemorative pilgrimage almost twenty years later, Hunter-Weston's retort remained a bitter memory for Paris.[72] Yet, for Mackenzie, these were the thoughts of a 'logician of war' rather than a 'mere butcher', who spoke from the conviction that casualties were of no consequence provided that the planned objective was gained – 'Actually', he commented, 'no man I have met brimmed over more richly with human sympathy'.[73]

New Methods – New Enemies

Hunter-Weston's geniality was fully restored by the arrival of the first troops from the 52nd Division who began to disembark at Helles in early June. He was already well acquainted with this Territorial unit, which was

---

71   *Gallipoli Memories*, 151–2.
72   IWM interview 8201: Joseph Murray (Hood Btn. RND).
73   *Gallipoli Memories*, 152.

recruited from across the Scottish lowlands.[74] Among the first arrivals from 155th Brigade were twenty neighbours from the village of West Kilbride, including some young men among their number who had grown up on the Hunterston estate. Hunter-Weston had them marched from the rest camp for tea at his HQ and regaled them with selections from his gramophone.[75]

The presence of the Division's GOC, Major-General Granville Egerton, was rather less congenial. Another enthusiastic contributor to Hunter-Weston's 'butcher' image, his acerbic diaries and post-war correspondence have been accepted uncritically by later historians who have portrayed him as a caring officer damned by Hunter-Weston for protesting at the handling of his men.[76] In fact, 'the Duke' was a rather more complex character who elicited strong reactions from his colleagues. He had served in colonial campaigns from Afghanistan to the Sudan, and although he claimed not to covet Hunter-Weston's command, he was taken aback that his Corps Commander, six years his junior, had risen so quickly.[77] An officer of the old school, he found it difficult to adjust to conditions at Gallipoli. Mackenzie found him 'a man of much charm and fine courtliness', but Arthur Lynden-Bell, who knew Egerton from his service with the Lowland Division before the war, considered him 'just the pestilential type of fellow who ought to be eliminated with a firm hand from our army'.[78] He was already 'very seedy and full of indigestion' when he arrived

---

74   Earlier in his career, he and Grace had spoken of the 52nd as a pleasant command, as its Glasgow HQ would have been convenient for Hunterston: HW Private War Diary, HW to GHQ, 10 June 1915, 48364, BL.
75   HW to C. Wigram, 6 May 1915, Hunter-Weston Papers, 6503/39/21, NAM; *Largs and Millport Weekly News*, 10 July 1915. He later made two brothers from the estate orderlies at his HQ: HW to GHW, 11 June 1915, HW Private War Diary, 48364, BL.
76   James, *Gallipoli*, 231. He left two diaries: a short manuscript diary, compiled while on the peninsula (Acc.1669/10, NLS) and a later typescript version which incorporated material from his letters and was sprinkled with bitter marginal comments made seventeen years after the events described (CAB 45/249, TNA).
77   Egerton Diary, 24 June 1915, CAB 45/249, TNA.
78   *Gallipoli Memories*, 166–7; E. Girdwood to S. Hare 17 July 1915; A. Lynden-Bell to S. Hare, 2 August 1915, Hare Papers, 66/85/1, IWM. Lynden-Bell was a friend of Hunter-Weston's from their time together at Staff College.

A Dealer in Hope – The Last Battles

at Helles, prompting Hunter-Weston to give him his own bed to sleep in, but his relationship with this 'real good Samaritan' deteriorated sharply over the next few weeks.[79]

Egerton's advent coincided with the successful French assault on Kereves Dere Ravine on 21 June, the first stage of the new limited operations approach. Hunter-Weston was 'proud as a dog with two tails' at this vindication of concentrated artillery support; in the spirit of competitive emulation, he was also ready to mount his own operation on the left of the line.[80] He entrusted planning for the infantry component of the action to the new commander of the 29th Division, Beauvoir De Lisle, whom he considered by far the best of his divisional commanders.[81] A welcome face from Flanders, De Lisle was already well known as another 'thruster' who did not allow his first negative impressions of the military situation to influence his outwardly aggressive persona.[82]

The action sought to advance astride Gully Ravine to outflank the enemy in front of Krithia. As well as his own division, De Lisle was given the 156th Brigade from the 52nd Division. His plan was to use the 29th to capture the deep and heavily wired 'J' trenches which criss-crossed Gully Ravine, while the Territorials would seize the first two 'H' trench lines at Fir Tree Spur on the right. This division of labour posed one of Hunter-Weston's 'interesting problems' for artillery support, which remained the responsibility of VIII Corps HQ. The supply of guns and munitions was still severely limited. Except for the 640 rounds of HE ammunition fired off during the 4 June battle, no further HE shells had arrived until the end of July; nor were the French able to assist.[83] Hunter-Weston was concerned that the original plan did not allot enough artillery to the 156th Brigade sector, but as only a finite amount of resources were available,

---

79 Egerton Diary, 21 June 1915, CAB 45/249, TNA.
80 Davidson, *Incomparable 29th*, 109.
81 HW to I. Hamilton, 7 July 1916, Hamilton Papers, 7/7/16, LHCMA.
82 Henry de Beauvoir De Lisle, 'My Narrative of the Great German War', vol. 1, 75, GB99/1, LHCMA; Egerton Diary, 22 June 1915, CAB 45/249, TNA; Churchill and Gilbert, *Churchill: 1914–16. Companion*, 1073.
83 Simpson-Baikie notes, Hamilton Papers, 7/10/2, LHCMA.

Simpson-Baikie assured him that reducing the bombardment of the trenches on the left would prejudice success at the most vital point, where resistance was likely to be strongest. Prior finds it puzzling that Hunter-Weston did not simply shorten the front of the attack and spare the Territorials their baptism of fire, but he calculated that both sides of the ravine needed to be cleared to secure the position and avoid enfilading counter-attacks.[84] The 156th Brigade, who landed on 14 June, had only had a relatively brief period of acclimatisation to front-line conditions, but Hunter-Weston considered them stronger than most of the brigades from the 42nd Division, and certainly better than the RND; his only worry was that their Brigadier, W. Scott-Moncrieff, might not stand the strain.[85]

The two-hour bombardment opened at 9 a.m., with predictable results. On the right, the concentration of howitzers, French mortars and 'accurate and efficient' naval gunfire practically destroyed the first two Turkish trench lines.[86] Advancing a thousand yards, Marshall's men met their objectives, while Wolley Dod's 86th Brigade passed through them as planned to capture the eastern bank of Gully Ravine.[87] On the left, apart from one French howitzer on loan, the 156th Brigade attack relied on 4½ batteries of 18 pounders, which were only able to fire shrapnel. Even the division's antiquated howitzer battery that had seen service at Omdurman was diverted for use in the 29th Division sector.[88] The attack met with heavy resistance, but while the 1/4th and 1/7th Royal Scots battalions were able to push on, the rest of the brigade who were advancing on the right, led personally by Scott-Moncrieff, were cut to pieces. Their losses for the day amounted to 1,353 officers and men killed, missing and wounded.[89]

---

84 Prior, *Gallipoli*, 155.
85 HW to W. Braithwaite, 25 June 1915, Hamilton Papers, 7/1/21, LHCMA.
86 HW to Admiral J. De Robeck, 28 June 1915, De Robeck Papers, DRBK 4/43, CCC.
87 HW Private War Diary, 28 June 1915, 48364, BL.
88 Forman, Evidence to the Dardanelles Commission, CAB 12/29, TNA; R. R. Thompson, *The Fifty-Second Lowland Division, 1914–18* (Glasgow: Macklehose, Jackson & Co., 1923), 45.
89 Thompson, *Fifty-Second Lowland Division*, 67.

A Dealer in Hope – The Last Battles

Gaining ground was only the first phase of the plan; a process of attrition now followed over the next week in which repeated counter-attacks cost the Turks an estimated 10,858 casualties.[90] These tactical subtleties were lost on the 52nd division. Already resentful that the 29th Division had been given the best artillery support, they were infuriated by Hamilton's failure to acknowledge their contribution in his despatches.[91] The camaraderie that had once bound the MEF had been replaced by ongoing inter-unit rivalry, which Hunter-Weston's championing of the 'incomparable' 29th Division could only fuel.[92] Egerton, who had watched the battle from VIII Corps HQ, was depressed by his brigade's losses, bitterly commenting that 'they were lent to the 29th Division for the day and were nobody's children'.[93] When Hunter-Weston arrived with Hamilton to inspect the survivors, he could barely conceal his contempt for this 'mountebank' general.[94]

The partial success at Gully Spur caused Hunter-Weston's stock to rise at GHQ, just as Hamilton's was dwindling. Far from resenting the situation, staff officers Orlo Williams and Wyndham Deedes placed their chief confidence in the energetic 'Hunter-Bunter' and their colleague Major Guy Dawnay, in the belief that that Sir Ian 'really does nothing at all'.[95] For his own part, Hunter-Weston remained stubbornly loyal to his 'dear chief', while discreetly prodding him for promotion to the permanent rank of

90 Erickson, *Gallipoli*, 127; VIII Corps to GHQ, 2, 3 July 1915, HW Official War Diary: 48356, BL.
91 Thompson, *Fifty-Second Lowland Division*, 72–3; Capt. Weir to C. F. Aspinall, 30 April 1929; F. A. Wynter to C. F. Aspinall, 11 April 1929, CAB 45/242, TNA.
92 Jerrold, *Royal Naval Division*, 127.
93 Egerton Diary, 28 June 1915, Acc.1669/10, NLS; Egerton Diary, 1 July 1915, CAB 45/249, TNA.
94 It was at this visit that Hunter-Weston allegedly made an infamous remark describing the Territorials' exposure to battle conditions as 'blooding the pups'. The phrase came naturally to a bluff hunting man, but Egerton was infuriated by it: James, *Gallipoli*, 231; Egerton Diary, 29 June 1915, Acc.1669/10, NLS.
95 Orlo Williams Diary, 30 June 1915; 21 July 1915, 69/78/1, IWM; James, *Gallipoli*, 201. Dawnay felt 'quite in favour' at VIII Corps HQ, where he spent a large part of the time discussing operations and higher strategy with Hunter-Weston: G. P. Dawnay to C. Dawnay, 24 June 1915, Dawnay Papers, 69/21/1, IWM.

Lieutenant-General.[96] Nevertheless, his frustration over Hamilton's ineffectual lobbying for War Office resources led him to bypass GHQ in order to take direct action. In the case of new technology, this was uncontroversial; he became a prominent supporter of the experimental Stokes mortar, a three-inch, smooth-bore trench mortar which contrasted favourably with ineffectual weapons available on the peninsula.[97] A much greater career risk was involved in leaking vital statistics on the munitions shortage to Lieut.-Colonel Sir Eustace Fiennes MP, a serving RND officer. Hamilton was aghast at this. Realising it would lead to Hunter-Weston's immediate sacking, he telegraphed Fiennes requesting him not to take the matter further.[98]

Despite pressure from Bailloud, Hunter-Weston was reluctant to renew the offensive until his corps reserve was strengthened.[99] In the meantime, his divisional commanders were exhorted to undertake ruses and demonstrations with the aim of making the Turks 'really jumpy'.[100] Marshall's response was to have an 'inspecting general' paraded on a pole to draw enemy fire – the dummy bore a suspiciously close resemblance to Hunter-Weston.[101] The respite was, however, only temporary. The failure of Turkish counter-attacks in early July and a rumoured ammunition shortage seemed to offer a further opportunity to wear down the enemy on the Helles front before Hamilton's new offensive got underway in the north of the Anzac sector.

The next attack was scheduled for 12 July, with the intention of pushing the allied centre forward east of Achi Baba Nullah to align with recent gains on each flank. When medical reports made it clear that the RND

---

96 HW to S. H. Pollen, 6 July 1915, Hamilton Papers, 7/1/24, LHCMA. Hamilton had hoped to get his name on the honours list, but having been given a temporary promotion, the convention was that he could not receive further recognition until the end of the campaign.
97 Griffiths, *Battle Tactics*, 105; Simpson-Baikie notes, Hamilton Papers, 7/10/2, LHCMA.
98 I. Hamilton to HW, 11 July 1915, Hamilton Papers, 7/1/33, LHCMA.
99 HW Official War Diary, 5 July 1915, 48356, BL.
100 C. Macmullen to GOCs Divisions, 9 July 1915, HW Official War Diary, 48356, BL.
101 Marshall, *Four Fronts*, 100.

were unfit to take part, Hunter-Weston assigned the two fresh brigades of the 52nd Division to the task in their place. They were instructed to assault along a 1,000 yard front, while the French made another attack on the right of the line at Kereves Dere. As at Gully Ravine, this advance was to be shaped by the availability of artillery, but a new solution had been devised which sought to avoid any costly disparity in support. The British attack was to take place in two consecutive halves in conjunction with the French, allowing the guns to concentrate on each operation in turn. If the first attack by the 155th Brigade on the extreme right of the British line failed in the morning, the action on the left by the recently arrived 157th Brigade, scheduled for the late afternoon, was to be abandoned, but if the morning operation was an immediate success, the follow-up attack would then be pressed home at once.

Egerton was deeply resentful of Street and Hunter-Weston's 'absurdly voluminous' orders and 'positively wicked' plans, that he felt left him no autonomy in arranging operations.[102] In fact, the instructions from VIII Corps HQ were meticulous in specifying attacking formations and arrangements for consolidation, but much less precise in spelling out the actual objectives for the attack.[103] This was not entirely surprising, as the Turkish forward trench system in front of the British line was an irregular and confusing network of curves and loops, with some defences still under construction and others which had fallen into disuse. Crucially, the plan of attack incorrectly described the two long Turkish fire-trenches and the complicated and partial system of communication systems as though they were three distinctly marked and continuous lines.[104] These were assigned to the two Territorial brigades as their objective, with both of the first two attack waves ordered to occupy the enemy's 'third trench' (E12), which at most points did not in fact exist, or was at best a series of a short and

---

102 Egerton Diary, 8 July 1915, Acc.1669/10, NLS; Egerton Diary, 9, 10 July 1915, CAB 45/249, TNA; G. G. A. Egerton to C. F. Aspinall (proofs comments), 8 June 1929, CAB 45/242, TNA.
103 Memorandum, 3 July 1915, HW Official War Diary, 48356, BL. Many elements of the 12 July attack were carried over from this earlier postponed operation.
104 Thompson, *Fifty-Second Lowland Division*, 84.

shallow scrapes in the ground. By 11 July, Hunter-Weston had personally begun to doubt whether the 'third trench' was an attainable objective. New aerial photography revealed that it would offer little cover in the 157th Brigade sector, although it looked deeper and more continuous towards the right of the line. He therefore had new instructions drawn up which proposed that the new objective for the 157th brigade should be the second trench line, but that they should also establish outposts in E12 to cover its consolidation if possible. Egerton received the change of plan and an amended trench diagram from Street on the eve of the battle, along with the promise of an extra allocation of howitzers, but while he later claimed that he passed the information to his Brigade HQs, Lieut.-Colonel R. R. Thompson, the divisional historian, was firmly of the view that this was incorrect.[105] This omission would contribute to the confusion and communication breakdown that distinguished the battle.

12 July was one of the hottest days yet experienced at Gallipoli. The first indications of possible success were good. GHQ had insisted on increasing the weight of the morning bombardment, which demolished the Turkish forward trenches.[106] At 7.35 a.m., the 155th Brigade surged across no-man's land with fixed bayonets, but the real fighting began when they entered the defensive maze, in which stubborn pockets of Turkish resistance impeded their progress and made it difficult to get messages back. The 1/4th Royal Scots Fusiliers (RSF), including the West Kilbride contingent, tried in vain to wheel over the labyrinth of trenches.[107] Efforts to capture the non-existent 'third trench' also caused unnecessary casualties, with the 1/4th KOSB, who had driven even further forwards, losing 60 per cent of their

---

105 52nd Division War Diary, WO95/4318; R. R. Thompson to C. F. Aspinall, 7 July 1915. Travers suggests otherwise, but Thompson is quite unambiguous on the point: *Gallipoli*, 108.
106 HW Official War Diary, 11 July 1915 48356, BL; Forman, Evidence to the Dardanelles Commission, CAB 12/29, TNA.
107 Total RSF casualties were 368 killed and wounded. The West Kilbride men named by Hunter-Weston got off relatively lightly, with only three wounded. For an account of the battle by one of their number, Sgt. William Tyre, see *Ardrossan and Saltcoats Herald*, 20 August 1915.

A Dealer in Hope – The Last Battles 203

numbers.[108] Hunter-Weston was stationed at his usual observation post, trying in vain to control the battle by telephone. By noon, he still lacked sufficient information from the 52nd Division HQ to decide whether to mount the afternoon attack and reports continued to drift in gradually over the next hour. On the right, the French attack was held up at the first Turkish trench. Pressed by Egerton, who had already committed his reserves, Hunter-Weston finally decided that the 157th Brigade assault should go ahead, in conjunction with a renewed effort by the French and the 155th. Again, most of the first wave had no difficulty in capturing the first and support trenches, but on reaching their third objective, they found it impossible to consolidate and fell back; the French attack made slight gains, while the 155th Brigade had been too exhausted to move.

During the night, the inexperience of the Territorials began to show as some battalions began to quit their trenches. The situation was quickly stabilised by their officers, but the lurid accounts which filtered back to VIII Corps HQ coupled with a continued lack of situational reports from Egerton, convinced Hunter-Weston that there was a serious risk of losing all they had gained during the day unless 'decisive action' was taken to increase the security of the front line.[109] He now decided to call on his RND reserve, which was kept back for use in this type of emergency. Rushing to the HQs of Egerton and Brigadier Charles Trotman, who was in temporary command of the RND, he ordered that the three available battalions should attack at 4.30 p.m. and capture all the trenches from the 52nd Division's original objectives which were still in enemy hands. Given the congestion of the communication trenches with allied wounded, he suggested that they should advance 'over the top' from the original British starting position.[110]

The RND attack was a shambles. After a poorly coordinated barrage, the Chatham battalion failed to attack, while the attempts of the Portsmouth and Nelson battalions to locate and consolidate the elusive

---

108 HW Report to GHQ, 12, 13 July 1915, HW Official War Diary, 48356, BL.
109 HW Report to GHQ, 13, 14 July 1915: HW Official War Diary, 48356, BL; see also HW Official War Diary, 12 July 1915: 48356, BL.
110 *OHG (2)*, 109; G. G. A. Egerton to J. E. Edmonds, 15 December 1929, CAB 24/242. He claimed that Hunter-Weston 'merely enunciated' his plan.

third trench position cost yet more lives.[111] Hunter-Weston reported to GHQ that their failure was 'inexplicable', but in reality the attack had simply been a hasty over-reaction to inaccurate information.[112] The staff of VIII Corps, nor 52nd Division HQ had not passed on the updated trench map, nor did they seem aware that the 157th Brigade had actually already regained their lost trenches. The concentration of dead, dying and wounded in a narrow half-mile front gave this action a particularly horrifying air. Over the next two days, entire battalions remained 'missing' and little clarity could be established as to who was actually in possession of key sections of the line.[113] Ashmead-Bartlett made the most of the chaotic situation. His dramatic testimony at the Dardanelles Commission later suggested that the situation was close to a 'mutiny', with 'brigadier-generals' refusing to follow Hunter-Weston's orders, as they blamed him for the 'muddle'.[114] The version that can be pieced together from the Divisional War Diary and Douglas Jerrold's later account is, however, rather different.[115] During the night of the 13 July, attempts were made to push up the remaining RND battalions to consolidate the line and to relieve the Portsmouth Battalion and units of the 52nd Division. VIII Corps HQ postponed a further full-scale assault by the Chatham and Hawke battalions on the third-line trenches that were assumed to be in Turkish hands, but orders were issued the next night for more limited operations, which were in any case thwarted by hostile fire. Events then descended into farce. On 15 July, the Hawke and Drake battalions, under the command of Ashmead-Bartlett's 'source', Leslie Wilson, were ordered to capture 'Position P'. This was believed by Hunter-Weston's

111 Chater Account, 12 July 1915, 74/101/1, IWM; see also Brigadier Trotman's report 18 July 1915, RND War Diary, WO 95/4290, TNA.
112 HW Report to GHQ, 13, 14 July 1915: HW Official War Diary, 48356, BL; F. W. H. Walshe to C. F. Aspinall, 30 June 1930, CAB 45/245, TNA; G. P. Dawnay to C. Dawnay, 15 July 1915, Dawnay Papers, 69/21/1, IWM.
113 The mystery of the 'missing regiment' of KOSBs gave rise to some black humour at Corps HQ which would have horrified Egerton: Davidson, *Incomparable 29th*, 131.
114 Evidence to the Dardanelles Commission, Hamilton Papers, 8/2/6, LHCMA.
115 Major-General Paris, Report of Operations, 13–16 July inclusive, RND War Diary, WO 95/4290, TNA; Douglas Jerrold, *The Hawke Battalion* (London: Ernest Benn Ltd: 1925), 92–4.

A Dealer in Hope – The Last Battles 205

staff to be a critical junction point in the Turkish lines, but was actually as insubstantial as the rest of the third line. The attacking company found nothing but a small hillock, but on doing so, decided to follow orders and bomb it anyway. The Turks, who were evidently as confused as the British, also shelled the position and the assaulting parties withdrew. Honour had been satisfied, and Wilson's decision not to press on with the attack, citing the battered state of the trenches, heavy artillery fire and large enemy numbers, was formally sanctioned by his divisional commander.[116]

Egerton left a withering description of the action at Achi Baba Nullah as 'a mere nibble out of the granite front facing us, in effecting which we lost most of our front teeth.'[117] At the cost of an estimated 5,000 casualties, two Turkish trench systems had been captured, and a solid advance made of 500 yards, securing a new defensive line that gave the Helles army their best field of fire to date. Hunter-Weston regarded it as 'another battle and another success', but still craved the additional howitzers and ammunition which he felt were needed to secure a real breakthrough.[118] Although the battle had already gone on for too long, he was hopeful of 'rounding off' the advance as soon as the French were ready to provide support with their guns. Hamilton refused to sanction any further attacks, preferring to conserve his strength for the Anzac initiative.[119] Nor would he send the complementary message to the 52nd that Hunter-Weston requested to 'buck them up for their next operation'; instead, his order balanced words of praise with a warning of the need for 'grip and determination', an approach which caused further murmurings among the division.[120]

This emotionally charged battle had a suitably dramatic postscript. On the evening of 13 July, while the fighting was still in progress, Hunter-Weston

---

116 Major-General Paris, Report of Operations, 13–16 July inclusive: RND War Diary, WO 95/4290, TNA.
117 G. G. A. Egerton to J. E. Edmonds, 15 December 1915, CAB 24/242, TNA.
118 HW to GHW, 13 July 1915, HW Private War Diary, 48364, BL.
119 HW to I. Hamilton, 16 July 1915, 7/2/5, Hamilton Papers, LHCMA; Official War Diary, 17 July 1915: 48356, BL.
120 I. Hamilton to HW, 16 July 1915, 7/2/5, Hamilton Papers, LHCMA; Egerton Diary, 19 July 1915, CAB 45/249.

arrived at Egerton's heavily shelled command post. Sensing that his subordinate was 'physically done', he sent him to get a couple of night's rest on board a hospital ship.[121] He did not relieve Egerton of command, and when he went to visit him on the ship at midnight, he was confident that he would be able to return once he had sufficiently rested. Nevertheless, Egerton was amazed and horrified, lashing out in his diary: 'Hunter-Weston is an oily humbug & I think has got a down on me, I mistrust him – he may be a great soldier but men call him the murderer – I can't describe the battle ...'[122] This was far from the end of the matter. Hamilton was furious at not being consulted, but later explained to Hunter-Weston that his real concern was with regard to the impact on Egerton's authority. Knowing him well, he believed that there was 'not a grain of generous inspiration in the whole of the man from the top of his head to the sole of his foot'.[123] His ability to command depended on fear and respect, but these had now been eroded by his Corps Commander's 'helpful' act. The rest of the story does not reflect well on Hamilton. Egerton did reassume his command, but his performance in doing so continued to give cause for concern. Hamilton placed the case before Kitchener, citing an officer from GHQ who had witnessed his excitability in battle conditions; his recall was ordered as soon as soon as operational conditions permitted.[124] Egerton was distraught when the telegram finally arrived ordering him to Alexandra, blaming his downfall on the altercation with Hunter-Weston. Hamilton preferred not to disabuse him and denied any personal involvement in his sacking.[125] An excellent hater – he hoped that Winston Churchill would 'shortly die of

---

121 Egerton Diary, 12, 13, 14 July 1915, Acc.1669/10, NLS. Temporary command was handed over to Major-General 'Fred' Shaw who had recently arrived with 13th division – the same officer whom Hunter-Weston had replaced as commander of the 29th Division.
122 Egerton Diary, 12 July 1915, Acc.1669/10, NLS; A. R. Chater Account, 12, 74/101/1, IWM.
123 I. Hamilton to HW, 15 July 1915, Hamilton Papers, 7/2/5, LHCMA.
124 I. Hamilton to Lord Kitchener, 11 August 1915; Lord Kitchener to I. Hamilton, 30 August 1915, Hamilton Papers, 7/2/5, LHCMA.
125 I. Hamilton to G. G. A. Egerton, 17 September 1915, Hamilton Papers, 7/2/5, LHCMA. Egerton Diary, 15 August 1915, Acc.1669/10, NLS.

cancer' – Egerton proceeded to direct a personal vendetta against Hunter-Weston, the 'mountebank bounder', for the rest of his life.[126]

New divisions were at last arriving at the peninsula, but there was a rising note of desperation in Hunter-Weston's analysis of the tactical situation. In mid-July, he wrote to Braithwaite and Major-General C. E. Callwell, Director of Military Operations at the War Office, proposing his own version of 'all out or get out'. The next two months, he argued, would be crucial. Rather than a half-hearted balancing act, there had to an honest recognition that the Gallipoli campaign could only be supported at the expense of the allied effort in Flanders. Either the whole enterprise should be abandoned, or sufficient resources had to be diverted immediately to secure victory before the autumn storms set in. If the full amount required could not be sent, then they should cut their losses and return as many men as possible to Britain: 'the remainder of us told to stick it out (as I shall be very glad to do) and kill as many Turks as possible before we run out of ammunition'.[127]

There would be no gallant last stand for Hunter-Weston. Within days, it was rumoured that he had been forced to leave the peninsula as the result of a nervous breakdown, or even that his departure had been engineered and welcomed by Hamilton.[128] While neither was the case, his alternative account of a sudden onset of sunstroke that began on 17 July was not entirely frank either.[129] Apart from a slight chill that worsened his throat condition, his physical health had been robust during the campaign, although he had visibly aged after almost three months on the peninsula.[130] Early on the morning of 11 July, a doctor had been called in as Hunter-Weston had

---

126 Egerton Diary, 22 July 1915, CAB 45/249. Egerton never held a front-line command again. His wrath also extended to Simpson-Baikie, whom he accused of inaccuracies in his contribution to Hamilton's *Gallipoli Diary*: G. G. A. Egerton to H. Simpson-Baikie, 31 May, 23 June 1915; 19 June 1921, Hamilton Papers, 7/10/11, LHCMA.
127 HW Official War Diary, 11 July 1915: 48356, BL: HW Private War Diary, 15 July 1915, 48364, BL.
128 Travers, *Gallipoli*, 110.
129 HW Official War Diary, 17 July 1915–31 July 1916, 48356, BL.
130 HW Private War Diary, HW to GHW, 10 July 1915, 48364, BL.

become very sick; this may have been the result of sunstroke or one of the many stomach conditions that plagued the army.[131] He improved during the day and by evening was much better, but any suspicion that he had not been in perfect health while fighting the battle of Achi Baba Nullah would have been a gift to the Gallipoli gossip mill, especially given his handling of the Egerton episode.[132]

Despite his temporary rally, he continued to feel unwell for the next few days. When he rode out on 17 July to inspect the 52nd Division, he was in a weakened state. He spent a very hot morning walking round the various battalions in his helmet and shirtsleeves talking to the troops, but became giddy and faint. Much to Egerton's delight, he got on his horse to ride back to his HQ, but he was forced to dismount after 200 yards and lie down in the shade.[133] He wired GHQ to suggest that Sir Frederick Stopford, the new commander of IX Corps, be placed in temporary command at Helles and then boarded the admiral's yacht *Triad*, hoping that he would be back at his post after a few days of leave.[134] In fact, this break from normal duties had the opposite effect. When Roger Keyes saw him later that evening he was in his usual high spirits, but the next day his condition deteriorated sharply, with severe headaches, disturbance of vision and persistent fever, all of which were consistent with his doctor's diagnosis of 'good old-fashioned sunstroke'.[135] Cumulative exposure to stress and exhaustion probably contributed to the speed of his final collapse – a similar episode had ended his service in South Africa.[136] His medical treatment may also have added to his woes, as 'heroic' purgatives like calomel,

---

131 HW Private War Diary, 11 July 1915, 48364, BL; Davidson, *Incomparable 29th*, 129.
132 Ashmead-Bartlett, Evidence to the Dardanelles Commission, Hamilton Papers, 8/2/6, LHCMA.
133 HW Official War Diary, 48356, BL7; Egerton Diary, 17 July 1915, CAB 45/249, TNA: 'He really was bad today. I wasn't'.
134 HW Private War Diary, 17 July 1915, 48364, BL.
135 Keyes, *Fight for Gallipoli*, 196; HW War Diary, HW to GHW 17 July 1915, 48364, BL; HW to Hamilton, 11 August 1915, Hamilton Papers, 7/1/33, LHCMA.
136 Hamilton suspected that it was the recent fighting combined with the Egerton episode that had finally worn him out: I. Hamilton to Lord Kitchener, 21 July 1915, PRO 30/57/61, TNA.

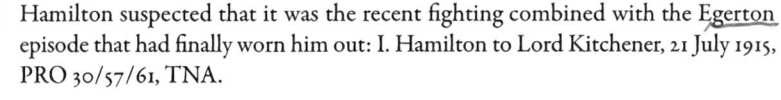

which were used to reduce his fever, were also likely to have compounded his severe dehydration.[137] It was clear that he would have to return home to recuperate. On 22 July, he staggered onto a launch bound for the hospital ship *Sicilia*, still suffering from an agonising headache.[138] Reaching Malta, he was swung over the side in a stretcher and immediately hospitalised. After resuming his journey, it was not until the ship neared Gibraltar that his temperature began to fall. By the time an anxious Grace arrived to pick him up in London on 7 August, he had lost 2½ stones in weight during eighteen days of fever.

Far from providing a convenient excuse to remove a failing general, Hamilton deeply regretted his loss, especially during the August offensive at Anzac where the performance of his senior commanders left much to be desired.[139] He therefore asked Kitchener to send Hunter-Weston back to Gallipoli once he was fit, offering a candid appreciation of his qualities as a man and a soldier:

> his departure leaves a blank it will be uncommonly difficult to fill. As a human being it is easy to pick holes in him. But as a Commander in the field he is really top hole. He is full of energy, is never down cast, is a man of ideas and expresses them excellently. 'Never say die' is his motto, and he has been a great support to me during the dark hours.[140]

Hunter-Weston was a world away from the slothful 'dugouts' that have become associated with Gallipoli. He had once believed that forcing the Dardanelles was 'the most hopeful method of finishing the war', but the campaign was strategically flawed from its outset and was further hindered by inadequate planning, resourcing and communication. Although he had grasped the military risks, his loyalty and ambition would not allow him to pursue the logic of his analysis. As a result, his 'glorious task' was a very mixed blessing indeed. Had he waited for a New Army division, he would have trained it and put his personal stamp upon it. As a divisional

---

137 HW Private War Diary, 17 July 1915, 48364, BL.
138 Sir Ian Hamilton, *Gallipoli Diary*, vol. 2 (London: Edward Arnold, 1920), 26.
139 I. Hamilton to Lord Kitchener, 11 August 1915, Hamilton Papers, 7/2/5, LHCMA.
140 I. Hamilton to Lord Kitchener, 27 July 1915, PRO 30/57/61, TNA.

commander in France in 1915, he would have found a greater abundance of resources, but a similar lack of solutions to the endemic problems of trench warfare. However, by sharing the frustrations of other new Major-Generals there, his failures would have remained less conspicuous than those which occurred in the small, toxic world of Cape Helles.

Proud of his reputation as a tactician, there was certainly a strong element of rigidity in Hunter-Weston's approach at Gallipoli – it seemed as though he was fighting the war he wanted to fight, rather than the one being waged by the Turks. For all his reputation for dash, he also appeared to lack an eye for exploiting opportunities as they arose. Yet, he developed to some extent in the course of the campaign, showing an increasing awareness of the role of heavy artillery and switching to small-scale operations that secured a modest and methodical advance. He had evidently failed to fulfil his early promise as a Brigadier, but given the scale of the systemic challenges that he faced, it could be argued that his performance was not the unmitigated disaster that is often assumed. In any case, the quality (or otherwise) of his generalship could hardly have been expected to transform the outcome of what had been a compromised, indeed, even a doomed, campaign.

CHAPTER ELEVEN

A Day of Disaster

At first, the failure of the Gallipoli campaign was eclipsed by the heroism of its participants. For all the mutterings on the peninsula, Hunter-Weston's name remained linked at home with the 'Incomparable' 29th Division. He was knighted by King George V on the day after his return to Britain and quickly received two prestigious job offers. Lord Kitchener wanted him as his Chief of Staff on his mission to the Balkans and the Dardanelles, while Sir John French invited him to become his deputy as Commander of the British Home Forces.[1] These approaches were extremely flattering, but there was no doubt that his real desire was for another field command. His patience was rewarded in March 1916 with a return to VIII Corps, which was reforming in Picardy in preparation for the next great offensive, which was to take place around the River Somme.

Although the Western Front seemed to offer a new beginning, ultimately it was corps command at the Somme that would decisively check Hunter-Weston's career ambitions. His role was not as conspicuous as it had been at Gallipoli, but historians have since been unrelenting in their analysis of the disaster that befell his men. Travers, for example, uses VIII Corps as a case study of what went wrong on the first day of the battle.[2] Prior and Wilson cite Hunter-Weston's 'malign effect' on corps artillery arrangements, while Farrar-Hockley categorises his pre-battle preparation

---

[1] Summary of Personal Movements, HW Official War Diary, 48357, BL. He was too ill to take up Kitchener's post, but he remained a staunch supporter of 'K', believing that French's GHQ had become the heart of an anti-Kitchener conspiracy: HW to C. Wigham 24 May 1915, Hunter-Weston Papers, 6503/39/21, NAM.
[2] Travers, *Killing Ground*, 157–60.

as born of 'mismanagement or carelessness'.[3] For good measure, Simpson remarks that his 'hands off' exercise of corps command resembled 'the steady plod of a sleepwalker', in marked contrast to his thrusting reputation.[4] Although the relationship between the two has not yet been systematically explored, a further feature of the historiography is a willingness to link Hunter-Weston's performance at the Somme with his previous command at Gallipoli. His failure appears prefigured, if not predestined, by his 'very mixed reputation' for over-optimism, recklessness and lack of imagination.[5] Crucially, his 'Westerner' superiors, Douglas Haig and Henry Rawlinson, the Fourth Army Commander who deplored the Gallipoli adventure, made a similar negative connection. Indeed, their willingness to focus on Hunter-Weston's 'different' experience may have diverted their attention from more endemic flaws in their own planning for the battle.[6]

In fact, the legacy of Hunter-Weston's Gallipoli command was highly complex. There is little doubt that he arrived in France desperate to win glory for his corps. His experience on the Gallipoli peninsula had strengthened his belief in the traditional 'moral' qualities of discipline and leadership, and instilled in him a fear of fractured, disorganised assaults.[7] He had also learned important tactical lessons. His experiment with 'bite and hold' tactics had been initiated out of necessity, but he had become increasingly convinced that carefully planned limited offensives, 'strictly in proportion to the men and munitions available', offered the only road to success.[8] Unfortunately, these good intentions were caught in the crossfire between Haig and Rawlinson as they stumbled towards a hybrid battle plan

---

3   Robin Prior and Trevor Wilson, *The Somme* (New Haven and London: Yale University Press, 2006), 304; Anthony Farrar-Hockley, *The Somme* (London: Pan, 1966), 113.
4   Simpson, *Directing Operations*, 198.
5   Peter Hart, *The Somme: The Darkest Hour on the Western Front* (London: Weidenfield and Nicholson, 2005), 134. See also Travers, *Killing Ground*, 157.
6   Prior and Wilson, *Somme*, 65–8.
7   HW Private War Diary, 25 April 1916, 48365, BL.
8   Note on action to be taken by his Corps, when acting on the left flank of the general attack from near Fonquevillers to near the River Ancre, 25 March 1916, HW Official War Diary, 48357, BL.

A Day of Disaster

that combined a wearing-down artillery assault with an unlimited offensive. Beguiled by the artillery apparently at his disposal, Hunter-Weston did not challenge their approach, even though the depth of penetration it demanded would weaken the intensity of his preliminary bombardment just as surely as his over-extended front had done at Gully Ravine. This equation was enough to deny success at the Somme, but the delegated decision-making structure of Rawlinson's Fourth Army also left sufficient room for active command errors at corps level. Far from sleepwalking to disaster, it was a combination of Hunter-Weston's energy and imagination – in particular, his fascination with 'scientific' planning, his faith in new technology and his fondness for imaginative *ruses de guerre* – that would increase the agony for VIII Corps on 1 July 1916.

A New Command

One of Haig's most biting criticisms of Hunter-Weston and fellow Gallipoli veterans was that they were 'amateurs in hard fighting'.[9] Passing judgment on a soldier who was deeply engaged in his profession, this was wide of the mark. Hunter-Weston was well aware that there had been many changes since he had left Flanders a year before. Not only had the BEF expanded to a force of one and a half million men, but there had also been a dramatic increase in the numbers of heavy guns available to them.[10] More subtle shifts had also taken place in the role of army corps. At Gallipoli, VIII Corps had emerged from a haphazard accumulation of units that could no longer be controlled by GHQ. On the Western Front, the development of the corps as the highest level of operational command had been stimulated by the need to coordinate artillery arrangements; as the numbers of corps

---

9 Haig Diary, 30 June 1916, Acc. 3155/96, NLS.
10 Prior and Wilson, *Command on the Western Front*, 137–8.

expanded, their responsibilities also increased, thereby requiring a more centralised model of command.[11]

Keen to investigate the latest fighting methods, Hunter-Weston decided to visit France prior to taking up his new posting.[12] During a seventeen-day trip, he studied artillery techniques and the intricacies of corps administration, but it was his conversation with Major-General Frederick McCracken, who had commanded the 15th (Scottish) Division at Loos the previous September, that made the deepest impression on him.[13] Many features of the battle were familiar from his time on the peninsula, not least the lack of operational experience to mount a large-scale offensive, but the 'three main facts' that he drew out were the failure of reserve arrangements; the allocation of objectives that were too distant; and the lack of infrastructural preparation to facilitate rapid troop movement. Where the attack had succeeded, this was 'because of the extreme care with which all details for the attack were gone into before the day itself'.[14]

Before he could put these insights into practice, Haig gave him a secret mission. Despite his views on Gallipoli, he was happy to use Hunter-Weston's expertise in planning a daring expedition to capture the port of Ostend.[15] Haig cared deeply about this project, as he viewed the Belgian coast as having great strategic significance for future offensive operations in Flanders. He therefore deputed Hunter-Weston to draw up a scheme in collaboration with Rear-Admiral Reginald Bacon, a controversial officer noted for his technical acumen. In the past Hunter-Weston might have relished leading such an enterprise, but recent experience had given him a more realistic attitude. Lacking the ability to land on a broad enough front to prevent hold ups, he argued that the assault would have to be made on

---

11   Simpson, *Directing Operations*, 19.
12   HW Private War Diary, 29 January-17 February 1915, 48365, BL.
13   Hunter-Weston also received a personal tactical briefing from Haig: Haig Diary, 8 February 1916, Acc. 3155/96, NLS.
14   HW Official War Diary, 9 February 1916, 48357, BL.
15   HW Official War Diary, 18 February 1916, 48357, BL; for Haig's views on Gallipoli evacuation, see Haig Diary, 20 December 1915, Acc. 3155/96, NLS; John Terraine, *Douglas Haig: The Educated Soldier* (London: Leo Cooper, 1990), 146.

A Day of Disaster

the heavily defended harbour. Even if the attackers survived the onslaught of German heavy artillery, any radial advance could easily be blocked and there would be no chance of the 'rapidity and vigour of action' that such an operation would require.[16] Bacon grasped this, but Haig was still convinced that the plan had potential if the military situation were to change. When the three next met again in Dover, there was agreement that any attempt to take Ostend would require the enemy's reserves to be drawn off beforehand, but Haig ordered a detailed exposition of the scheme nevertheless.[17] For the next two months, alongside planning for the Somme, Hunter-Weston would also be absorbed in the Ostend project.[18]

It was mid-March before he finally arrived at his new HQ, the imposing pre-revolutionary Chateau Marieux.[19] His new accommodation was much more spacious than his previous dugout, but his experience as a 'chateau general' still left much to be desired. The existing lavatories emptied into an ancient cesspit and the sanitary officers immediately replaced them with a bucket system of latrines situated well clear of the house – 'far from convenient on a wet night'.[20] Nevertheless, he was extremely pleased that fate had brought him to this part of the British lines. The rolling chalk landscape was a striking contrast from 'horrible' Flanders; there was plenty of scope for riding through charming little woods, carpeted with wild daffodils and anemones. He also liked his new commander, Rawlinson– 'a clever man and pleasant' – and rejoiced that he had avoided the ill-tempered Allenby and the Third Army.[21]

---

16 A Note on the Projected Landing at Ostend, 24 February 1916, HW Official War Diary, 48357, BL.
17 Haig Diary, 25 December 1915, Acc. 3155/96, NLS.
18 It was not until 18 April that Haig allowed him to devote his time exclusively to corps planning, but he continued to advise Bacon until the operation was shelved in June 1916 pending progress at Ypres: Haig Diary, 12 June 1916, Acc. 3155/96, NLS; Andrew Wiest, 'The Planned Amphibious Assault' in Peter Liddle (ed.), *Passchendaele in Perspective: the Third Battle of Ypres* (London: Leo Cooper, 1997), 201–14.
19 HW Official War Diary, 18 March 1916, 48357, BL.
20 HW to C. Wigram, 2 April 1916, HW Private War Diary, 48365, BL.
21 HW to GHW, 25 April 1916, HW Private War Diary, 48365, BL.

His four divisions had already begun assembling. The first to arrive from Egypt was the 31st Division, a New Army unit, which contained a number of North Country 'Pals' battalions; they were commanded by Major-General Robert Wanless O'Gowan (*né* Smith), who had been rescued from the half-pay list to become Assistant Quartermaster General in 1914. Representing the Territorial Force were the 48th (South Midland) Division, under the popular Major-General Edward Fanshawe.[22] Balancing these units were two regular divisions, both very familiar to Hunter-Weston. The 4th Division joined the corps in May along with the 11th Brigade, which was now commanded by Bertie Prowse. The division had suffered heavy losses over the past year, but was 'fighting fit' and almost back to its August 1914 standard following impressive new drafts from its traditional recruiting areas; the GOC was Lord French's former Military Secretary, 'Billy' Lambton, reckoned by Margot Asquith to be 'no genius, but sound and straight'.[23] Making an even more welcome reappearance were the 29th Division, even though the nucleus of officers and men who had survived Gallipoli was painfully small; their commander, De Lisle, remained one of Hunter-Weston's closest associates.[24] In moulding together a disparate force, the Corps Commander could not disguise his sentimental attachment to this unit. Perhaps he sensed that they shared similar challenges in readjusting to the Western Front. Just as he had exchanged his singular authority at Helles for being one of five Corps Commanders in the Fourth Army, the 29th Division could no longer count on being 'the cynosure of every eye, the "backbone" of every enterprise'.[25]

22 Carrington, *Soldier from the Wars Returning*, 102.
23 C. M. Vallentin, to J. E. Edmonds, Notes on Draft, nd., CAB 45/138; Holmes, *Little Field Marshall*, 255.
24 Hunter-Weston campaigned for De Lisle to be rewarded for his services on the peninsula – the lack of decorations for the 29th Division was a concern shared by both men: HW Official War Diary, 22 March 1916, 48357, BL.
25 Gillon, *Story of the 29th Division*, 77–8.

Planning

At the Chantilly Conference in December 1915, evacuation from the Gallipoli peninsula cleared the way for directing Britain's main military effort towards the Western Front.[26] By the time of Hunter-Weston's arrival, the broad outline of the new offensive had already been decided. His first task as Corps Commander during March was to direct the infrastructural preparations that now underpinned any major battle.[27] He had assistance in this massive logistical exercise from his new corps staff – a team he deemed 'excellent', although this was not a universally shared view. The rapid expansion of corps had led to a shortage of well-trained staff officers, but while his artillery commander Brigadier T. A. Tancred was considered an effective soldier, this was less true of his chief staff officer, Brigadier 'Jerry' Hore-Ruthven VC, a scion of the Scottish aristocracy who had been badly wounded at Gallipoli. Meeting him later in the war, a friend and colleague was astounded to find him in a senior staff position, regarding him as a 'thorough, good sporting, hard riding man with a minimum of intellect'.[28]

Hunter-Weston's second duty involved helping to plan the Fourth Army's outline scheme of attack. The challenge facing Rawlinson's force was formidable: they would be engaged in an offensive stretching from Serre in the north to a point just east of Mametz in the south. Facing them was a three-line trench network featuring deep dugouts and a series of fortified villages. Behind this system was another defensive line 2,000–4,000 yards to the rear, with a series of strongpoints lying in between. The construction of a third line was also underway, but was not yet fully developed. Rawlinson's initial inclination was for a limited, two-stage advance. Having methodically calibrated his targets to allow for the number of heavy

---

26 For an overview of the extensive literature on the background to the Somme campaign, see Prior and Wilson, *Somme*, 15–34.
27 See VIII Corps G31, Preliminary Order for the Somme, 25 March 1916: HW Official War Diary, 48357, BL.
28 Travers, *Killing Ground*, 275. He was later raised to the peerage as the First Earl of Gowrie and became Governor-General of Australia.

howitzers available, his plan allowed for the initial seizure of the enemy's first-line defences. From here, the artillery could prepare the way for the next assault on the second-line position. This cautious approach took into account the strength of the German positions, but also reflected the weight of opinion among his Corps Commanders.

As always, Hunter-Weston had forcefully expounded his views at a Fourth Army Conference on 30 March.[29] Although VIII Corps had been assigned the sector from Serre to Beaucourt, specific objectives had not yet been agreed beyond securing a defensive flank for the main advance. He argued that the depth of penetration should be conditional on the number of troops available and the weight of the artillery that could be brought up to support the infantry. At this stage, he showed an acute tactical awareness of the strong likelihood that any initial attempt to storm the German defences that crowned the Serre-Beaucourt ridge would result in very heavy casualties, calculating that each of his two main attacking divisions would be lucky to have a brigade in hand when they reached their objective. The only way that he could contemplate a further 2,000-yard advance to take the enemy's second line was if he was to have five divisions at his disposal, plus one in reserve – anything else would be 'foolish generalship'.[30] He was also adamant that any advance must be approached in a step-by-step fashion, as the main Serre-Grandcourt objective was not within range of his field artillery. Far being from an advocate of the gallant 'hooroosh', as he is often caricatured, Hunter-Weston actually argued that too often in the war substance had been lost 'by grasping at the shadow':

> I am strongly opposed to a wild rush by the advance line of troops for an objective 4000 yards away from their trenches of departure. Even if they get over the intervening line of trenches, the remnant of the line that started cannot but arrive as a widely spread and disordered rabble, with no power to overcome even a feeble

---

29 Battle of the Somme: Preparations by the Fourth Army, Fourth Army: Operations, WO 158/233, TNA.
30 Note on action to be taken by his Corps, 25 March 1916, HW Official War Diary, 48357, BL.

resistance in the enemy back trenches and with but little chance of being able to maintain themselves therein.[31]

Rawlinson endorsed his caution, noting in his diary that both he and Thomas Morland of X Corps 'had good ideas in their heads and will do well'.[32] Accordingly, Hunter-Weston had little hesitation in presenting his views to Haig when he visited Marieux on 7 April, explaining to the Commander-in-Chief that he intended to take the enemy's first trench system, proceeding slowly, stage by stage.[33] His timing, however, was unfortunate, as only two days earlier, Haig had dismissed Rawlinson's preliminary scheme for the attack as lacking in ambition, and instead had proposed 'getting as large a combined force of French and British across the Somme and fighting the enemy in the open'.[34] In Hunter-Weston's sector this meant that Serre should be captured 'fairly quickly' to enable mounted troops and machine-guns to be sent immediately to occupy Miraumont and Grandcourt and then to take the Theipval defences in reverse. Deeming the high ground west of Serre to be suitable terrain for tank operations, Haig was in no mood for conservatism, stressing that VIII Corps needed to be fully prepared to take advantage of surprise.[35] He raised the 'attack problem' again with Rawlinson the next day, impressing upon him that he must insist on Hunter-Weston gaining his objectives 'at one single effort', as the alternative would allow the enemy to bring up reserves as at Verdun, making the efforts to gain the Serre-Grandcourt position even more costly.[36]

As the discussions between Haig and Rawlinson continued over the next few weeks, an uneven compromise emerged.[37] It was everything that Hunter-Weston had feared. A total of eleven divisions were now to mount

---

31 Note on action to be taken by his Corps, 25 March 1916, HW Official War Diary, 48357, BL.
32 Sir Henry Rawlinson Diary, 10 April 1916, Rawlinson Papers, RWLN 1/5, CCC.
33 Haig Diary, 7 April 1915, Acc. 3155/96, NLS; Rawlinson Diary, 8 April 1916, Rawlinson Papers, RWLN 1/5, CCC.
34 Haig Diary, 5 April 1915, Acc. 3155/96, NLS.
35 Haig Diary, 7 April 1915, Acc. 3155/96, NLS.
36 Haig Diary, 8 April 1915, Acc. 3155/96, NLS.
37 See Prior and Wilson, *Command on the Western Front*, 146–53.

the offensive along a 24,000-yard front, involving a diversionary attack Gommecourt in the north and an extension of the main assault to include a junction with the French at Montauban in the south. Rawlinson's lengthy preliminary bombardment with 220 howitzers was retained, but between Serre and Pozières, including the VIII Corps sector, there was to be a rush to take the German second line, with the depth of the advance ranging from 3,000 to 4,000 yards. The northern corps would then attempt to roll up the rest of this line, which would also be attacked by a thrust from the south along the Contalmaison-Montauban position.

Many crucial issues were left unresolved by this composite plan. These included the problems of wire cutting and providing artillery support at such an extended distance; the need to neutralise the enemy reserves before the assaulting troops reached the second line; as well as the challenge of maintaining coherence in inexperienced units. These doubts would resurface in Hunter-Weston's own planning. It was even more significant to the success of the enterprise that these distant objectives had the effect of doubling the number of yards of trench requiring a heavy howitzer bombardment, thus diluting the destructive power to be brought to bear on the enemy defences. This was artillery warfare, but without a proportionate increase in the guns and ammunition available it was unlikely that even the German front-line positions would fall to infantry assault.

While he was aware of this risk, Rawlinson also knew his place in the command hierarchy. Bound by the same authority structure, Hunter-Weston and his fellow Corps Commanders fell into line. With the revised Fourth Army plan now in place detailed preparations could begin in earnest at corps level, but as they hammered out their methods of attack, the objectives for the offensive continued to change and grow as the French contribution steadily diminished. By end of June, 'the great advance' had become a largely British affair, with the towns of Bapaume, Monchy and Douai designated as distant but 'achievable' targets for Haig's cavalry push.

The challenge facing Hunter-Weston at the Somme was probably greater than that facing any other Corps Commander. Forming the northern anchor of the Fourth Army offensive, VIII corps would attack along a three and a half mile front on either side of Beaumont Hamel village. Not only did the natural landscape of the chalk heights north of the Ancre overwhelmingly favour his opponents, but the Germans had also maximised their advantage through their extensive defensive preparations. His corps front was marked by a series of large spurs running south-eastwards towards the winding river. Lying in the shallow valley between the Auchonvilliers spur and the Beaucourt spur was the village of Beaumont Hamel, while at the northern end of the Grandcourt spur was the village of Serre. The enemy positions in this sector were held by an estimated nineteen and a half battalions from the 52nd Division, mainly drawn from the Grand Duchy of Baden, and from the 26th Reserve Division, from the neighbouring Württemberg.[38] The succession of valleys and ridges gave them protection from shelling, while also offering an excellent view of the British, whose own artillery observation was limited by the location of their trenches on a convex slope.[39] The defenders were assisted by two further natural features: Y Ravine, a deeply cut defile in the Beaumont Hamel valley which provided good cover for reserves and supports; and the nearby Hawthorn Ridge, whose commanding presence made any approach extremely dangerous.

The main German artillery positions were on the reverse of the Beaucourt and Grandcourt spurs. Frontline trenches had been constructed on the forward slopes running from the eastern slope of the Auchonvillers spur and passing round the head of Y Ravine to Hawthorn Ridge. Here, a redoubt of machine-gun posts had been built. The line then crossed the Beaumont Hamel valley and continued across the Beaucourt spur towards the knoll upon which Serre was perched. Stretching along the summit behind these trenches was another strong intermediate line – the Munich Trench – with the second main line dug out on the reverse slopes running from Grandcourt to Puisieux, followed by the third trench system three

---

38 Appreciation of the probable line of defence which the enemy may reasonably be expected to adopt against an attack by VIII Corps [A. Hore-Ruthven], 12 April 1916, HW Official War Diary, 48357, BL; Christopher Duffy, *Through German Eyes: The British and the Somme, 1916* (London: Phoenix, 2006), 138.

39 J. E. Edmonds, *History of the Great War Based on Official Documents by Direction of the Historical Section of the Committee of Imperial Defence: Military Operations in France and Belgium, 1916. Volume I: Sir Douglas Haig's Command to the 1st July: Battle of the Somme* (London: Macmillan, 1932), 426–7 [*OH 1916 (1)*].

miles further to the rear. Well-protected with belts of wire, the German trenches had been ingeniously designed, incorporating minor salients to allow interlocking fields of fire, as well as switch trenches and covered communication systems; miners from the Rhineland had been busy since the winter of 1914 building great tunnel-like dugouts to give troops additional protection and allow lateral movement underground.[40] As the lynchpin of defensive system, the vital high ground around Serre in the second line had been turned into miniature fortress, while to the south the Quadrilateral strongpoint that jutted out from the German front line had been packed with explosives to form a massive booby trap for attacking infantry. Another hazard was the low-lying Beaumont Hamel village, 500 yards behind the front line, which contained a formidable defensive system of cellars, dugouts and machine-gun posts. No Man's Land offered little cover, with distances from the German line ranging from 200 yards in the north to an average of 500 yards in the south.[41]

The undulating terrain and impressive scale of the German defences limited Hunter-Weston's attack options and made interlocking success in the centre and on the major spurs essential.[42] It may seem strange that his notorious 'cheeriness' survived, but just a week after he had questioned Haig's unlimited offensive tactics he had become increasingly confident that his guns could indeed carve a way through for the infantry. Even though there would clearly be no fifth division arriving to strengthen VIII Corps, the appreciation prepared by his Chief of Staff struck a defiant note:

> It is assumed that the intensive preliminary bombardment and the elan of the assaulting infantry will carry them through to the first objective within half-an-hour of the commencement of the assault except at the re-entrant east of Serre and the re-entrant west of Beaucourt where it will take ten minutes longer. It is assumed that the artillery bombardment will pin the troops holding the front line to their positions and

40 R. Spencer Smith to J. E. Edmonds, 17 July 1930, CAB 45/137, TNA; Duffy, *Through German Eyes*, 143.
41 VIII Corps, G31, Preliminary Order for the Somme, 25 March 1916, HW Official War Diary, 48357, BL.
42 Farrar-Hockley, *Somme*, 98; for 'Code Blue' risk, see Fourth Army Plan of Attack: Haig Diary (typescript), Acc. 3155/106, NLS.

A Day of Disaster 223

at the same time batter down Beaumont Hamel and Serre to such an extent as to nullify all resistance in these two villages.[43]

While Hunter-Weston's optimism at Gallipoli had been presented for public consumption, it now seemed to be fuelled by genuine conviction. An explanation for this was the remarkable array of heavy guns accumulating under his command. He detailed his new armoury to the long-suffering Grace with customary precision – although his list did not include his eight obsolete 4.7" guns, which would have an important role in counter-battery work:

> I have in all under my command at the present time 600 pieces of Ordnance, less 4, i.e. 596 VIS:
> 15" Howitzers, which fire a shell weighing   1300lbs
> 12" Howitzers "   "   "   "   750lbs
> 9.2" Howitzers   280lbs
> 8" Howitzers   200lbs
> 6" Howitzers   100lbs
> 6" guns, which fire a shell weighing 100lbs but of course to a very much greater distance than the Howitzers.
> 5" guns i.e. 60 prs which fire a shell weighing 60lbs.
> The above are the Heavy Howitzers, & Heavy guns, then come the Field Howitzers and Field guns, viz:
> 4.5" Howitzers which fire a shell weighing 37lbs, & the ordinary Field guns (18 prs) which fire a shell weighing 18lbs.
> Also the 75mm French guns, which fire a shell weighing about 14lbs, at the rate of 20 rounds a minute.
> Then come the Trench mortars:
> Heavy Trench mortars which fire a shell weighing about 192lbs.
> Medium Trench Mortars which fire a shell weighing about 50lbs
> Light Trench Mortars which fire a shell weighing about 11lbs.[44]

After being starved of resources at Gallipoli, his exhilaration at the possession of this firepower was understandable – indeed, he boasted that with a sixth of the weaponry available to him at the Somme, he would have

---

43 Appreciation of the probable line of defence, 12 April 1916, HW Official War Diary, 48357, BL.
44 HW to GHW, 26 June 1916, HW Private War Diary, 48365, BL.

reached Constantinople and shortened the war. Unfortunately, the sheer amount of heavy ordinance diverted him from the question of how far this could be effectively concentrated relative to the area of attack. Edmonds, for example, suggests that VIII Corps Heavy Artillery, totalling eighty-one guns, worked out at around one per forty-four yards of front, while the divisional artillery had one field gun per twenty yards.[45] This appeared rather more favourable than the Fourth Army average of one per forty-nine yards for heavy guns, and one per twenty-three yards for field guns, but these calculations did not take into consideration the actual area of the enemy's multi-layered trench system that was to be assaulted. Although he would never have admitted it, Hunter-Weston also lacked experience in commanding heavy artillery. Like most senior officers at the Somme, this led him to overestimate the technical capability of his guns and to neglect consideration of problems of gun design, ammunition supply, shell power and mechanical reliability.[46]

'Faulty optimism' may have influenced Hunter-Weston's plan of attack, but he also remained aware of risks surrounding deep incursion.[47] Ruthven's appreciation had suggested that gaining their objectives would depend on the amount of warning given and the length of time which the enemy took to bring up his reserves. If there was a short, intense bombardment along the line and a simultaneous infantry assault with the artillery lifting from the first to the second trench line, then the attackers might be able to move to the second line, but they could also be easily caught between the two. However, if the preparatory bombardment was a long one ('over two hours') it was difficult to see how the Grandcourt-Serre line could be won without a second bombardment on an equally large scale, as anything less would allow the enemy reserves to reach the line in sufficient force to hold it.[48] By May, it had become clear that the preliminary bombardment

---

45 Hunter-Weston's list corresponds to that given in the *Official History* with the exception of the 4.7 inch guns: *OH 1916 (1)*, 427.
46 Prior and Wilson, *Command on the Western Front*, 164–6.
47 J. Hartley to J. E. Edmonds, 5 November 1929, CAB 45/134, TNA.
48 Appreciation of the probable line of defence, 12 April 1916, HW Official War Diary, 48357, BL.

was to be methodical and very lengthy indeed; Hunter-Weston's persistent fear of a disorganised advance beyond the support of his field artillery now added to the complexity of his task.[49]

As at Gallipoli, his approach to planning was directive rather than consultative in nature. The preliminary schemes of attack from his divisions were refined during a series of planning conferences which took place from March onwards. The essentials of the Fourth Army Plan and Rawlinson's *Tactical Notes* were communicated at these meetings amid a mass of directives from Corps HQ setting out guiding principles for the attack, as well as addressing grimly practical necessities such the burial of the dead.[50] Hunter-Weston was well to the fore at such occasions, but they also provided an opportunity for developing a shared approach to common problems. Unlike Rawlinson, the Corps Commander's practice was to set out a firm framework for decision-making at divisional and brigade level, inviting plans of attack that would subsequently be 'critiqued' – a process from which even De Lisle's 'excellent' tactical scheme did not emerge unscathed.[51] With the lessons of Loos (and Third Krithia) fresh in his mind, for example, he also made it abundantly clear to his divisional commanders that the use of reserves would be tightly monitored, as their proper deployment required 'the highest moral courage as well as deep military knowledge'.[52]

As he drove his staff on during these busy weeks, Hunter-Weston was also under pressure from his superiors. His relationship with his Army Commander was still on a sound footing. While Rawlinson doubted the abilities of some of his VIII Corps subordinates (particularly O'Gowan), he found Hunter-Weston to be 'intelligent and very keen', although he

---

49 VIII Corps Conference, 23 May 1916, Corps Commander's Remarks, HW Official War Diary, 48357, BL.
50 Notes of Two Conferences held at Corps Headquarters, 21, 23 June 1916, HW Official War Diary, 48357, BL.
51 HW to H. B. De Lisle, 21 June 1916, HW Official War Diary, 48357, BL.
52 HW to W. Lambton, R. W. O'Gowan and H. B. De Lisle, 28 June 1916, HW Official War Diary, 48357, BL.

cautioned him against overwork.[53] In contrast, Haig's apprehensions had not abated. On 10 May, he joined 'Rawly' on a visit to VIII Corps HQ, seizing the opportunity to quiz Hunter-Weston personally on his plans. The session did not go well. Hunter-Weston respected Haig as 'an old friend' but he could not conceal his continuing worries over advancing towards distant objectives at full tilt. The exasperated Commander-in Chief set him straight:

> I impressed on him that there must be no halting at each trench in succession for rear lines to pass through! The <u>objective</u> must be as far off as our guns can prepare the enemy's position for attack – and when the attack starts, it must be pushed to the final objective with as little delay as possible. His experiences at Gallipoli were under very different conditions; then he landed in ships, a slow proceeding; now his troops can be formed in succession of lines in great depth, and all can start from the same moment![54]

When the VIII Corps scheme was issued on 11 June, it bore the imprint of this exchange. As an administrative order it was not much different from other corps plans, but it was remarkable for its sedulous presentation. The accumulation of minute detail in a bid to control uncertainty had been a feature of Hunter-Weston's approach even as a junior officer; the situation on the Somme now gave free rein to this tendency, as though to squeeze out the possibility of failure. A thirteen-page summary was followed by a full exposition of sixty-nine pages, with twenty-eight headings which included: dispositions of infantry and artillery; employment of aircraft; trench mortars; mining; machine-guns; ammunition; signals; water; rations; roads forward; and the evacuation of the wounded.[55] Not surprisingly, Rawlinson

---

53   Rawlinson Diary, 2 May 1916, Rawlinson Papers, RWLN 1/5, CCC.
54   Haig Diary, 10 May 1916, Acc. 3155/96, NLS.
55   VIII Corps Scheme for Offensive, [11 June 1916], HW Official War Diary, 48357, BL. In comparison, the XIII Corps plan takes up twenty-nine pages in the *Official History* and is succinct enough not to require a summary. Even the VIII Corps précis was more than twice the length of any other in the Fourth Army Plan of Attack: Haig Papers, Acc. 3155/106, NLS.

A Day of Disaster

considered it 'well worked out and nothing forgotten', but Brigadier Hubert Rees of the 31st Division felt it was a 'terrible document'.[56]

In fact, the difficulty lay less with the document itself than with the planning process. As an outsider who had only joined VIII Corps two weeks before, Rees immediately grasped its deadening effect when he discovered that his own division had produced a further 365 pages of supplementary instructions, which now had to be hacked down into manageable brigade orders.[57] Further down the military pecking order, Captain Vallentin also waded through a blizzard of directives, three quarters of which he found to be irrelevant to his field battery.[58] While it was unlikely that the enemy would be flattened into submission by this onslaught of paper, the rigidity of such an approach was liable to frustrate improvisation if events did not unfold according to plan. The culture of precision which had gripped VIII Corps in the weeks before the Somme Battle was vividly captured at the conference of 4th Division Staff Captains on 16 June where the first item on the agenda was the question of what breakfast should be served to the men on the morning of the assault ('a cold bacon sandwich and in some cases hot tea').[59]

The most important part of the VIII Corps scheme was, of course, the arrangements for the attack. The scene had already been set by Haig and Rawlinson's commitment to a common advance across the Fourth Army front rather than attacks at selected tactical points. However, Hunter-Weston's experience of the chaotic battlefields of Gallipoli and his awareness of the dangers of unsupported infiltration reinforced the emphasis on uniformity. Indeed, controlling his own troops seemed almost as important as suppressing the defenders. At the heart of his offensive scheme was an

---

56   Rawlinson Diary, 12 June 1916, Rawlinson Papers, RWLN 1/5, CCC; H. C. Rees to J. E. Edmonds, 14 November 1929, CAB 45/137, TNA; Griffiths, *Battle Tactics*, 58; *OH 1916 (1)*, 270.
57   For the 4th Division's administrative preparations, see H. F. Davies to J. E. Edmonds, 29 November 1929, CAB 45/132, TNA.
58   C. M. Vallentin to J. E. Edmonds, Notes on Draft, n.d., CAB 45/138, TNA.
59   Notes on Conference of Staff Captains, 14 June 1916, 4th Division War Diary, WO 95/1444, TNA.

ambitious and highly structured timetable. He believed that if they could get the infantry forwards to the Grandcourt-Serre ridge in three hours from the moment of the assault, they would 'have done very well indeed'.[60] Leaving a only modest margin for delay, the 29th Division in the south were ordered to make a 4,000-yard advance eastwards, pushing into the Beaumont Hamel valley and through Munich Trench until they reached their final objective, the enemy's second line, in just three and a half hours. On their left, operating within the same time frame, the 4th Division was to spearhead an equally ambitious assault along the heavily fortified Redan Ridge. Both operations involved complex arrangements for fresh brigades passing through initial assault units to maintain the momentum of the attack. Meanwhile, in the north the 31st Division had been set target of a 3,000-yard advance. They were to roll up the village of Serre and form a protective 'shoulder' as the main assault progressed, their left brigade pivoting at right angles to the main advance while the right was to swing forwards to keep in touch with the 4th Division attack.[61]

Hunter-Weston had equally firm ideas of how his troops should negotiate no man's land. For all his new-found eagerness for speed over a staged advance and his injunction that 'ALL UNITS MUST PUSH FORWARDS RESOLUTELY', he warned his heavily laden troops against advancing at the double except over short distances such as twenty yards, as doing so would exhaust them and cause the impulsion of the attack to dissipate.[62] The operational conditions across his front would make these strictures difficult to enforce, but he believed that it was not only the pace of the assault but also the effective alignment of his troops that would deliver the maximum physical and 'moral' blow.

Specifying the deployments in some detail, VIII Corps orders were therefore intended to maximise energy and cohesion. In the 29th Division

60 Notes of Two Conferences, HW Official War Diary, 48357, BL.
61 The 48th Division formed the corps reserve, to be used 'Offensively not Defensively' and 'not dribbled up to reinforce part of the line that may be hard pressed': Notes of Two Conferences, HW Official War Diary, 48357, BL.
62 VIII Corps Scheme for Offensive; see also Notes of Two Conferences, HW Official War Diary, 48357, BL.

each battalion was to attack on a three-company front with one in support. Although the Corps Scheme did not specify which attack formation they should adopt to reach their first objective, they were instructed to move beyond it in columns and to be ready to extend when necessary. The 4th Division were also to assault their first objective on a three-company front, with battalions attacking in four waves. The less experienced 31st Division were to attack closest to the enemy front line positions. Here the eight platoons from 94th Brigade forming the first wave were to lie down in No Man's Land ten minutes prior to zero hour, while the 93rd Brigade advanced on a two-company front, with the first two waves extended to an interval of three paces. In all cases, the Corps Commander was keen to emphasise the importance of the attacking units lining up parallel with the enemy trenches that formed their objectives. Immediately prior to the attack, the plan was that the leading waves would emerge and form up in this alignment, supported by a hurricane barrage from the trench mortars – as an early supporter of the light Stokes mortar, Hunter-Weston continued to be impressed by the tactical flexibility and destructive power of its larger cousins.[63]

Considerable preparatory work was necessary before his men could reach this critical point. As a prelude to the offensive, Hunter-Weston's heavy guns were to play their part in the slow bombardment intended to subdue enemy resistance across the Fourth Army's area of operations. He knew that his artillery would also have to silence the enemy during the actual attack, as his infantry lacked the weapons to do so. Fire and movement tactics were still at a basic stage, but the solution he arrived at was an early version of the creeping barrage, designed to move at a pre-arranged pace in front of the infantry to neutralise enemy troops still in the trenches and eliminate machine-guns between defensive lines. Indeed, the VIII Corps Scheme was one of the first times that the 'creeping' terminology was explicitly used and the concept was novel enough to require explaining

---

63 VIII Corps Scheme for Offensive, HW Official War Diary, 48357, BL. After one training exercise he remarked that the largest mortar left a crater thirty feet deep and forty feet wide: HW Private War Diary, 14 April 1916 48365, BL.

to his divisional commanders more than once.[64] The guiding principle was that a shrapnel barrage should progress on the basis of strictly timed lifts, conforming to the infantry's rate of advance, which had been calculated at fifty yards per minute. At the beginning of each infantry attack, the divisional guns would lift 100 yards and continue lifting at the rate of fifty yards a minute to the objective, firing three rounds of gunfire at each step.[65] A total of six lifts were laid down, with the Corps Heavy Artillery lifting in all cases five minutes beforehand and moving straight to the objective. For the 29th Division, this highly structured programme was timed to finish precisely at 4.40 p.m., 'when the division will have met all its objectives'.[66]

Despite all the hunger for certainty and completeness that drove the VIII Corps Scheme, two decisions taken during the final days before the battle were to become associated with the scale of loss on 1 July. The most controversial of these was the order to detonate over 40,000lbs of explosive under Hawthorn Redoubt 10 minutes before zero hour.[67] The origins of the idea lay in an earlier proposal from Hunter-Weston to schedule the detonation at 6 p.m. the evening before the attack.[68] By creating uncertainty over the timing of the impending assault, he hoped to regain the element of surprise lost by the lengthy bombardment, reasoning that a platoon with a machine-gun would be ample to hold the crater without giving the enemy a 'magnificent target'.[69] Although, like artillery lifts, the deployment of mines had been left to corps discretion, GHQ vetoed his proposal on the advice of Major-General R. N. Harvey, the Inspector of Mines, who was sceptical that the position could be captured and held.[70] The mine was

64 VIII Corps G1585, HW Official War Diary, 48357, BL. See Major A. F. Becke, 'The Coming of the Creeping Barrage', *Journal of the Royal Artillery* 58/1 (1931/2), 19–42.
65 VIII Corps Scheme for Offensive, HW Official War Diary, 48357, BL; see Section 13 on 'Artillery Lifts'.
66 VIII Corps G1585, HW Official War Diary, 48357, BL.
67 Simon Jones, *Underground Warfare, 1914–18* (Barnsley: Pen & Sword, 2010), 115–17.
68 *OH 1916 (1)*, 429; R. N. Harvey to J. E. Edmonds, 21 January 1930, CAB 45/189, TNA.
69 HW to H. B. De Lisle, 21 June 1916, HW Official War Diary, 48357, BL.
70 R. N. Harvey to J. E. Edmonds, 28 October 1929, CAB 45/189.

A Day of Disaster

consequently timed to explode at zero hour in the original corps plan of attack, but Ruthven believed that the compromise time of 7.20 a.m. had been agreed at a conference held around 29 June.[71] Writing to Edmonds thirteen years later, Hunter-Weston accepted full responsibility for the order as Corps Commander, arguing that, 'the reasons which lead to the issue of any Army Corps order are only of academical interest'.[72] His generosity in this respect was commendable, as none of his colleagues wanted to admit involvement in such a disastrous decision. As a result, the official historian found it difficult to get to the bottom of the issue. Comparing notes with Ruthven, Hunter-Weston recalled that De Lisle and Brigadier W. de L. Williams of the 86th Brigade had persuaded him to change the original orders, arguing that the mine would do as much damage to the assaulting troops as the Germans.[73] In contrast, J. F. C. Fuller, GSO3 of the 29th Division, rather unconvincingly placed the responsibility squarely on the shoulders of Major Reginald Trower, the O.C. 252nd Tunnelling Company, who had expressly requested ten minutes grace to ensure the mine exploded properly.[74] De Lisle attempted to distance himself even further by suggesting that he had complained to Haig and Rawlinson about the early detonation, but that his superiors sanctioned the measure to divert the enemy's attention away from the main attack, which was to be made by XIII and XV corps south of the Ancre.[75]

Such claims aside, the balance of probability is that 'Hunter-Bunter's folly', as Harvey termed it, lay in the Corps Commander's willingness to

---

71   This probably refers to the conference of divisional commanders which took place on 30 June: J. Ruthven to J. E. Edmonds, 30 October 1929, CAB 45/137, TNA.
72   HW to J. E. Edmonds, 12 December 1929, CAB 45/138, TNA.
73   Another motivation at Corps HQ may have been the wish to let poisonous gases dispel: W. Dobbie to J. E. Edmonds 31 October 1929, CAB 45/132, TNA.
74   J. F. C. Fuller to J. E. Edmonds, 24 January 1930, CAB 45/133, TNA. Harvey placed considerable blame on Fuller, whose opinion was allegedly accepted at 29th Division HQ to because he was a sapper: R. N. Harvey to J. E. Edmonds, 27 February 1930, CAB 45/189.
75   H. B. De Lisle to J. E. Edmonds, 12 November 1929, CAB 45/134, TNA. Edmonds included this interpretation in his narrative: *OH 1916 (1)*, 430. See also De Lisle, 'My Narrative of the Great German War', vol. 2, 9, GB99/1, LHCMA.

oblige his most trusted division. Although he was a sapper, he had no experience of the effects of mining on this scale and may also have been influenced by the 'magnificent waterfall of earth' that he witnessed following a large mine explosion at an earlier training exercise.[76] Horrified at the latest change in orders and certain that the impetus had come from 29th Division officers, Lieut.-Colonel Frank Preedy, the Controller of Mines, asked Major-General Reginald Buckland, the Fourth Army's Chief Engineer, to take up the matter at VIII Corps HQ. This was to no avail because, as Buckland informed him, 'it had been decided to stick to the arrangement made and the Corps did want not to force the 29th Division against its will'.[77]

This fateful departure from Hunter-Weston's normal planning methods had a further knock-on effect. The Corps Heavy Artillery could not continue to fire while the Hawthorn crater was under attack. However, rather than limiting the lift to this immediate sector, the decision was taken to apply this all along the line, so that all his heavy guns would move to target the rearward defences ten minutes prior to the assault. This is another rather murky episode, not least as the original artillery order was not widely circulated and has apparently not survived. As far as the tasks of the Corps Heavy Artillery were concerned, the Corps Commander considered it unnecessary to 'burden' the infantry with detailed information.[78] He had, of course, shown a similar eagerness for an early lift at the Third Battle of Krithia, but this time the experiment was prompted by lingering concerns over how to meet his ambitious objectives. He was confident of taking the front line trenches, but had concerns about how to hold them and assault the second line, as he realised that the prolonged barrage would give the Germans time to bring up reserves. A rapid, coordinated movement to bombard the reserve trenches would pin the enemy down while

---

76   HW to GHW, 20 May 1916, HW Private War Diary, 48365, BL.
77   F. Preedy to J. E. Edmonds, 22 March 1930, CAB 45/136.
78   VIII Corps G1585, HW Official War Diary, 48357, BL. The first operational order for the heavy artillery has very little information on 'Z Day' – arrangements were to be notified later: Operational Order No. 1 by D. F. F. Logan Commanding VIII Heavy Artillery, 16 June 1916: VIII Corps Artillery War Diary, WO 95/825, TNA.

A Day of Disaster

also keeping his corps in line as they attacked. In place of the corps artillery, he placed his faith in new military technology – in the ten minutes prior to the assault, enemy fire would be suppressed by the planned trench mortar barrage as well as intensified fire from the divisional artillery.[79] Despite protests from his officers, he remained resolute in his decision and on this occasion GHQ did not intervene to contradict him.[80]

Preparing

Preparations gathered momentum as the day of battle drew closer. The lack of labour battalions meant that the construction work required tended to detract from the training schedule across the Fourth Army, but in the case of VIII Corps, Hunter-Weston ensured that the time dedicated to brigade and divisional training was greater than in other formations, even though it alternated with wearying fatigues.[81] He had devolved training down to divisional level in April but ensured that this was being carried out to his scrupulous standards. As a result, he was constantly on the move in the weeks before the offensive, motoring and riding round his corps.[82]

If the training received by Hunter-Weston's troops was regarded as 'excellent', the same could not be said of his artillery preparation.[83] The

---

79 The corps contained eight heavy mortar batteries, nineteen medium batteries and thirty-two light batteries: VIII Corps Scheme for Offensive, HW Official War Diary, 48357, BL.
80 Travers, *Killing Ground*, 158; Farrar-Hockley, *Somme*, 113; J. H. Gibbon to J. E. Edmonds 13 February 1930, CAB 45/132, TNA.
81 Time Allotted for Brigade and Divisional Training by Corps, Haig Diary (typescript), Acc. 3155/106, NLS. Work on the 31st Division front alone included thirty-eight miles of trenches, eighty-six dugouts and thirty-four observation posts: J. P. Macready to J. E. Edmonds, 17 December 1929, CAB 45/136, TNA.
82 Notes on a Conference held at VIII HQ, 1 April 1916, HW Official War Diary, 48357, BL. For a typical day's activity, see HW Private War Diary, 22 May 1916, 48365, BL.
83 A. Johnston to J. E. Edmonds, 21 December 29, CAB 45/135, TNA.

preliminary five-day bombardment began on 24 June and was directed at wire cutting, destroying trench systems and machine-gun posts and subduing enemy batteries. The bulk of this destructive work fell to the VIII Corps Heavy Artillery, which was divided into four groups, two in the northern sector and two in the south.[84] The task of destroying machine-guns and dugouts near the front line was assigned to trench mortars and the 4.5-inch divisional field howitzers, while the field artillery attempted to disrupt communications, especially at night, to prevent the enemy from repairing the damage. No single Corps Heavy Artillery group had been allotted to counter-battery work, and when not being used for this task, their 60 pounders and 4.7-inch guns were switched to distant wire-cutting duties, which were beyond the range of the flat-trajectory 18 pounders.[85]

It soon became clear from night-time reconnaissance raids that the artillery programme was having very mixed results. In the 31st and 29th Division sectors, patrols were continually unsuccessful due to uncut wire and prompt artillery retaliation.[86] Wire was reported to be 'fairly well cut' in the 4th Division area, but here the enemy dugouts were found not only to be intact, but even still 'in excellent repair and scrupulously clean'.[87] The 1/Rifle Brigade's experience on one of these adventures also gave an early warning of the 'very unsatisfactory' performance of trench mortars, with bombs falling sixty yards short of the German front line.[88] Without more comprehensive intelligence it was difficult to judge the effects of the bombardment on the German defensive network, although there were worrying signs that strong-points had not been eliminated. On the 4th Division's front, C. B. Simonds of the 170th Artillery Brigade recalled his frustration when the Corps Heavy Artillery was unable to respond to requests for assistance to blast a suspected machine-gun nest, an omission which would

84 Fourth Army Plan of Attack: Haig Diary (typescript), Acc. 3155/106, NLS.
85 Artillery Programme V Day, HW Official War Diary, 48357, BL.
86 GHQ War Diary, 27–9 June 1916, Haig Papers, Acc.3155/191, NLS.
87 Report of a raid carried out by the 1/Lancashire Fusiliers on the night of 3/4 June, HW Official War Diary, 48357, BL.
88 1/Rifle Brigade War Diary, 29 June 1916, WO 95/1496, TNA.

A Day of Disaster

later lead to a heavy toll of casualties.[89] Meanwhile, regular reports of 'fairly active' hostile shelling suggested that the lack of effective massed artillery was also limiting VIII Corps counter-battery work; this was in addition to the use of maps showing enemy batteries that were 'incomplete and so misleading'.[90] Not surprisingly, when poor weather caused a two-day postponement of the offensive, the gunners took the opportunity to accelerate wire-cutting activity and give further attention to the latent artillery threat, while also shelling distant billets and communication lines.[91]

For Douglas Haig, the negative reports issuing from Hunter-Weston's HQ confirmed his doubts over the 'amateurism' of VIII Corps. He believed that failures in trench-raiding indicated a lack of leadership, and after visiting the 29th and 31st Divisions on 28 June, he commented that both seemed 'poor'.[92] Counter-battery work was a particular worry – indeed, this was one of the few occasions in his later typescript diary that he added comments to underline his original judgement.[93] Despite his earlier confidence in Hunter-Weston, Rawlinson's worries were also growing. At a meeting with Joffre on 28 June, he openly shared with the French commander that he was dissatisfied with VIII Corps artillery preparation; indeed it was clear from his diary that by the eve of battle he viewed Hunter-Weston's corps as the weak link in an attacking force of otherwise 'proven fighters'.[94] How far this criticism was personally directed at the Corps Commander is unclear. It may be that both he and Haig preferred to localise these issues rather than confront the evidence that artillery problems were actually undermining the planned offensive across most of the Fourth Army front.

---

89 C. B. Simonds to J. E. Edmonds, 3 February 1930, CAB 45/137, TNA.
90 GHQ War Diary, 26–8 June 1916, Haig Papers, Acc. 3155/191, NLS; C. M. Hogg to J. E. Edmonds, 4 November 1929, CAB 45/134, TNA.
91 VIII Corps Artillery War Diary, 29–30 June 1916, WO 95/824, TNA.
92 Haig Diary, 28 June 1915, Acc. 3155/96, NLS.
93 See his typescript entry for 10 May 1916 Acc. 3155/106: 'The hostile fire, moreover, is very different here. We must silence the hostile guns, and push on our infantry while the hostile guns are quiet'. Note also his addition to the entry for 29 June 1916 regarding his fears for the leadership at company and platoon level after the failure of the trench raids.
94 Rawlinson Diary, 28, 30 June 1916, Rawlinson Papers, RWLN 1/5, CCC.

Prior and Wilson suggest, for example, that counter-battery work was only being taken seriously in the XIII Corps sector, while success in wire cutting and trench destruction appeared generally to be patchy, with poor results and limited information also evident in the central area assigned to X and III Corps.[95]

The most critical of these observations remained private for the time being and Hunter-Weston remained in high spirits as 'Zero Day' approached – not least because intelligence from prisoners suggested that the Germans in the north expected only a series of raids or a 'minor enterprise' rather than a major attack.[96] His job was now to instil similar confidence into his troops. Visiting the 4th Division on the afternoon of 30 June, he addressed the CO of the 2/Lancashire Fusiliers – 'Splendid, Freeth! The enemy's trenches are full of Germans, they will be blown to pieces in the morning'. When these comments were conveyed to the men, Major Collis-Brown recalled 'we though this must be the start of the end of the war!!!'[97] Trusting his regulars, Hunter-Weston devoted most of his attention that day to the 'new blood' of the 31st Division by personally addressing each of its eight battalions.[98] Even Rees had to admit that his 'magnificent speech' at Observatory Wood strongly impressed his men, although for one young soldier of Sheffield City Battalion the uplifting effect was rather spoiled by the band playing 'When You Come to the End of a Perfect Day'.[99] Despite Hunter-Weston's best efforts, optimism was not universal across VIII Corps. Gloom had descended on the officers of the 1/Royal Warwickshire with the news of the early detonation of the Hawthorn Redoubt mine, while 12th Brigade also anticipated heavy

95 Prior and Wilson, *Somme*, 65–9.
96 HW to GHW, 27 June 1916, HW Private War Diary, 48365, BL.
97 J. Collis-Brown to J. E. Edmonds, 12 November 1932, CAB 45/132.
98 HW to GHW, 30 June 1916, HW Private War Diary, 48365, BL.
99 IWM Interview 16467: Donald Cheshire Cameron (12/York and Lancaster Regiment). Note also the testimony of IWM Interview 16473: Reginald Glenn from the same battalion.

casualties and sought permission to bury their dead on the spot – this request was refused.[100]

Writing to Grace on the eve of battle had become a ritual, but Hunter-Weston's letter on this occasion went beyond his usual self-congratulatory forecasts. As had been the case at Gallipoli, there was something about the scale of the enterprise that encouraged him to place his faith in a Higher Power. His Commander-in-Chief would have applauded his piety, if not the estimation of his corps:

> Tomorrow is the great day, & by this time tomorrow another great page in History will be turned. Everything promises well for the success of the great Venture & I have never entered a campaign with so many chances in our favour. The result is in the hands of God, but I can say that all has been done to done by Haig, by Rawlinson, and by my staff.
>
> Difficulties, disappointments, contretemps & heavy losses there are sure to be, but I rejoice in difficulties & pray God that I may be given strength & judgement to put right the matters that require to be put right, as the difficulties arise.[101]

Fighting

The narrative of VIII Corps seems curiously unbalanced. After months of planning and preparation, its fate was quickly, brutally and finally decided in a few minutes. Hunter-Weston later commented that offensives were decided by luck, but at the Somme 'luck' lay overwhelmingly with the defenders.[102]

Dawn promised a warm day. Hidden saps and tunnels had already been opened up towards the enemy, and at 5 a.m. VIII Corps heavy howitzers began their steady bombardment of the first and second German positions,

---

100 C. J. P. Ball to J. H. Gibbon, n.d., CAB 45/132; H. F. Davies to J. E. Edmonds, 29 November 1929, CAB 45/132, TNA.
101 HW to GHW, 30 June 1916, HW Private War Diary, 48365, BL.
102 HW to GHW, 9 April 1917, HW Private War Diary, 48366, BL.

gradually increasing their rate of fire until intensity was reached at 7.10 a.m. After ten minutes, in accordance with the corps artillery programme, the howitzers firing on the first line lifted to the reserve trenches, followed at 7.25 am by those that had been firing on the support trenches.[103] At Corps HQ, the detonation of the Hawthorn Ridge mine was recorded at 7.21 a.m.; the trench mortars and divisional guns had already begun their fusillade as leading assault battalions assembled in No Man's Land prior to zero hour at 7.30 a.m.

The attack of the 29th Division unravelled immediately. The Germans had begun appearing in their front trenches even before the heavy artillery barrage had lifted and easily won the race for the vast Hawthorn Ridge crater, creating a serious obstacle to any further advance.[104] The explosion was also the signal for a machine-gun barrage that caught the leading companies of the 87th Brigade as they formed up outside their trenches.[105] At this crucial moment, the thin shrapnel barrage from the British lines was further weakened by the division's decision that field batteries should adopt a phased lift from the front line three minutes before zero hour.[106] As the brigade attacked downhill at the deadly Y Ravine, struggling through partially cut wire and blasted by batteries firing unchecked from behind the Beaucourt Ridge, the guns continued their timetabled 'creep', removing any chance of receiving the close support that they desperately needed. By 8 a.m. their advance was at a standstill, while back at the brigade's empty 'Cage' for German prisoners there was a sickening awareness that something was going badly wrong.[107] On their left, having failed to secure the mine crater, the 86th Brigade's attempt to seize Beaumont Hamel made even less progress. Here, an artillery barrage was placed on the British front trenches as soon as the leading battalions began to advance. Starved of ammunition, the trench mortars could make little impact in the face of

---

103 Action of VIII Corps Heavy Artillery on 1 July 1916, VIII Corps Artillery War Diary, 98/825, TNA.
104 J. Hamilton Hall to J. E. Edmonds, 30 December 1929, CAB 45/134, TNA.
105 G. T. Raikes to J. E. Edmonds, 28 October 1930, CAB 45/137, TNA.
106 *OH 1916 (1)*, 431; E. W. S. Sheppard to J. E. Edmonds, n.d., CAB 45/137, TNA.
107 A. Stair Gillon to J. E. Edmonds, 6 September 1929, CAB 45/134, TNA.

A Day of Disaster

heavy machine-gun fire.[108] Exaggerated reports of a breakthrough in the 87th Brigade sector encouraged De Lisle to use his reserves aggressively, as Hunter-Weston had envisaged. He urgently sent forward the 1/Essex and 1/Royal Newfoundland Battalions 'to clear the whole front system', but after two disastrous assaults he was forced to suspend operations at 10.05 a.m.[109]

The 4th Division's attack on Redan Ridge began more hopefully, but also quickly fell victim to poor preparatory work. Although the wire had been more effectively cut in this sector, the main danger came from undisturbed machine-guns and from defenders emerging from deep dugouts. Again, the German machine-guns had continued to operate even during the final heavy artillery bombardment up to 7.20 a.m., with their reserves already massed in trenches on the Beaucourt spur in anticipation of any attack. Some observers felt 'practically nothing' of the Beaumont Hamel explosion, but enemy batteries now became increasingly active in bombarding No Man's Land before shifting their attention to the British front line.[110] Nevertheless, the advance battalions of the 11th Brigade were largely spared casualties in their assembly trenches; some companies rushed out of tunnel exits while others were seen advancing at a slow trot.[111] Together they were able to seize a foothold in the German front lines, although their right was badly mauled by machine-gun fire. Here, the creeping barrage was apparently more successful. Assisted by the enemy's mistake in detonating the mine under the Quadrilateral position, they managed to penetrate even further into the defensive network. A confused grenade fight followed,

---

108 Report on Operations of 29th Division from 30 June to Night of 1/2 July, HW Official War Diary, 48357, BL. Fuller later admitted that they had overestimated the effectiveness of these bulky and inaccurate weapons: J. F. C. Fuller to J. E. Edmonds, 24 January 1930, CAB 45/133, TNA.
109 HW Official War Diary, 1 July 1916, 48357, BL; G. A. Mackay Paxton to J. E. Edmonds, 19 December 1929, CAB 45/136, TNA.
110 G. C. Robson to J. E. Edmonds, n.d., CAB 45/137 TNA; *OH 1916 (1)*, 438. Before setting off, the CO of the 1/East Lancashires counted five machine-guns on the frontage assigned to his battalion: J. Green to J. E. Edmonds, 19 November 1930, 95/134, TNA.
111 1/Somerset Light Infantry War Diary, 1 July 1916, WO 95/1499, TNA.

but the failure to 'mop up' during the advance again led to growing casualties.[112] The assault was fast losing any cohesion and Lambton ordered a halt at 9.30 a.m., since throwing in more men looked like an 'unwarranted gamble'.[113] His signal did not reach the 10th and 12th Brigades, who continued to advance in accordance with the strict timetable set out in VIII Corps orders. As a result, there was confusion in the communication trenches; their Brigadiers lost control as their battalions advanced too soon and became mixed with units of the 11th Brigade.[114] It was now only a matter of time before the survivors would be driven out as their ammunition ran low and enemy bombers worked round their flanks.

The efforts of 4th Division to consolidate their desperate grip were greatly handicapped by the failed attacks taking place on either side of them.[115] The limitations of counter-battery work were clearest and most costly on the 31st Division's front. Given the excellent observation in the north, the Germans hardly needed the Hawthorn Ridge explosion or the lifting of the Corps Heavy Artillery to tell them that an attack was imminent.[116] Machine-guns opened up on the 94th Brigade as the first waves of infantry moved into No Man's Land at 7.20 a.m., but the intensity of the barrage from the trench mortars and eighteen pounders encouraged Rees to hope that success might be still possible.[117] All doubt was removed at zero hour when the full weight of the enemy's artillery was felt along the British front line and support trenches, reminding him of a 'thick belt of poplar trees'.[118] The fire was particularly destructive on the division's unprotected left flank, but it was impossible to stop the advance of either

---

112 Three companies of the 1/East Lancashires were reported to have been captured by Germans coming out from cover at 7.35 a.m.: War Diary, 1 July 1916, WO 95/1498, TNA.
113 W. Bartholomew to J. E. Edmonds, n.d., CAB 45/132, TNA.
114 W. Lambton to J. E. Edmonds, 29 October 1929, CAB 45/135, TNA. See also F. A. Wilson to J. E. Edmonds, 17 July 1930, CAB 45/138, TNA.
115 Lieut.-Colonel Dannerman to J. E. Edmonds, 23 December 1929, CAB 45/132, TNA.
116 E. P. Lambert to J. E. Edmonds, 1 November 1929, CAB 45/135.
117 Memoirs of H. C. Rees, 77/179/1, IWM.
118 H. C. Rees to J. E. Edmonds, 14 November 1929, CAB 45/137.

A Day of Disaster

brigade as they had already been ordered to move immediately in order to reach their objectives on time; in the event, only a few isolated parties managed to reach the German front line and enter Serre village, with entire battalions from the 93rd Brigade virtually wiped out by the wall of machine-gun and artillery fire.

Ten miles away at Chateau Marieux, Hunter-Weston was apparently fighting a different battle. For the first hour of the action, initial summaries were 'rosy', and it was not until 8.40 a.m. that the first real check, involving the 31st Division, was reported.[119] An avalanche of bad news then cascaded in, but he responded quickly by abandoning any attempt to capture the German second position by 10.25 a.m. and instead concentrating on consolidating the gains made by the 4th Division in Munich Trench.[120] He ordered the divisional and heavy artillery to redirect their bombardment to a 1,000-yard frontage in preparation for a combined operation by the 88th and 10th Brigades at 12.30 p.m., while also moving up the 48th Division in readiness. However, it was impossible to regain the tactical initiative given the congested trenches and fractured communication lines involved; the attacks were therefore cancelled by mid-afternoon. By this point, De Lisle and Lambton had made it clear that they were no longer capable of undertaking offensive action; the 86th Brigade had 'practically no one left' and the 87th was 'all but used up', while the shredded battalions of the 4th Division were slowly drifting back to their starting positions.[121] In the 31st Division sector, rumours that Serre village had been captured gave Hunter-Weston some lingering hope, but Rees and O'Gowan were reluctant to risk further assaults without confirmation.[122] Desperate to salvage something from the day, Hunter-Weston ordered the 92nd Brigade to attack under cover of darkness and join up with any remaining forward units, but then

---

119 VIII Corps Narrative of Operations of 1st July 1916. Showing the Situation as it Appeared to General Staff, VIII Corps from Information Received During the Day, HW Official War Diary, 48357, BL.
120 VIII Corps Narrative of Operations, HW Official War Diary, 48357, BL.
121 HW Official War Diary, 1 July 1916, 48357, BL. The Quadrilateral position was finally abandoned the next morning.
122 Memoirs of H. C. Rees, 77/179/1, IWM.

wisely countermanded this order at 9.45 p.m. As dusk fell, his men began organising their defensive lines and counting their dead.

The defeat of VIII Corps on 1 July was total. Its casualties were estimated at over 14,000 or around 50 per cent of its strength, a figure greater than any other corps in the Fourth Army.[123] Hunter-Weston appeared to absorb the shock philosophically, admitting to Grace with characteristic understatement that 'we have not attained the success we had hoped for'.[124] Elsewhere along the line the story was similar. On the left, a diversionary attack at Gommecourt, led by Snow, had been a miserable failure, while on the right the assaults by Morland's X Corps on the strongpoints of Thiepval and Mouquet Farm had also been repulsed at the cost of some 10,000 men. In the centre of the Fourth Army front, the sector most vital to Haig's plans, Pulteney's III Corps had sustained 12,000 casualties without making a breakthrough. Only in the south was there any positive news, as XV Corps, and XIII Corps in particular, had achieved better results, assisted by favourable terrain, weaker German defences and more effective counter-battery work.

Although he was far from alone in his lack of success, there was little safety in numbers. Despite his apparent composure, Hunter-Weston was steeped enough in the culture of the British officer corps to know that it was not only his corps that he now had to rebuild, but also his professional reputation.

---

123 *OH 1916 (1)*, 450.
124 HW to GHW, 1 July 1916, HW Private War Diary, 48365, BL.

A Day of Disaster 243

Aftermath

Convinced that VIII Corps wanted 'looking after', Haig and Rawlinson assigned it to Hubert Gough's Reserve Army along with X Corps, in the hope that he could 'push them on again'.[125] The vigorous Gough immediately motored northwards on the night of 1 July, but after discussing the situation with Hunter-Weston he knew that further attacks were futile.[126] Instead, the massive task of clearing of the battlefield now began. Despite the careful preparations which had been made for the disposal of the dead, the trench tramway set aside for the purpose proved to be completely inadequate, leading in some sectors to 'an enormous stack of corpses which were extremely bad for morale'.[127] Among the casualties were some of the last of the colleagues who had sailed with Hunter-Weston for France in August 1914, including Bertie Prowse, who had been shot in the back while rallying his brigade. Prowse was at least spared the ignominy of mass burial; the Corps Commander later arranged railings and a 'pretty cross' for his grave at Vauchelles.[128]

Expectations of victory made the disappointment across VIII Corps all the more painful.[129] Hunter-Weston decided to direct the full force of his personality towards rebuilding morale by visiting battalions who had been in action and circulating a printed message to every soldier in his command. His address acknowledged the difficulty of their undertaking at Serre and Beaumont Hamel, while saluting 'a magnificent display of disciplined courage worth of the best traditions of the British race'.[130] The number of copies carefully preserved by survivors suggests that his consoling

---

125 Haig Diary, 1 July 1915, Acc. 3155/96, NLS.
126 Hubert Gough, *The Fifth Army* (London: Hodder & Stoughton, 1968), 137.
127 W. P. H. Hill to J. E. Edmonds, 13 January 1930, CAB 45/134, TNA; H. F. Davies to J. E. Edmonds, 29 November 1929, CAB 45/132, TNA.
128 HW Private War Diary, 15 July 1916, 48365, BL.
129 J. C. Hawkhurst to J. E. Edmonds, 5 November n.d., CAB 45/134, TNA.
130 Message from Lieut-General SIR AYLMER HUNTER-WESTON to ALL OFFICERS, N.C.O.s and MEN of the VIII Army Corps, 4 July 1916, HW Official

sentiments struck a resonant note.[131] The return to familiar military routine also helped. VIII Corps was ordered to take over the line held by the 36th Division as far as the Ancre on 2 July, and battalions began the work of digging, patrolling and absorbing reliefs; in less than a fortnight, survivors from the 29th Division were parading in Paris in celebration of Bastille Day.[132] Nor did Hunter-Weston give up hope of returning to the offensive. As Anglo-French operations continued against the German Second Army during July, he prepared his corps to move forward by sapping and mining in anticipation of an enemy withdrawal in the north.[133]

Whether a similar sense of normality would return to his career was another matter. The war had elevated 'whitewashing' to a new military art form, of which the key components were speed and consistency. Hunter-Weston's mission to explain began when he offered to drive over to visit Sir William Robertson after breakfast on 2 July.[134] Whether briefing the Chief of the Imperial General Staff, writing to well-wishers or lunching informally at GHQ, his consistent strategic priority was to divert attention from any personal planning failures, particularly with regard to artillery support. With this in mind, he cited verbal testimony from Brigadier Lees which highlighted that the strength of the bombardment immediately before the assault was timely and helpful, and duly embellished it with some heroic rhetoric – much to Lees' later embarrassment.[135]

His own account stuck doggedly to four themes. The first was that he and his staff 'could not have done more' in view of the lack of surprise and the strength of the enemy's defences and massed artillery. Second, he

---

War Diary, 48357, BL. For his visit to the 1/8 Warwicks and his address to the 93rd and 94th Brigades, see 4 July 1916, HW Private War Diary, 48365, BL.

[131] This was certainly the case for one old soldier who 'would not part with his for anything'; see *Yorkshire Evening Post*, 23 March 1940.

[132] HW Official War Diary, 2 July 1916, 48357, BL.; HW Private War Diary, 14 July 1916, 48365, BL.

[133] Notes of a Conference at Corps HQ, 16 July 1916, HW Official War Diary, 48357, BL.

[134] HW to W. Robertson, 2 July 1916, Robertson Papers, 7/5/26, LHCMA.

[135] H. C. Rees to J. E. Edmonds, 14 November 1929, CAB 45/137. Hunter-Weston enclosed a copy for Robertson.

A Day of Disaster

argued that although the losses from the German artillery barrage were heavy, they were not enough to stop his men – 'it was the machine guns that finally wiped them out'. Third, he suggested, in complete contrast to his initial optimism, that a major contributory cause of the defeat was the inadequacy of his artillery and ammunition; he explained to Robertson that his howitzers could not stand continuous fire and that he had insufficient heavy howitzer shells with which to concentrate his fire on the enemy's front-line trenches. Fourth, he stressed that the gallantry and discipline and devotion of his troops on the day had been beyond praise.[136] Indeed, while whitewashing was often accompanied by scapegoating, Hunter-Weston remained fiercely loyal to his officers and men, including his divisional commanders, although his special fondness for the 'supra-excellent' 29th Division remained.[137] In time, he would weave these themes into a larger explanatory framework which banished failure even further from view. After Joffre publically acknowledged the contribution made by the 'hard fighting in the north', he felt entitled to claim that while the VIII Corps attempt had not been 'directly' successful, it had 'indirectly' made the victories on the British right possible by pinning down the enemy in a vital position.[138]

Self-preservation and wishful thinking aside, Hunter-Weston was stumbling close to the truth of the Somme. He had believed that the result of the battle would be determined by 'the spirit and fighting power of the men', but gallantry had not been enough to prevail against modern firepower.[139] While he could share the 'unpleasant and dangerous facts' of his artillery weakness with Robertson, it was more difficult to admit that it was Haig and Rawlinson's plan that had spread these resources even more thinly in the first place. Nor was he able (or willing) to confront his own shortcomings in command. While high-level decision-making had ultimately determined the outcome the Fourth Army's offensive, poor

---

136 G. S. Clive Diary, CAB 45/201; HW to W. Birdwood, 10 July 1916, HW Private War Diary, 48365, BL; HW to W. Robertson, 2 July 1916, 7/5/26, LHCMA.
137 HW to L. Kiggell, 22 July 1916 [draft], HW Official War Diary, 48357, BL.
138 HW to J. E. Edmonds, 12 December 1929, CAB 45/138, TNA.
139 HW to GHW, 30 June 1916, HW Private War Diary, 48365, BL.

counter-battery work, a very rigid plan of attack and the failure to integrate the mine explosion with his infantry assault had made the disaster all the more complete for VIII Corps. For the second time in his career, Hunter-Weston had set aside his own initial scepticism and decided to embrace a flawed strategy rather too enthusiastically.

If the failure of his corps had been due to a lack of offensive spirit, as Haig had originally believed, Hunter-Weston's dismissal would have been easy, but as the scale of loss became apparent, more complex considerations intervened to save him.[140] Competent corps commanders were fairly thin on the ground and the summary removal of Hunter-Weston without a credible replacement might have had a demoralising effect. Besides, as Carrington pointed out, 'the hero of Gallipoli' ... could not be 'sacked like an office boy'.[141] His qualities as a trainer were also to his credit, and Haig no doubt calculated that he would be eager and conscientious in any new defensive role that he was given. At any rate, no more could be expected of his depleted force. On 19 July, the Commander-in-Chief gave orders for his corps to be withdrawn from active operations at the Somme and exchanged with XIV Corps on the Ypres sector.[142] Haig let Hunter-Weston down as gently as possible, asking his Chief of General Staff, Sir Launcelot Kiggell, to write to him with personal assurances that the move would allow him to refit and be ready for any new campaign in the north, especially if this involved an amphibious element.[143] Nevertheless, Hunter-Weston was bitterly disappointed for himself and for his men, who would not now have the opportunity to 'get a bit of their own back.'[144] While happy enough to escape from Gough, whose 'impetuosity' and 'over-optimism' had become trying, it was galling that club drawing room gossips would assume that he had been 'stellenbosched'.[145] He would spend the months ahead trying to rationalise his fate, but for Grace's benefit, at least, he remained robust

---

140   Haig Diary, 1 July 1916, Acc. 3155/96, NLS.
141   Carrington, *Soldier from the Wars Returning*, 119.
142   GHQ War Diary, 19 July 1916, Acc 3155/191, NLS.
143   L. Kiggell to HW 22 July 1916, HW Official War Diary, 48357, BL.
144   HW to D. Haig, 22 July 1916 [draft], HW Official War Diary, 48357, BL.
145   Brigadier Philip Howell Diary, 16 July 1916, 6/2/1, LHCMA.

and unapologetic: 'As a matter of fact, this humble one and the whole of VIII Corps is very highly thought of ... Don't let it worry you. It doesn't disturb me in the least. He is a poor fellow that can't stand the rebuff of fortune ... If things go wrong under my Command, I accept all blame. In this case, however, there has been no blame'.[146]

---

146   HW to GHW, 27 July 1916, HW Private War Diary, 48365, BL.

CHAPTER TWELVE

Holding On

After his departure from the Somme, the record of Hunter-Weston's military career seems to disintegrate into anecdotes. Many of these are probably apocryphal, but they evoke a powerful personality confined by routine duties. He still attracted his admirers, but more commonly, it was disgruntled subordinates who bemoaned the 'madness' of their corps commander. A particularly perceptive portrait from this period emerges from the letters of Cuthbert Headlam.[1] A 'clever outsider' drawn into the BEF at the outbreak of war, the former civil servant was in close contact with Hunter-Weston, as GSO2 Intelligence, VIII Corps, between November 1916 and April 1918. Despite his Corps Commander's personal kindness towards him, he found Hunter-Weston to be an intensely conceited, loquacious and meddling little man who generated much fuss, bustle and extra work for his staff merely by his presence. Nevertheless, he remained rather sorry for him, grasping the misfortunes of his later career. While he thought Hunter-Weston 'a tremendous windbag' with 'the hide of an elephant and the vanity of a peacock', he also seemed a rather pathetic figure, 'no longer appreciated at his proper value'.[2] Headlam recognised his soldierly qualities, but with more Corps HQs in existence than active sectors it was painfully clear that he had been sidelined during a critical period of development for the BEF. Instead, he played the part of the general to perfection, hosting parliamentary delegations and entertaining allied statesmen, before later making his own flamboyant leap into politics as 'The Soldiers' MP'.

1   Jim Beach, ed., *The Military Papers of Lieutenant Colonel Sir Cuthbert Headlam, 1910–42* (London: Army Records Society, 2010).
2   *Headlam Military Papers* (5 July 1917), 170.

On balance, Hunter-Weston amused Headlam more than he annoyed him. At a time when many young officers took it for granted that the army was 'an odious necessity, a ghastly interruption of rational life', the Corps Commander's obsession with 'flummery' coupled with a fondness for heroic oratory meant that he cut a rather comical figure: 'the very image of a brass-hat'.[3] Mercifully, his lack of self-awareness shielded him from this fact. Yet there still remained a serious soldier behind the idiosyncrasies. He understood, for example, the scale of the task that lay ahead in training the new mass army; and while he may have done less actual fighting than many of his fellow Corps Commanders, the 'quiet' sectors garrisoned by VIII Corps were nonetheless tense and vulnerable places.[4] Indeed, his highly strung nature found the strains of command during these months even greater to bear in defence than they had been in attack.

'The Most Important Part of the Whole Line'

The tiny Ypres salient was a dismal place in the autumn of 1916. The enemy guns searched and probed from the safety of their concealed positions, and communications and drainage were a constant worry to the British defenders.[5] Military logic suggested withdrawal to a stronger line, but the symbolic significance of the salient made this impossible. For a soldier whose mind was filled with 'glorious stands' and 'gallant efforts', it was in some ways the ideal posting. Indeed, Hunter-Weston quickly convinced himself that his relocation was actually a mark of favour. After all, he had been entrusted with 'the most important part of the whole line' while Snow,

---

3 C. S. Lewis, *Surprised by Joy: The Shape of My Early Life* (London: Fount 1977), 145; see Carrington, *Soldier From the Wars*, 119.
4 Simpson notes that their time spent fighting battles was 'surprisingly small': Haig 63.16 per cent; Haldane 18.77; Congreve 14.38; Rawlinson 9.03; Hunter-Weston 4.85; Wilson 0.29: *Directing Operations*, 182.
5 De Lisle, 'My Narrative of the Great German War', vol. 2, 10, GB99/3, LHCMA.

Holding On

who 'was not so highly though of', was left at the Somme with a depleted corps.⁶ The inclination to overstate the importance of his new defensive role came naturally to him, but this was nevertheless a sector of real strategic significance. Its closeness to the Belgian coast meant that it held the key to Haig's continuing hopes for a further great offensive in 1917, while any German breakthrough would immediately threaten the BEF's lifeline of the Channel ports.

Hunter-Weston was fortunate that his arrival coincided with an unusually peaceful spell in the salient, with the Germans' attention diverted by operations at the Somme. Joining the Second Army and taking possession the comfortable Chateau Lovie, he was delighted to serve under Herbert Plumer, whom he considered to be a 'delightful man' and a 'thorough gentleman'.⁷ He reassured his wife, who was now running a soldiers' canteen in Euston Station, that his workload was not excessive, but his new area was large; it took an hour and a quarter in a fast car to reach the front line from his HQ.⁸ The notoriety of the salient also meant a that it received a steady stream of official guests including King George V, the Prince of Wales – 'a first rate youngster' – and King Albert of the Belgians, all visits requiring hectic bursts of trench cleaning and equipment polishing.⁹ He enjoyed the ceremonial aspects of military leadership and took an obvious delight in being one of the 'extra special big wigs' on such occasions, but his immediate priorities during these first months at Ypres were maintaining a strong defensive position and running an efficient corps.¹⁰ Looking ahead, however, he realised that future offensive capacity could only be assured

6   HW to GHW, 31 September 1916 [sic], HW Private War Diary, 48365, BL.
7   HW to GHW, 3 August 1916, HW Private Diary, 48365, BL. Gough was less complementary about the chateau, which later became his HQ, describing it as 'large, pretentious and ugly': *Fifth Army*, 193.
8   HW to GHW, 16 August 1916, HW Private War Diary, 48365, BL.
9   HW to GHW, 23 August 1916; 28 September 1916 HW Private War Diary, 48365, BL.
10   HW to GHW, 8 January 1917, HW Private War Diary, 48366, BL; Notes of a Conference of Divisional Commanders held at VIII HQ, 29 August 1916; Notes of a Conference of Battalion Commanders of 38th and 55th Divisions held at Corps HQ, 13 October 1916: HW Official Diary, 48358, BL.

through effective training. Units such as the 29th Division had lost over 5,000 casualties, but the problem went deeper than the ability to absorb new recruits.[11] As Griffiths suggests, the hugely expanded BEF was now a generally deskilled army, where basic tactical know-how had vanished due to the loss of experienced veterans; the challenge was how to break out of the vicious spiral where 'inexperience in one battle ensured the perpetuation of inexperience in the next'.[12]

The scheme of trench raids drawn up by VIII Corps provided one method of instruction, but a more significant and sustained method was Hunter-Weston's creation of a Corps School, a forerunner of the 'archipelago' of training schools that multiplied throughout the BEF over the next two years. The higher authorities were initially hesitant and funding remained tight, but he knew that the project was essential since many new company commanders were so poorly acquainted with 'the ABC of soldiering'.[13] Following Ruthven's recommendation, an experienced trainer, Lieut.-Colonel J. H. Levey, a former Sergeant Major in the Scots Guards, was sent out to get the venture under way in September 1916. Although specialist instruction was later given in areas such as air reconnaissance work, the School's most basic task was to teach junior officers and NCOs to think for themselves and lead instinctively, just as Hunter-Weston had learned from his own colonial apprenticeship.[14] Nor were senior officers exempt from the classroom. The ethos of professionalism was designed to permeate the whole corps; indeed, the Corps School was intended to stimulate comprehensive training systems at division and brigade level.[15]

Hunter-Weston was a constant visitor to his new creation and liked to address each intake. He considered himself a gifted teacher and was always happy to expound on 'the art of teaching', which he believed required

---

11 De Lisle, 'My Narrative of the Great German War', vol. 2, 10–12, GB99/3, LHCMA.
12 Griffiths, *Battle Tactics*, 64.
13 HW to GHW, 26 August 1916, HW Private War Diary, 48365, BL.
14 HW Private Diary, 12 September 1916, 48365, BL.
15 Address given by the Corps Commander at Senior Officers' School held at VIII HQ, 23 November 1916, HW Official Diary, 48358, BL.

'thought and system'.[16] One of his favourite techniques was the use of alliteration to drive a lesson home. His maxim, 'T.T.T. before T.T.T.' (Teach the Teachers what to Teach <u>before</u> Teacher Teaches Tommy) was one such attempt to communicate the cascade principle that was central to his approach.[17] He was also keen to give a higher meaning to even the most mundane tasks, impressing on his young audiences the 'glorious position of company commander' and the 'great duty' of training their men that lay ahead of them.[18] Above all, he wanted to instil the same qualities of character and professional knowledge that he had championed in his pre-war manual, *Training and Manoeuvre Regulations*. The idea of officers being 'a model to their men' had been second nature in the old army but now needed to be taught. Besides the need for personal smartness and turnout, he stressed their duty of care for their men in order to ensure that they would be 'in the very best condition at the right time to take their place against the enemy'.[19] When that time came, they should lead by example. He liked to illustrate this point by recalling the 11th Brigade's attack on Le Gheer:

> That terrible word 'Retire' was said. (Mark you my lads, have nothing to do with that word 'Retire'. Never listen to it. It is generally started by a coward who ought to be shot). One glorious fellow – a Drummer – (whom I salute) rushed forwards shouting: 'There is no such word "Retire" in our Battalion'. He walked up and down repeating this, and by so doing managed to save the situation and make of it the big success that it was.[20]

16 Notes on a Conference on Educational Training held at HQ VIII Corps, 5 January 1919, Official War Diaries of the 8th Army Corps Vol. VI. Reserve, Fourth French Army, Vimy Front and Final Advance. 1 May 1918-Jan. 1919, Add. MS 48360 British Library, [HW Official War Diary, 48360, BL].
17 Example of the Preparation of a Training Scheme, 25 May 1918, Some papers from the Official War Diaries of the 8th Army Corps, Vol. VII, France and Flanders, 1916–19, British Library, Add. MS 48361 [48361, BL].
18 Notes of a Conference held at VIII HQ, 4 August 1916, HW Official War Diary, 48358, BL.
19 Corps Commander's Address to officers attending the first course at the VIII Corps Senior Officers' School, 12 September 1916, HW Official War Diary, 48358, BL.
20 Corps Commander's Address to the NCOs and men of the training company at the VIII Corps Officers School', prior to their departure, 5 January 1917, HW Official Diary, 48358, BL.

The impact of this exhortation is not recorded – it may, of course, only have been a coincidence that the cover of the Corps School magazine 'The Bugle' bore the cartoon of a clown blowing a hunting horn.[21] However, there is no doubt that Hunter-Weston's oratorical powers attracted genuine respect. Rev James Wishart, a visiting military chaplain, reported that he held his audience in the palm of his hand, playing on their emotions 'as the great violinists play on the strings of their instruments'.[22] Unfortunately for some colleagues who had heard the story of 'the drummer of the good old 11th Infantry Brigade' once too often, the mixture of bathos and bombast wore thin; meanwhile, other new officers resented having to 'bow down and worship the remnants of the Regular Army', when they had learnt their own soldiering in the thick of modern battle.[23]

Spirited personal interventions aside, the divisions that passed through the hands of VIII Corps from the autumn of 1916 onwards do seem to have benefited from Hunter-Weston's commitment to officer education. One of the first of these was the 38th (Welsh) Division, which had been downgraded to line-holding duties after their failure at Mametz Wood in July 1916. After making 'great progress in military efficiency', the New Army division emerged as a very credible fighting unit a year later.[24] Following heavy losses at the Somme, the Territorials of the 55th (West Lancashire) Division were also sent to the Ypres sector in October 1916 for refitting and the training of new drafts. They went on to win a reputation as one of the BEF's 'premier league' divisions, performing well at the Third Battle

---

21   See HW Private War Diary, (1918) 48367, BL.
22   *Ardrossan and Saltcoats Herald*, 19 April 1918.
23   R. J. Pinney Diary, 17 March 1918, 66/257/1, IWM; *Headlam Military Papers* (13 March 1917), 159.
24   Message from Lieutenant-General Sir Aylmer Hunter-Weston, KCB, DSO, MP to The Officers, Warrant Officers, Non-commissioned Officers and Men of the 38th (Welsh) Division, HW Private War Diary, HW Private War Diary, 48366, BL. This was a highly political formation with strong links to Lloyd George: J. E. Mumby, *A History of the 38th (Welsh) Division* (London: Hugh Rees Ltd, 1920), 1–14. For Captain Wyn Griffith's experiences of VIII Corps and its commander during this period (15/Royal Welch Fusiliers), see *Up to Mametz ... and Beyond*, 131–8.

of Ypres and beyond.[25] A pattern was already being established whereby Hunter-Weston would rebuild units for others to command in active operations. Later in the war even this subsidiary role diminished, as declining manpower levels and the rapid turnover of divisions made it increasingly difficult to organise the sustained instruction in the battlefield skills that he considered essential for future success.[26]

The Honourable and Gallant Member

It was during his first months at Ypres that Hunter-Weston discovered a further non-military outlet for his energy. On 10 September, he received a telegram requesting permission to put his name forward as the Coalition candidate for his home constituency of North Ayrshire.[27] The alacrity with which he responded suggests that the approach not entirely out of the blue. He was also quick to gain the endorsement of his military superiors, who could see the advantages of having an unofficial spokesman in parliament. Haig communicated his entire approval with a 'charming letter', although Robertson stipulated that Hunter-Weston's services would still be required at the front until the war was over.[28]

Cynical observers suggested that this new opportunity offered some welcome compensation for his stalled military career, but his interest in home-front politics was in fact long-established.[29] He had viewed the war from the outset as a struggle of 'nations against nations' in which the mobilisation of Britain's whole productive power was essential to victory;

25 Griffiths, *Battle Tactics*, 82; Rev J. O. Coop, *Story of the 55th (West Lancashire) Division* (Liverpool: *Daily Post* Printers, 1919), 46.
26 HW to GHW, 28 March 1918, HW Private War Diary, 48367, BL.
27 HW to H. Blair, 10 September 1916, HW Private War Diary, 48365, BL.
28 HW to GHW, 26 September 1916; W. Robertson to HW, 26 September 1916, Private War Diary, 48365, BL.
29 *Town Topics*, 21 October 1916.

he had also been quick to contrast the 'selfless sacrifice' of the soldiers with what he saw as the squabbles on Clydeside over shorter hours and 'a paltry two-pence halfpenny of pay'.[30] While he had not personally been politically active in the constituency, generations of his family had been pillars of the local Conservative party and his uncle Robert Cochran-Patrick had served as the local MP between 1880 and 1885.[31]

While his path was smoothed by the decision of local Liberals not to field a candidate, an unlikely rival did emerge in the shape of the Rev. Humphrey Chalmers. Standing as the 'Independent Anti-Coalition Candidate', the radical cleric had the support of some prominent Glasgow-based Independent Labour Party figures.[32] 'The Baptist v. the General' caught the popular imagination during a whirlwind election campaign in early October 1916. Sympathetic to the Union for Democratic Control, Chalmers addressed nearly a hundred meetings across the constituency, calling for the formation of a new government and 'the cessation of the growing militarist domination of our own land'.[33] In contrast, Hunter-Weston's position as an absentee candidate was rarely questioned. His platforms were filled by local Unionist and Liberal figures, who presented the election as an opportunity to re-affirm national unity. The result was hardly in doubt; the voters did their duty and returned 'The General' with a majority of nearly 6,000.

The new member for North Ayrshire attracted national press coverage when he appeared in the House of Commons in full field uniform, with 'a face weather-beaten and wreathed in smiles'.[34] As Hew Strachan remarks, this was a remarkable example of the link between parliamentary and

30 *Scotsman*, 5 December 1914.
31 *Glasgow Herald*, 11 September 1884; 21 November 1885. North Ayrshire had also become known as a 'soldier's seat'. The 1916 vacancy had been created by the death of the sitting member, Lieut.-Colonel Duncan Campbell DSO, from wounds received on the Western Front.
32 *The Times*, 2 November 1916; *Daily Sketch*, 4 October 1916.
33 *Ardrossan and Saltcoats Herald*, 6 October 1916; *Evening Times*, 9 October 1916; *Labour Leader*, 12 October 1916; *Glasgow Herald*, 13 October 1916.
34 *Spectator*, 4 November 1916.

Holding On

military service.[35] Recently the traffic had been in the opposite direction, although most parliamentarians who had become soldiers during the war had been Territorials or had already given up their professional military careers. In contrast, Hunter-Weston was actually elected as MP while still a Corps Commander on active service on the Western Front.

He was lecturing to some of his men when the news came through of his victory and immediately requested that they heckle him for the sake of practice.[36] Over the next two years he developed a proprietorial attitude both to 'his' constituency and 'his' corps, even though his military duties meant that he could only keep in touch with the former through regular addresses and infrequent visits. It was therefore hardly surprising that the boundaries between his two roles became blurred. His acerbic staff officer Headlam was scathing over a ruse to send Christmas cards to North Ayrshire at public expense, but Hunter-Weston was equally willing to use his position to help his constituents who had relatives missing in battle.[37] As he settled in to his new project, his finest hour as a wartime parliamentarian was yet to come.

Assisting Operations

During early 1917 the Second Army front was sparsely defended, with intermittent mine warfare and the use of trench mortars compensating for the lack of heavy artillery.[38] VIII Corps held the extreme left of the British line – a 'place of honour' according to Hunter-Weston. The work of the

---

35 Hew Strachan, *The Politics of the British Army* (Oxford: Oxford University Press, 1997), 32.
36 Dunn, *War the Infantry Knew*, 408.
37 *Headlam Military Papers* (26 December 1917), 159; *Ardrossan and Saltcoats Herald*, 8 February 1918.
38 Cyril Falls, *History of the Great War based on official documents by direction of the Historical Section of the Committee of Imperial Defence: Military Operations in France*

corps benefited from Herbert Plumer's more coordinated and consultative command style, with notable progress made in refining trench raiding techniques.[39] Reduction to a line-holding formation inevitably meant that Corps HQ lost many experienced staff. Fortunately, the capable new Brigadier-General, General Staff (BGGS), Edward Ellington, was a man of few words who acted as a perfect foil to his Corps Commander.[40] Almost hoping for a small enemy attack, Hunter-Weston kept himself busy during these wearisome months with paperwork and inspections.

As he delivered yet another broadside on the care of gumboots and the issue of dry socks, Gallipoli must have seemed a lifetime away; but Hunter-Weston received an uncomfortable reminder of his former command when he was summoned to give evidence before the Dardanelles Commission in February 1917.[41] He was more than a match for the government-appointed commissioners, providing testimony that ran to forty-four typescript pages. He was given the opportunity to air his objections to the enterprise and to comment on its logistical shortcomings, but he also faced some tough questioning on his policy of 'small frontal attacks'.[42] However, as the conduct of operations was not the primary concern of the enquiry, it was to be another two years before its military findings were formally released.

On his return from London, Hunter-Weston's hopes rose that a strengthened VIII Corps might be allotted to the First Army in preparation for the spring offensive at Vimy Ridge, but this came to nothing.[43]

---

      and Belgium, 1917. Volume I: The German Retreat to the Hindenburg Line and the Battle of Arras (London: Macmillan, 1940), 533 [*OH 1917, (1)*].

39 These now followed 'general principles' which were set out at Army level: see reports from 55th, 38th and 39th Divisions (29, 30 April; 11, 12 May 1917): HW Official War Diary, 48358, BL.

40 *Headlam Military Papers* (6 January 1917), 153; Griffith, *Up to Mametz ... and Beyond*, 136. He became Air Marshal Sir Edward Ellington, who rose to become Chief of the Air Staff and retired as Inspector General of the RAF in 1940.

41 HW Private War Diary, 9 February 1917, 48366, BL.

42 Hunter-Weston, Evidence to Dardanelles Commission, 12 February 1917, Hamilton Papers,: 8/2/50, LHCMA.

43 *OH 1917, (1)*, 128. He had to content himself writing a tactical appreciation of Byng's 'simply magnificent' victory.

Holding On

Indeed, it was not until May 1917 that the pace of life began to quicken in anticipation of the Second Army's attack against Messines Ridge planned for the following month. This was the 'essential preliminary' for the main Flanders offensive that Haig hoped would clear the Belgian coast.[44] Having amassed nearly three times as many heavy guns per yard for the preliminary bombardment than were available at the Somme, Plumer intended to launch three assaulting formations, with VIII and II Corps in support.[45]

As planning for the battle intensified in early June, Hunter-Weston had by no means given up on his imaginative attempts to mislead the enemy. On this occasion, however, his suggestion for a 'demonstration' on his front five minutes five minutes before zero hour, using his heavy artillery to draw the fire of enemy batteries, was quickly brushed aside by the Army Commander, who was anxious to maximise the element of surprise.[46] Even so, he still hoped for some follow-up role if the initial phase of the battle was successful. His corps was due to pass into reserve with the Fifth Army after the battle, but Plumer suggested that it might join with II Corps in an attack along the Menin Road. Advancing some 1,200 yards north and south of the Bellewaarde Lake, the aim would be to open up the high ground at the western end of the Gheluvelt Plateau for use as a jumping off point for the main offensive, which Haig had entrusted to Gough's Fifth Army.[47]

Even if Plumer's plan suggested a measure of confidence in VIII Corps, Douglas Haig remained less than convinced. Visiting its sector on the eve of battle on 6 June, the Commander-in-Chief commented that it had taken the appointment of a new artillery commander, Brigadier Henry Ward,

---

44 J. E. Edmonds, *History of the Great War based on official documents by direction of the Historical Section of the Committee of Imperial Defence: Military Operations, France and Belgium, 1917. Volume II: Messines and Third Ypres (Passchendaele) 7 June–10 November* (London: HMSO, 1948), 88–9 [*OH 1917, (2)*].
45 *OH 1916 (1)*, 300–1; see, Griffiths, *Battle Tactics*, 150.
46 VIII Corps G8670; Second Army G 597, 3 June 1917, Second Army Headquarters Papers, WO 158/291, TNA.
47 HW Private War Diary, 25 May 1917, 48366, BL; *OH 1917, (2)*, 88–9.

to rescue the corps from a 'too defensive' attitude.[48] The next day, Hunter-Weston waited on the left of the Second Army ready to repel any centre thrusts made by the Germans on Plumer's flank. The morning began with the detonation of nineteen mines, creating a huge tactical advantage along the British line. VIII Corps artillery opened up immediately at 3.10 a.m., pouring neutralising fire onto enemy batteries in the northern sector; their counter-battery work had evidently improved, as the guns were able to reply to as many as seventy zone calls throughout the day, many of which were silenced.[49] The battle itself was savage and successful, eventually removing the Germans from the dominating southern face of the Ypres salient, but for VIII Corps Messines was poor revenge for the Somme; their marginal contribution to victory was evident from a casualty list of 203, compared with 24,567 for the Second Army as a whole.[50]

Nor was Hunter-Weston allowed his own moment of glory in the aftermath. On 8 June, his patrols reported the enemy's new line to be strongly held; Plumer then sensibly requested extra time from Haig for the transfer of medium and heavy artillery to allow the exploitation phase to proceed.[51] This was refused and control of II and VIII Corps was handed immediately to Gough, who had little appetite for an immediate attack and allowed the impetus to lapse. Whether this was a prudent policy or a costly mistake, it meant that VIII Corps would enter the reserve as planned, with its battle-ready 38th and 55th Divisions detached for Gough's use in the great offensive at Ypres.[52]

Handing over the last section of his old front line on 14 June, Hunter-Weston moved his HQ to the moated chateau at Esquelbecq. Even though

48 Haig Diary 6 June 1917, Acc. 3155/96, NLS.
49 HW to GHW, 7 June 1917, HW Private War Diary, 48366, BL; HW Official War Diary, 7 June 1917, 48358, BL.
50 *OH 1917, (2)*, 87.
51 HW Official War Diary, 8 June 1917, 48358, BL; Haig Diary 8 June 1917, Acc. 3155/97, NLS.
52 Second Army Headquarters, Letters, G906, W158/301, TNA. For a discussion of the failure to follow up after Messines, see Nigel Steel and Peter Hart, *Passchendaele: The Sacrificial Ground* (London: Phoenix, 2001), 59.

Holding On

his corps would not be involved in active operations, he was anxious to share his views on the coming offensive.[53] Fearing his superior's rashness, his main message was that Gough should adopt 'bite and hold' tactics. He rehearsed the classic argument that the depth of the attack on the first day of the offensive should be limited to the distance that the infantry could go without losing momentum and outrunning their artillery support. He had also given much thought to ground and weather conditions and to the risk of counter-attacks, which he thought were most likely to occur when the attackers had advanced furthest from their original artillery support; with this in mind, he insisted that the reserves should be as strong as number of troops taking the objective.[54]

His advice went unheeded and the new few weeks were frustrating for both commanders. In Hunter-Weston's case, life in reserve brought the usual challenges. He had been allotted the 61st Division (2nd South Midland), a second-line Territorial unit that had suffered a disastrous first engagement at Fromelles in July 1916. The Division displayed persistent weaknesses in patrolling and in the tactical handling of weaponry and would clearly require substantial retraining if it were to be properly equipped for the stress of battle.[55] During early July, gossip was already circulating around VIII Corps HQ was that Hunter-Weston had been summoned back from extended leave by Gough, and that he was 'quiet and below par'; he seemed to recover his spirits, but a month later it was again rumoured that he had been taken off by his ADCs to the sea for 'a change of air'.[56]

53 Tim Hannigan to HW, 9 June 1917, HW Private War Diary, 48366, BL.
54 VIII Corps G9448, 8 August 1917, Official War Diary of the 8th Army Corps [VIII Corps]. Vol. V. Ploegsteert and Passchendaele. 3 July 1917–25 April 1918, Add. Ms 48359 British Library [HW Official War Diary, 48359, BL].
55 Note by Corps Commander for 61st Division apropos of the Scheme for the Exercise Carried out on the 7th of August, HW Official War Diary, 48359, BL. The Division continued to be a source of worry when Lieut.-Colonel John Brough (GSO1) committed suicide at the end of July 1917.
56 *Headlam Military Papers* (5 July 1917; 16 August 1917), 170, 176.

As he lazed in the sun and watched cricket for the first time in years, things were going badly wrong for the Fifth Army at Ypres.[57] The first day of the offensive which opened on 31 July resulted in some 15,000 casualties. As Hunter-Weston had feared, Gough had overstretched himself by failing to secure the vital high ground on his right and exposing his exhausted assault troops elsewhere to enemy counter-attacks.[58] Hampered by rain and low cloud, he had then spent the next three weeks battering away at Gheluvelt and Langemarck until his attacks finally ground to a halt against strengthening German defences. Haig's grand strategic design for a landing from the sea combined with a thrust towards the coast by Rawlinson's Fourth Army now lay in ruins, as this had depended on the earlier success of Gough's break out. On 25 August, Haig belatedly entrusted the main effort of the offensive to Plumer in the hope that that the BEF's frontage could be extended at a more acceptable cost.

After more than two months in reserve, an augmented VIII Corps now re-joined the Second Army. Hunter-Weston rejoiced to be serving under such a 'topper' of a commander, and fully supported his tactical scheme for a staged advance on the Gheluvelt Plateau, which was submitted to Haig on 27 August.[59] However, he was fully aware that his own role in these operations would be a limited one. On taking his place in the line on 2 September with two divisions, he seemed to be travelling backwards in his career, revisiting the same flooded trenches between the River Douve and the Lys that he had held as an ambitious brigadier three years before. The heat was oppressive as he made his new HQ in a dilapidated little modern villa in the small village of Flêtre, near Hazebrouck. The departing corps had left their trenches in a filthy state and Headlam, returning from a short break with XIX Corps, found his Corps Commander 'madder than ever', with both his ADCs threatening to resign.[60]

57   HW to GHW, 17 August 1917, HW Private War Diary, 48366, BL.
58   Farrar-Hockley, *Gougie*, 221; Robin Prior and Trevor Wilson, *Passchendaele: The Untold Story* (New Haven and London: Yale University Press, 1996), 75.
59   HW to GHW, 21 September 1917, HW Private War Diary, 48366, BL.
60   HW to GHW, 26 August 1917, HW Private War Diary, 48366, BL; *Headlam Military Papers* (30 August 1917; 7 September 1917). 178–9.

Holding On

The Second Army's step-by-step approach was initially successful, crushing the opposition through concentrated artillery barrages. VIII Corps extended their frontage to allow I Anzac Corps to undertake the main assault at Menin Road on 20 September. Taking their place on the southern defensive flank of the Second Army, Hunter-Weston's guns simulated preparation for an attack at Zandvoorde and Warneton, bringing down very heavy shelling and machine-gun fire onto the enemy's front and support lines. Nevertheless, his artillery were able to carry out a considerable counter-battery programme, chiefly assisting the neighbouring IX Corps with their 60 pounders and 9.2 howitzers in shelling various sites during the day; six days later they reprised their supporting role as Plumer attacked at Polygon Wood.[61] Both the tempo and the ambition of operations were quickening, but the Battle of Broodseinde on 4 October marked the high point of the Second Army's efforts. In the face of unusually heavy rain and a partial check eight days later at Poelcappelle, the decision of Haig and Plumer to drive on to seize Passchendaele Ridge meant the continuation of a brutal struggle of attrition amid torrential rain and appalling ground conditions. Despite its defensive role, VIII Corps paid a heavy price, with 285 officers and men killed, wounded and missing during a typical week in late October.[62]

After Plumer's departure for the Italian front, command of the Second Army passed to Henry Rawlinson. Hunter-Weston continued to support the final attacks made by the Canadian Corps east and northwest of Passchendaele, employing his well-practised diversionary activities.[63] By the time the Third Ypres Battle was finally wound down on 10 November the Canadians had consolidated their grip along on the main ridge at the cost of 16,000 casualties, but the frontage of the assault had progressively narrowed, creating a precarious salient straddling the blasted high ground with an advanced outpost line precariously clinging to its eastern slopes.[64]

---

61   HW Official War Diary, 26 September 1917, 48358, BL.
62   Weekly report on operations for week ending 6.00 am Thursday 25 October, 1917, HW Official War Diary, 48359, BL.
63   VIII Corps Order 34, 4 November 1917, HW Official War Diary, 48359, BL.
64   *OH 1917, (2),* 358.

Five days later, this delicate morsel was handed over to a half-strength VIII Corps in the still-pouring rain.

The 'Silly Salient'

There was little sense of victory anywhere in the allied ranks after Passchendaele, and certainly not for Hunter-Weston, who was reaching one of the lowest points of his military career. Writing to Grace in a rare moment of tenderness and vulnerability, he was haunted by the fear of failure:

> The Army Commander has given over the defence of the whole Passchendaele salient to me. An honour, but a perfectly damnable position to hold. If the Germans think it worthwhile to put in an attack in force on this silly salient, we are, I fear, certain to lose it. However, I'll do my little bit to get the horrid place in the best order possible and will do all that is humanly possible to safeguard it. I have and have had many damnable and difficult jobs, and as someone has to do them, it is just as well it should be me, for I am so happy that if the whole world tumbled about my head and everything went wrong (which with God's help it shall not do here) I should still be a happy and contented man in the possession of your wondrous love ...[65]

When ordered to prepare his sector for a future offensive in the spring, he was extremely critical of the decisions that had led to this desperate situation, blaming Haig's preoccupation with 'knocking out the Bosche to get the cavalry through'.[66] On moving into the line in November, he had asked his new BGGS, Cecil Aspinall – already well known to him from Hamilton's GHQ at Gallipoli – to prepare a tactical appreciation. The result made disturbing reading. Command responsibility for the salient was initially shared with II Corps, with the front of the VIII Corps sector forming an almost exact semi-circle. The entire corps area, which

---

65 HW to GHW, 3 December 1917, HW Private War Diary, 48366, BL.
66 HW to GHW, 18 December 1917, HW Private War Diary, 48366, BL.

Holding On

was only 1,000–3,000 yards wide, was exposed to continuous shellfire on a 240 degree arc.[67] Matters had not been greatly improved by an ill-fated attack which was ordered by Rawlinson on 2 December. Undertaken jointly with II Corps, the aim had been to capture valuable observation points and improve defensive security near Passchendaele village, but the operation was poorly coordinated and hampered by bright moonlight, resulting in heavy casualties for both assaulting divisions.[68] It was the on following day that Rawlinson had assigned the entire responsibility for the salient to VIII Corps.

Operational conditions, as wearily detailed by Hunter-Weston, were deplorable. The ground was 'completely smashed up, with no tree, nor building, nor road remaining – only a few pill boxes'; it was impossible for troops to move across a landscape of deep mud pitted with shell holes, where duckboards, plank roads and tramlines were constantly being destroyed by artillery; positions were cramped and too closely concentrated, with often as many as ten field guns damaged and put out of action every day. In addition, holding the salient meant constant losses in both men and material, so that cadres which began weak soon became weaker, a situation that was 'bad for work, bad for training, and bad for morale'.[69]

Hunter-Weston's despondency was symptomatic of the general gloom that had settled over the Western Front by the end of 1917. This new mood was signalled by GHQ's acceptance of the general principle of a three-zone defensive system, disseminated via Haig's Armies during December to

---

67 Appreciation of the Situation on the VIII Corps Front: November 1917, Some Papers from the Official War Diaries of VIII Corps, 48361, BL. At this point, command responsibility for the salient apparently overlapped with II Corps in the northeast.
68 Hunter-Weston later claimed a measure of success for his 8th Division: An Outline of the Operations of VIII Corps, November 1917–November 1918, HW Official War Diary, 48360, BL. A detailed analysis of the action is contained in Michael LoCicero, 'A Moonlight Massacre: The Night Operation on the Passchendaele Ridge, 2nd December 1917', PhD Thesis, University of Birmingham, 2011.
69 HW to GHW, 15, 18 December 1917, HW Private War Diary, 48366, BL. De Lisle agreed that it was the worst sector that he ever occupied: 'My Narrative of the Great German War', vol. 2, 70, GB99.3, LHCMA.

ensure that corps defensive schemes were in alignment.[70] Hunter-Weston had already put his engineering knowledge to use in adapting VIII Corps defences to the dangerous local conditions; his outpost line was a series of small defensive positions organised chequer-wise in depth, while his frontline system involved a series of camouflaged defensive localities giving mutual support; these were protected by a carefully coordinated system of machine-gun defences and strengthened by an extensive switch system to localise incursions.[71] He had even begun to develop a miniature railway system to circumvent communication difficulties and ensure a supply of men and munitions when required.[72]

In his heart, he knew that he was wasting his energy in a sector that would be indefensible in the event of any serious German attack. Aspinall's report had floated the idea that the salient might not be worth keeping and suggested withdrawing 8,000 yards westwards to the line of Westhoek-Pilkem Ridge.[73] If defence was problematic, then the recent failed night attack further convinced Hunter-Weston that any idea of pushing forwards in anticipation of future offensive action was 'criminal folly' – particularly given the impending transfer of enemy troops from the Russian front.[74] He felt that there was no option but to confront his superiors. On 7 December, he went to see Rawlinson, threatening resignation unless he was allowed to pursue his plans for the immediate construction of a strong defensive position at Pilkem Ridge, while leaving only enough of a forward garrison to bluff the enemy.[75] It was fortunate that 'Rawly' shared his concerns; indeed, an Army Commanders' Conference on the same day confirmed the

70 Notes for Army Commanders' Conference on 7 December, 1917, Haig Diary, Acc. 3155/97, NLS; Proceedings of a Conference held at Second Army Headquarters at 11 am, 9 December, 1917, Rawlinson Papers, RWLN 1/10, CCC.
71 VIII Corps Conference held at HQ 33rd Division, 23 November 1917; VIII Corps Conference, 24 December 1917, HW Official War Diary, 48359, BL.
72 G. S. Hutchison, *The Thirty-Third Division in France and Flanders, 1915–19* (London: Warlow & Sons, 1921), 77.
73 Appreciation of the Situation on the VIII Corps Front: November 1917, VIII Corps War Diary, TNA: WO 95/821.
74 HW to GHW, 18 December 1917, HW Private War Diary, 48366, BL.
75 HW to GHW, 7 December 1917, HW Private War Diary, 48366, BL.

Holding On 267

seriousness of the manpower situation.[76] On 19 December, Hunter-Weston had a further interview with Rawlinson, Haig, and his artillery adviser, Noel Birch, who was 'nervous' about the number of guns in vulnerable forward positions in the salient.[77] Again, he sketched out the grim tactical situation and – in his own estimation at least – prompted the Commander-in-Chief 'furiously to think'.[78] Haig seems to have appreciated the risk, as he ordered half of the field artillery batteries to be moved back as soon as possible, leaving howitzers to undertake the barrage work.[79]

Rawlinson worried that this removal would leave the defensive barrage too weak, but Hunter-Weston was happy at these 'sane and proper' steps.[80] However, as he toured the corps defence zone in January 1918 under his Army Commander's disapproving eye, his fears grew that a fatal gap existed between the adoption of a realistic defensive policy and its implementation.[81] A deliberate retirement from the Passchendaele salient still made the best military sense to him, but the barrier lay not so much in the shortage of labour to build a new defensive line as in the difficulty of giving up ground which had so dearly been gained. As a consequence VIII Corps would remain in their blighted shell-trap for another three months.

Beneath his customary good humour, Hunter-Weston had by now become a bitter man. He still found solace in the company of his troops, rising early on Christmas morning to greet them on their way up the line, but there was a new asperity towards senior colleagues like 'Rozy' Wemyss, whose careers had prospered while his had not.[82] He looked older than his years, and the strains of command at Passchendaele were beginning

---

76 He feared that 'we shall be thrown on the defensive and shall have to fight for our lives as we did at the first Ypres': Rawlinson Diary, 7 December 1916, Rawlinson Papers, RWLN 1/9, CCC.
77 Rawlinson Diary, 12 December 1916, Rawlinson Papers, RWLN 1/5, CCC.
78 HW to GHW, 19 December 1917, HW Private War Diary, 48366, BL.
79 Haig Diary, 19 December 1917, Acc. 3155/97, NLS; Rawlinson Diary, 19 December 1917, 5201/33/27, NAM.
80 HW Private War Diary, 2 January 1918, 48367, BL.
81 Rawlinson Diary, 2 January 1917, Rawlinson Papers, RWLN 1/9, CCC.
82 *Headlam Military Papers* (25 December 1917), 187. He believed that the appointment of Weymss as First Sea Lord was 'nothing less than a national misfortune', due

to affect his behaviour in other ways. Always punctilious, his attention to detail had now developed into an obsession with minutiae, leading him to interfere in matters more appropriate for a junior staff officer than a Corps Commander. His refusal to delegate was in direct contradiction to *Field Service Regulations II*, which emphasised the need for decentralisation among subordinates, but he had lost the steadying hand of Ellington, and Aspinall was still struggling to find his feet.[83]

Controlling detail had perhaps become Hunter-Weston's way of coping with the tense military situation in his sector. However, his pursuit of perfection was also firmly rooted in the traditional paternalism of the British officer corps. His carefully choreographed parades and medal ceremonies were time-honoured mechanisms to be used for bolstering morale and esprit de corps in difficult situations. Many of his other pet enthusiasms were similarly based on a shrewd concern for the welfare of his troops. He was a firm believer that an efficient, well-scrubbed military machine could do much to overcome the sordid horror of life in the trenches. His critical gaze extended to kitchen ranges, stockpots and (a particular favourite focus for his attention) battalion water carts. Well aware that dysentery that could rapidly reduce the fighting capability of a battalion, he had also developed 'a nose like a setter for a trench latrine'.[84] The result of one of these was recalled by Eric Harrison, a young staff officer with the 58th Division: 'Inspecting a certain unit he went behind the latrines and had the buckets pulled out for inspection. When a fresh turd, uncovered by earth, was exposed, there was trouble, until his ADC, returning from the front of the latrines murmured, "You know, General, the bird's still on the nest"'.[85]

---

to his complete absence of brains: HW to GHW, 28 December 1917, HW Private War Diary, 48366, BL.

83   *Headlam Military Papers* (20/11/1917), 184. Hunter-Weston had earlier been supportive of Aspinall in his earlier attempts to obtain promotion: HW to C. F. Aspinall, 4 May 1916, Aspinall-Oglander Papers, OG/AO/G/28, County Records Office, Isle of Wight.
84   J. K. Stanford Papers, DS/Misc/75, IWM.
85   Harrison, *Gunners, Game & Gardens*, 51. See also Points Brought to Notice and Lessons Taught by the Corps Commander, VIII Corps, on his First Visit to the

His tireless admonitions clearly effected relationships with colleagues – one 'witty officer' who did not understand the depth of his frustration and unease at the end of 1917 described him as acting as though he were 'on heat'.[86] During this period, the ceaseless churn of units through VIII Corps brought him into contact with a succession of divisional commanders. The surviving diaries of two of these officers, William Heneker (8th Division) and Reginald Pinney (33rd Division) present a most unflattering portrait of a difficult superior. Both were returning to the irksome routines of a line-holding corps, after leading their units with some distinction in active operations. As career-minded soldiers they may also have feared guilt by association with a commander whose professional star was obviously no longer in the ascendant. A protégé of Sir Ivor Maxse, Heneker was an expert 'small wars' tactician who did not demur from describing Herbert Plumer as 'talking balls'.[87] When he heard that VIII Corps was about to take over his sector in August 1917 and that its commander was rumoured to be 'an ass', he decided to avoid him as much as possible.[88] His personal antipathy towards Hunter-Weston's grew after the latter's support of the set-piece attack on 2 December, which cost his division over 600 casualties.[89] Despite sharing a similar commitment to intensive training and the maintenance of 'smartness', he found his superior to be 'very mad' on the occasions when they did meet.[90]

Pinney, who was immortalised as 'the cheery old card' in Sassoon's poem 'The General', found it more rather difficult to keep his distance, although he discovered that if he stopped answering his Corps Commander

---

Front of a Division, September, 1917, HW Official War Diary, 48358, BL. One of his points was as follows: 'Latrines to be covered with lids; soiled paper prevented from blowing about'.
86   *Headlam Military Papers* (14 December 1917), 186.
87   W. C. G. Heneker Diary, 22 August 1917, 66/154/1, IWM; see John Bourne, 'Major General W. C. G. Heneker: A Divisional General of the Great War', in Hughes and Seligman, *Leadership in Conflict*, 54–67.
88   Heneker Diary, 26 August 1917, 66/154/1, IWM.
89   Heneker Diary, 19–21 November 1917, 66/154/1, IWM.
90   Heneker Diary, 2–8 January 1917, 15 February 1917, 66/154/1, IWM.

during 'one of fussy phone calls about gas or draining posts', he would eventually ring off.[91] His arrival at VIII Corps in November 1917 had got off to a bad start when his predecessor Philip Wood claimed that Hunter-Weston had bullied him out of his command, although the caustic Heneker commented that his sacking was 'a good job too'.[92] Pinney initially found his new chief to be very hospitable, but his habit of being 'most discursive on many subjects' soon wore him down, and his diary soon became peppered with instances of Hunter-Weston's patronising omniscience.[93] His training methods were a particular bone of contention. After delivering a lecture to the officers of 33rd Division, Hunter-Weston required Pinney's staff to submit their notes in the form of 'well-arranged paper'.[94] Reviewing the submission of the GOC 19th Infantry Brigade, the Corps Commander discovered a serious omission – the officer in question had failed to pay adequate attention to the chopping board issue. He reminded him:

> In order to preserve the kitchen tables, a small chopping board should always be provided on which to place meat which has to be chopped up. A small handing board can be easily scrubbed and kept clean, and when finally its service becomes too bad from the destructive action of the chopper, this board can be used as firewood and another board taken into use.[95]

The eccentricities of many senior commanders on the Western Front often caused consternation and sometimes offered comic relief, but in Hunter-Weston's case the gap between impact and good intentions is particularly striking. He was genuinely proud of his 'educative' approach to inspections:

> I always make a point when going round to make my inspections quite different to the ordinary general's inspections. I never go round to find fault. I only go round to assist & help, which I do by hanging talks on a big principle on to some good or bad

---

[91] Pinney Diary, 28 November 1917, 66/257/1, IWM.
[92] Pinney Diary, 17 March 1918, 66/257/1, IWM; Heneker Diary, 26 August 1917, 66/154/1, IWM. Robbins accepts Wood's claims at face value, but there was evidently more to this case: *British Generalship*, 32.
[93] Pinney Diary, 3 December 1917, 66/257/1, IWM.
[94] Pinney Diary, 28 December 1917, 66/257/1, IWM.
[95] VIII Corps G 3268 [December 1917], HW Official War Diary, 48358, BL.

point ... My inspections, I think, are therefore enjoyed rather than dreaded, except by the real slackers.[96]

Unfortunately, harassed subordinates experienced these visitations rather differently, even devising code words – 'GAWDHELPUS' – to extricate themselves.[97] The most revealing portrait of the Corps Commander at work is contained in Bernard Freyberg's unpublished war memoirs. Freyberg was certainly no 'slacker'. A Gallipoli veteran and VC-winner, he had recently taken command of the 87th Brigade aged only twenty-eight. He was, in Hunter-Weston's opinion, 'a wonderful fellow'.[98] Indeed, he was so eager to inspect the billets of his new brigadier that not even the opening of the great German offensive on 21 March could deter him. The visit started badly with Hunter-Weston reprimanding Freyberg for not having tacked down the carpet on the stairs leading to his bedroom. His 'prolific brain' then proceeded to suggest many improvements for the billets. He next decided to inspect the Mess of 4/Worcesters, where he had kitchen hygiene firmly in his sights:

> On arrival, he asked to see the mincing machine and by a happy chance it was produced, shining like a new penny. No fault could be found. Even its blades for cutting meat were clean, too clean, in fact. Doubts were expressed by the angry critic as to whether the machine was used.
> The mess cook was sent for:
> 'Yes, he used it frequently.'
> 'What did he make with it?'
> 'Oh! Lots of things.'
> But when forced out into the open, he could only think of 'rissoles.'
> Now followed triumphantly a long list of dishes that could be prepared by its aid, which included six methods of employing waste bread, and various ways of cutting up vegetables.
> 'Did the Worcesters cut up their bread with the same blades as they used for their meat?'

---

96 HW to GHW, 8 September 1918, HW Private War Diary, 48367, BL.
97 Pinney Diary, 30 March 1918, 66/257/1, IWM; Griffith, *Up to Mametz ... and Beyond*, 136.
98 HW to GHW, 21 February 1918, HW Private War Diary, 48367, BL.

'Where were the blades supplied for that purpose?'

After a hunt for a few minutes the missing parts were guiltily produced, dirty and completely blocked up with rust.

This was a great stroke of luck. All further inspection of the mess ceased, and for five minutes we listened breathlessly to a list of the diseases that were directly attributable to dirty mincing machines. The ten plagues of Egypt faded into obscurity.[99]

In a way, such encounters are rather poignant given Hunter-Weston's original reputation for dash and military risk-taking. For officers of Freyberg's generation, he had become a pompous irrelevance, displaying qualities that would have made 'an admirable plumber or a medical officer of health', but which were hardly appropriate to a fighting general.[100]

---

99 'A Linesman in Picardy, transition between Gallipoli and France', CAB 45/208, TNA.
100 Stanford Papers, DS/Misc/75, IWM.

CHAPTER THIRTEEN

Breaking Through

Amid the anxieties and disappointments of the Passchendaele front, politics came to Hunter-Weston's rescue. In January 1918 he made a remarkable parliamentary debut, delivering what was hailed at the time as 'the war's greatest speech'.[1] More importantly, the final year of hostilities also brought the resumption of mobile warfare and the return of VIII Corps as a fighting formation. In the battles of the Hundred Days it would no longer be necessary to use his infantry to compensate for the lack of firepower as had been the case at Gallipoli, or to exploit the application of brute force as at the Somme. Instead, control of the battlefield had shifted to the attacker and it was now possible to conduct a material-based offensive without a costly sacrifice of manpower. As an early advocate of the combined arms approach, Hunter-Weston's command philosophy continued to develop during this period, ensuring that when the final advance began in August 1918 his corps would make a modest yet creditable contribution to the allied victory.

The Speech of the War

The essential background to Hunter-Weston's triumph as a parliamentarian was the end of the government's commitment to a 'large army first' principle. After Passchendaele, the prospect of continuous battles of attrition without decisive results, coupled with doubts over the long-term sustainability of the British war effort, had led policymakers to attempt to

---

1 *Newcastle Illustrated Chronicle*, 28 February 1918.

find a balance between military manpower demands and the competing claims of agriculture and the war industries.² This process also marked the beginning of greater political control over Haig's conduct of the war, even though there was little consensus over an alternative military strategy. On the home front, morale was plagued by severe food shortages, industrial unrest and an unrestricted night bombing campaign directed at London.³

Hubert Gough later claimed that it was he who had begged Hunter-Weston to make a speech to put the army's case and to 'cheer and hearten our people'.⁴ In fact, as the commander of a depleted corps in a fragile sector – and someone who enjoyed the limelight – Hunter-Weston needed little encouragement. He set off from his HQ at Vogeltje on 13 January in 'a monstrous exhibition of weak-headed vanity and unscrupulous extravagance' that affronted the prim Headlam.⁵ On his arrival in London, the preparations for his speech hint at how well connected he had become; apparently the time spent entertaining the great and the good on the Western Front had been well spent. First, he discussed his ideas with Lord Northcliffe and Geoffrey Dawson, editor of *The Times*, later circulating the text to Lloyd George and Lord Derby, the Secretary of State for War, both of whom gave their approval.⁶

When he rose to address the House of Commons on 24 January 1918 during the debate on Clause Two of the new Military Service Bill, Hunter-Weston cut a dashing figure, complete with monocle and three rows of medal ribbons.⁷ Claiming that he rose only with 'great diffidence', the oration that followed was a tour de force, balancing his desire to bring home

---

2   Keith Grieves, 'The "Recruiting Margin" in Britain: Debates on Manpower during the Third Battle of Ypres', in Peter Liddle, ed., *Passchendaele in Perspective: The Third Battle of Ypres* (Leo Cooper, 1997), 53; David Stevenson, *With Our Backs to the Wall: Victory and Defeat in 1918* (London: Allen Lane, 2011), 259–60.
3   Adrian Gregory, *The Last Great War: British Society and the First World War* (Cambridge: Cambridge University Press, 2008), 213.
4   Gough, *Fifth Army*, 242.
5   *Headlam Military Papers* (13 January 1918), 189.
6   HW Private War Diary, 13 January 1918, 48367, BL.
7   *Hansard*, House of Commons Debates, 24 January 1918, vol. 101, cc. 1160–265; *Daily Graphic*, 27 January 1918.

the facts of the manpower crisis with the need to maintain confidence in the army's ability to deliver ultimate victory. His message on the indivisibility of the home and fighting fronts was a simple one, and while his sentiments were neither profound nor very original, they were expressed forcibly and eloquently, drawing on all of his authority and experience as a senior commander.

His main argument was that the army needed the full support of those on home front, rather than 'destructive and ill-informed criticism'. National solidarity was vital, as the present conflict was a struggle for Britain's very existence, but military claims for manpower must remain paramount:

> We need men. We specially need young men. We need men to hold and work and fight on our front. We need men to continue working on our many defensive lines. We need men to continue to improve the communications, on which so enormous an amount of work has been done during this past year. Above all, we need men to train for offensive and counter-offensive action, so that we may have strong, well-trained divisions with which to meet and defeat the enemy.

If the army represented 'the nation at the front', then industrial workers, 'the army at home', also had their part to play:

> Guns, aeroplanes, munitions, are our lifesavers. Without them our men suffer heavy casualties. With them, we can so deal with the enemy that our losses are reduced to a minimum. Therefore, I would beg them to remember that any interruption or cessation of work means wounds and death to the brave lads who are fighting for you.

He concluded by offering an emotionally uplifting morale-booster in the form of one of his characteristic extended metaphors:

> I say, therefore, to all: Have Courage Confidence and Resolution! ... A great flood of liberty and justice has been surging against the great dam, formed by the Prussian desire to attain world domination, based on might and long-prepared military force. To the superficial observer that dam still seems to stand fast. But under the dam a steady, if unseen, process of disintegration has been going on, and someday the dam of might will burst, and the great flood of right will carry all before it.[8]

---

8   *Hansard*, House of Commons Debates, 24 January 1918, vol. 101, cc. 1160–265.

Hunter-Weston's speech, of course, could hardly resolve the manpower crisis by itself, and indeed the issue continued to convulse Parliament for the rest of the year. However, his 'thrilling appeal' seized the national imagination just as public confidence in the government's handling of the war had reached a low ebb. Newspapers hailed the military parliamentarian as an authentic 'voice from the trenches', 'a healthy breeze' in contrast to the jaded factionalism of civilian politicians; copies of 'the Man-Power Speech' were also printed for distribution in factories, schools and clubs.[9] The effusive reaction of the press was matched by a flow of personal congratulations from luminaries such as Lord Londonderry, Henry Rawlinson and a 'delighted' Douglas Haig, but the ultimate accolade came from the King, who discreetly conveyed his appreciation via Lady Hunter-Weston.[10]

Escape from Passchendaele

Back at his Corps HQ, Hunter-Weston was observed basking in the glory with a conceit so spontaneous that it was difficult to take offence.[11] His new role as unofficial 'liaison officer' between the Army and Parliament brought him a great deal of personal fulfilment, but the urgency of his call for front-line manpower and national unity was fully vindicated when the Germans launched their long-awaited offensive eight weeks after the speech, on 21 March.[12]

---

9   *Daily Mail*, 25 January 1918; *Daily Sketch*, 25 January 1918; *Reynold's Newspaper*, 27 January 1918; *Lloyd's Weekly News*, 27 January 1918; *Scots Pictorial*, 2 February 1918.
10 HW to GHW, 5 February 1918, HW Private War Diary, 48367, BL.
11 *Headlam Military Papers* (5 February 1918), 191.
12 The description was Herbert Samuel's: *Hansard*, 24 January 1918, vol. 101, cc. 1160–265. For the March offensive, see Martin Middlebrook, *The Kaiser's Battle* (Barnsley: Pen & Sword, 2007); Samuels, *Command and Control*, 230–69; Tim Travers, *How The War was Won: Command and Technology in the British Army on the Western Front, 1917–18* (London and New York: Routledge, 1992), 50–90.

Breaking Through

Despite the acceleration of hostile raids at Passchendaele during that month, he had correctly forecast that that no major attack was imminent in his sector due to the 'horrible' ground conditions. This was a calculation which may explain his decision to continue with the routine inspection of Freyberg's brigade even after the first blow had fallen in the south; he was also prescient that Germany's military leaders would face 'a revulsion of feeling' on the home front if their all-out gamble failed.[13] Even so, his mood swung violently from complacency to alarm as news of the dramatic British retreat in the south filtered back to his HQ.

Sending home a present of artichokes and prunes with one of his officers who was going off on leave, he blithely assured Grace on 22 March that although the previous day's fighting had delivered 'a distinctly hard knock', things probably looked much worse from the perspective of the home front.[14] Twenty-four hours later his views had changed dramatically. Like Haig, he was shocked by the speed of the British withdrawal and the apparent lack of resistance, particularly from Gough's Fifth Army, asking his wife to keep the secret that: 'we may be in view of a grave disaster'. From his own bitter experience, he added that one of the main causes of the reversal was that under-trained British divisions were less efficient than their German counterparts in a war of movement.[15]

Yet, the situation was not as dangerous as it first appeared. 'Operation Michael' was the first of five German offensives that would be delivered with diminishing force between March and July. Over the next week, logistical failings, exhausted attackers and a British recovery under unified allied command helped to stabilise the line in front of Amiens. As the immediate crisis subsided in the south, Hunter-Weston's thoughts returned to the defence of the Passchendaele salient. He worried that his 'very unsound' position would become even less defensible after his best units were replaced by weak, tired divisions from the southern battlefront.[16]

---

13   HW to GHW, 18 February 1918, HW Private War Diary, 48367, BL.
14   HW to GHW, 22 March 1918, HW Private War Diary, 48367, BL.
15   HW to GHW, 23 March 1918, HW Private War Diary, 48367, BL.
16   He was losing the 1st and 33rd divisions as well as the returned 29th. These were replaced by the 9th and 41st Divisions, which had been in action in the battles of

Secret plans for a phased withdrawal to a strengthened battle-zone position at Pilkem ridge had already been put in place, but he was desperate to quit the salient immediately.[17] He put his case to Plumer as soon as the latter returned to command of the Second Army in March, but found that he remained 'on the crest of a wave' after his recent victories on the Ypres front, and was consequently unwilling to yield even an inch of captured ground; nor could Hunter-Weston convince his fellow Corps Commanders to abandon their advanced positions, due to their fear that any withdrawal might provoke attack.[18]

Deeply concerned, he shared his fears with Grace that that history was about to repeat itself:

> It is a curious fatality that at Gallipoli, on the Somme and here again now, I have to carry out a policy with which I disagree, and as to which I have expressed myself strongly to commanders. However my duty as a subordinate commander is, after making my point of view quite clear to my superior and making him see the reasons for my point of view, my duty, as I say then, is to carry on to the best of my ability whatever is decided. There must be only one man to make a plan, and that must be the Commander-in-Chief. If an attack is made from southeast of Ypres on a broad front on each side of the Menin Road, and if it succeeds, the troops holding the salient would be cut off, and large proportion of field and corps artillery of VIII Corps lost ... Plumer and Haig know this but still hold that best course overall is to remain in salient.[19]

On 7 April, the Germans began their second great offensive, 'Georgette', with the objective of capturing Ypres and forcing the British back to the Channel ports. Two days later, as he waited in expectation of an enemy attack on the right of his corps, the war hit home personally to Hunter-Weston. He was visiting the 86th Brigade when his groom, John Ramsay,

---

St Quentin and Bapaume: HW to GHW, 1 April 1918, HW Private War Diary, 48367, BL.

[17] HW Official War Diary, 20 February 1918, 48359, BL.
[18] HW to GHW, 23 March 1918, HW Private War Diary, 48367, BL; Minutes of Corps Commanders' Conference, 23 March 1918, HW Official War Diary, 20 February 1918, 48359, BL.
[19] HW to GHW, 23 March 1918, HW Private War Diary, 48367, BL.

Breaking Through 279

was killed by shellfire on the main Poperinghe-Ypres road, after he had gone on ahead with the horses. A Gallipoli veteran, 'dear little Ramsay' had been 'a very good friend'. The Corps Commander was observed at his funeral 'standing erect and unmoved at the salute', but wrote privately that he had not felt the death of anyone in the war as deeply as that of 'this splendid little man'.[20]

Ramsay's death was one misfortune among many as the Germans continued to advance, but this latest enemy onslaught also finally extricated VIII Corps from Passchendaele, thus avoiding a third and potentially career-wrecking disaster for its commander. Under the pressure of a general attack along the Second Army front on 10 April, Plumer was forced to relinquish Messines and the other gains he had made the previous autumn but he still could not bring himself to give up Passchendaele.[21] Tim Harrington, his Chief of Staff, motored north to consult Hunter-Weston, who again advised immediate withdrawal to prevent the enemy pinching off the salient, but another emotional meeting was required before Plumer accepted the inevitable.[22]

Hunter-Weston showed no such hesitation. Spared the attentions of the enemy, VIII Corps began moving back its artillery to the battle-zone on the night of 11 March, with its infantry following the next night.[23] Although this phased withdrawal followed a prearranged schedule, the *Official History* suggests that its speed may have caused some difficulties to the neighbouring II Corps Commander, Lieutenant-General Claude Jacob, who had planned a more gradual movement.[24] With a shorter and better line now in place, a relieved Hunter-Weston handed over his 41st

20 HW to GHW, 4 April 1918; HW to Mrs Ramsay, 9 and 12 April 1918, HW Private War Diary, 48367, BL; see also *Ardrossan and Saltcoats Herald*, 17 May 1918.
21 Haig Diary 11 April 1918, Acc. 3155/125, NLS.
22 Charles Harrington, *Plumer of Messines* (London: John Murray, 1935), 161.
23 VIII Corps Order 150, HW Official War Diary, 12 May 1918, 48360, BL.
24 J. E. Edmonds, *History of the Great War based on official documents by direction of the Historical Section of the Committee of Imperial Defence. Military Operations. France and Belgium, 1918. Volume I: The German March Offensive and its Preliminaries* (London: Macmillan, 1935), 274–5.

Division to Jacob at 8 a.m. on 13 April, and moved out of the line and 'clear of the horrid PASSCHENDAELE salient'.[25]

As Harrington recalled, the next weeks were momentous for the Second Army – 'we were literally hanging on by our eyelids'.[26] It was not until the end of April that the offensive began to dwindle, by which time the British had given up of most of the territory they had held around Ypres. Meanwhile, VIII Corps was relegated to the digging of new back lines at Cassel and receiving exhausted divisions from the south. Much of his time as a Corps Commander in reserve was spent in conferences, but there were plenty of opportunities to indulge his passion for strenuous exercise, galloping over the nearby wheat fields. He was also invited to deputise for Plumer at the visit of the French Premier, Georges Clemenceau, who at the age of seventy-six astonished him by displaying the energy of a man twenty years younger.[27]

Hunter-Weston's diplomatic skills and fluent French became even more valuable the next month when Haig ordered VIII Corps to join the French Fourth Army front in the Champagne-Argonne region.[28] This was in response to a request from Foch, the new Commander-in-Chief of the Allied Armies, that a large number of reserve units should be withdrawn from the British zone in anticipation of a renewed enemy offensive.[29] Haig, who was 'very nice' to the departing Corps Commander, drew Hunter-Weston aside and asked him to report personally from time to time.[30] The responsibilities of his corps remained limited to line holding for the moment. His new HQ was a villa on the outskirts of Challons, whose proximity to Paris meant frequent shopping trips and even an extended visit from Grace. The move also allowed him to renew his acquaintance with Henri Gouraud, who had taken command of the Fourth Army, as well as bringing him into the orbit of other luminaries, such as Pétain and

25 HW to GHW, 13 April 1918, HW Private War Diary, 48367, BL.
26 Harrington, *Plumer*, 160.
27 HW to GHW, 22 April 1918; HW Private War Diary, 48367, BL.
28 VIII Corps Orders, 130, 132, HW Official War Diary, 20 February 1918, 48359, BL.
29 Haig Diary 6 June 1918, Acc. 3155/130, NLS.
30 HW to GHW, 13 May 1918; HW Private War Diary, 48367, BL.

Breaking Through

Franchet d'Espèrey. This pleasant interlude ended in sudden and dramatic fashion on 19 June, when a despatch rider arrived at the Ritz Hotel, where Hunter-Weston was sipping coffee, with the news that VIII Corps was to be broken up in five days' time; he was ordered to take over command of XVIII Corps on the Vimy front.[31]

Prompted by Haig's fears that the Germans were preparing to seize the tempting bait of Vimy Ridge, Hunter-Weston's sudden recall had only been decided after a tug-of-war between the British Commander-in-Chief and an equally anxious Foch.[32] Having escaped the grip of the *Généralissime*, he arrived on the front of General Sir Henry Horne's First Army, which stretched from Hill 70, east of Loos, via Lens and Vimy Ridge, south towards Willerval. He had already changed armies more frequently than most Corps Commanders, but he always nurtured cordial personal relations with his various superiors – Gough, for example, assured him that the letter he sent him on leaving the Somme in July 1916 would remain one of his 'most cherished possessions'.[33] However, although Horne was an old friend, the temperaments of the two men were quite different. Famed for his quietness and restraint, Horne respected Hunter-Weston as a 'gentleman' but found his voluble, emotional nature difficult to handle. His doubts over his suitability for active service had begun shortly after Hunter-Weston's return from Gallipoli and he now complained to his wife that he found his subordinate 'rather "cracky"' and apt to fuss over trifles; typically, one of his most pressing concerns on arrival had been the redesignation of XVIII Corps as 'VIII Corps'.[34]

---

31 HW Private War Diary, 19 June 1918, 48367, BL.
32 On his dealings with Foch, see Haig Diary 6 June 1918, Acc. 3155/130, NLS.
33 H. Gough to HW, 27 July 1916, HW Private War Diary, 48365, BL; Simpson, *Directing Operations*, 191.
34 Horne to Lady Horne, 7 October 1918, Horne Papers, 73/60/1–2, IWM; HW Official War Diary, 2 July 1918, 48359, BL. Like many commanders, he had been keen to stamp his personal identity on VIII Corps, devising hunting horn badges (the Hunter Clan Crest) for the Corps Cyclists Battalion and for his staff: HW to GHW, 13 March 18, HW Private War Diary, 48367, BL.

Despite these misgivings, their professional relationship began on a sound footing. Horne was open with Hunter-Weston that his predecessor, Ivor Maxse, was leaving after a difference of opinion over defensive arrangements.[35] Hunter-Weston heard both sides of the debate, but after reading Maxse's dossier he found that he could not agree with it.[36] This was a matter of tactical judgment as much as professional self-interest. Taking to the sky in an R.E.8 reconnaissance plane, he decided to see his new sector for himself, 'to the detriment to the comfort of [his] interior economy'.[37] The line-holding policy that he subsequently developed reflected official First Army practice, but it also had the support of his divisional commanders; 'all nice men' whose opinion he had canvassed.[38] His scheme was for an outpost system held by a garrison strong enough to beat off anything but a general attack, while the front edge of his battle-zone served as the main line of resistance.[39] Equally to his taste was Horne's determination to maintain the upper hand in No Man's Land through a policy of active aggression. This meant frequent bombardment schemes, nightly raiding patrols and the harassment of the enemy by machine-guns and trench mortars.[40] As well as keeping the enemy permanently on edge, Hunter-Weston remained determined to combat 'trench lethargy' among his own troops, not least his artillery commanders who he felt were 'dreadfully heavy, dull creatures'.[41] At times, commented one disgruntled officer, it seemed that the

---

35 John Baynes, *Far From a Donkey: The Life of Sir Ivor Maxse* (London: Brassey's, 1995) 209; Don Farr, *The Silent General: Horne of the First Army* (London: Helion, 2007), 193–4; Robbins, *British Generalship During the Great War*, 192.
36 HW Private War Diary, 22 June 1918, 48367, BL.
37 HW to GHW, 25 June 1918, HW Private War Diary, 48367, BL.
38 HW Private War Diary, 23 June 1918, 48365, BL.
39 Conference Held by the Corps Commander at 20th Division HQ after his Lecture on 21 August, 1918, HW Official War Diary, 48360, BL.
40 An Outline of the Operations of the VIII Corps, November 1917–November 1918, HW Official War Diary, 48360, BL.
41 HW to GHW, 26 July; 8 September 1918; HW Private War Diary, 48367, BL. On a single day, he inspected two brigades in training and divisional and brigade billets in twelve different locations: HW Official War Diary, 13 July 1918, 48360, BL.

'real day-by-day contest for all units in the area was not with the Germans, but with the Corps Commander'.[42]

'Lombard Street to a China Orange'

Just as VIII Corps' three-line defence system was nearing completion in late July, there was a complete change in the tactical situation on the Western Front. A new German offensive directed against his friend Gouraud's Fourth Army in the Champagne region two weeks before had been repulsed by a decisive counterstroke that drove the enemy from most of the ground that they had captured in the spring. This reversal signalled to the allies that Ludendorff's earlier attacks had been made at a massive cost to German manpower and morale. In Hunter-Weston's view, however, the real turning of the tide came three weeks later with the successful British attack at Amiens, in which Rawlinson's Fourth Army advanced eleven miles in a single day. He was ecstatic at this 'perfectly marvellous' turn of events, although his experiences over the past few years had taught him to restrain his natural optimism.[43] Impatient with 'futile prophecies' that the end of the war was close, he predicted much hard fighting and many reversals and trials ahead but could not resist hinting to Grace that 'the chances of peace coming next year are very great'.

The impact of events in the south was felt immediately through the more passive attitude of the enemy facing VIII Corps.[44] Byng's Third Army, which had taken over the main effort of the Amiens offensive, continued to make progress towards Bapaume; on 15 August Horne was ordered by Haig to stand in readiness to exploit any enemy withdrawal by seizing

42 Stanford papers, DS/Misc/75, IWM.
43 HW to GHW, 14 August 1918; HW Private War Diary, 48367, BL.
44 An Outline of the Operations of the VIII Corps, November 1917–November 1918, HW Official War Diary, 48360, BL.

the heights south of the Scarpe River.[45] The First Army's main task was to secure Byng's left flank as the latter attempted to break the Hindenburg line between St Quentin and Cambrai. For the moment though, Hunter-Weston could put the strains of Passchendaele behind him and enjoy being a Corps Commander again.

It was during this period that he made a powerful and lasting impression on two officers joining his staff. Charles Bonham-Carter was attached to VIII Corps in mid-August as the temporary replacement for Aspinall, who had injured his knee. As Brigadier General Staff (Training) at GHQ, he was already well acquainted with Hunter-Weston's technical expertise, but a month spent working as his chief staff officer revealed a whole new dimension to this 'extraordinary man'.[46] On arrival, he was faced with a mass of instructions, suggestions and information from the Corps Commander in response to what he had seen on his recent tours of inspection. When Bonham-Carter asked for advice on what to do with these notes, the BGRA, Henry Ward, explained the normal procedure:

> Some of them are ridiculous and disappear into the wastebasket. Some seem sensible but are different or impossible to carry out; explain the difficulty to the CC and the reasons. He is always considerate and listens, indeed he is a great gentleman; he is never unreasonable. Some are sound and in regard to these make sure that he realises that his wishes have been carried out.[47]

Suitably briefed, Bonham-Carter went on to develop a shrewd and nuanced judgement of Hunter-Weston, which echoed some of Cuthbert Headlam's more cutting observations:

> he has fine brains and remarkable knowledge of his work & yet he has not been a complete success out here as he finds it impossible to curb his love and keenness for detail so his subordinates have rather a worrying time. His love of advertisement &

---

45 Haig Diary, 15 August 1918, Acc. 3155/130, NLS.
46 HW to C. Bonham-Carter, 28 May 1918, HW Official War Diary, 48360, BL; Headlam found Bonham-Carter 'boring' on first acquaintance, but they later became firm friends: *Headlam Military Papers* (13 April 1918), 196.
47 Autobiography (Chapter IX), Charles Bonham-Carter Papers, BHCT, 9/2, CCC.

heroics have also led to his being generally regarded as a bit of mountebank. It is a real pity as I can [sic] help feeling that he is really a very big man. I find him rather a worrying master though he is always quite charming to me.[48]

It was precisely these 'heroics' that fascinated Lieutenant F. L. Freeman, who took over as GSO3 at VIII Corps HQ in July 1918. In later life he remembered Hunter-Weston as 'an astonishing character' with great panache. What others regarded as fripperies, he considered essential to the visibility and dignity of command, although the end result was often rather different. Typically, the Corps Commander disliked wearing a steel helmet and had a pith version made of same size and shape. When he wanted to congratulate his pioneers who had undertaken tunneling in the front line – strictly against First Army orders – he had them drawn up on parade. He got out of his car and walked over to the horses, which were tethered out of sight. Mounting his charger, he applied his spurs and his cavalcade of staff and orderlies made a theatrical entrance into the parade ground. At this moment, a gust of wind caught his helmet and it went flying into the air before bouncing several times on the ground. It was impossible for the troops to conceal their amusement and the parade dissolved into laughter.[49]

The Corps Horse Show held on 24 August went rather more smoothly, but also did little to enhance Hunter-Weston's image. Upon his return from leave, Freeman found preparations in full swing. These morale-boosting sporting events were common throughout the BEF during the war, but a recent I Corps extravaganza had featured fresh salmon, ices and peaches and champagne, setting a new benchmark that Hunter-Weston was determined to exceed. The ingenuity and mastery of detail that had once been expended on plans of attack and defensive schemes was now directed at the sourcing of quantities of turbot and grouse. For Freeman, it seemed as though the participation of VIII Corps in 'the great advance' was being

---

48 C. Bonham-Carter to J. Bonham Carter, 25 August 1918, Charles Bonham-Carter Papers, BHCT, 2/1, CCC.
49 F. L. Freeman to V. Bonham-Carter, 25 August 1950, Charles Bonham-Carter Papers, BHCT 9/2, CCC.

delayed simply as a result of the Corps Commander's self-indulgence.[50] His burst of indignation some forty years after the event has been taken at face value by Travers who uses the horse show episode as evidence of the often 'doubtful quality' of command at corps level.[51] In reality, VIII Corps was still holding a quiet part of the line and was not yet engaged in active operations, with the result that even the First Army Commander found time to present the prizes at the show.[52] Within days, Hunter Weston had switched his attention to more weighty matters. As the battle began to edge northwards, he inspected dressing stations and ensured that administrative arrangements were in place to allow the rapid absorption of new divisions during the coming offensive.[53] When the Battle of the Scarpe finally opened on 26 August, VIII Corps played a useful supporting role. Operating as Horne's extreme left corps, it protected the flank of the Sir Arthur Currie's Canadian Corps and maximised the surprise of their advance through a series of diversions, feints and minor operations, including a 1,000-yard advance carried out by night patrols from Heneker's 8th Division.[54] This pattern continued during the battles to break the Hindenburg Line. Indeed, there was by now little alternative, as Hunter-Weston's corps had become a very slim outfit, with tired divisions strung out over a lengthening front.

The reasons for British success in the 'Hundred Days' battles are open to debate. Travers suggests that despite the BEF developing a successful attack formula, victory was more the result of German exhaustion; in contrast, Prior and Wilson stress the irresistible nature of new British firepower-based tactics, while Simpson's analysis of corps command highlights the

50   F. L. Freeman to V. Bonham-Carter, 25 August 1950, Charles Bonham-Carter Papers, BHCT 9/2, CCC.
51   Travers, *How The War was Won*, 5.
52   Horne found Hunter-Weston's obsession with the prize medallion that he had designed for the event to be rather odd: Horne to Lady Horne, 7, 12 October 1918, Horne Papers, 73/60/1–2, IWM.
53   HW Private War Diary, 26, 27 August 1918, 48367, BL.
54   J. E. Edmonds, *History of the Great War based on official documents by direction of the Historical Section of the Committee of Imperial Defence. Military Operations. France and Belgium, 1918. Volume IV: 8 August–26 September: the Franco-British Offensive* (London: HMSO, 1947), 297 [*OH 1918, (4)*].

greater sophistication and flexibility in the BEF's offensive methods, arguing that it contributed to a greater operational tempo.[55] The experience of VIII Corps would tend to support the latter argument, because although enemy resistance did increasingly crumble as it pressed ahead during the last weeks of the war, its divisions also showed themselves capable of rising to the challenge of open warfare, illustrating the diffusion of innovation even in the case of a corps that had not been recently engaged in major offensive activity. Hunter-Weston also made a personal contribution in this respect. Despite his apparent professional marginalisation, he ensured that he had remained fully engaged with recent tactical and technological developments, not only benefiting from the expertise of divisions that had recently been through heavy fighting, but also using engagements like the Second Battle of the Marne as instructional tools to underline the integration of the latest infantry weapon systems and artillery support in both defence and attack.[56] Indeed, it was impossible for any commander to ignore the rapidly changing nature of warfare, as the speed of the enemy's retreat made even 'bite and hold' tactics increasingly irrelevant. The result, as Travers suggests, was a period of 'useful anarchy', from which a range of simple but effective techniques emerged to neutralise defensive fire power and increase the ability to manoeuvre.[57]

The growing sense of improvisation was clear from the instructions received by VIII Corps in advance of the resumption of the Canadian attack at the Scarpe on 3 September.[58] They were asked to prepare for three possible operations: an attack on the current front; an advance to follow up an enemy withdrawal; and a gradual extension of the battle front northwards. Tanks and cavalry were attached to the corps, but in all of the possible scenarios,

---

[55] Travers, *How the War Was Won*, 175–82; Prior and Wilson, *Command*, 289–91; Simpson, *Directing Operations*, 155–75.

[56] Conference Held by the Corps Commander at 20th Division HQ after his Lecture on 21 August, 1918, HW Official War Diary, 48360, BL. See also HW to I. Maxse, 17 September 1918, Maxse Papers, 69/53/14 File 60, IWM.

[57] Travers, *How the War Was Won*, 149; Alun Thomas, 'Open Warfare during the "Hundred Days" – 1918', *Stand To!* 96 (2013), 24–7.

[58] VIII Corps Order No 7, 3 September 1919, HW Official War Diary, 48360, BL.

additional divisions would only become available at the last minute. In these conditions, Hunter-Weston could hardly expect to replicate the detailed, centralised planning in place ahead of the Somme. Instead, more flexible methods of command developed, although Corps HQ retained the responsibility for coordinating set-piece attacks. This process was in alignment with the precepts set out in the official pamphlet *The Training and Employment of Divisions, 1918 (SS135)*, as well as with traditional pre-war deference to the 'man on the spot', but the calibre of Hunter-Weston's divisional commanders also assisted the process of delegation. He had always been ruthless in replacing doubtful subordinates and the energetic new breed of Western Front commanders were well represented in VIII Corps. Besides Heneker and the tough and experienced H. W. Higginson, (12th (Eastern) Division), the officers included G. G. S. Carey, (20th (Light) Division), who had prevented a German breakthrough during the March offensive by assembling a scratch force of British and American troops.[59]

Anticipating the pursuit of the enemy in the event of a further withdrawal in mid-September, it was notable that Hunter-Weston was content to set out general principles while devolving operational planning and control to his Divisional HQs.[60] His intention was to encourage independent action rather than to curb it. Although a continuous line was laid down for the objective of each 'bound', it was stressed that this did not imply advancing in regular lines; instead, the recommendation was for 'wedges' to be thrust where the enemy was weak with proximate fire support. Where enemy strong points held out, these were to be dealt with by outflanking manoeuvres using artillery, his beloved Stokes mortars and machine-guns. Indeed, it was only in cases of advances beyond designated objectives that Corps HQ sought to retain control. The policy of devolved

---

59 Hunter-Weston had known Carey at Shorncliffe before the war when he was still a Major commanding a battery: HW to GHW, 29 June 1918, HW Private War Diary, 48367, BL. For the sudden departure of Sir Percy Wilkinson (50th Division), see Heneker Diary, 24 February 1918, 66/154/1, IWM; Everard Wyrall. *The History of the 50th Division, 1914–19* (London: Percy Lund, Humphries & Co. Ltd, 1939), 285.
60 VIII Corps Instructions No 1 – Action in Case of an Enemy Withdrawal, 15 September 1918, HW Official War Diary, 48360, BL.

initiative brought early results on the night of 26 September when the 8th and 20th Divisions attacked at Arleux-en-Gohelle. Although this 'very successful little affair' was intended as a diversionary operation to assist the main Canadian thrust across the enemy's last prepared defensive position at the Canal du Nord, it was a success in its own right. Not only did it capture the town, but it also created a substantial breach in the enemy defences to the north along a length of 2,000 yards.[61]

After the collapse of Germany's ally, Bulgaria on 30 September, Horne was well aware of the need to push back the enemy as quickly as possible. The next few days brought a lull in operations as the Canadians regrouped, but having beaten off a series of counter-attacks in the south around Cambrai, the First Army's progress continued. In response to intelligence that the enemy were planning a withdrawal to the Haute Deule Canal, strong patrols from the 58th Division were pushed out either side of Lens.[62] The south of the city was still strongly held, but troops from the 174th Brigade were able to reach the railway line and maintain pressure from the northeast. Working southwards, the encirclement was complete the next day when they linked up across the Souchez River with the 20th Division which had fought its way north. By the time that the ruined city was reported captured at 12.15 a.m., the enemy had already disappeared.[63]

That morning, Horne summoned Hunter-Weston and told him to 'push on.'[64] Chilled and feverish from the influenza that was beginning to grip the army, he returned immediately to brief his divisional commanders. The speed of the advance continued to wrong-foot him. He had been certain that the war still had a long way to run, to the extent that he had given orders a few days before for his office at Corps HQ to be cleaned

---

61   HW to GHW, 27 June 1918, HW Private War Diary, 48367, BL; Haig Diary 27 September 1918, Acc. 3155/131, NLS; Major-General Sir H. Anderson, 'The Crossing of the Canal du Nord – 27th September 1918' Horne Papers, 62/54/1, IWM.
62   Resume of Events, HW Private War Diary, 48367, BL; An Outline of the Operations of the VIII Corps, November 1917–November 1918, HW Official War Diary, 48360, BL.
63   HW Official War Diary, 3 October 1918, 48360, BL.
64   Horne Diary, 3 October 1918, 62/5/4, File 26, IWM.

and redecorated.[65] He now explained to his team that the enemy would not go back until they were 'properly pressed', and that a fighting retreat through France and Belgium was still the most likely outcome; it would take a spring and possibly even a summer campaign, before the Germans could be forced back far enough to guarantee their surrender.[66]

Instead, the coming weeks brought the 'victorious advance' that had been in Hunter-Weston's mind since 1914. The attention of VIII Corps now turned southeast, and Grace could trace her husband's progress against stiff but patchy resistance on the Douai front using the sketch map he had sent her.[67] On 4 October, the 20th and 58th Divisions advanced to line from north of Oppy to the railway line running to Pont-à-Vendin through Fresnoy, Acheville and Méricourt. Two days later, Carey's brigades advanced their outposts to the east of Fresnoy, while Henecker moved forwards in preparation for an attack on the powerful Fresnes-Rouvroy defence line. By evening on 7 October, 8th Division had gained most of its objectives along a two-mile front, completing the task by daylight the following day when outposts were established on the western edge of Vitry-en-Artois and in the Vitry marshes.[68] Incursions into the enemy's defensive positions were becoming self-sustaining, but Horne was anxious to maintain the tempo of operations.

Over the next week, Grace was able to tick off even more villages taken by the British: Rouvoy and Loison fell on 10 October; by the next evening the 8th Division had taken Brebiers and Petit Cuinchy, completing an advance of five miles during the day; the 12th Division had also captured Billy Montigny, while the 58th had seized the collection of fosses north of canal at Noyelles.[69] For the next five days, the advance continued towards the Haute Deule canal, and despite poor weather, impassable roads and resistance from machine-gun outposts, landmines and booby traps,

---

65   HW to GHW, 27 September 1918, HW Private War Diary, 48367, BL.
66   HW to GHW, 30 October 1918, HW Private War Diary, 48367, BL.
67   HW to GHW, 5 October 1918, HW Private War Diary, 48367, BL.
68   HW Private War Diary, 7 October 1918, 48367, BL.
69   VIII Corps General Staff Report on Operations for Week Ending 6am 11.10.18, HW Official War Diary, 48360, BL.

a further procession of villages continued to fall – Dourges, Courrières, Wagonville, Flers, Auby and Courcelles; by 16 October the whole corps front had managed to draw level with the line of the canal, with Hunter-Weston comfortably installed in a house that only a few days before had been a German dressing station.[70]

Now that they were on the tail of a rapidly retreating enemy, his earlier predictions of peace in 1919 were forgotten; instead, he now fully expected 'considerable movement' for his Corps HQ, with continuous fighting over the winter that would force the Germans to acquiesce to whatever terms the allies saw fit to impose. Yet, even though Horne thought his corps had made 'very good progress', Hunter-Weston was less than satisfied.[71] The terrain was flooded and traversed by mine workings, trenches and wire entanglements and it therefore presented one obvious barrier to further advance, but another worry was the state of his new divisions. While Henecker's refitted 8th Division had performed 'remarkably well', the battered and understrength 12th and 58th Divisions had been put straight back into the line with drafts of new conscripts, and were 'hardly as good as they should have been'.[72] The 52nd Division, which he had famously 'blooded' at Gallipoli, was also in a weakened state. Returning to the front line on 19 October, it arrived just in time to join VIII Corps in its final advance, much to Hunter-Weston's delight.

If momentum was to be maintained at a minimum cost, it was vital to feed recent combat experience back into the planning of operations. In line with practice across the BEF, VIII Corps HQ now increasingly functioned as a clearing house for new ideas, providing a tactical menu for subordinate commanders to draw upon as the situation demanded. The notes circulated by HQ around commanders of divisions, brigades and battalions on 6 October, for example, drew lessons from the fighting to

70   HW Private War Diary, 16 October 1918, 48367, BL.
71   Horne to Lady Horne, 12 October 1918, Horne Papers, 73/60/1–2, IWM.
72   HW to GHW, 11 October 1918, HW Private War Diary, 48367, BL. The 12th (Eastern) Division had already made a costly contribution in the earlier battles of the Hindenburg line, while the 58th (2/1st London) Division had been heavily involved in the defensive battles in the spring.

date while also offering a valuable glimpse of how VIII Corps were developing their 'art of attack'. Operations were now divided into two categories. Against 'organised resistance', the previous year's set-piece approach still held: the barrage should keep as straight and simple as possible, with tanks and infantry formed up on a tape line. However, 'disorganised resistance' from scattered machine-gun posts had now become far more common and required new attacking methods to be developed to counter it. These included the use of broad front attacks to avoid enfilading fire and advancing by bounds from cover to cover, using machine-guns from the rear to provide fire support. Experience had also taught that as few men as possible should be deployed in the initial stages of attacks in order to reduce casualties from surprise fire, while the maximum number should be kept under the commander's hand to allow freedom of movement. In a final departure from Hunter-Weston's previous practice, commanders were counselled to support the advance 'where it is succeeding, not where it is held up'. Beside these broad principles, the notes offered many practical ideas on the conduct of mobile warfare. Some of these, like hip-firing from Lewis guns, reflected the increasingly aggressive use of new weaponry, while 'the old saw "use the rifle"' suggested the need to relearn basic infantry skills after months spent in the trenches. From a certain perspective it was also rather encouraging that souvenir hunting had again become a problem, as it had been in 1914.[73]

As the First Army prepared to cross the River Selle in conjunction with Byng's force, there were even clearer signs of the enemy's slackening resolve. On 17 October, the Canadians pushed across the Sensée Canal, helping to prepare the way for VIII Corps to approach Douai from the west; by early afternoon, the Germans had pulled out, leaving much of the town in flames. Hunter-Weston's divisions were now operating on a narrowed two-brigade front, with the Corps Cyclists and detachments from the 4th (Queen's Own) Hussars placed under their direct command; the latter were accompanied by field guns, as well as performing their normal

---

73   Notes Gleaned from the Recent Fighting of Value to Divisional, Brigade and Battalion COs, VIII Corps GA 289/17, 6 November 1918, HW Official War Diary, 48360, BL.

Breaking Through

reconnaissance duties.[74] Rearguard activity was weak and resistance was mainly limited to long-range artillery fire, but progress remained frustratingly slow, averaging five to six miles per day. Besides the fatigue of marching and skirmishing in unfamiliar territory, the main problems were those of supply. The enemy had deliberately smashed roads and railways, but off-road travel was also very difficult due to the flooding caused by the destruction of culverts.[75] While liberating recently occupied towns was a pleasant sensation, this too added to the logistical crisis, as thousands of civilian inhabitants now had to be fed.[76] By 23 October, VIII Corps were beginning to fall behind the Canadian Corps to their right and were ordered to push towards and cross the River Scarpe to restore alignment. As they advanced, they discovered that the German Army had not yet disintegrated but were in fact still capable of mounting determined, if sporadic, resistance. The Scarpe proved less of a barrier than the Escaut Canal, which the 8th Division attempted to cross in three places in the face of strong enemy counter-attacks.[77] Nevertheless, the cumulative effect of the previous week's fighting was inescapable; along the British line the Battle of the Selle had resulted in the capture of 20,000 prisoners and 475 guns, an enormous blow to Germany's exhausted reserves.[78] The next objective for the First Army was the communications hub of Valenciennes, the last major French city in enemy hands. VIII made their usual contribution, holding the flank to the north, while Horne launched a three-stage attack that finally succeeded in driving out the enemy on 2 November.[79]

The open countryside of the Selle area had now given way to a more rolling, enclosed landscape, where densely populated villages and narrow

---

74 HW Official War Diary, 21 October 18, 48360, BL.
75 VIII Corps General Staff Report on Operations for Week Ending 6 am 25.10.18, HW Official War Diary, 48360, BL; H. K. D. Evan and N. O. Laing, *The 4th (Queen's Own) Hussars in the Great War* (Aldershot: Gale and Polden, 1920), 158.
76 HW to GHW, 20 October 1918, HW Private War Diary, 48367, BL.
77 HW Official War Diary, 24 October 1918, 48360, BL.
78 OH 1918, *(4)*, 383.
79 VIII Corps General Staff Report on Operation for Week Ending Week Ending 6 am 1.11.18, HW Official War Diary, 48360, BL.

roads created new problems for the advance. The drive eastwards continued, but still faced stubborn opposition at times, as VIII corps discovered on 4 November when attempts to get patrols across the Jard canal, northeast of Condé, were checked by heavy machine-gun fire.[80] Over the next few days, Hunter-Weston's troops continued to be held up by artillery, machine-guns and trench mortars, as the Germans clung on along the Schelde River, despite a general withdrawal northwards towards Mons. It was not until the early morning of 8 November that the enemy finally melted away, enabling leading brigades to cross the Jard and Escaut canals by rafts and pontoon bridges and to occupy Condé.[81]

A complete German collapse now looked inevitable to Hunter-Weston. Although daily supply challenges continued to absorb him, the simpler, more spontaneous form of warfare over the past few weeks had reduced his responsibilities as Corps Commander. Now that divisions were being given general objectives along with the flexibility to achieve them, his diminished managerial role allowed him greater personal mobility across the battlefield. Like the thrusting brigadier of 1914, he personally reconnoitred his front and toured his division HQs and advanced brigade posts to urge his commanders on, sometimes motoring but often travelling on horseback to avoid the many craters in the roads. Anxious to prevent the enemy from settling into organised defensive positions before the winter, he fully appreciated that military operations were closely interrelated with political developments on the German home front. There was also a new bitterness in his attitude towards the Germans due to the malicious destruction that he had witnessed in occupied towns like Douai and St Amand, which fuelled his determination to seek revenge against 'a damnable people'.[82] Yet, this was not a reckless, 'at all costs' advance. One restraining factor was the pressure from Haig and the politicians at home to minimise casualties, but the desperate manpower situation in VIII Corps, where troops were

---

80 HW Official War Diary, 4 November 1918, 48360, BL.
81 VIII Corps General Staff Report on Operations for Week Ending 6 am 8.11.18, HW Official War Diary, 48360, BL.
82 HW to GHW, 24 October 1918, HW Private War Diary, 48367, BL.

Breaking Through

thinly spread between front-line duties and rebuilding communications, also encouraged a circumspect approach. Indeed, on this occasion it would not be Hunter-Weston, but the Canadian commander, Arthur Currie, who was accused after the war of being cavalier with his men's lives in the pursuit of personal glory.[83]

On the afternoon of 9 November news of the Kaiser's abdication reached Hunter-Weston; 'the betting', he assured his wife, 'is Lombard Street to a China Orange that the Armistice will be signed tomorrow, though probably we shall not know about it till Monday'.[84] Advance guards from VIII Corps continued to trudge through the sodden, wooded landscape in an attempt to catch up with the Canadian advance towards Mons; by marching eight miles on 10 November, they had almost succeeded.[85] Still trying to draw level, patrols from the 52nd Division on the left and 8th Division on the right pushed forwards early the next morning towards the Nimy-Jourbise road, north of Mons. They met with no opposition and easily took their objectives by 10.25 a.m.. When the formal end to hostilities came into effect shortly afterwards, the Scottish Territorials were too weary and mindful of their losses to celebrate; in a similar spirit, the 4th Hussars simply dismounted and sat by the roadside, lighting their cigarettes. The only remark to be heard was: 'well, thank God that's over'.[86]

The day was also a quiet one for Hunter-Weston, who spent the morning doing routine paperwork and conferring with his divisional commanders. He heard that evening that First Army would not be marching to the German frontier to participate in the occupation of the Rhineland. On the grounds of seniority, that honour would go to Plumer and Rawlinson.

It was not until midnight that he sat down to write his last wartime letter to Grace: 'Such a wonderful day! And so we have won, and won at

---

83   Robert Sharpe, *The Last Day, The Last Hour: The Currie Libel Trial* (Toronto: University of Toronto Press, 2009).
84   HW to GHW, 9 October 1918, HW Private War Diary, 48367, BL.
85   An Outline of the Operations of the VIII Corps, November 1917–November 1918, HW Official War Diary, 48360, BL.
86   Thompson, *Fifty-Second Lowland Division*, 572; Evan and Laing, *4th (Queen's Own) Hussars*, 133.

the end so quickly. It is incredible, it is glorious. Wonderful old Britain ... It has been a privilege to have been through it all from start to finish. And how delightful to feel that the long period of separation is nearly over.'[87]

87   HW to GHW, 11 November 1918, HW Private War Diary, 48367, BL.

CHAPTER FOURTEEN

The Man That Gets Things Done

The first days of peace were spent in a blur of speeches, lunches and civic ceremonies as the liberated towns of Flanders celebrated their deliverance.[1] However, as the pleasures of victory subsided, those who had progressed quickly in their careers began to fear for the future. While successful Army Commanders could expect plum imperial postings, temporary Lieutenant-Generals would be lucky if they were selected to command a division in the Army of Occupation.[2] Some of Hunter-Weston's colleagues later proved remarkably enterprising in adapting to civilian life: Beauvoir De Lisle trained polo teams for the Maharaja of Kashmir; Sir Ivor Maxse became a fruit-grower; while Hubert Gough experimented rather less successfully with raising pigs, cows and chickens. In contrast, Hunter-Weston's victory in the December 1918 General Election meant that he was to remain a public figure, serving as MP for Bute and North Ayrshire for the next seventeen years and successfully defending his parliamentary seat at six General Elections. His time as an MP spanned the glory years of Scottish Unionism as the party grew in vitality and confidence against a background of economic crisis and social strife. As a Tory landowner, he proved to be remarkably adept at rebranding himself as a hard-working, 'non-political' local representative – 'the man that gets things done'. He could not escape the scrutiny of his war record, especially regarding Gallipoli, but while more illustrious military contemporaries became mired in controversies over their past campaigns, he found a new mission in campaigning for the

---

1 HW to GHW, 27 November 1918, HW Private War Diary, 48368, BL. In one of the more bizarre episodes of the liberation, Hunter-Weston met a remarkable mule that had spent the past four years of the occupation hidden in a dwelling house.
2 Haig Diary, 10 February 1919, Acc. 3155/136, NLS.

virtues of 'cheerfulness, devotion to duty, and above all, comradeship' to be carried forwards into peacetime.

A Working MP

Hunter-Weston liked to explain his decision to contest the new seat of Bute and North Ayrshire as a response to the call of 'his ain folk'.[3] Whatever his actual motivations, his election emphasised the continuing electoral dividends of military service. As a wholehearted supporter of the reconstruction policy of Lloyd George's Coalition, the keynote of his intense and dramatic campaign was unity, efficiency and self-sacrifice. His platform personality was also credited with the ability to sway voters, while the local press flagged up his relationship with the 52nd Division, both at Gallipoli and Mons, suggesting that constituents hungered 'to share some of the glory which attaches to this great soldier'.[4] His opponents, an Aberdeen law professor and a local councillor, could not complete and he galloped home in the 1918 election with a handsome majority of nearly 7,000 votes.[5]

Aware that he would not be continuing with soldiering after the war, he was anxious to finish the job and 'clear out'.[6] He worked till 2 a.m. on 16 January finishing his paperwork; then, having torn strips off two divisional generals for insubordination, he put on his coat and left the mess for the last time, cheered on his way by the VIII Corps Cyclists.[7] The war had taken its toll – he could be no longer be taken for a 'young general'.

---

[3] 1929 General Election leaflet, West Kilbride Museum; *Ardrossan and Saltcoats Herald*, 13 December 1918.
[4] *Kilmarnock Standard*, 14 December 1918; *Glasgow Herald*, 7 December 1918.
[5] *Ardrossan and Saltcoats Herald*, 30 December 1918.
[6] HW to GHW, 11 November 1918, HW Private War Diary, 48367, BL. He was promoted to the substantive rank of Lieutenant-General at the beginning of 1919.
[7] HW Private War Diary, 16 January 1919, 48368, BL.

A routine operation to open up his nasal passages in the hope of curing his long-standing laryngitis proved much more serious than expected and resulted in a lengthy convalescence.[8] His sick leave lasted until 28 April and he was placed on half pay. Upon taking up his duties in parliament the next day, his active military career was formally over.

History has not been kind to the first post-war Parliament, but Hunter-Weston at least added colour to a rather grim assemblage, famously described by Stanley Baldwin as 'a lot of hard-faced men who look as if they had done very well out of the war'. Already 'the most talked about man in the army', his arrival was a gift for parliamentary sketch writers who were quick to single out his slight and well-groomed figure, 'with wonderfully bright eyes and a remarkable characteristic nose'.[9] His military background also placed him in good company, as between 1919 and 1939, regular officers were second only to lawyers as the largest occupational group in the House of Commons.[10] They included senior career soldiers, such as Sir Henry Wilson and even Archie Hunter, who spent an uncomfortable four years as MP for Lancaster.[11]

Hunter-Weston had always been a clubbable individual and he fitted easily into the social life of Westminster, becoming president of the local British Legion Branch. He also contributed to the grind of committee work, including membership of the Parliamentary Army Committee. Yet, despite the impact of his maiden speech, he did not become a prolific performer in the debating chamber. Indeed, he made only nine speeches in twenty years, mostly on issues of imperial defence and the organisation of the armed forces. The early 1920s certainly gave him plenty of scope for comment in these areas. As Philpott suggests, the crippling cost of the war had inspired the spirit of retrenchment that shaped defence policy, with the three services fighting against Treasury-led spending reductions

---

8   HW Private War Diary, 16 January 1919, 48368, BL; The *Buteman*, 24 January 1919.
9   *The World*, 10 May 1919.
10   Strachan, *Politics of the British Army*, 26.
11   Hunter, *Kitchener's Sword Arm*, 231–2.

while battling each other for a share of the cake.[12] It is therefore hardly surprising that in March 1922, Hunter-Weston rose to berate the severity of the defence cuts proposed by the Committee for National Expenditure, chaired by Sir Eric Geddes. He explained that the dangers facing the regular army in 'safeguarding our far-flung frontiers in every corner of the world' had actually increased, as the internal condition of Britain's dependencies had not become any more tranquil. Closer to home his argument that the cuts would threaten the county regiments with their historic territorial connections was equally passionate, seeing them as 'the mother liquor into which the manpower of this country was poured'.[13]

Given this climate of economy and efficiency, questions of administrative centralisation and coordination were inevitably also raised. As a member of the Parliamentary Army Committee, Hunter-Weston was part of the rather uncertain lobby pressing for the creation of a Ministry of Defence. Following Henry Wilson in the debate on defence forces organisation in March 1922, he insisted that a more contextualised discussion of defence needs was desirable, rather than placing the army in a watertight compartment. He drew on the bitter legacy of war to buttress his position:

> We won, but at what a cost! We have lost countless millions of treasure. Far more than that, we have lost the flower of the younger generation. Make no mistake about it. The most enterprising, the most go-ahead of our race, the potential leaders of the future, are lying amongst the dead, and the nation is irreparably poorer for their loss ... Ought we not to see how we can utilise our great and terrible experiences so as to prevent the recurrence of such losses?[14]

Despite his best efforts, this was a specialist controversy that failed to grip the popular imagination. As Britain settled into the habits of peacetime, concerns about imperial defence gave way to economic and labour issues,

---

12   William Philpott, 'The Campaign for a Ministry of Defence, 1919–36' in Paul Smith, ed., *Government and the Armed Forces in Britain, 1856–1990* (London: Hambledon, 1995), 109.
13   *Hansard*, House of Commons Debates, 1 February 1922, vol. 151 cc. 448–531. See also *The Times*, 12 February 1922.
14   Hansard, House of Commons Debates, 13 March 1922, vol. 151, cc. 2258–9122.

about which Hunter-Weston felt less comfortable, meaning that his parliamentary contributions tailed off after 1924. Yet he was by no means a passive observer, as he doggedly pursued the interests of ex-servicemen (of which he, of course, was now one) in the areas of pensions, death duties and disability. One such campaign, directed at the Ministry of Pensions, was on behalf of 'mentally broken' ex-servicemen, of whom an estimated 6,000 ended up in pauper lunatic asylums in the early 1920s.[15] He also busied himself with local government issues, transport and rural affairs, raising written questions on a number of arcane topics from railway rates to agricultural liming.[16] Herein lay the secret of his political success. As a diligent local MP, he looked after his constituency as he had his corps, eagerly promoting its welfare and development, in return receiving the affection and recognition he had craved throughout his army career.

Bute and North Ayrshire was by no means an easy constituency to represent. It was mostly rural, including the Isles of Bute and Arran and Great and Little Cumbrae, but there was also a large working-class presence in the industrial towns of the Garnock Valley and the Clyde Coast. Hunter-Weston made his Hunterston estate his new 'HQ', using its grounds for fetes and garden parties.[17] It was also fortunate that he was an early motoring enthusiast, enabling him to keep in touch with his scattered constituents by touring with Lady Hunter-Weston every autumn during the parliamentary recess. His 1922 tour, for example, involved spending every weekday evening for four weeks visiting farmers' dances, jumble sales and 'conversaziones' from Millport to Kilbirnie.[18]

Hugh MacDiarmid dismissed inter-war politicians in Scotland as 'futilitarians, openers of bazaars', but in Hunter-Weston's case, such anodyne public activity was backed up by assiduous efforts made behind the

---

15 *Beith Supplement*, 25 December 1924.
16 *Hansard*, House of Commons Debates, 23 November 1920, vol. 135, cc. 242; 1 March 1927, vol. 203, cc. 220.
17 *Largs and Millport Weekly News*, 31 August 1925.
18 *Ardrossan and Saltcoats Herald*, 6 October 1922; *Bulletin*, 20 October 1935.

scenes to help individual constituents amid worsening economic conditions.[19] By the early 1930s he was dealing with an estimated mailbag of 6,000 letters per year; many of these were concerned with pension issues, which he took up directly with the ministries concerned, drawing on the web of personal contacts which he had developed during his long army and parliamentary career.[20]

The Politics of Remembrance

The first call from his constituency had been symbolic rather than material. As the local MP and a distinguished solider he was expected to lead public commemoration of the war dead. These acts had a special poignancy, as some of the heaviest losses in north Ayrshire had been suffered by local Territorials in the July battles at Gallipoli. The early 1920s were the peak years of monument building, which resulted in scores of dedication ceremonies in schools, workplaces and civic spaces. The sheer volume of ceremonies, sometimes occurring on a weekly basis, meant that Hunter-Weston was often tempted to reuse entire speeches. More commonly, though, he interwove sections on themes dear to his heart, crafting his overall remarks to suit the local conditions. The fragmented nature of local press coverage meant made this creative recycling difficult to detect. At the unveiling of Dalry War Memorial in June 1929, for example, those who were hearing it for the first time believed he had delivered 'the speech of his life', quite

---

19 Quoted in Catriona Macdonald, *Whaur Extremes Meet: Scotland's Twentieth Century* (Edinburgh: John Donald, 2010), 208.
20 *Ardrossan and Saltcoats Herald*, 9 September 1931. Hunter-Weston's patronage extended to colleagues as well as constituents. He lobbied the then Scottish Secretary, Sir John Gilmour, to secure a KBE for his constituency chairman, Neil Cochran Patrick, who was also married to his cousin: HW to J. Gilmour, 1 January 1934, GD 383/51, National Archives of Scotland, Edinburgh.

unaware that the 'unseen spirits of dead heroes' were making one of their frequent appearances.[21]

This limited repertoire did not, however, imply insincerity. As a commander, Hunter-Weston had been required to remain personally detached from the human cost of war. Now that he was directly confronted by the sorrow of the bereaved, the unveiling of memorials gave him the opportunity to express his emotions. It is difficult to imagine what the audience at Stewarton Parish Church made of one such typical (and in this case, original) flight of oratory in July 1921. In a powerful voice that reached every listener, he proclaimed:

> Time is a great consoler. Time blurs the sharp outlines of memory. Is it so with your memory of these dead heroes? No! A thousand times, no! Do you, the mothers of these dead heroes forget the babe you bore – the little mouth that suckled you? Do you fathers forget the wee baby hands and feet, the dimpled wrinkles forming bracelets around his wrist, and the pride and pleasure and happy trouble he was to you?[22]

Such outpourings were unusual in Scottish war commemoration, which was generally characterised by reticence and simplicity, but his rhetoric echoed two prominent themes that structured remembrance at a local and national level.[23] The first was that the war-dead were 'ideal citizens' whose sacrifice imposed duties on their survivors. Typically, he assured the congregation of Kilmaurs Parish Church in July 1922 that 'the best memorial we can dedicate to their memory is the dedication for their sake and the sake of the country they died for that we will do our bit and do it cheerily, for

---

21 *Ardrossan and Saltcoats Herald*, 10 June 1929. Hunter-Weston's address at the unveiling of the Beith War Memorial was the same speech as that which he had delivered at Craigie Parish Church two months before: *Kilmarnock Standard*, 17 September 1920; *Beith Supplement*, 12 November 1920. Similarly, his speech at Ardrossan Academy on Monday 28 May had already been delivered at the unveiling of the 29th Division Memorial at Leamington the previous Saturday: *Ardrossan and Saltcoats Herald*, 2 June 1922; *Royal Leamington Spa Courier*, 2 June 1922.
22 *Ardrossan and Saltcoats Herald*, 8 July 1921.
23 Elaine McFarland, 'The Great War' in T. M. Devine and Jenny Wormald, eds, *The Oxford Handbook of Scottish History* (Oxford: Oxford University Press, 2012), 553–68.

others not ourselves'.[24] The second theme was the celebration of the wartime achievements of Scottish soldiers as the product of a unique 'national character'. For most of his life, Hunter-Weston's Scottishness had comfortably nested within a larger British identity, but at unveiling ceremonies he now gave it free rein, reinforced by a stout Ayrshire patriotism. Dedicating the Dreghorn War Memorial in November 1921, he explained that those whose names were written on it had now joined 'the great company of Ayrshiremen, including Wallace'.[25]

Nevertheless, these themes were secondary to the main message he sought to convey through commemoration. Above all, he aimed to glorify the wartime spirit of 'comradeship and cheerfulness', which he believed was equally essential in facing the challenges presented by unemployment and industrial strife. One of the first memorial tablets he unveiled was in Rothesay Parish Church in April 1920. On this occasion, he accorded 'the spirit of comradeship' shown by soldiers during the war the highest ethical value:

> It showed itself as true religion, not necessarily in adherence to the dogmas of a particular church, but in carrying out the religion of Christ, that we should love one another, that we should be comrades ... Do not let us lose it now. We need it now so badly. Christ's commandment that we love one another is the true remedy for our present and future ills.[26]

Hunter-Weston had now become a professional politician, despite his claims to the contrary. His solemn invocation of the common bond of service and suffering at dedication ceremonies found expression in the 'mutual cooperation against class hatred' that he campaigned for on electoral platforms. Besides being able to exploit his personal celebrity, his ability to construct a local power base also reflected broader developments in the Scottish political landscape. During the inter-war years, Scottish politics became increasingly polarised along class lines. Once a dispirited redoubt

---

24 *Kilmarnock Standard*, 10 July 1922.
25 *Kilmarnock Standard*, 21 November 1921.
26 *Ardrossan and Saltcoats Herald*, 9 June 1920.

in Scotland, the Unionist Party made striking electoral advances, benefiting from their identification with winning the war: in 1918, half of their MPs had done military service, compared with only a tenth of Liberals.[27] The Labour Party, too, had been boosted during the conflict through increased trade union membership and industrial struggles waged against the Liberal-led government. Indeed from 1922 onwards, it was Labour who increasingly filled the vacuum in working-class politics left by a retreating and bedraggled Liberal Party, who had lost their pre-war reputation for radicalism.

Concerned over the expanded electorate and the reduced power of the House of Lords, the main response of the Scottish Unionists was to capture the support of former Liberal middle-class voters. The rallying call of a coalition against 'Socialism' was to dominate successive elections, but the party also adopted a more interventionist stance on social and economic issues. Hunter-Weston vociferously embraced both the Socialist bogey and 'one nation' politics, although his support for anti-socialism and corporatism was instinctive rather than intellectual. He remained more comfortable as an old-fashioned Tory paternalist than as a class warrior. He made work for local ex-servicemen by extensively landscaping his estate grounds, while his general prescription for unemployment was for an industry-based insurance scheme to be financed by employers and workers.[28] Similarly, his 1922 election address explained that he was a 'Unionist' not in the old party sense, but in the sense that he supported, '... the union of all classes and all interests in the Nation.'[29]

Hoping to blunt the local Labour threat, he actively courted the Orange vote in the working-class areas of his constituency, commending the Orange Order's appeal to young people and its encouragement of 'solidarity and

---

27   Iain Hutchison, 'Scottish Unionism between the Two World Wars', in Catriona Macdonald, ed., *Unionist Scotland, 1800–1997* (Edinburgh: John Donald, 1996), 73–99.
28   *Ardrossan and Saltcoats Herald*, 9 September 1921; HW to E. Spears, 3 March 1931, Sir Edward Spears Papers, 1/172, CCC.
29   *Ardrossan and Saltcoats Herald*, 3 November 1922.

comradeship'.[30] However, he was happiest fighting on his own record as a constituency MP. His plea to electors in the 1929 contest, for example, was unintentionally self-deprecating: 'In the belief... that I can be of MORE USE TO THE CONSTITUENCY AND ITS INHABITANTS than anyone else, however gifted, I venture again to appeal to you for your vote'.[31] The creation of the National Government, the resultant crisis of Labour and the self-destructive tendencies of local Liberalism made his position in North Ayrshire increasingly unassailable; the average majority in his various contests was 6,365, but this rose at the 1931 General Election to a huge victory by a margin of 14,620 votes.[32]

He was also becoming a parliamentary institution at Westminster, with few MPs able to boast a longer record.[33] A picturesque figure with silver hair and abundant moustache, he had become one of the House's 'silent members'. Now over sixty, his agility and brisk walk surprised many onlookers, but severe rheumatoid arthritis was beginning to set in and his doctors had already forbidden him to travel to parliament.[34] In 1931, he reached the age limit for reserve officers and the following year contracted double pneumonia, forcing him to spend the spring and summer recuperating. In typical fashion, he sealed his recovery by taking his wife on a strenuous semi-official tour of East Africa, with the aim of inspecting the work of Toc H, St John of Jerusalem and the British Legion.[35] Asked by a local journalist if he had any decided opinion on racial issues, he replied, 'I am pro-Empire', adding that he not met a single 'rotter' on his tour, and that 'every Britisher in East Africa is a credit to their race'.[36]

30 Orange Halls were regularly used for Unionist meetings and Hunter-Weston and his wife reciprocated by attending Orange Order functions: *Ardrossan and Saltcoats Herald*, 30 May and 18 November 1927.
31 *Ardrossan and Saltcoats Herald*, 3 November 1922.
32 *Ardrossan and Saltcoats Herald*, 21 January 1935.
33 *Daily Express*, 23 March 1930.
34 *Ardrossan and Saltcoats Herald*, 22 February 1930.
35 *Edinburgh Evening News*, 7 November 1932.
36 *East African Standard*, 6 December 1932.

Memory and Reputation

Just as Hunter-Weston was attracting mounting respect as a public figure, his performance as a wartime commander began to attract renewed attention. When the military report of the Dardanelles Commission had appeared at last in 1919 it had been an insipid affair focusing on bureaucratic bungling rather than tactics, which had not questioned the fighting ability of the expeditionary force. Hunter-Weston specifically escaped censure on the issue of frontal attacks, as 'without more intimate knowledge of the locality and conditions', the commission found it impossible to express an opinion on whether these were justified. Nor did its members find any evidence that 'useless' attacks had been undertaken because of the neglect of senior commanders and their staffs to visit the trenches.[37] Thereby officially vindicated, he had gone on to become one of the main creators and beneficiaries of the heroic-romantic 'myth' of Gallipoli, which emphasised the campaign's strategic value and the sacrifice of its participants.[38] Returning to the high ground over W and V beaches in April 1921 to help to select a site for a national memorial, he paid homage to his 'wonder-working warriors' in spirited fashion: 'To the Dead – Honour! They have gained each to his own memory praise that shall never die. And with it the noblest of all sepulchres, not the place where their bodies are laid, but an everlasting place in the minds of men'.[39]

After talking to the Turkish War Minister and Chief of Staff on the eastern tour that followed, he had become even more convinced that the campaign had never stood a chance of success once the opportunity of surprise had been lost. Despite this, he still refused to view it as a failure. The original strategic conception had, in his opinion, been a noble one and the landings themselves were 'the achievement of the impossible'. More

---

37 Defeat at *Gallipoli*, 299.
38 Macleod, *Reconsidering Gallipoli*, 6–15.
39 *The Times*, 7 June 1921. A version was also published in the *Army Quarterly*, now edited by Cuthbert Headlam: *Military Papers* (25 July 1915), 244.

than this, through their sacrifice, the men of Gallipoli had made a vital contribution to the outcome of the war:

> It was their deeds that made possible the historic victories gained by Britain at Baghdad, at Jerusalem, and in Syria. The tenacity and pugnacity of our troops at Helles and Anzac killed off the German-trained regulars, broke up the Turkish Army, and made it incapable of further well-organized offensive action, either against Egypt, or against our troops in Mesopotamia, or in Palestine.[40]

This consolatory tone had already been strongly echoed in the first histories of the campaign, of which Hunter-Weston's personal favourite was John Masefield's *Gallipoli* (1916).[41] In these war narratives he claimed his place as a tough and resolute commander, a judgement confirmed in the various unit histories that also began to appear from the early 1920s, especially Captain Stair Gillon's, *Story of the 29th Division*.[42] Despite lingering criticisms over some of his decisions, the image of a 'slashing man of action' gained further confirmation in Ian Hamilton's diaries, published in 1920, which found a treasured place in his library at Hunterston.

An air of romance therefore continued to cloak the Gallipoli campaign, but by the end of the decade it seemed that sufficient emotional distance had developed to allow criticism of its military conduct, without devaluing the suffering and heroism of those who had participated. It was at this point that the rumours and criticisms that had surrounded Hunter-Weston on the peninsula increasingly began to enter the public realm. A new wave of personal memoirs appeared that were less than kind to him. Ashmead Bartlett's *Uncensored Dardanelles* was published in 1928, followed the next year by Marshall's *Four Fronts*, which gained enhanced credibility as the unexpected literary product of a fellow soldier. More criticism followed with the appearance of the first volume of the painstaking *Official History* in 1929. Its author, Cecil Aspinall (now Aspinall-Oglander) was concerned to emphasise the enormous political and logistical challenges that had

---

40 See *Wellington Post*, 6 August 1921.
41 HW to I. Hamilton, 31 December 1928, Hamilton Papers, 13/11, LHCMA.
42 See, for example, H. W. Nevison, *The Dardanelles Campaign* (London: Nisbet & Co., 1918), 200–1; Gillon, *Story of the 29th Division*, 9–10.

frustrated the enterprise, but he did not let his old Corps Commander off lightly. Written for a professional audience, his criticism of Hunter-Weston's tactical decisions and inflexible orders – sometimes muted but often more direct – suggested that he may have thrown away major opportunities. Far from readdressing the balance, the florid portrait offered by his admirer Compton Mackenzie in his tragi-comic *Gallipoli Memories* (1929) only served to anchor Hunter-Weston's reputation for callous eccentricity. The French commentator, Edmond Delage, for example, was one of the first to draw selectively on Mackenzie's account in his scathing attack on British strategy and tactics at Gallipoli. By the time the translation of his work *Tragedy of the Dardanelles* appeared in 1932, any exculpatory nuances had been excised, and the image of Hunter-Weston as a butcher and a bungler was becoming firmly established.[43]

There was little respite in the attacks on Hunter-Weston's reputation, as the focus soon shifted to his performance on the Somme. Like many participants in the battle, he had received drafts of the *Official History* account from J. E. Edmonds, which he thought 'excellently pieced together'.[44] However, when the volume finally emerged, again in 1932, it was critical of the preparations and tactics of VIII Corps, including the detonation of the Hawthorn Ridge mine and the premature artillery lift; only scant consolation was given by the fact that he was clearly not the only culpable commander on one of the BEF's blackest days.

Hunter-Weston was reported to be planning an autobiography in 1926, but whether due to lack of time or simply because he found fighting old battles 'unprofitable', he ultimately declined to enter 'the war of the memoirs'.[45] Instead, as president of both the RE Old Comrades Association and the 29th Division Association, he directed his energy into work with ex-servicemen at a local and a national level. This put him in close and

---

43 Edmond Delage, *The Tragedy of the Dardanelles* (London: John Lane, 1932), 177, 182.
44 HW to J. E. Edmonds, 11 February 1930, CAB 45/138, TNA.
45 *Glasgow Evening News*, 23 September 1926. His papers contain a substantial archive of correspondence, mementos and reminiscences from 1922–1936: Hunter of Hunterston Papers, NRAS852/325. See HW to I. Hamilton, 18 April 1923, Hamilton Papers, 13/11, LHCMA.

regular contact with Sir Ian Hamilton, who had become Scottish President of the British Legion. Their friendship now matured into real affection – to Hamilton, he became 'my dear, in fact beloved, Hunter-Bunter'.[46] As well as his practical welfare work, he was a strong believer in the support which could be generated by 'cheery' reunions, arguing that 'by our cheeriness, we help each other'.[47] Despite the literary onslaught it seems that survivors' memories had softened, so the presence of their old commander became a reminder of shared adversity and the spirit of comradeship; at the commemoration of the twenty-first anniversary of the landings, he was carried shoulder-high through the streets of Coventry by veterans of the 29th Division.[48]

As another election approached in 1935, he announced that he had decided to retire from his constituency to make way for a younger man. His constituents presented him with a bound illuminated volume, containing 10,000 signatures.[49] Yet, Hunter-Weston's parliamentary retirement was far from marking the end of his public life. Having been appointed Commandant of the Royal Engineers in 1921, he continued to relish his obligations and embarked on an official eight-month tour of India in September 1937.[50] The end of his political career also allowed him to take an even more active role in local affairs, looming large in the Ayrshire branches of the British Legion and Toc H, as well as in the Boys Brigade and the Scouts, St Andrews Ambulance Brigade and the Red Cross; Freemasonry, with its fraternal ideals, also attracted him as 'vital force in Britain and the Empire', and he became an office bearer at lodge and provincial level.[51]

---

46 I. Hamilton to HW, 21 January 1938, Hamilton Papers, 13/11, LHCMA. See also *Chatham News*, 11 December 1925 and *Aberdeen Press and Journal*, 22 June 1925.
47 *Newcastle Chronicle*, 21 November 1929.
48 *Daily Mail*, 27 April 1936.
49 *Glasgow Evening News*, 24 May 1935. He was succeeded by Col. C. G. McAndrew, MP for Partick; another future MP for Bute and North Ayrshire, the soldier and writer, Sir Fitzroy Maclean, would almost certainly have met with Hunter-Weston's approval.
50 His cruise with Grace to the West Indies the following year also included visits to RE establishments: *The Gleaner*, 28 February 1938.
51 *Ardrossan and Saltcoats Herald*, 21 December 1927.

He was further energised by the outbreak of war in 1939, even though he was unable to take an active part in home defence. By now aged seventy-five and still a 'keep fit' enthusiast, he was in habit of climbing the stairs onto the flat-roofed belvedere tower of Hunterston House to perform exercises to help ease his arthritis while enjoying the view over Firth of Clyde. On the morning of Monday 18 March 1940, he went up as usual at around 10.30 a.m.; shortly afterwards, a number of men working in the grounds heard a thud on the veranda above the ground-floor windows. They rushed to investigate, but found Hunter-Weston lying on the veranda roof, having fallen a distance of forty-five feet. He was already dead when they carried him into the house, where Lady Hunter-Weston was at home.[52]

Local legend suggests that he jumped from the tower while in the grip of a mortal illness, or even that he was pushed to his death by a grieving relative of one of his soldiers. Both tales are equally improbable. In fact, his general health had been good, despite his arthritis, and he had attended a number of public functions in the weeks before his death. Besides, a gentleman of his upbringing would never have chosen to take his life in this way while Grace was close at hand to witness the consequences. The most likely explanation for the fall is that he had an attack of dizziness and overbalanced over the low iron railings. The morning rain had made the lead floor of the tower slippery and the stiffness of his legs would have made it difficult for him to regain his balance.[53] His wife reacted with a stoicism that he would have admired. She wrote to Ian Hamilton: 'It is all just a terrible tragedy. But for him a merciful end. Perfect health and happiness to the last moment of his life, and then: instantaneous death. No illness,

---

52 *Largs and Millport News*, 22 March 1940; *Ardrossan and Saltcoats Herald*, 22 March 1940.
53 There is no system of Coroner's Inquests in Scotland. His death, registered 9 April, was attributed by the Procurator Fiscal (the local Crown agent) to an accidental fall. He had sustained a fracture of the base of the skull, a compound fracture of his right thigh and general severe bruising: Scotland's People: Statutory Deaths 620/00/0025.

no suffering. And with his disability, if the parting had to come, it is better than I should be the one to be left, I know'.[54]

In accordance with his wishes, he was given a private funeral. He was buried in the little local cemetery at West Kilbride. Few dignitaries were in attendance and the mourners were mostly estate workers and old local friends. The only wreaths placed on the grave were from Ian Hamilton and from his old corps, the Royal Engineers.

Aylmer Gould Hunter-Weston longed to be a great captain. Starved of glory, he instead became a political soldier; a 'survivor' clinging on to senior command despite a chequered military performance. And yet, his standard portrayal as a classic military buffoon is too harsh. While it is true that he often displayed a lack of proportion in carrying out his role as Corps Commander, he was an intelligent solider who thought deeply about his profession. Despite an abiding commitment to the doctrine of the offensive, he was open-minded and enthusiastic in embracing developments in military technology. He was energetic in carrying out orders, even when he profoundly disagreed with them, but his deference to military authority was balanced by a loyalty to his subordinates and a strong emotional bond with the units under his command. While his showmanship may have alienated (and sometimes amused) his more reticent colleagues, it anticipated the charismatic command style of World War Two generals such as Montgomery and Patton. Unfortunately, when compared to this later generation of commanders, Hunter-Weston had much less access to the sophisticated firepower that might have subdued his opponents and protected his soldiers' lives.[55] Whatever his failures, it should always be borne in mind that the tactical challenges that he faced were truly formidable.

Beyond the usual conventional piety of obituaries, his death provoked some shrewd insights into the complex mix of strengths and weaknesses that marked his personality. The usual stories of his exhibitionist

---

54   GHW to I. Hamilton, 1 April 1940, Hamilton Papers, 14/10/5, LHCMA. She outlived him by fourteen years, and continued to ably manage the estate farms: *Ardrossan and Saltcoats Herald*, 12 March 1954.
55   J. E. Edmonds to G. G. A. Egerton, 21 October 1945, Egerton Papers, Acc.1669/27, NLS.

postures, speeches and discomfitures were dusted down, but he was also presented as 'a man of uncommon character', whose unflagging energy, self-confidence and optimistic outlook had been evident throughout his military career.[56] Driven by a strong will to succeed, he was described as going 'all out', whether in oratory or in conversation, with the result that his keen intelligence and deep knowledge of the world were hidden beneath a cloak of flamboyant pride. His full grasp of military minutiae and ability to provoke inspiration, irritation and affection in equal measure were also recognised. Indeed, *The London Illustrated News* perceptively summed him up as 'something of a d'Artagnan and something of a Cyrano, with a dash of Quixote'.[57]

The last word may safely be left to Hunter-Weston himself. Just two weeks before his death, he distributed one of his famous personal printed messages to the men of the Ayrshire Construction Company of the Royal Engineers, who were leaving on active service. Included among his 'one or two words of homely advice' was a fitting epitaph for a soldier who had experienced many reversals of fortune:

> DO NOT LOSE CONFIDENCE IN YOURSELF WHEN THINGS GO WRONG AND YOU MAKE MISTAKES: We all make mistakes. Successful men take stout-heartedly and calmly the consequences of their mistakes and the criticism and blame they get from their superiors. They acknowledge their faults, learn from their failures, and, without ever being bumptious, never lose confidence in themselves.
>
> DO NOT WORRY. Never let your mind distress itself about its past mistakes, or about slights whether real or imaginary. A man who worries can never be a successful man. He becomes a nuisance to others as well as to himself.[58]

56 *The Times*, 19 March 1940; *The Royal Engineers Journal*, March 1941, 131–6.
57 *Illustrated London News*, 30 March 1940. On receiving a note from Lady Hunter-Weston in answer to his note of condolence, Headlam commented, 'He was an odd personality: a fine soldier, I suppose, in his day: brave, optimistic, kind-hearted – but vain and futile in many ways – very human nevertheless – always nice to me': *Headlam Military Papers* (18 April 1940), 309.
58 Printed Personal Message to each member of the Ayrshire Construction Company, Royal Engineers, from Brother Sapper Sir Aylmer Hunter-Weston, Hunter of Hunterston Papers, NRAS852/ 320.

Bibliography

Unpublished Primary Sources

The National Archives

Cabinet:
CAB 19/28–33, CAB 45/133–8, CAB 45/189, CAB 45/201, CAB 45/208, CAB 45/259, CAB 45/249
War Office:
WO 33/713, WO 95/821, WO 95/824–5, WO 95/1444, WO 95/1495–8, WO 95/2366, WO 95/4264, WO 95/4290, WO 95/4311; WO 95/4312; WO 158/191, WO 158/233, WO 159/13
Field Marshall Lord Kitchener Papers (PRO 30/57/61)

British Library, Department of Manuscripts

Lieutenant-General Sir Aylmer Hunter-Weston Papers
India Office Records and Private Papers

Churchill Archives Centre, Churchill College, Cambridge

General Sir Charles Bonham-Carter Papers
Sir Winston Churchill Papers
Field Marshal Lord Rawlinson Papers
Admiral Sir John de Robeck Papers
Robert Rhodes James Papers
Major-General Sir Edward Spears Papers

County Records Office, Isle of Wight

Aspinall-Oglander Papers

Liddell Hart Centre for Military Archives, King's College London

Captain H. T. Cawley Correspondence
General Sir Henry de Beauvoir De Lisle Papers
Brigadier-General Sir J. E. Edmonds Papers
General Sir Ian Hamilton Papers
Sir Basil Liddell Hart Papers
Field Marshall Sir William Robertson Papers
Brigadier-General Sir H. A. D. Simpson-Baikie Papers

Hunterston House, Ayrshire

Hunter of Hunterston Papers

Imperial War Museum

Anonymous account of the 1st Battalion East Lancashire Regiment, August – September 1914
Major C. L. Brereton Diary
Major-General A. R. Chater Papers
Major-General G. P. Dawnay Papers
Sir Philip Game Papers
Lieut.-Colonel G. W. Geddes Papers
General Sir W. S. G. Heneker Diary
General Lord Horne Papers
Private S. L. Lambert Diary
General Sir Ivor Maxse Papers
Major-General Archibald Paris Correspondence
Major-General R. J. Pinney Diary
Lieut.-Colonel J. K. Stanford Papers

Lieut.-Colonel G. B. Stoney Papers
The story of the doings of the 4th Division B.E.F. Aug. & Sep. 1914. Maj. Gen. T. D'Oyly Snow.
Captain A. D. Talbot Papers
Dr Orlo Williams Diary

National Army Museum

Lieutenant-General Sir Aylmer Hunter-Weston Papers
Lieutenant J. R. E. Charles Correspondence
Eight Months Record of Service of 1st Bn., East Lancashire Regiment in Flanders, 28 Sept. 1914–21 May 1915; written by its commanding officer, Lieut.-Col George Henniker Lawrence, CMG
Major-General C. A. Milward Diary
Field Marshal Lord Rawlinson Papers

National Library of Scotland

Major-General G. G. A. Egerton Papers
Field Marshal Earl Haig Papers
Lieutenant-General Sir J. A. L. Haldane Papers

Newspapers and Periodicals

Aberdeen Free Press; Aberdeen Press and Journal; Ardrossan and Saltcoats Herald; Army and Navy Quarterly; Beith Supplement; Blackburn Standard; The Bulletin; Chatham News; Daily Express; Daily Graphic; Daily Mail; Daily Telegraph; East African Standard; Eastern Counties Advertiser; Edinburgh Evening News; Essex County Telegraph; Essex Standard; Glasgow Evening News; Glasgow Herald; Irish News; Kilmarnock Standard; Largs and Millport Weekly News; Lloyd's Weekly News; Morning Post; London Gazette; Newcastle Illustrated Chronicle; Newcastle Chronicle; Pall Mall Gazette; Reynold's Newspaper; Royal Engineers Journal; Royal Leamington Spa Courier; Scots Pictorial;

The Sketch; *The Standard*; *The Times*; *Town Topics*; *United Services Gazette*; *Wellington Post*; *West Suffolk Gazette*; *Windsor Magazine*; *The World*.

Official Publications

Aspinall-Oglander, Cecil F., *History of the Great War Based on Official Documents by Direction of the Historical Section of the Committee of Imperial Defence: Military Operations, Gallipoli. Volume I: Inception of the Campaign to May 1915* (London: William Heinemann, 1929).

——, *History of the Great War Based on Official Documents by Direction of the Historical Section of the Committee of Imperial Defence: Military Operations, Gallipoli. Volume II: May 1915 to the Evacuation* (London: William Heinemann, 1932).

Defeat at Gallipoli: The Dardanelles Part II, 1915–16 (London: The Stationery Office, 2000).

Edmonds, J. E., *History of the Great War Based on Official Documents by Direction of the Historical Section of the Committee of Imperial Defence: Military Operations in France and Belgium, 1914. Volume I: Mons, the Retreat to the Seine, the Marne and the Aisne, August to October, 1914* (London: Macmillan, 1922).

——, *Military Operations in France and Belgium, 1916. Volume I: Sir Douglas Haig's Command to the 1st July: Battle of the Somme* (London: Macmillan, 1932).

——, *Military Operations, France and Belgium, 1917. Volume II: Messines and Third Ypres (Passchendaele) 7 June-10 November* (London: HMSO, 1948).

——, *Military Operations. France and Belgium, 1918. Volume I: The German March Offensive and its Preliminaries* (London: Macmillan, 1935).

——, *Military Operations. France and Belgium, 1918. Volume IV: 8 August-26 September: the Franco-British Offensive* (London: HMSO, 1947).

——, and C. G. Wynne, *Military Operations in France and Belgium, Winter 1915. Volume I: Battle of Neuve Chapelle: Battles of Ypres* (London: Macmillan, 1927).

Falls, Cyril, *Military Operations in France and Belgium, 1917. Volume I: The German Retreat to the Hindenburg Line and the Battle of Arras* (London: Macmillan, 1940).

General Staff, *Field Service Regulations, Part 1, Operations (1909)* (London: HMSO, 1909).

General Staff, *Training and Manoeuvre Regulations, 1913* (London: HMSO, 1913).

Report of the Examination for Admission at Staff College Held in August, 1896 (London: HMSO, 1896).

Autobiographies, Memoirs and Other Contemporary Works

Alford, H. S. L., and W. D. Sword, *The Egyptian Soudan: its Loss and Recovery* (London and New York: Macmillan, 1898).
Amery, L. S. ed., *The Times History of the War in South Africa, 1899–1902*, 7 vols (London: Sampson, Lowe, Marsden and Company, Ltd, 1900–9).
Ashmead-Bartlett, Ellis, *The Uncensored Dardanelles* (London: Hutchinson, 1920).
Atteridge, A. Hilliard, *Towards Khartoum: The Story of the Soudan War of 1896* (London: A. D. Innes & Co., 1897).
Beach, Jim, ed., *The Military Papers of Lieutenant Colonel Sir Cuthbert Headlam, 1910–42* (London: Army Records Society, 2010).
Berkeley, G. F. H., *My Recollections of Wellington College* (Newport: R. H. Johns Ltd, 1945).
Birdwood, William, *Khaki and Gown: an Autobiography* (London: Ward Lock, 1942).
Buck, E. I., *Simla Past and Present* (Calcutta: Thackray, Spinks and Co., 1904).
Burnham, F. R., *Scouting on Two Continents* (New York: Doubleday, 1926).
Calwell, C. E., *Small Wars: Their Principles and Practice* (London: HMSO, 1906).
——, *Stray Recollections* (London: Edward Arnold & Co., 1923).
Carrington, Charles, *Soldier from the Wars Returning* (London: Hutchinson, 1965).
Churchill, Randolph, and Martin Gilbert, *Winston S. Churchill: 1914–16, the Challenge of War. Companion* (London: Heineman, 1972).
Conan Doyle, Arthur, *The Great Boer War* (London: Smith and Elder & Co., 1902).
Cook, Arthur, *A Soldier's War* (Taunton: Goodman and Sons, 1957).
Creighton, Oswin, *With the 29th Division in Gallipoli: A Chaplain's Experiences* (London: Longmans, 1916).
Creswick, Louis, *South Africa and the Transvaal War* (Edinburgh: T. C. and E. C. Jack, 1902).
Earl of Cromer, *Modern Egypt*, 2 vols (London: Macmillan, 1908).
Davidson, George, *The Incomparable 29th and the River Clyde* (Aberdeen: Bissett, 1919).
Dunn, Captain J. C., *The War the Infantry Knew, 1914–19* (London: Abacus, 1994).
Edmonds, J. E., 'Four generations of Staff College students – 1896 to 1952. Part I, 1896', *Army Quarterly* LXV/1 (1952), 42–9.

——, 'The "Shop" sixty years ago', *The Royal Engineers Journal* (December 1940), 523–9.
French, Sir John, *The Complete Despatches of Lord French, 1914–16* (London: Chapman and Hill Ltd, 1917).
Forrest, G. W., *Sepoy Generals, Wellington to Roberts* (Edinburgh: Blackwoods, 1901).
Gillam, John Graham, *Gallipoli Diary* (London: Allen & Unwin, 1918).
Goldman, Charles, *With General French and the Cavalry in South Africa* (London: Macmillan, 1902).
Gough, Hubert, *The Fifth Army* (London: Hodder & Stoughton, 1968).
Griffith, L. Wyn, *Up to Mametz ... and Beyond* (Oxford: Casement, 2010).
Groome, F. H., *Ordnance Gazetteer of Scotland. A Study of Scottish Topography. Statistical, Biographical and Topographical* (London: William Mackenzie, 1892).
Hamilton, Sir Ian S. M., *Gallipoli Diary*, 2 vols (London: Edward Arnold, 1920).
Harrington, Charles, *Plumer of Messines* (London: John Murray, 1935).
Harrison, Eric, *Gunners, Game and Gardens: An Autobiography* (London: Leo Cooper, 1978).
Horan, F. S., *From the Crack of the Pistol: A Personal Saga* (Dorchester: Longmans, 1955).
Kannengiesser, Hans, *The Campaign in Gallipoli* (London: Hutchinson, 1927).
Keyes, Sir Roger, *The Fight for Gallipoli* (London: Eyre and Spottiswood, 1941).
Lockyer, H. C., *Gallipoli, Cape Helles, April 1915. The Tragedy of 'The Battle of the Beaches'. Together with the proceedings of HMS Implacable* (n.p., 1936).
Low, William, *Lieutenant-Colonel Gould Hunter-Weston of Hunterston, Knight of Justice and honorary commander of the Order of St John of Jerusalem in England, one of the defenders of Lucknow during the Indian Mutiny 1857–8: a biographical sketch* (Selkirk: *Scottish Chronicle* Office, 1914).
Mackenzie, Compton, *Gallipoli Memories* (London: Cassell, 1929).
Marshall, William, *Memories of Four Fronts* (London: Edward Benn Ltd, 1929).
Masefield, John, *Gallipoli* (London: Heinemann, 1916).
Mason, Capt. A. H., 'The Miranzai Expedition of 1891', *Journal of the Royal United Services Institution* XXXVI/168 (1892), 109–23.
Maurice, Frederick, *History of the War in South Africa, 1899–1902*, 4 vols (London: Hurst and Blackett, 1906–9).
Maxse, F. I., *Seymour Vandeleur: the story of a British officer: being a memoir of Brevet-Lieutenant-Colonel Vandeleur, D.S.O., Scots Guards and Irish Guards, with a general description of his campaigns* (London: National Review, 1905).
Neville, Capt. H. L., *Campaigns on the North-West Frontier* (London: John Murray, 1912).
Nevison, H. W., *The Dardanelles Campaign* (London: Nisbet & Co., 1918).
Parrott, J. E., *The Children's Story of the War, 10 vols* (London: Nelson, 1915).

Ruutz Rees, L. E., *A Personal Narrative of the Siege of Lucknow* (Oxford: Oxford University Press, 1858).
Smith-Dorrien, Herbert, *Memories of Forty-Eight Years Service* (London: John Murray, 1925).
Steevens, G. W., *With Kitchener to Khartum* (Edinburgh: Dodd, Mead & Co., 1898).
The Sudan Campaign 1896-99 [by An Officer], (London: Chapman & Hall, 1899).
The Wellington College Register 1859-1923 (Wellington College: The Old Wellingtonian Society, 1926).
Wemyss, Admiral Rosslyn, *The Navy in the Dardanelles Campaign* (London: Hodder Stoughton, 1924).
de Wet, Christiaan, *Three Years War* (New York: Charles Scribner, 1902).

Histories of Specific Units, Formations and Services

Atkinson, Christopher T., *The Royal Hampshire Regiment, 1914-18* (Glasgow: Maclehose & Co., 1952).
Baker Brown, W., *History of the Corps of Engineers* (Chatham: Institution of Royal Engineers, 1952).
Becke, Major A. F., *The Royal Regiment of Artillery at Le Cateau, 26 August 1914* (Woolwich: Royal Artillery Institution, 1919).
Berkeley, R., and W. W. Seymour, *History of the Rifle Brigade in War of 1914-18*, 2 vols (London: Rifle Brigade Club, 1927).
Coop, Rev J. O., *Story of the 55th (West Lancashire) Division* (Liverpool: *Daily Post* Printers, 1919).
Evan, H. K. D., and N. O. Laing, *The 4th (Queen's Own) Hussars in the Great War* (Aldershot: Gale and Polden, 1920).
Gillard, Brian, *Good Old Somersets: An 'Old Contemptible' Battalion in 1914* (Leicester: Matador, 2004).
Gillon, Captain Stair, *The Story of the 29th Division: A Record of Gallant Deeds* (London: Thomas Nelson, 1925).
Godwin-Austen, A. R., *The Staff and the Staff College* (London: Constable, 1927).
Haldane, J. A. L., *A brigade of the old army: Relating to operations of 10 Infantry Bde, France, Aug-Nov, 1914.* (London: Edward Arnold, 1920).
History and Digest of Service of the 1st King George's Own Sappers & Miners (Roorkee: 1st King's Own Press, n.d.).

Hopkinson, E. C., *Spectamur Agendo. 1st Battalion The East Lancashire Regiment. August and September, 1914* (Cambridge: W. Heffer & Sons Ltd, 1926).
Hutchison, G. S., *The Thirty-Third Division in France and Flanders, 1915–19* (London: Warlow & Sons, 1921).
Jerrold, Douglas, *The Hawke Battalion* (London: Ernest Benn Ltd, 1925).
——, *The Royal Naval Division* (London: Hutchinson, 1923).
Mumby, J. E., *A History of the 38th (Welsh) Division* (London: Hugh Rees Ltd, 1920).
Sandes, Lieut.-Col. E. W. C., *The Indian Sappers and Miners* (Chatham: Institution of Royal Engineers, 1948).
——, *The Military Engineer in India* (Chatham: Institute of Royal Engineers, 1933).
——, *The Royal Engineers in Egypt and the Sudan* (Chatham: Institution of Royal Engineers, 1937).
A Short History of the London Rifle Brigade (Aldershot: Gale and Polden, 1916).
Stacke, H. F., *The Worcester Regiment in the Great War* (Kidderminster: G. T. Cheshire & Sons, 1928).
Thompson, R. R., *The Fifty-Second Lowland Division, 1914–18* (Glasgow: Macklehose, Jackson & Co., 1923).
Ward, Col. B. R., *The School of Military Engineering, 1812–1909* (Chatham: Royal Institute of Engineers, 1909).
Wyrall, Everard, *The History of the 50th Division, 1914–19* (London: Percy Lund, Humphries & Co. Ltd, 1939).
——, *The Somerset Light Infantry, 1914–19* (London: Methuen & Co., 1927).

Other Published Sources

Allan, Stuart and Allan Carswell, *The Thin Red Line: War, Empire and Visions of Scotland* (Edinburgh: National Museum of Scotland, 2004).
Ascoli, David, *The Mons Star* (Edinburgh: Birlinn, 1981).
Asher, Michael, *Khartoum: The Ultimate Imperial Adventure* (Harmonsworth: Penguin, 2006).
Ashworth, Tony, *Trench Warfare, 1914–18: The Live and Let Live System* (London: Pan Books Ltd, 2000).
Asprey, Robert, *The First Battle of the Marne* (New York: Lippincott, 1962).
Badsey, Stephen, *Doctrine and Reform in the British Cavalry, 1880–1918* (Aldershot: Ashgate, 2008).

Balmer, Elizabeth, 'General Hunter-Weston's Appreciation of the Dardanelles Situation', *Stand To!* 79, (April 2007).

Barr, Niall, 'Command in the Transition from Mobile to Static Warfare, August 1914 to March 1915', in Gary Sheffield and Dan Todman, eds, *Command and Control on the Western Front: The British Army's Experience, 1914–18* (Staplehurst: Spellmont, 2004), 13–38.

Baynes, John, *Far From a Donkey: The Life of Sir Ivor Maxse* (London: Brassey's, 1995).

Beattie, Hugh, *Imperial Frontier: Tribe and State in Waziristan* (Richmond: Curzon, 2002).

Becke, Major A. F., 'The Coming of the Creeping Barrage', *Journal of the Royal Artillery* 58/1 (1931/2), 19–42.

Beckett, Ian, 'Campaigning under Kitchener', in Edward Spiers, ed., *The Sudan: The Reconquest Reappraised* (London: Frank Cass, 1998).

——, 'King George V and his Generals', in Mathew Hughes and Matthew Seligman, eds, *Leadership in Conflict, 1914–18* (Barnsley: Pen & Sword, 2000), 247–64.

——, *The Victorians at War* (London: Hambledon, 2006).

——, *Ypres: The First Battle, 1914* (Harlow: Pearson, 2006).

——, and Steven Corvi, eds, *Haig's Generals* (Barnsley: Pen & Sword, 2006).

Bevir, J. L., *The Making of Wellington College* (London: Edward Arnold, 1920).

Bidwell, Shelford and Domenick Graham, *Fire-Power: The British Army Weapons and Theories of War, 1904–45* (Barnsley: Pen & Sword, 2004).

Bond, Brian, *The Victorian Army and the Staff College, 1854–1915* (London: Eyre Methuen, 1972).

——, *The First World War and British Military History* (Oxford: Clarendon, 1991).

Bourne, John, 'British Generals in the First World War', in Gary Sheffield, ed., *Leadership and Command: The Anglo-American Military Experience Since 1861* (London and Washington: Brassey's, 1997), 93–116.

——, 'Major General W. C. G. Heneker: A Divisional General of the Great War', in Matthew Hughes and Matthew Seligman, eds, *Leadership in Conflict, 1914–18* (Barnsley: Pen & Sword, 2000), 54–67.

Carlyon, Les, *Gallipoli* (London: Bantam, 2001).

Cawthorne, Nigel, *The Beastly Battles of Old England: The Misguided Manoeuvres of the British at War* (London: Piatkus, 2013).

Chasseaud, Peter, *Rat's Alley: Trench Names of the Western Front, 1914–18* (Staplehurst: Spellmount, 2006).

Collin Davies, Cuthbert, *The Problem of the North West Frontier, 1890–1908* (Cambridge: Cambridge University Press, 1932).

Delage, Edmond, *The Tragedy of the Dardanelles* (London: John Lane, 1932).

Dixon, Norman, *On the Psychology of Military Incompetence* (London: Pimlico, 1994).

Duffy, Christopher, *Through German Eyes: The British and the Somme, 1916* (London: Phoenix, 2006).
Erickson, Edward, *Gallipoli: The Ottoman Campaign* (Barnsley: Pen & Sword, 2010).
Farr, Don, *The Silent General: Horne of the First Army* (London: Helion, 2007).
Farrar-Hockley, Anthony, *Gougie* (London: Granada, 1975).
——, *The Somme* (London: Pan, 1966).
French, David, *Military Identities: the Regimental System, the British Army, and the British People c. 1870–2000* (Oxford: Oxford University Press, 2005).
Gardner, Nikolas, *Trial by Fire: Command and the British Expeditionary Force in 1914* (London: Praeger, 2003).
——, 'Command in Crisis: the BEF and the Forest of Mormal, August 1914', *War and Society* 16/2 (1998), 13–32.
Gooch, John, *The Plans of War: The General Staff and British Military Strategy c. 1900–16* (London: Routledge and Kegan Paul, 1974).
Green, Andrew, *Writing the Great War: Sir James Edmonds and the Official Histories, 1915–48* (London: Frank Cass, 2003).
Gregory, Adrian, *The Last Great War: British Society and the First World War* (Cambridge: Cambridge University Press, 2008).
Grieves, Keith, 'The "Recruiting Margin" in Britain: Debates on Manpower during the Third Battle of Ypres', in Peter Liddle, ed., *Passchendaele in Perspective: The Third Battle of Ypres* (London: Leo Cooper, 1997).
Griffith, Paddy, *Battle Tactics of the Western Front: the British Army's Art of Attack, 1916–18* (New Haven and London: Yale University Press, 1996).
Harris, Leslie, 'A Scientific Frontier for India: Background to the 'Forward Policy of the Nineties', *Canadian Journal of History* 1/1 (1966), 46–71.
Hart, Peter, *Gallipoli* (Oxford: Oxford University Press, 2013).
——, *The Somme: The Darkest Hour on the Western Front* (London: Weidenfield and Nicholson, 2005).
Holmes, Richard, *Little Field Marshal: A Life of Sir John French* (London: Cassell, 2005).
Hughes, Clive, 'The New Armies', in Ian Beckett and Keith Simpson, eds, *A Nation in Arms: A Social Study of the British Army in the First World War* (Manchester: Chandler & Beckett, 1985), 100–23.
Hunter, Archie, *Kitchener's Sword Arm: The Life and Campaigns of General Sir Archibald Hunter* (Staplehurst: Spellmount, 1996).
Hutchison, Iain, 'Scottish Unionism between the Two World Wars', in Catriona Macdonald, ed., *Unionist Scotland, 1800–97* (Edinburgh: John Donald, 1996), 73–99.
Hutton, John, *August 1914: Surrender at St Quentin* (Barnsley: Pen & Sword, 2010).

Hynes, Samuel, *A War Imagined: The First World War and English Culture* (London: The Bodley Head, 1990).
Jones, Simon, *Underground Warfare, 1914–18* (Barnsley: Pen & Sword, 2010).
Keegan, John, *The Mask of Command: A Study of Generalship* (Harmonsworth: Penguin, 1988).
Kendall, Paul, *Aisne 1914: The Dawn of Trench Warfare* (Stroud: Spellmount, 2012).
Keown-Boyd, Henry, *A Good Dusting: A Centenary Review of the Sudan Campaigns, 1883–99* (London: Leo Cooper, 1986).
Kochanski, Halik, 'Planning for the Final Years of the *Pax Britannica*, 1889–1903', in David French and Brian Holden Reid, *The British General Staff: Reform and Innovation, 1890–1939* (London: Frank Cass, 2002), 9–25.
Laffin, John, *The Agony of Gallipoli (London: The History Press, 2005)*.
Lamb, Peter, *He-who-sees-in-the-dark; the Boys' story of Frederick Burnham, the American Scout* (London: Brewer, Warren and Putnam, 1932).
Lee, Celia, *Jean, Lady Hamilton, 1861–1941: A Soldier's Wife* (London: Celia Lee, 2001).
Lee, John, *A Soldier's Life: General Sir Ian Hamilton, 1853–1947* (London: Macmillan, 2001).
Macdonald, Catriona, *Whaur Extremes Meet: Scotland's Twentieth Century* (Edinburgh: John Donald, 2010).
McFarland, Elaine, 'The Great War', in T. M. Devine and Jenny Wormald, eds, *The Oxford Handbook of Scottish History* (Oxford: Oxford University Press, 2012), 553–68.
Mackenzie, John, *Imperialism and Popular Culture* (Manchester: Manchester University Press, 1986).
Macleod, Jenny, *Reconsidering Gallipoli* (Manchester: Manchester University Press, 2004).
Middlebrook, Martin, *The First Day on the Somme: 1 July 1916* (Harmondsworth: Penguin, 2006).
——, *The Kaiser's Battle* (Barnsley: Pen & Sword, 2007).
Mombauer, Annika, *Helmuth von Moltke and the Origins of the First World War* (Cambridge: Cambridge University Press, 2001).
Moreman, Tim, 'The British and Indian Armies and North West Frontier Warfare, 1849–1914', *Journal of Imperial and Commonwealth History* 20/1 (1992), 35–64.
Murland, Jerry, *Retreat and Rearguard 1914: The BEF's Actions from Mons to the Marne* (Barnsley: Pen & Sword, 2011).
Newsome, David, *A History of Wellington College, 1859–1959* (London: John Murray, 1959).
Pakenham, Thomas, *The Boer War* (London: Harper, 1992).

Palazzo, Albert, *Seeking Victory on the Western Front: The British Army and Chemical Warfare in World War I* (Lincoln, Nebraska and London: University of Nebraska Press, 2000).

Philpott, William, 'The Campaign for a Ministry of Defence, 1919–36', in Paul Smith, ed., *Government and the Armed Forces in Britain, 1856–1990* (London: Hambledon, 1995), 109–54.

Pollock, John, *Kitchener: The Road To Omdurman* (London: Constable, 1998).

Prior, Robin, *Gallipoli: The End of the Myth* (New Haven: Yale University Press, 2009).

——, *The Somme* (New Haven and London: Yale University Press, 2006).

Prior, Robin and Trevor Wilson, *Command on the Western Front: The Military Career of Sir Henry Rawlinson 1914–18* (Oxford: Blackwell, 1992).

——, *Passchendaele: The Untold Story* (New Haven and London: Yale University Press, 1996).

Reader, W. J., *'At Duty's Call'. A Study in Obsolete Patriotism* (Manchester: Manchester University Press, 1988).

Rhodes James, Robert, *Gallipoli* (London: Pimlico, 1999).

Robbins, Simon, *British Generalship During the Great War: The Military Career of Sir Henry Horne (1861–1929)* (Farnham: Ashgate, 2010).

——, *British Generalship on the Western Front 1914–18: Defeat into Victory* (London: Frank Cass, 2005).

Royle, Trevor, *The Kitchener Enigma* (London: M. Joseph, 1985).

Samuels, Martin, *Command or Control?: Command, Training and Tactics in the British and German Armies, 1888–1918* (London: Frank Cass, 1999).

Senior, Michael, *Lieutenant General Sir Richard Hacking: XI Corps Commander, 1915–18: A Study in Corps Command* (Barnsley: Pen & Sword, 2012).

Sharpe, Robert, *The Last Day, The Last Hour: The Currie Libel Trial* (Toronto: University of Toronto Press, 2009).

Sheffield, Gary, *The Chief: Douglas Haig and the British Army* (London: Aurum, 2011).

——, *Forgotten Victory: The First World War – Myths and Realities* (London: Headline, 2001).

——, *Leadership in the Trenches: Officer-Man Relations, Morale and Discipline in the British Army* (London: Macmillan, 2000).

——, *The Somme* (London: Cassell, 2003).

——, and Geoffrey Till, eds, *Challenges of High Command in the Twentieth Century* (London: Macmillan, 2003).

——, and John Bourne, eds, *Douglas Haig: War Diaries and Letters, 1914–18* (London: Phoenix, 2006).

Sheffy, Yigal, 'The Chemical Dimension of the Gallipoli Campaign: Introducing Chemical Warfare to the Middle East', *War in History* 12/3 (2005), 278–317.

Simpson, Andy, 'British Corps Command on the Western Front, 1914–18', in Gary Sheffield and Dan Todman, eds, *Command and Control on the Western Front: The British Army's Experience 1914–18* (Staplehurst: Spellmont, 2004), 97–118.
——, *Directing Operations: British Corps Command on the Western Front, 1914–18* (Stroud: Spellmount, 2006).
Snow, Dan and Mark Pottle, eds, *The Confusion of Command: The War Memoirs of Lieutenant General Sir Thomas D'Oyly Snow, 1914–15* (London: Frontline, 2011).
Spiers, Edward, *The Late Victorian Army, 1868–1902* (Manchester: Manchester University Press, 1992).
Steel, Nigel, and Peter Hart, *Defeat at Gallipoli* (London: Macmillan, 1994).
——, *Passchendaele: The Sacrificial Ground* (London: Phoenix, 2001).
Stevenson, David, *With Our Backs to the Wall: Victory and Defeat in 1918* (London: Allen Lane, 2011).
Strachan, Hew, *The Politics of the British Army* (Oxford: Oxford University Press, 1997).
Talboys, R. S., *A Victorian School: The Story of Wellington College* (Oxford: Basil Blackwell, 1944).
Terraine, John, *Douglas Haig: The Educated Soldier* (London: Leo Cooper, 1990).
——, *Mons: the Retreat to Victory* (Barnsely: Pen & Sword, 1991).
Thomas, Alun, 'Open Warfare during the "Hundred Days" – 1918', *Stand To!* 96 (2013), 24–7.
Till, Geoffrey, 'The Gallipoli Campaign: Command Performances', in Gary Sheffield and Geoffrey Till, eds, *The Challenges of High Command. The British Experience* (London: Palgrave, 2003), 34–56.
Travers, Tim, 'Command and Leadership Styles in the British Army: the 1915 Gallipoli Model', *Journal of Contemporary History* 29 (1994), 403–42.
——, *Gallipoli 1915* (Stroud: Tempus, 2003).
——, *How The War was Won: Command and Technology in the British Army on the Western Front, 1917–18* (London and New York: Routledge, 1992).
——, *The Killing Ground: The British Army, the Western Front and the Emergence of Modern War, 1900–18* (Barnsley: Pen & Sword, 1987).
——, 'Learning and Decision-making on the Western Front, 1915–16: the British Example', *Canadian Journal of History* 18 (1983), 87–97.
——, 'The Offensive and the Problem of Innovation in British Military Thought, 1870–1915', *Journal of Contemporary History* 13/3 (1978), 531–53.
——, 'Technology, Tactics and Morale: Jean de Bloch, the Boer War and British Military Theory, 1900–1914', *Journal of Modern History* 51 (1979), 264–86.
Turner, John, *British Politics and the Great War* (New Haven and London: Yale University Press, 1992).

Wiest, Andrew, 'The Planned Amphibious Assault', in Peter Liddle, ed., *Passchendaele in Perspective: the Third Battle of Ypres* (London: Leo Cooper, 1997), 201–14.

Zuber, Terence, *The Mons Myth: A Reassessment of the Battle* (Stroud: History Press, 2010).

Unpublished Theses

LoCicero, Michael, 'A Moonlight Massacre: The Night Operation on the Passchendaele Ridge, 2nd December 1917', PhD Thesis, University of Birmingham, 2011.

Robbins, Simon, 'British Generalship on the Western Front in the First World War, 1914–18', PhD Thesis, Kings College London, 2001.

Index

Achi Baba 128, 132, 136, 140, 141, 145, 150, 159, 160, 161, 162, 165, 166, 167, 169, 170, 176, 177, 180, 190
Achi Baba Nullah, Battle of (1915) 200–5, 208
Aisne, Battle of the (1914) 96, 99, 100–2
Albert I, King of the Belgians 257
Allenby, General Sir E. H. H. 34, 37, 41, 58, 61, 215
d'Amade, General A. G. L. 130, 131, 133, 158, 159, 167, 173, 175
Amiens, Battle of (1918) 283
Ashmead-Bartlett, Ellis 189, 190, 204
Aspinall (Oglander), Brig.-Gen. C. F. 138, 156, 264, 266, 268, 284, 308

Bacon, Rear-Admiral Sir R. H. S. 214–4
Bailloud, General M. C. 186, 200
Beaumont Hamel (1916) 220, 221, 222, 223, 228, 238–40
Bengal Miners and Sappers 22
the 'Birdcage' (1914) 115–17
Birdwood, General Sir W. R. 126 n., 129, 131, 133, 134 n., 143
Bloemfontein (South African War) 46, 47–9, 50, 100
Bonham-Carter, General Sir C. 284–5
Botha, Louis 50, 55, 57
Braithwaite, Lt.-Gen. Sir W. P. 35, 38, 77, 131, 132, 139, 150, 153, 182
Breeks, Brig.-Gen. R. W. 14, 170, 175

British Imperial and Commonwealth Forces
Armies
First Army 258, 281, 282, 284, 289, 292–3, 295
Second Army 251, 257, 259, 260, 262, 263, 278, 279, 280
Third Army 283
Fourth Army 213, 216, 217–18, 220, 224, 225, 227, 229, 233, 235, 242, 245, 262, 283
Fifth Army (Reserve Army) 259, 262, 277
Brigades
2nd Australian Brigade 174
7th Brigade 92
10th Brigade 80, 86, 89, 99, 241
11th Brigade 80–1, 82, 84, 85–96, 100–3, 107–9, 113, 118, 239, 240, 253
12th Brigade 80, 86, 89, 92, 109, 236, 240
19th Brigade 98
29th Indian Brigade 168, 169, 173, 184, 185
86th Brigade 138, 150, 153, 162, 164, 178, 1198, 231, 232–8, 241, 278
87th Brigade 140, 142, 159, 161, 143, 169, 174, 238, 239, 271
88th Brigade 140, 149, 161, 162, 163, 164, 169, 172, 173, 184, 185
92nd Brigade 241

93rd Brigade 229, 241
94th Brigade 229, 240, 244
125th Brigade 168, 169, 172, 181
127th Brigade 181
174th Brigade 269
New Zealand Brigade 173
Corps
  ANZAC (Australian and New Zealand Army Corps) 124, 129, 132, 141, 158, 168, 263
  I Corps 84, 87
  II Corps 84, 85, 86, 94, 264–5, 297
  III Corps 97, 98, 108
  IV Corps 105
  VIII Corps
    formation (1915) 178–9, 213
    Gallipoli 181–90, 197–205
    Hundred Days (1918) 285–95
    Passchendaele Salient 264–7, 276–80
    redesignation of XVIII Corps as 281
    reformation on Western Front (1916) 211, 216
    Somme *see under* Somme, Battle of the (1916)
    training 233, 252–5
    transfer to First Army (Vimy) 281
    Ypres Salient 250–5
  IX Corps 208
  X Corps 219, 242, 243
  XVIII Corps 281
  Canadian Corps 263, 286, 287, 289, 293, 295
Divisions
  3rd Division 89, 92, 110
  4th Division 80, 83, 84–6, 89, 94, 95, 97, 110, 116, 132, 216, 227, 228, 229, 234, 236
  5th Division 89, 102
  8th Division 269, 286, 290, 291, 293, 295
  12th Division 290
  20th Division 289
  29th Division
    at Alexandria 132
    formation 121, 126
    Gully Ravine 197–9
    First Battle of Krithia 161–4
    Old Comrades Association and commemoration 303 n., 309
    Second Battle of Krithia 166–74
    Somme and aftermath 228–9, 230–2, 235, 238–9, 241, 244, 245, 252
    Third Battle of Krithia 180–5
    transfer to Western Front 216
    see also Gallipoli campaign; Gallipoli landings
  31st Division 216, 227, 228, 229, 235, 236, 240–2
  36th Division 244
  42nd Division 254, 260
  48th Division 216, 228 n., 241
  52nd Division 180, 195, 197–9, 201–4, 208, 291, 295, 298
  55th Division 254, 260
  58th Division 268, 289, 290, 291
  61st Division 261
  63rd (Royal Naval) Division 124, 130, 132, 138, 162, 180, 182–4, 185, 186, 189, 198, 200, 203–4
    Collingwood Battalion 184, 185
    Hawke Battalion 185, 189, 204

Index

Cavalry (South Africa) 41, 43–6, 55, 65
GHQ (British Expeditionary Force) 95, 100, 230, 233, 244
GHQ (Mediterranean Expeditionary Force) 131, 139, 140, 141, 154, 156, 164, 167, 169, 173, 179, 180, 181, 183, 192, 194, 199, 200, 202, 203, 208, 213, 264
Regiments/Battalions
  1/East Lancashire Regiment 81, 82, 85, 88, 90, 99, 109, 114, 116, 117
  1/Essex Regiment 126 n., 149, 151, 239
  2/Essex Regiment 108
  1/Hampshire Regiment 81, 88, 91, 92, 100, 109
  1/Kings Own Scottish Borderers 126 n., 139, 142, 157, 184
  1/Lancashire Fusiliers 126 n., 147, 188
  2/Lancashire Fusiliers 236
  1/Prince Albert's (Somerset Light Infantry) 81, 82, 85, 88, 90, 99, 109, 114, 116, 117
  1/Rifle Brigade (Prince Consort's Own) 81, 87, 88, 90, 93, 101, 102, 116, 117, 118, 234
  1/Royal Dublin Fusiliers 126 n., 138, 148
  2/Royal Fusiliers 126 n., 146
  1/Royal Munster Fusiliers 126 n., 152, 176
  1/Royal Newfoundland 239
  1/Royal Warwickshire 236
  2/South Wales Borderers 126 n., 139, 145
  4/Worcester Regiment 126 n., 151, 271–2

4th (Queen's Own) Hussars 292, 293, 295
London Rifle Brigade 111
Royal Field Artillery
  XXXII Brigade 91
  68th Field Battery 98, 103
Royal Engineers 15–16, 22, 65
  Field Troops (South Africa) 40, 41, 42, 43, 44, 46, 50, 53
  First Division, Telegraph Battalion 18
Royal Marines 139, 142, 145
British Fleet
  Albion 148
  Cornwallis 148
  Euryalus 139, 143, 145, 146, 149, 153, 158, 159
  Implacable 146, 154
  Lord Nelson 149
  Queen Elizabeth 135, 139, 143, 149, 153, 156
  River Clyde 139, 148, 152
  Sapphire 153
  Swiftsure 135
Boyd, Maj. G. F. 93
Brereton, Maj. C. L. 98–9, 103
Broodseinde, Battle of (1917) 263
Bucy-le-Long (Aisne) 101, 103, 104
Bulfin, Maj.-Gen. E. S. 109
Burnham, F. R. 50–1, 52, 53–4
Bute and North Ayrshire (constituency) 297, 298, 301
Byng, General the Hon. Sir J. H. G. 59, 68, 258, 283, 284, 292

Callwell, Maj.-Gen. C. E. 32, 70, 207
Canal du Nord, Battle of the (1918) 289
Carey, Maj.-Gen. G. G. S. 288, 290
Casson, Lt.-Col. H. 146, 153
Charles, Lieut. Ronald 47, 49, 53
Churchill, Capt. Jack 192

Churchill, (Sir) Winston Spencer 118, 124, 125, 127
Colesberg (South African War) 43, 44, 55, 62
Currie, Lt.-Gen. A. W. 286, 295

Dawnay, Maj. G. P. 199
De Lisle, Maj.-Gen. H. de B. 108, 197, 216, 225, 231, 239, 241, 297
De Robeck, Vice-Admiral J. M. 117, 153
Department of Military Training (War Office) 73–4
Derby, Lord 247
Dongola campaign (1896) 27–33
Douglas, Maj.-Gen. Sir W. 178, 188

Edmonds, Brig.-Gen. J. E. 16, 34, 224, 231, 309
Egerton, Maj.-Gen. G. A. A. 196, 199, 201, 202, 203, 205–8
Ellington, Brig.-Gen. E. L. 238, 268

Fanshawe, Lt.-Gen. Sir E. A. 216
Firket, Battle of (1896) 31–33
Foch, Marshal, F. 280, 281
French, Field Marshal Sir J. D. P. 41, 43–4, 45, 46, 47, 49, 50, 53, 55–61, 65, 66, 77, 81, 83–4, 95, 97, 102, 109, 110, 119, 121, 193, 211
French Forces
  Fourth Army (Gouraud) 280, 283
  89th Infantry Brigade 104
  Corps Expéditionnaire d'Orient 167
    Brigade Coloniale 172
    Brigade Metropolitaine 172
Freyberg VC, Lt.-Comm. B. C. 271–2, 277
Fuller, Lt.-Col. J. F. C. 231, 239 n.

Gallipoli campaign
  inception 124–5
  conditions 166, 174, 189, 194
  logistics and resourcing 125, 130, 164–5, 175–6, 179, 207
  memoirs and accounts 308–9
  strategic aims 121, 124
  see also Achi Baba; Achi Baba Nullah, Battle of (1915); Gallipoli landings; Gully Ravine, Battle of (1915); Krithia, First Battle of (1915); Krithia, Second Battle of (1915); Krithia, Third Battle of (1915)
Gallipoli landings
  planning 131–3, 138–40
  S Beach 132–3, 139, 145–6, 152–3
  V Beach 132–3, 139, 140, 146, 148–9, 150, 151–2, 157
  W Beach 132–3, 139, 146, 148–9, 150, 151–2, 157
  X Beach 132–3, 139, 140, 146, 151, 154
  Y Beach 132–3, 139, 145, 149–50, 151, 152–7
Geddes, Capt. G. W. 175
Geddes, Sir Eric 300
George V, HM King 3, 78, 126 n., 211, 251
German Forces
  2nd Cavalry Division 90
  26th Reserve Division 221
  52nd Division 221
Gough, General Sir H. de la P. 37, 78, 121, 243, 246, 251 n., 259, 260, 261, 262, 274, 277, 281, 297
Gough VC, Brig.-Gen. J. E. 68
Gouraud, General H. J. E. 180, 182, 184, 185, 186, 194, 280, 283
Gully Ravine, Battle of (1915) 197–8, 201, 213

Index

Haig, Field Marshall Sir D. 3, 34, 38, 41, 45, 46, 57, 74, 84, 96, 212, 213, 214–15, 219, 220, 222, 226, 227, 231, 235, 237, 242, 243, 245, 246, 250 n., 251, 255, 259, 260, 262, 263, 264, 265, 267, 274, 276, 277, 278, 280, 281, 283, 295
Haldane, General Sir J. A. L. 80, 103
Hamilton, General Sir I. S. M. 2, 14, 15, 66, 68, 77, 122, 123, 125, 126 n., 127, 129–30, 131, 132, 133–4, 136, 137, 139, 142, 150, 153–4, 156, 157, 158, 159, 162, 163, 164–5, 167, 168, 170, 172, 173, 174, 175, 176, 180, 188, 192, 199, 200, 205, 206, 207, 209, 310, 311, 312
Hamilton, Maj.-Gen. H. I. W. 110
Hare, Maj.-Gen. Sir S. 137, 138, 139, 147
Hasler, Brig.-Gen. J. 133
Headlam, Cuthbert 240–50, 257, 262, 274, 284, 313 n.
Henderson, Colonel G. F. R. 36
Heneker, General Sir W. C. G. 269, 270, 286, 288
Hildyard, General Sir H. J. T. 33, 35, 66
Hore-Ruthven VC, Brig.-Gen. A. G. A. 217, 224, 231, 252
Horne, General Sir H. S. 281, 282, 283, 286, 289, 290, 291, 293
Hunter, General Sir A. 28 n., 33, 299
Hunter, Robert Caldwell 8, 10, 13 n.
Hunter-Weston, Lt.-Gen. Sir A. G.
appearance 3, 24, 131, 168, 267–8, 306
appointment as GOC 29th Division 121, 125, 126
attitude to casualties 2–3, 114–15, 123–4, 188–9, 191, 195, 302–4
to Germany 294
to war strategy 111, 122, 283, 289–90, 291, 294–5
'cheeriness' 3, 113, 222, 298, 310
command style 80–1, 87–8, 91, 102, 107, 112–13, 179, 190, 225, 268–72, 282–3, 288–9, 294
commands VIII Corps (Hundred Days, 1918) 286–96
commands VIII Corps (Messines) 259–60
commands VIII Corps (Passchendaele) 264–72
commands VIII Corps (Vimy Sector) 281–4
commands VIII Corps (Ypres) 250–2, 257–8
commands 11th Brigade:
Aisne 97–105
Colchester 80–2
Le Cateau 87–93
Ploegsteert (1914–15) 109, 113–9
commands column in South Africa 58–62
education (school) 13–15
education (military) 16–18
enters parliament 255–7
death and funeral 311–12
defence schemes (1917–18) 265–7, 282
and Douglas Haig 212–13, 214, 219, 222, 226, 227, 235, 243, 245, 246, 255, 259, 264, 267
family and early upbringing 7–11
health 104, 118, 207–9, 311
and Henry Horne 281, 282, 283
and Henry Rawlinson 105, 212, 213, 215, 219, 220, 225, 226, 231, 235, 243, 245, 265, 266, 267, 276
horses and horsemanship 37, 41, 45, 91 n., 118

and Hubert Gough 246, 261, 274, 281
and Hunterston Estate 9, 10, 73, 103, 163, 301, 308
Indian service 21–7
and John French 41, 43, 47, 50, 56, 211
and Kitchener 28, 29–32, 70, 109, 121, 125, 178, 209
love of detail 18, 36, 226–7, 268
loyalty to superiors 5, 80, 168, 199, 211 n.
'Manpower Speech' (1918) 273–6
marriage 67
and new technology 2, 18, 69, 78, 200, 213, 233, 312
optimism 130, 117, 179, 180, 212, 223, 224, 236, 245, 283, 313
oratory 250, 254, 273–6, 303, 313
personality 3, 24, 37, 79–80, 81, 82, 88, 193, 243, 249, 298, 312
post-war political career 298–310
and other ranks 81–2, 113–14, 188
reputation 1–5, 49, 75, 79–80, 112–13, 119, 177, 187–95, 210, 211–13, 246, 249, 268–72, 284–6
on role of Brigadier 112
on role of Corps Commander 179, 225
sentimentality 81, 94, 110, 174–5, 193
at Staff College 34–38
as staff officer (peacetime) 66–78
as staff officer (South Africa) 41, 56, 57–8
and subordinates 101–2, 130, 140, 141–2, 155, 179, 192, 220, 225, 245, 249, 268, 270–2, 284–5, 291–2
Sudan service 27–33
and tactical theory 70–2, 73–5, 77–6, 288, 291

as trainer 68, 70–1, 75–7, 81, 181, 233, 246, 250, 251–5
and trench raids 234, 236, 252, 282
and VIP visitors 118, 250, 251, 274, 280
and war memorials 302–4
wounded 26
see also VIII Corps; 29th Division; Gallipoli campaign; Gallipoli landings; Gully Ravine, Battle of (1915); Krithia, First Battle of (1915); Krithia, Second Battle of (1915); Krithia, Third Battle of (1915); Somme, Battle of the (1916)
Hunter-Weston, Lt.-Col. Gould Read 7–10, 21, 66
Hunter-Weston, Lady Grace 4, 6, 83, 94, 103, 113, 115, 127, 136, 143–4, 160, 166, 171, 178, 196 n., 209, 223, 237, 243, 246, 264, 276, 277, 278, 280, 283, 290, 296, 301, 310, 311–12
Hunter-Weston, Jane Caldwell 8–11, 73
Hunter-Weston, Reginald Hugh 10, 15, 26
Hunter-Weston Hill (Gallipoli) 166, 194

Jacob, Lt.-Gen. Sir W. C. 279–80
Joffre, Marshal J. C. C. 235, 243

Keyes, Commodore R. 141 n., 150, 208
Kiggell, Lt.-Gen. Sir L. E. 246
Kimberly, Relief of (1900) 43–7
Koe, Lt.-Col. A. S. 142, 153, 155
Krithia, First Battle of (1915) 161–6, 168
Krithia, Second Battle of (1915) 169–74, 191
Krithia, Third Battle of (1915) 180–6
Kroonstat Raid (1900) 50–3

Index

Lambton, Maj.-Gen. the Hon. W. 216, 240, 241
Le Cateau, Battle of (1914) 87–91
Le Gheer (1914) 108–109, 115, 253
Limpus, Vice Admiral A. H. 127
Lloyd George, D. 254 n., 274, 298
Lockhart, Sir William 22–3, 25, 26
Lucknow, Siege of (1857) 8
Lynden-Bell, Maj.-Gen. Sir A. 35, 196

Macmullen, Capt. (C.) N. 178
Marshall, Lt.-Gen. Sir W. R. 126, 138, 140, 143, 146, 151, 153, 159, 163, 164, 171, 181, 186 n., 193–4, 198, 200, 308
Matthews, Lt. Col. G. E. 141, 145, 153, 154–6, 157
Maxse, Lt.-Gen. Sir F. I. 269, 282, 297
Messines, Battle of (1917) 259, 260
Middelburg (South African War) 55, 59
Milne, Field Marshal G. F. 35
Milward, Capt. C. A. 143, 152, 155 n., 157, 160
Miranzai Expeditions (1891) 22–3
Mons, Battle of (1914) 83–4
Moore, Capt. C. D. H. 178
Morland, Lt.-Gen. Sir T. L. N. 219, 242
Murray, Sir A. Wolfe 123

Napier, Brig. H. E. 140, 149
Nicholson, Rear Admiral W. S. 153
North Ayrshire (constituency) 255–6, 257
Northcliffe, Lord 274

O'Gowan, Maj.-Gen. R. W. 210, 225, 241
Ostend (landing scheme) 214–5
Outram, Sir James 8

Paardeburg, Battle of (1900) 46–62
Paris, Maj.-Gen. A. 130, 168, 195
Passchendaele Salient (1917–8) 264–7, 277–80
Passchendaele, First Battle of (1917) 261–2
Passchendaele, Second Battle of (1917) 263–4
Petain, General H. P. 280
Pilkem Ridge 266–78
Pinney, Maj.-Gen. Sir R. J. 269–70
Ploegsteert ('Plugstreet') Wood 108–9, 111, 113, 116, 118
Plumer, General Sir H. C. O. 251, 258, 259, 260, 262, 263, 269, 278, 279
Pretoria–Delagoa Railway 53–4
Prowse, Brig.-Gen. C. B. 109, 113, 216, 243

Ramsay, Admiral Sir A. R. M. 135
Rawlinson, General Sir H. S. (Bt.) 105, 212, 213, 215, 217, 219, 220, 225, 226, 227, 231, 235, 243, 245, 262, 263, 265, 266, 267, 276
River Clyde (transport) 139, 148, 152
Roberts, Lord 44, 45, 46, 47, 48, 49, 50, 53, 55, 66, 149
Robertson, General Sir W. R. 68, 121, 244–5
Royal Military Academy (Woolwich) 16, 17, 18, 21, 34, 35

School of Military Engineering (Chatham)
Scott-Moncrieff, Brig-Gen. W. 198
Scottish Unionist Party 297, 305
Selle, Battle of the (1918) 292–3
Serre (1916) 217–18, 219, 220, 221, 222, 224, 228, 241, 243
Shaw, Lt.-Gen. Sir F. C. 126, 140, 206 n.

Smith Dorrien, General Sir H. L. 37, 84–5, 87, 89, 93, 95, 108
Snow, General Sir T. D'O. 68, 80, 85, 86–7, 89, 93, 94, 110, 242, 250–1
Somme, Battle of the (1916)
  background 117
  casualties 242
  operations (VIII Corps 1 July) 237–41
  planning (Fourth Army) 217–20
  planning (VIII Corps) 222, 224–32
  preparation (VIII Corps) 233–7
  terrain 221–2
Staff College (Camberley) 33, 34–38
Street, Brig.-Gen. H. E. 148, 157, 161, 164–5, 178, 179 n., 181, 189, 201, 202
switch system 104, 266

Territorial Force 70, 73, 216
Training and Manoeuvre Regulations, 1913 75, 253
trench mortars 200, 223, 226, 229, 233, 234, 238–9, 240, 257, 282, 288, 294
trench naming 104, 118
Trotman, General Sir C. N. 203

Turkish Forces
  9th Division 147, 167
  19th Division 147

Venerable Order of St John of Jerusalem 11, 24, 300
Venizel (Aisne) 100
Vimy Ridge 258, 281
Von der Marwitz, General Georg 90

Walford VC, Capt. G. N. 152, 157
Ward, Brig.-Gen. H. D. O. 259–60, 284
Waziristan Expedition (1884–5) 24–6
Wellington College 13–15
Wemyss, Rear-Admiral R. E. 134, 135, 139, 147, 150, 267
West Kilbride 28 n., 196, 202, 312
Williams, Orlo 131, 199,
Wilson, Lt.-Col. L. O. 189, 204–5
Wilson, Field Marshall Sir H. H. 66, 70, 121
Wilson, Maj.-Gen. Sir H. F. M. 80, 89, 97, 110
Wolseley, Field Marshal Viscount 34, 66

Ypres, First Battle of (1914) 107, 109
Ypres Salient 250–1, 257–8